D1065480

A HISTORY OF
COLONIAL BRAZIL,
1500–1792

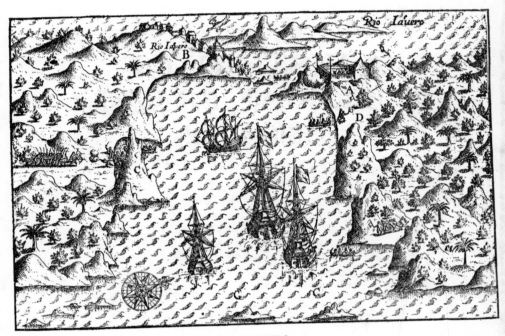

RIO DE JANEIRO, 1599.

From Olivier du Noort's *Description du penible Voyage* (Amsterdam, 1602).
KEY. — G, Anchorage of ships. A, Portuguese fort. B, The town of Rio de Janeiro. C, Sugar-loaf mountain. D, Place where prisoners were exchanged.
Cf. De Bry's *Additamentum nonæ partis* (1602) and Gottfriedt's *Newe Welt* (1655), p. 390.
Source: North Wind Picture Archives.

A HISTORY OF COLONIAL BRAZIL, 1500–1792

by

Bailey W. Diffie[†]
compiled with
the editorial assistance of
Edwin J. Perkins
Department of History
University of Southern California

ROBERT E. KRIEGER PUBLISHING COMPANY
MALABAR, FLORIDA
1987

Original Edition 1987

Printed and Published by
ROBERT E. KRIEGER PUBLISHING COMPANY, INC.
KRIEGER DRIVE
MALABAR, FL 32950

Library of Congress Cataloging-in-Publication Data
Diffie, Bailey W. (Bailey Wallys), 1902-1983.
  A history of colonial Brazil, 1500–1792.

  Bibliography: p.
  1. Brazil—History—To 1821. I. Perkins, Edwin J.
II. Title.
F2524.D53 1987   981   85–25605
ISBN 0–89874–685–X (Cloth)
ISBN 0–89464–214–6 (Paper)

A HISTORY OF COLONIAL BRAZIL, 1500–1792

HOW SHOULD HISTORY BE WRITTEN?
O Historiador Deve Escrever as Cousas como Ellas Passaram
José de Cunha Brachado
1651–1733

Wie es Eigentlich Gewesen
Leopold von Ranke
1795–1886

For my beloved wife, Edilla, and granddaughter, Rima

and

All my former students and friends

IN GRATITUDE

Bailey lived with a consuming passion in his later years: to complete this particular book! If he must leave it unfinished, he had a boundless and sound faith that his friends would step into the breach. From the coterie of companions at the University of Southern California, Edwin Perkins assumed the painstaking editorship of the manuscript. Later, Mario Rodríguez read the work carefully and put together the bibliography. Francis A. Dutra of the University of California in Santa Barbara and Dauril Alden of the University of Washington in Seattle offered their expertise. There was no hesitation—Bailey meant that much to them. It was remarkable, moreover, to watch Isabel Mahony, Brenda Rena Johnson, and especially Martha Rothermel—the secretaries in the Department of History—groping with Portuguese words and book titles, not to mention the Luso-Brazilian quirks in accentuation. It was such a noble effort on the part of so many! I am deeply impressed with their loyalty and with what they have done to nurture my husband's memory. I thank them all so much. *Abraços*.

Edilla Diffie
Los Angeles

Contents

EDITOR'S PREFACE

Bailey Diffie died unexpectedly from a stroke on January 12, 1983. He was alert and active right up until the end; I saw him that very morning and we joked and laughed as usual about whatever was the general topic of conversation that day. Frequently in those last few weeks, we talked about ongoing negotiations with the publisher related to the contract for this book and about his trials and tribulations in trying to master, at age 80, the word processing program for the home computer just recently purchased.

This volume represents over a quarter century of Bailey Diffie's research on the one subject most dear to his heart—Colonial Brazil. The manuscript he left for posterity was essentially a rough first draft; many pages were partial sheets with faint, almost illegible type. In the course of my editorial work, I added nothing in the way of new data to the text. I trimmed perhaps one-quarter of the original text —much of it background information on events in Portugal and Europe generally and therefore only tangentially related to Brazil per se. In the interest of clarity and a tighter organization, the original 36 chapters were consolidated into 27 chapters. Most of the sentences were edited and restructured, but I tried to remain faithful to his general style of presentation. No new introductions or closing paragraphs were drafted for any of the chapters; they start and end as he left them. This book is Bailey Diffie's legacy.

Endnotes are available only for the first two chapters and the final appendix. Notes for the other chapters were either still in the process of formulation or in such a jumbled state that I could not decipher them. Some readers may be disturbed because of the fairly frequent use of unattributed quotes from primary and secondary sources. I decided to leave them in the text because Bailey had selected these quotations with great care and intended to use them.

No bibliography for this text was ever discovered in Bailey's files. What I originally believed was the proper bibliography turned out to be instead the list of sources for his previous book on Portuguese expansion. The selected bibliography at the back of this volume was generously compiled by Mario Rodriguez, a Latin American specialist and one of Bailey's closest and best friends over the last decade of his life.

I volunteered for this project because of my respect and love for Bailey Diffie, a wonderful friend and colleague who was here at USC as an adjunct professor for nearly a decade after his "retirement" from CCNY. Although unfamiliar with the field of Latin American history, I had been an editor of *Pacific Historical Review* since 1979 and therefore felt sufficiently qualified to undertake this project. I also felt this was an opportunity for me to give back something to the historical profession which has been so generous to me over the last two decades.

Others who contributed their time and efforts included two diligent secretaries in the USC history department, Sharon Mather and Brenda Johnson, as well as Martha Rothermel, who put most of the text on the computer and also acted as production manager in coordinating the movement of the manuscript through various stages of completion involving our word processing and printing equipment. Edilla Diffie was extremely helpful in locating material; she spent much time going through stacks of files and boxes in search of misplaced or incomplete chapters. Frank Mitchell, as always, offered guidance and support. Mario Rodriguez, Dauril Alden, and Francis Dutra carefully reviewed copies of the final manuscript. I join the entire Diffie family in thanking Dean Paul Bohannan of the USC Division of Social Sciences and Chair Mauricio Mazon of the USC History Department for approving grants for secretarial assistance on this project.

MEMORIAL TRIBUTE TO BAILEY W. DIFFIE

by

Frank Mitchell

*Prepared for oral presentation at memorial service on February 7, 1983, at the University of Southern California:

I wish to pay tribute to the memory of Bailey Diffie as our beloved colleague in the Department of History of the University of Southern California. Our collegiate association with Bailey began in the fall of 1970, when he first joined us as a visiting professor of Latin American history. He did not know at the time, nor did we, that that association would continue until the last day of his life. But we knew from the beginning that we were forging a lasting friendship with a warm and remarkable man.

The dozen and a half years that we were privileged to know Bailey were barely one-seventh of his life. From this vantage point, as his colleague and friend during his winter season, we knew the man grown old in years, but ever young in spirit. We came to know, too, through the wonderful stories he shared with us of his youth and middle years, the life of the whole man. We knew him best as one who embraced life lovingly and to its fullest measure.

Each of us will have special memories of Bailey. We knew him in the classroom, the colloquia, meetings of the History Guild, visits in his home, or at ours, at departmental social gatherings, such as softball games and picnics, the annual Christmas party, and in innumerable other ways. The common thread that runs through all of these activities is the collegiality he engendered and his zest for life.

Bailey had a wonderful capacity for transforming the routine experiences of day-to-day living into a pleasurable time of fellowship. Consider the luncheons many of us shared with him over the years at the Faculty Center. Characteristically, Bailey would take the lead in rounding up as many as possible for lunch. How many times did he provoke us to laughter by carefully reading the menu but almost always ordering the Mexican plate of the day? And what did we talk about? The subjects were as diverse as the experiences of his life. We loved to engage him in telling us about growing up in Texas; going to college in Oklahoma; living in Spain as he studied for his doctoral degree. We learned of his love for his family; we learned about the middle years of this century as he had experienced those decades as a professor at City College of New York; we learned of his many travels abroad, his trips to Latin America, Europe, India, and Japan. We talked about football, religion, politics, the state of the economy, and, yes, history.

All of these subjects were interesting, but most important, we wanted to learn about Bailey, *his* life, *his* times. It was as though there was something mysterious about the source of his energy, his vitality, the breadth and depth of his interests, and his engaging capacity for fellowship. But there was no mystery at all, for Bailey was an authentic person with a consistent adventurous bearing. He was forever putting out to sea, taking the tide at floodtime, sailing on new realms of discovery and adventure. When he was with us, he was like the sailor happy to be home, but eager to embark upon the next voyage. His personal odyssey intrigued and inspired us; he dared us to dream bold dreams, to make no small plans, and to never grow old in spirit.

Yes, he knew that he had grown old in years during the time he was our colleague, but he never lost that capacity for living life to the fullest and of inspiring others to do the same. And he took his declining years in stride. I remember his good humor when we were returning late one Friday evening from a dinner meeting of the Los Angeles

History Guild. He was my regular companion on these thrice-yearly meetings and appreciated not having to drive his car after dark. "Frank," he joked, "how will *we* get to the guild meetings when *you* become too old to drive at night?"

We who were his colleagues will remember and cherish Bailey for teaching us to live with a spirit of adventure; and, when one *dream* is fulfilled, to dream again, pressing on, "still tackling plans unfinished, tasks undone."[1]

In celebrating the life Bailey Diffie has lived, ". . .we celebrate the possibilities of our own living, to walk undaunted, to live as freely as we can, to invest ourselves in sharing, and to see the value of today and the promise of tomorrow."[2]

1. S. Hall Young, in *Into the Sunset* quoted in Paul Irion, *A Manual and Guide* (Baltimore: Waverly Press, Inc., 1971), p.44.
2. Adapted from Paul Irion, *ibid.*, p.43.

INTRODUCTION

This history has been written for those seriously interested in Brazil, either the lay reader or the advanced university student. The style is narrative and chronological; it is not quantitative in the recent vogue, nor topical, although statistics are used where applicable and a few topics are treated in their proper place. Insofar as material allows, I have followed events in the order that they occurred. Brazil is such a large and complicated country, however, that it has often been necessary to pursue topics to dates that overlap. For example, in discussing the bandeiras beginning in the sixteenth century, it is impossible to follow simultaneously the conquest of the East-West coast which took place at the same time. Another example is my treatment of the seventeenth century when four principal inland expansionist movements were in progress simultaneously; in this case there is some imbalance in the chronology. I do not, however, as some books in English, and as is the rule in histories of Brazil by Brazilians (with a few exceptions), carry topics through three centuries before returning again to the sixteenth to start anew.

In adopting the chronological approach, I have customarily tried to take up any given subject at the moment it became most pertinent to Brazil, going back in time to trace its development. For example, the Jesuits came to Brazil in 1549; thus I immediately review the origins of the Jesuits before their arrival. Or, to cite another case, in explaining the significance of the royal decree of 1551, which made the king Permanent Grandmaster of the Order of Christ, I trace the history back to Portugal and the long struggle of the king for power over the clergy, culminating in the decision to make the clergy a branch of royal government. I believe this procedure will enable readers to refresh their memories and become more aware of the pertinence of this background information without resorting immediately to other books. [*A substantial amount of this background material was edited out of the final draft due to considerations of length, although much still remains. —E. Perkins]

Although I hold to no single interpretation of history—such as economic, cultural, religious, or geographic—I do place a great deal of emphasis on economic interests as a motivation for human conduct, and I may seem at times to offer readers an economic interpretation. My treatment of the land system created by the Portuguese in Brazil may be cited. This system was started in Portugal as a method of dividing land into small holdings which would be cultivated. In Brazil, on the other hand, it became a system for placing thousands of acres, even hundreds of thousands, in a single ownership.

These are but a few examples of the approach of this book. I hope readers will acquire a good knowledge of Colonial Brazil and how it foreshadowed in many respects the Brazil of today. For, it is certain, that nations do not dig up their historical roots and kill them; rather they sink them deeper into the soil and grow from them.

1

DISCOVERY AND PRELUDE: HOW PORTUGAL DEVELOPED THE CAPACITY FOR WORLD EXPLORATION

On Wednesday, April 22, 1500, as the sun was setting over the coastal mountain range, "at the hour of vespers, we caught sight of land . . . a huge mountain . . . . The captain named it Monte Pascual; and he called the land Terra de Vera Cruz."

The official European discovery of Brazil had been made. Pedro Álvares Cabral, in command of an armada en route to India, made the sighting that was to establish Portugal's claim to lands east of the Line of Demarcation agreed upon in the Treaty of Tordesillas with Spain on June 7, 1494.

Cabral remained along the coast of Brazil for ten days, trying without success to talk to the Indians and to judge the nature of the newly-found land. After consultation with others in his fleet, he dispatched a ship to Portugal to announce the discovery to his king. On May 2 he sailed on toward India, never to return to Brazil.[1]

For more than a century an unnecessary, harmful, and rancorous controversy has raged over the question of whether Cabral followed "secret" orders to sail intentionally to a land already known to the Portuguese or whether he discovered Brazil accidentally, pushed farther west than intended by winds and ocean currents. But whether "intentional" or "accidental," the presence of Cabral's armada in the western Atlantic was not the result of mere accident or chance.

Many centuries of advancement in shipbuilding and navigational science, improvements in commercial and economic systems, and political growth, lay behind Cabral, thus making possible his expedition. It was no accident that Europeans discovered the New World, rather than the Indians the Old World. And it was Portugal, more than any other nation, that led the probing of the Atlantic Ocean.

When the Portuguese began their explorations early in the fifteenth century, Europe knew little of any other part of the world. The Western Hemisphere was unknown, except briefly by the Vikings centuries before.[2] The East—India, China, Japan—was a jumble of names, and seldom the right names. Europe knew itself only as far north as Scandinavia (with its settlements in Iceland and Greenland), the western edge of Russia, the Mediterranean with a small part of the Near East known to the Europeans of the time as the Levant, and the northern rim of Africa. Within one century Portuguese navigators would reveal almost the entire globe to the Europeans.[3]

No other people in prior history made such extensive geographical discoveries as the Portuguese. They were the first to reveal to Europe the unknown coast of Africa, advancing by stages along the West African coast until Bartolomeu Dias passed the Cape of Good Hope and returned to Portugal in 1487–88. They were the first to sail from Europe to India when Vasco da Gama reached Calicut and returned home in 1497–99. Cabral's voyage came next in 1500–01. Other fleets followed Cabral to India and on to Malacca in 1511, China in 1513, and to other parts of the East in the following years.

We need to look far back in history to understand the special significance of leadership in Atlantic exploration by Portugal and Spain. From the third century B.C. to the third century A.D., Portugal had been the western end of a trade area reaching from the Atlantic to the Pacific Ocean. This vast area comprised the Roman dominions from Scotland to the Persian Gulf, the Han Dynasty of China which had established the Pax Sinica as far west as the Caspian Sea, and the Parthian Empire whose borders touched the Han on the east and the Roman on the west. Together they afforded protection for merchants who put the spices of the East on Roman tables and the silks of China on Roman ladies. With the decline of the three great empires in the third century after Christ, most of the interchange ceased, to be renewed only in the thirteenth and fourteenth centuries. At the end of the fifteenth century, Portugal had established East-West contacts by the ocean route, avoiding for the first time the land barrier that divides the Mediterranean Sea from the Indian Ocean. A thousand years of decline and regrowth in the West separated the fall of Rome from the voyage of Cabral. Only the Byzantine Empire survived as a continuation of the eastern part of the Roman Empire to hold off the rising power of Islam from the seventh to the fifteenth centuries.

The rise of Islam profoundly influenced the Christian world, and particularly Portugal and Spain. In one century from its origin in Arabia, Islam spread from Mecca to northern France, where it was turned back after suffering defeat by Charles Martel at Poitiers (Tours) in 732. Retreating, the Muslims settled in the Iberian Peninsula. Slowly the Christians drove southward the Arabic-led people known to the Portuguese and Spaniards as "Moors." The process took more than four hundred years in Portugal and almost eight hundred in Spain, leaving indelible influences in the peninsula that would later become characteristic of the lives of those who settled in the New World, among them the colonizers of Brazil. Brazil's origins in a sense begin with Portugal's—in 1095.

The year 1095 was a key date in both the Iberian Peninsula and in all Europe. In that year Portugal achieved for the first time a separate status under the Castilian kings; and the Pope's call for rescue of the Holy Land from the Muslims set in motion the First Crusade. Thousands of French and other northern Europeans came to the peninsula during the eleventh century. Many fighting men were among them, and the most important were two noble cousins from Burgundy, Raymond and Henry. Raymond married the daughter of Alfonso VI of Castile and was thereby heir to the throne, but died before he could inherit. Henry fared better. He married another daughter, Teresa, born outside canonical wedlock, but granted along with her husband a part of Alfonso VI's dominions known as O Porto, the port, around the mouth of the Douro River. This area they and their son, Afonso Henriques (1128–1185), converted into a kingdom separate from Castile after a long struggle that engendered bitter feelings between the peoples only later known generally as Portuguese or Spaniards. The bitterness and rivalry carried over to America when they colonized their territories; the mutual hostility becoming like the marrow in their bones.

The Crusades to the Levant stimulated contacts between northern Europe and the new Portuguese nation. In 1147 Afonso Henriques persuaded the Crusaders sailing along the coast of Portugal to the Holy Land to stop over and help him conquer Lisbon from the Moors. Lisbon, the finest port in the Iberian Peninsula, thus became a Christian bastion rather than a Muslim barrier to Christian expansion southward. Other Crusaders later again allied themselves with the Portuguese and contributed to the expulsion of the Moors from Portugal in 1249. The south of Portugal, Algarve, also contained good harbors which, though not comparable to Lisbon, served later as points of departure for Portuguese expansion overseas.

Meanwhile, the rise of the Mongol Empire in the thirteenth century once again made trade and cultural contacts possible between the East and the West. The great distances that had to be traveled overland from China to the Mediterranean still hampered this trade, of course, and only articles of great value relative to their weight could be exchanged. For the Christians the necessity of trading through Muslims who held the eastern end of the Mediterranean added further burdens and expense. They began to seek actively a way to avoid the Muslim restraints; and it is pertinent to note that the nations dependent on the Italian cities, who held a near-monopoly over trade with Muslims, began thinking of a way to avoid the Italian merchants.

Western Christians, who naively thought of all non-Muslims as fellow Christians, or at least as potential allies, nourished a belief in a Prester John, supposedly a great Christian monarch who could be brought into an alliance to deliver a crushing blow to the Muslims. Missionaries went to the Mongol rulers. They were received with respect, but they made no progress in converting the Mongols to Roman Catholicism. The threat of Mongol expansion westward against the Muslims, and sometimes the reality of such invasions, nevertheless took some pressure off the Christian West.[4]

Traders as well as missionaries found their way to the East. Eastern spices, gems, silks and other articles of trade enriched many cities along the Mediterranean, the most important being Venice, Genoa, Marseilles, and to some extent Barcelona and other cities of the Iberian Peninsula.

The Polos of Venice became the most famous of all westerners who went to the East. Marco Polo, son of Nicolo and nephew of Maffeo, traveled to the Mongol Empire with his father and uncle in 1271, becoming a favorite of the Khan and then serving him in diplomatic missions. He left China in 1292 on a mission to Persia and was back in Venice in 1295. Marco's wild tales, for they were thought so by many, became very popular, stimulating greater interest in travel and trade. Other writers who had traveled in the East or Africa, or who claimed to have done so, added to the literature about areas outside Western Europe. Marco Polo's book inspired Columbus two centuries later.

While Marco was still in the East, the last of the Crusader's strongholds in the Levant, Acre, fell to the Muslims in 1291. The military aspects of the Crusades were a failure, but commercial and cultural consequences became permanent. Although Christian trade with the East was not by any means cut off by the fall of the last Christian stronghold, it was still more under Muslim control and subject to such tariffs as the Muslims could exact. In times of war, trade could be, and sometimes was, interrupted entirely.

Venice and Genoa were the richest Christian cities, holding a near-monopoly on the products coming from the East. They fought frequent wars for the control of this trade. When Venice at times predominated, Genoa sought other ways to find a route around the Venetian, as well as Muslim, power. In 1291, the same year as the fall of Acre, two Genoese brothers, Ugolino and Vadino Vivalde, sailed out through the Straits of Gibraltar to beyond Safi (Safim), where the Genoese had established trade as early as 1253, in an attempt "to go to the East, to the region of the Indies."[5] Their fate is unknown, but rumors about them persisted for a century and a half.

Other Genoese settled in the Canary Islands, with the island of Lanzarote taking its name from Lanzarote Marocello. The cross of Genoa appears on a map of Lanzarote as early as 1339. The expansion of Europeans into the Atlantic had begun. Other expeditions sailed from Catalonia, Mallorca, Seville, and Portugal during the fourteenth century.

Portugal was in an advantageous geographical location for expansion into the unknown ocean. Situated at the southwest corner of Europe, pinned in by Spain on its east and north, having good ports on both its western and southern shores, its people could not avoid cultivating the arts of shipbuilding, commerce, and fishing. From its origin as a nation in the twelfth century, Portugal had traded with northern Europe, the nearby Spanish ports, and North Africa. If, on the one hand, most Portuguese were still rural dwellers, the coastal inhabitants by necessity faced the sea. Even the earliest kings were business-minded. They built houses as rental properties for income and kept their own shops in the markets, to which they sent their own produce for sale. It is of no small significance to later expansion that the Portuguese monarchs took an active part in economic affairs.

The development of the trading post known as the feitoria, somewhat awkwardly translated into English as "factory," illustrates this point. The trading post was a formal organization of merchants on foreign soil. It was not unique to the Portuguese. The Italians established their trades in African and Mediterranean ports, and similar trade centers were founded by other European nations. In no case, however, was the foreign trading post more important to overseas expansion than to the Portuguese. Its role in Africa and Europe, as well as Brazil, became very important in later times. The feitoria established by the Portuguese merchants in Bruges (Belgium) received royal support in 1293, when King Dinis (ruled 1279–1325) gave his approval to a fund contributed by members of the merchant community to a mutual insurance and protection organization. Dinis also subsidized shipbuilding and promoted the planting of forests to provide lumber for shipyards.

The grandson of Alfonso the Wise of Castile, Dinis, was vigorous in every aspect of kingship: cultural promotion (he was himself a poet and founder of the university), control over the clergy, and economic activities. In his time contacts with the Mediterranean became frequent.

Portugal was an intermediate stopover for the Italian galleys making the run from the Mediterranean to northern ports. Among them was the famous Venetian Galere de Fiandra that left Venice for the North Sea annually beginning in 1293, the same year that King Dinis approved the Portuguese feitoria in Bruges. Genoa was, however, more closely tied to Portugal in commerce than to Venice. In 1317 Dinis brought a Genoese nobleman, Manuel Pessagno (later spelled Pessanha or Peçanha in Portugal), to serve as admiral of the fleet and to bring with him twenty captains to command ships. Thus did Portugal add to its knowledge of the sea from the Genoese. By 1336 or 1341, or possibly both years, a fleet under Italian command with sailors from many different areas sailed from Lisbon for a voyage to the Canaries. Although no other Portuguese expedition to the Canaries can be documented during the fourteenth century, there is no reason to doubt the boast of Afonso IV (1325–57) that his mariners were "the equals of any in Europe."[6]

If Portugal engaged in no other known voyages of venture in the fourteenth century, it did continue the developments that enabled its mariners to explore overseas in the next century. Trade agreements and trade privileges were negotiated with England, France, and Spanish and Italian cities. Fernão Lopes, famous Portuguese historian of the Middle Ages, noted that Lisbon "swarmed" with foreigners during the fourteenth century. Among these were Catalans, Castilians, Mallorcans, Lombards, Milanese, Biscayans, Aragonese, Venetians, Florentines, Piacenzans, Flemings, French, English, and Cahorsians. Far from being isolated, Portugal was a veritable "wharf between the seas" in the Mediterranean-Northern Europe exchange.

Portuguese legislation continued to encourage trade. In 1377 an act that regulated trade between Portuguese and foreign merchants contained a hundred pages of items. The same year, and again in 1380, other acts granted subsidies to shipbuilders. The formation of a Companhia das Naus renewed maritime insurance.

King Dinis also contributed to the process that slowly gave the state control over the secular affairs of the church. Portuguese monarchs were ever respectful (ultramontane) in their attitude toward the spiritual powers of the papacy, but equally diligent in resisting clerical control within their own realms over lands and other economic matters. As an example we may cite the establishment of the Order of Christ. When the papacy, then in Avignon under the influence of the French kings, abolished the Knights Templar, Dinis persuaded the Pope to give Templar properties in Portugal to the new Order of Christ founded in 1319. It received the special mission to carry on the struggle against the infidels wherever they were found. For the time being this meant the Muslims, but later it was interpreted to include all non-Christians. Under royal control, the Order came to be the most important vehicle for carrying the crown to dominance over the church in Portuguese territories. Henry the Navigator was governor and administrator from 1420 to his death in 1460, a post later assumed by the kings themselves.[7]

A change of dynasty in 1385 brought João I, Master of the Order of Aviz, to the throne. He granted special favors to the merchants of Lisbon and Oporto in return for the aid they had given him in his accession to the kingship. He also created a new group of nobles by bestowing on his followers the estates seized from his defeated opponents. The part played by the nobles during the next century was more conspicuous than that of the merchants.

João I also received aid from the English in his struggle against

Portuguese and Spanish opponents, thereby fomenting closer ties between the two peoples. The Treaty of Windsor, in 1386, remained in nominal force for centuries through affirmations in later treaties. It led to the marriage of João to Phillipa, daughter of John of Gaunt, in 1387. One of their sons, Henry, later known as Henry the Navigator, has already been mentioned as head of the Order of Christ from 1420 to 1460.

João's reign (1385–1433) saw the beginning of Portuguese expansion overseas. As previously noted, the Canary Islands were the first European objective in the fourteenth and fifteenth centuries. Populated at the time of discovery, as the other off-Africa islands were not, the Canaries attracted Italians, Mallorcans, Catalans, and other Spaniards in the last half of the fourteenth century. Castile established the first permanent European colony, when it supported Jean de Bettencourt and Gadifer de la Salle who made a settlement in 1402.

Portugal began its overseas expansion in 1415 with the capture of Ceuta in Morocco opposite Gibraltar. Thereafter, it held this important Moorish trade center from which ships had tapped the commerce of the Mediterranean and caravans brought products from the Sahara and West Africa south of the Sahara.[8] Among other objectives sought in capturing Ceuta, Portugal wished to block Castile from further expansion along the Atlantic coast of Africa.

Portugal also discovered the Madeira Islands, uninhabited, possibly as early as 1418, and the uninhabited Azores between 1427 and 1432. The Madeiras lie about 400 miles west of the African coast near the 32nd parallel, and the Azores more than eight hundred miles west of Portugal about 38° to 40°. The ability to make such voyages reveal that the art of navigation had advanced enough to free Portugal from mere coastwise sailing.

The west coast of Africa south of the Canaries remained still unknown to the Europeans. We can say it was unknown to the Africans too, for there is no evidence they had the ships or enough navigational science to pursue even modest coastwide trade, much less adventures on the high seas. Trade and fishing were carried on by the Portuguese and Spanish as far south as the Canaries; but sailing beyond Cape Bojador, situated on the African coast just south of the Canaries, was considered impossible for several good reasons, which we now know, as well as for fancied reasons now known to be nonexistent. The Portuguese, nevertheless, persistently pushed further southward along the coast.[9] Their efforts became more persistent after Prince Henry, "the Navigator," was granted exclusive rights beyond Cape Bojador in 1433. He acted in various capacities and joined his exploratory efforts with those of his experienced mariners. As head of the Order of Christ after 1420, he led the mission of this Order to carry on the fight against the Muslims or any other non-Christian wherever they were. He and the king were also able to obtain several papal bulls granting to Portugal jurisdiction over all areas discovered and to be discovered, if occupied by non-Christians or unoccupied.

Alvise Cadamosto, a Venetian merchant sailing with Portuguese captains in Portuguese caravels, discovered the Cape Verde Islands in 1456, which were uninhabited. A feitoria and fort established on the island of Arguim about 1456 protected the mariners and provided a center for trade. Portuguese mariners had advanced as far as modern Sierra Leone by the time of Henry's death in 1460.

The result of the discoveries was the settlement of people on hitherto unpeopled islands and the development of agriculture and livestock raising. The art of shipbuilding and navigation also progressed while ships were bucking the high waves of the rough Atlantic Ocean. The sailing vessel known as the caravel came into existence along the Portuguese and south Spanish coast sometime after 1434. Alvise Cadamosto, the Venetian merchant who made two voyages in Portuguese caravels in 1455 and 1456 called them "the best sailing ship in the world."

The Spaniards also traded along the African coast. They expanded their hold in the Canary Islands and defended them from Henry the Navigator's efforts to take them by diplomacy or force. The outlines of future Portuguese-Spanish rivalry for supremacy in overseas territories were firmly traced during this period.

There were other results of Portuguese discoveries. The most lucrative African trade became capturing, buying, and selling the Africans themselves. Slavery and the slave trade had existed before European participation, but their entry served to increase the amount of trade greatly. The future of Africans brought into slavery by the Europeans was set from the beginning. Gomes Eanes de Zurara (Azurara), the Portuguese chronicler from whom we learn most of what is known of the early discoveries, describes the large batches of slaves first brought into Lagos on the south coast of Portugal from 1441 onward. They were divided, sold, and separated: "the father in Lagos . . . the mother in Lisbon . . . the children some other place." He also thought it a beautiful thing that they had been enslaved, for, he said, it was better to have a "Christian" soul in an enslaved body than a "lost soul" in a free body. The following centuries would hear this repeated frequently as the standard justification for slavery. The price for a slave was low in European monies. Cadamosto traded at the rate of ten slaves for one horse, and even more at times—for example, King Budomel gave him 100 slaves for seven horses.

Gold, elephant tusks and the tusks of other animals highly regarded as aphrodisiacs, malagueta pepper, the skins of sea lions and other fur-bearing sea creatures, dye-producing plants, and many different forms of wealth led the Europeans to a stronger determination to discover and develop new lands. The Azores and Madeira Islands, by 1460 settled and producing wheat, wine, sugar and various crops, had been parceled out to donataries (donatários) or captains (capitães) who brought in settlers and developed the resources. In many aspects, the characteristics of the future Brazilian colony could be envisaged before Brazil was known to exist.

After 1460 the Portuguese continued to push further south along the African coast. Development began about 1460–62 in the Cape Verde Islands, granted to Prince Fernando, brother of King Afonso V, as governor and to António de Noli, an Italian merchant and one of the discoverers, as captain. The coast of the Gulf of Guinea was discovered, along with some of the islands during the 1470s.

Dynastic rivalry and contradictory claims to African coastal territories and islands brought war between Portugal and Spain in 1475. Both disputes were settled in 1479-80, one known as the Treaty of Alcáçovas, allotting the Canary Islands to Spain and the Madeiras and Azores to Portugal. It also gave to Portugal the coast "from the Canary Islands beyond towards Guinea (contra Guinea)." The doubts about the meaning of this phrase brought further disputes between Portugal and Spain after Columbus discovered America.

João II did not delay reinforcing his claims. He established a feitoria and fort at São Jorge da Mina (El Mina) near present-day Cape Three Points in 1482. Christopher Columbus went with the expedition or was there soon after. The same year Diogo Cão sailed on the king's order to explore further along the coast and discovered the Zaire River (Congo), sailing as far as about 13° S in 1482–84. On a second voyage in 1484–85 he reached almost to the Tropic of Capricorn, 23° S. Bartolomeu Dias completed the task of discovering the coast and rounded the Cape of Good Hope and continued for a distance up the east coast before returning to Portugal in 1487–88. One of those present to see his ship was Columbus. Four years later, in 1492, Columbus, who lived a total of about eight years in Portugal from 1476 to 1484 and learned much of what he knew about navigation while there, discovered America for Spain while attempting to go to the East by the western route.

Portugal thought the lands found by Columbus belonged to it. Spain reinforced its claims with four papal bulls in 1493, the last of which set aside all the rights Portugal had won to undiscovered lands by earlier bulls. Negotiations with the threat of war hovering over the two countries led to the signing of the Treaty of Tordesillas on June 7, 1494. By this treaty Portugal was to have all lands as far as 370 leagues west of the Cape Verde Islands. Spain gained those to the west of this demarcation.

Portugal sent Vasco da Gama in 1497 to establish the route to India within the bounds laid down in the treaty. When he returned in 1499 he had achieved two great objectives: he had circumvented the great land mass that had made overland trade difficult for centuries; and he had freed the Christians from dependence on the Muslim merchants of the eastern Mediterranean.

Portuguese exploration brought great progress in ocean navigation.[10] The compass, manufactured mainly in the Balearic Islands and Italy, was the one indispensable instrument of navigation. The astrolabe, used for centuries by astrologers to chart the stars, was refined and simplified near the end of the fifteenth century, or early in the sixteenth, to determine latitude at sea by observing either stars or the sun. It would evolve to become the sextant of later times. Longitude still could not be determined at sea with exactitude; but observance of the relative positions of moon and the planets gave a rough calculation, as noted by Amerigo Vespucci in 1499. The essential thing was that sailors could go thousands of miles from land, and even around the world, and still return to their home ports. Only after 1764 when John Harrison made the first successful chronometer that kept time at sea was it possible to determine longitude wherever desired.

Ships had also greatly improved. The caravel had retained its place as the best vessel for exploration; but it was larger and better rigged. Stronger vessels, usually called naus in Portuguese, with better sailing qualities than in earlier times, enabled the sailors to live months at sea, albeit still with a high incidence of scurvy that often killed a large portion of the crew and passengers. The art of map and chart making gave the sailors a visible record of where they had been and of the lands they had discovered. Weapons too had improved; the Europeans armed their ships and their land forces with guns and cannons superior to any used by the people they discovered. The rise of a strong merchant class, who supported the king and were protected by him, supplied the indispensable organization needed for sustained overseas exploration and colonization.

In all these matters Portugal led Europe at the time. When Vasco da Gama returned to Portugal with knowledge of how to sail to the East, as well as samples of the riches that abounded there, Portugal now possessed all the elements needed for opening up a new trade empire.

Thus it was not mere chance that permitted Portugal to fit out an armada of thirteen ships; nor chance that they could be supplied with many goods to exchange for the spices and silks of the East. Enroute to India, now known, Cabral discovered a portion of the Brazilian coast, the unknown.

PART II

King Manuel dispatched his second expedition to India with three objectives: to found feitorias for trade; to show off the armed might of Portugal to the Arab merchants and native rulers who had caused Vasco da Gama much trouble; and to establish diplomatic relations with the eastern rulers.

He prepared a strong armada of thirteen ships and placed it under the command of Pedro Alvares Cabral, accompanied by the flower of Portugal's navigators. The departure of the armada was the occasion for elaborate ceremony. After a solemn mass, the king escorted Cabral to the embarkation on March 8, 1500. The next day, when a favorable wind arose, Cabral put to sea. The weather continued good. On March 23, after passing the Cape Verde Islands, one of the ships disappeared "without rough seas or contrary winds to account for it," says Vaz de Caminha. Failing to find the lost ship after two days of search, "we continued our way through the sea," Caminha reported, until there appeared a "huge mountain, high and round." It signalled the discovery of Brazil.

The site lay a bit more than 16° S. latitude. The name given by Cabral was changed by the king to Terra da Santa Cruz, and soon called by the sailors "Land of the Parrots" for the many beautiful types found there. This name was also ephemeral, changed to "Brazil" as soon as it was discovered that an abundance of this dye-wood could be shipped to Europe with profit.

From another source, an anonymous chronicler who accompanied Cabral, there is an account to bear out Caminha's description: "We came in sight of land and went to see what land it was."[12] Cabral sent a boat ashore "to see what people they were." He found them to be "between white and black . . . nude as they were born, without shame . . . . No one understood their language." Bartolomeu Marchioni, a Florentine merchant established in Portugal who owned one of the ships in Cabral's fleet, wrote, after the fleet returned from India, that Cabral "has just discovered a 'New World' " but the voyage was very long and dangerous.[13] Amerigo Vespucci, on his 1501 voyage to Brazil, met some of Cabral's ships at Cape Verde on their return from India and talked with members of the expedition. Brazil, Vespucci said, was the same land he had discovered in 1499.[14]

Forced by high winds, Cabral sailed his fleet a few leagues north of his original sighting. On the morning of April 24 he anchored in a sheltered area to which he gave the name of Porto Seguro. Historians still differ about the exact site. On Sunday, April 26, Franciscan Frei Henrique de Coimbra said Mass on a small island near the mainland. The nude Indians gathered around to form a part of his congregation. What the Indians thought of the procedure cannot be known. The thoughts of the Portuguese who found the nude Indian women and girls attractive, and who for the first time in their lives were attending Mass with naked females, can be more easily surmised. Before Cabral sailed away some days later another Mass was said, and a Christian wooden cross was erected to signify Portuguese sovereignty.

Vaz de Caminha's letter contains the best description of the new discovery. He wrote to the king that the men were naked, "well built," somewhat reddish in color, having "good faces" and "well-shaped noses." They carried bows and arrows, but had not used them against the Portuguese. When shown a sheep, they were indifferent; but the sight of a chicken frightened them and at first none would touch it.

With obvious savor Caminha reported that the young women were just as nude as the men and "not displeasing to the eye." One had painted her body black from knees to thighs, exposing her shameful parts naked and uncovered with such innocence that there was no indecency whatever." Caminha's thoughts seem equally exposed.

The relations between the Indians and the Portuguese were good throughout the entire ten-day visit. Some of the Portuguese went to a village a short distance inland, trading trinkets, bells, and other triffles for feathers, bows, caps made of bird feathers, and "long and beautiful red parrots." The men returned to the ship with the report that they and the Indians "had a lot of fun together."

Caminha saw a divine purpose in the discovery and so advised the king. "Since our Lord who gave them fine bodies and good faces . . . brought us here . . . Your Highness . . . should take measures for their salvation." He thought they would be easily converted to Christianity because they had "no idolatry and no worship."

The Indians led a simple economic life. They had no ox, no cow, goat, sheep, hen, "or any domestic animal." They cultivated manioc and maize and had an abundance of seeds and fruits which, Caminha concluded, made them "stronger and better fed" than the Portuguese.

From where the armada lay, "as far as the eye could reach," Caminha estimated "land and forests" extending twenty or thirty leagues. Neither Caminha nor Cabral nor anyone could imagine the immensity of the newly-discovered land. Mestre João, a Galician astrologer-astronomer who was with the armada to make celestial observations, reported to the king. "Yesterday," he wrote, "we almost understood that this is an island and that there are four in all," from which "men come in dugout canoes (almadias) to fight them."[15]

The mestre had come closer than Caminha to understanding the nature of the Indian society, so falsely peaceable on this first visit, and of the size of the country. Nobody yet knew that from the site where they had landed Brazil would eventually stretch some 1500 miles to the south and 2000 or more to the north, embracing territory between 5° N and 32° S approximately. Caminha's "as the eye could reach" to the west would eventually extend Brazil hundreds of miles beyond the Line of Demarcation to the foothills of the Andes Mountains, the geography influencing history more than the parchment of the Treaty of Tordesillas. Brazil would in time become an empire in size and fact, and would yield far greater riches than the legendary East toward which Cabral was sailing when he made his brief landing in Brazil.

There was undoubtedly a great deal more discussion among the Portuguese than our sources reveal. Caminha reports that Cabral called in his chief men, Caminha among them, for consultation. They agreed that a report to the king must be made about "the finding (achamento) of this land of yours which was just found on this voyage." Cabral, we know, made his own report, for Caminha begins his letter by saying: "Inasmuch as the capitão-mor of this your fleet" and other captains had written, Caminha had decided to do the same. Alas for the gap in our documented history! If Cabral's report lies hidden somewhere, it has not been found. But for Caminha's letter to the king, we would know little about the Cabral days in Brazil. Cabral unloaded his supply ship and sent it home with the message. Caminha's and Mestre João's letters are our only proof of its arrival.

Leaving two degredados (degraded men, or criminals condemned to exile) ashore to survive, if they could, and learn the language of the Indians, and joined allegedly by two sailors who jumped ship to remain with the nude Indians, the fleet sailed on for India. The custom of leaving men behind to learn the languages and gather knowledge about the natives had been started in the African voyages, where it served well. The custom was useful in Brazil also. Two of those left behind by Cabral were back in Portugal in 1502, as we know from Valentim Fernandes, a German printer living in Lisbon. He wrote that he had his information about the 1501 expedition, in which Vespucci participated, from two men who had lived twenty months in Brazil.

Cabral left Brazil en route for India on May 2, 1500, never to see Brazil again, and indeed condemned after his return to Portugal in 1501 to live on his estate and not to be entrusted with another service for his king. No document reveals the reason for his disgrace. Vaz de Caminha, whose informative letter was later to be dubbed "the birth certificate of Brazil," was killed in India during an uprising against Cabral's men.

When the news about Brazil reached King Manuel, he acted at once to find out more about the new discovery. He changed the name to Santa Cruz and dispatched a fleet of three vessels in May 1501. Vespucci sailed with this expedition, in what capacity is not known but certainly in part as an astronomical observer, or as representative of the Medicis bankers and rulers of Florence for whom he worked. It is important to note that Vespucci was the most highly educated man of his time connected with exploration. Though never a mariner or navigator by profession, he was a student of astronomy who calculated longitude by observing the moons of Jupiter some fifteen years before this method was published. It is one of the misfortunes of history that so little of what Vespucci wrote has been preserved, and that some of his writings have come down to us in disputed and disputable versions.

The navigators from the time of da Gama onward began realizing one very important fact about sailing the Atlantic Ocean: the route from the north to India or to Brazil was essentially the same. They had to cross the equator at not less than 20° W to avoid falling into the doldrums off the West Africa coast and not more than 30° W if they were not to be drawn by winds and ocean currents into the West Indies. The instructions for sailing from that day to the present are the same for ships departing either European or American ports.

It was just such a course that the 1501 expedition was sailing when it met at Cape Verde with some of Cabral's ships returning from India. The three ships continued to Brazil, running along the coast a distance estimated variously at 760 to 800 leagues. Neither the point they first touched Brazil nor their utmost limit is known for certain. Somewhere along the coast two men went ashore to trade with the Indians. They soon found the prospects far different from those of India. No rich trade-goods existed here, and no markets for spices. When the men failed to return to the ships, a landing party went ashore to search for them, without success. After all but one of this party was back on the ship, he was surrounded by people Vespucci calls women but some modern authors have decided were men mistaken for women because of their long hair. Initially they seemed friendly, but one of them clubbed him over the head from behind. They then proceeded to cut him up as if he were a side of beef, roasting and eating him in view of the Portuguese, while making signals that the men still in the ships understood to mean that the other two men had met the same fate.

The Spaniards had already encountered cannibalism among the Indians of the Caribbean, and the Portuguese had seen it in Africa; but this was their first recorded experience with it in Brazil. Caminha would probably have been surprised to see the people he described as so peaceable acting so barbarously. The Indians whose souls he urged the king to save had just eaten three of his fellow Christians. As the historian and student of the Indian languages João Capistrano de Abreu wrote: "Cannibalism did not arouse a feeling of repugnance and seems to have been very common. Some tribes ate their enemies, and others their relatives and friends—this was the difference." [17]

In civilization and culture the people of Brazil resembled much more closely those found by the Spaniards in the Caribbean than they did the sedentary Indians of Mexico or Peru, although the people of Mexico also practiced cannibalism on a large scale. In Brazil there were no empires like the Aztec or Inca, no monumental stone and mortar buildings, no large sedentary agricultural societies, no great market places and no surplus to trade with others, and no domestic animals to facilitate life for humanity.

The Indians of Brazil were nomadic, moving frequently from place to place as the soil of their small plots of manioc or maize grew thin or the game that provided their meat (except the flesh of those they ate) became scarce. The rotting of their houses made from uncured wood also encouraged frequent moving and rebuilding.

Although the numerous splits produced hundreds of different groups of Indians, for practical purposes we may note that in the sixteenth century the Europeans faced two main groupings. The Tupi-

Guarani linguistic family, referred to above, lived mainly on the coast and included peoples as far apart as Paraguay and Venezuela. They spoke the lingua geral, or common language, with many dialects but closely related "like Spanish and Portuguese." The other principal grouping, called the Tapuias by the Portuguese, were much more diverse linguistically. They spoke a great many different languages, not dialects of one language family. These Indians the Portuguese called linguas travadas (tongue tied or stuttering), perhaps because the great variety made them less easy to learn. The Tapuias lived mainly in the interior, the sertão, but in some cases fought their way to the coast. They were generally considered more savage and warlike than the Tupi. The Portuguese, as well as the French in the sixteenth century and the Dutch later, used Indians as auxiliary troops against other Indian groups, thereby accelerating the conquest of Brazil. The English and French in North America and the Spaniards elsewhere followed the same strategy of temporary military alliances with Indians hostile to other tribes.

The Indians were powerful warriors. They were armed with bows that could kill a man at a hundred yards or more. Merciless and savage in battle, they gave no quarter except when they were seeking a live captive for ceremonial cannibalism. They might have held off the European invaders for decades if united. The Indians were, however, usually as intent in fighting one another as warring against foreigners. Only now and then did they join temporarily to confront the Portuguese. Given their tribal organization and the numerous subgroupings, union was inconceivable to them. Rather, it must have seemed to them that they were using the Portuguese, or other foreigners, to fight against those people they feared and hated the most— their immediate neighbors.

Usually living in small communities, their cane and straw houses could be rebuilt in a short time. Sometimes they migrated only short distances and at times hundreds of miles, invading the territory of others. From these invasions came the source of the unending wars that provided both sides with the victims killed and eaten in ceremonies attending cannibalism. Also such wars and moves resulted in frequent splits of tribes into separate branches, who continued to speak what became the lingua geral, the general language spoken by the Tupi from Venezuela to Paraguay.[19] Confined almost exclusively to the finite, rather than the infinite, the vocabularies could remain almost unaltered by the various tribes or groups.

Such were the people to whom the Portuguese brought their civilization. The natives were no match for the invaders in warfare, agriculture, commerce, structure of government, linguistic or literary development, or comprehension of what the meeting of two different peoples entailed. Inevitably, the Indians who did not succumb to warfare or disease became in time "Portuguese" in their culture, albeit with modifications. Like the ovary and sperm joining in the womb, a new being would be born, with predominance of the Portuguese male sperm.

ENDNOTES

1. Pero Vaz de Caminha was the scrivener of the trading post (feitoria) to be set up in India by Cabral. His *Carta a El-Rey Dom Manuel* is the most valuable record of Cabral's voyage as far as Brazil. Caminha was unfortunately killed in India during an uprising against the Portuguese, depriving us of further excellent descriptions from his pen. There are many editions of his letter in Portuguese and several different translations. The standard is in Greenlee, *Cabral*, from which this is taken, pp. 5–7. To save space, full titles are cited only in the bibliography. Appendix I discusses in more detail the controversies over the discovery of Brazil, where the principal works are cited. Metzner Leone's *Pedro Alvarez Cabral*, though it does not meet all the canons of academic scholarship is stimulating.

2. The Viking bibliography is abundant. Diffie and Winius, *Foundations of the Portuguese Empire*, has a brief sketch, pp. 9–10, and cites

some of the principal works, including Charles R. Beazley, Gwyn Jones, and Magnus Magnusson.

3. Appendix I for discovery of Brazil and discoveries in general. The principal histories of Portugal are by Fortunato de Almeida, Alexandre Herculano, H.V. Livermore, A.H. de Oliveira Marques, Stanley G. Payne, Damião Peres, Joaquim Veríssimo Serrão. Others are cited in the bibliography.

4. The significance of the Mongols to Portugal is treated briefly in Diffie and Winius, *Foundations*, pp. 15–16, 18. Among the principal works see Walter Heissig, C. Dawson, Eustace D. Phillips, and A.P. Newton, *Travel and Travellers of the Middle Ages*.

5. Diffie and Winius, *Foundations*, Ch. 2; Beazley, *Dawn of Geography*, III, 410–22; Florentino Perez Embid, *Los descubrimientos*, pp. 51–60; Damião Peres, *Descobrimentos*, pp. 13ff. of 2nd edition, 1960; Elias Serra Rafols, "Lançarotte Malocello en Canárias"; Francis M. Rogers, "The Vivaldi Expedition." Further information on the Canaries in Vitorino Magalhães Godinho, "Tentativas de antropologia histó-ricas os Guanchos," in his *Ensaios*, I, 173–78. This is also in the *Dicciónario Histórico de Portugal*, 3rd ed., III, 164–68.

6. For the alleged presence of the Portuguese in the Canaries about 1370, see Diffie and Winius, *Foundations*, p. 25, with notes; Fortunato de Almeida, *História de Portugal*, III, 759–89, where he produces doc-uments of doubtful authenticity on which some Portuguese historians base their arguments; and Rafols, "Lançarotte Malocello," who shows why the material in Almeida is not authentic.

7. A controversy has arisen as to whether Henry the Navigator should be called "Grandmaster" of the Order of Christ, the principal opponent being Charles Verlinden. Diffie and Winius, *Foundations*, p. 26, with references on why it is proper to give him the title.

8. The standard works on the capture of Ceuta are cited in Diffie and Winius, *Foundations*, ch. 3. The basic near-contemporary account is that of Azurara (Gomes Eanes de Zurara), *Crónica da tomada de Ceuta*; also Azurara's other chronicles of the expansion of Portugal in the fifteenth century. Diffie and Winius, *Foundations*, ch. 3–6 discuss Portuguese activity in Africa. Virgínia Ráu and Jorge de Macedo, *O açúcar da Madeira*, show the significance of Portuguese expansion and portents of methods to be used in Brazil later; and Maria de Lourdes Esteves dos Santos de Freitas Ferraz, "Povoamento e economia da Ilha da Madeira no século XV."

9. Diffie and Winius, *Foundations*, describe Portuguese activities along the African coast and in the Atlantic islands, citing the principal sources: Azurara, *Alvise da Ca da Mosto (Cadamosto)*; João de Barros, *Da Ásia*, particularly Decade I, books 2 and 3; Damião Peres, *Descobrimientos*; Pérez Embid, *Descubrimientos*; and F.G. Davenport, *European Treaties bearing on the History of the United States*. For a treatment different from Diffie and Winius, see Edgar Prestage, *The Portuguese Pioneers*. Manuel Nunes Dias in *O capitalismo monárquico Português* (2 vols) stresses the importance of the crown as a rising influence in the new capitalism, as his title shows, but also lays great stress on precious metals and other metals in creating the economic life of the late medieval and early modern periods. For less romantic views of slavery see Ronald Chilcoate, *Portuguese in Africa*, and James Duffy's books.

10. A standard study on the history of navigation is E.R.G. Taylor's *The Haven Finding Art*. A particularly good Portuguese work is Luis de Albuquerque, *Descobrimentos Portuguêses*, pp. 43–83, 129–81, 233–400. Duarte Leite, *Descobrimentos*, I, 375–410 and II, 455–511 is sound, though this writer holds some conclusions of Leite unjustified. Gago Coutinho (Coutinho in bibliography) defends the Portuguese view in numerous works—see his *A náutica dos descobrimentos*. Jaime Cortesão, his brother Armando, and Costa Brochado in numerous books and articles sustain Portuguese primacy over Spain and all other nations. For further bibliography, see Diffie and Winius, *Foundations*, ch. 8.

Vitorino Magalhães Godinho in his *Ensaios*, vols I and II, has several very pertinent articles on Portuguese navigation, with generally sound information and analysis. Duarte Leite, *História dos Descobrimentos*, 2 vols., edited by Godinho holds the same views. A. Teixeira da Mota, "As rotas marítimas Portuguêsas no Atlântico," and especially his *Mar, Alem Mar* (1972), contains excellent treatises on the Portuguese art of navigation and the discoveries. The best short treatment on the African coastal discoveries is by Eric Axelson, "Prince Henry the Navigator and the Discovery of the Sea Route to India." As a supplement to Portuguese discoveries see Peter E. Russel, "Fontes documentais castelhanas," in Do.T.e H.

11. See footnote 1.

12. The Anonymous Chronicler, quoted in Greenlee, Cabral, pp. 57– 58.

13. Marchioni, in *ibid.*, pp. 149–50.

14. Vespucci, in *ibid.*, pp. 154–55.

15. Mestre João, in *ibid.*, 37–38.

16. Bailey W. Diffie in *Latin American Civilization*, p. 633, incorrectly attributed the killing and eating of three members of the expedition to Cabral's voyage instead of to the 1501–02 expedition described in Vespucci's letter. Donald C. Worcester in *Brazil* repeats the same error. On the controversies surrounding the 1501 expedition see Damião Peres, "A expedição de 1501–02," and a strongly dissenting view in Marcondes de Souza, "A expedição de 1501–02," cited in bibliography. Robert Southey, *History of Brazil*, I, 14–16 covers this material.

17. Capistrano de Abreu *Capítulos de história colonial*, 1969 edition, p. 48. Florestan Fernandes in *A função social da guerra na sociedade Tup-*

inambá has a different point of view; Frederico G. Edelweiss, *Estudos Tupis e Tupi-Guaranis*, stresses the great influence of the Indians in the post-conquest period. His bibliography is extensive; Carlos Borges Schmidt, *Técnicas agrícolas primitivas e tradicionais*, shows native influences on early European colonization; Helza Cameu's *Introdução ao estudo da música indígena brasukeura*, although discussing modern Indians, no doubt indicates the past well, with many examples of music, songs, and photographs of modern Indians and their instruments.

18. Capistrano de Abreu, *Capítulos* (1969 ed.), pp. 47ff.; Lemos Brito, *Pontos de partida para a história econômica do Brasil*, 2nd ed., pp. 163–82.

19. Modern ethnologists classify the Indians into more exact divisions than those used in colonial times. With many variations in spellings, the three principal divisions are: (1) Tupi-Guarani = Potiguares, Caetés, Tupinambás, Tupininquins, Tamoios, Teminós, Carijós, Tabajaras; (2) Gés: = Aimorés, Botocudos, Apinajés, Xavantes; (3) Caribés or Caraíbas and Nuaraques, in the Amazon and parts of Mato Grosso. This classification is cited in Buarque de Holanda, *História do Brasil: Curso Moderno*, p. 40; and Holanda, *História geral*, passim and index of vol. II and vol. I, 72–86.

2

EARLY COLONIZATION

ortugal had the background of experiences needed for the colonization of Brazil. The century of exploration and settlement in the Atlantic islands and Africa evolved the two systems that were instituted in Brazil, the *feitoria* (trading post) and the *doação* (proprietary grant or captaincy). The feitoria had been developed in step with the increase of Portugal's trade with northern Europe.[1] Extended to the African conquests, it was both a trading post and a fortification for the protection of the colonists. Examples of these were the island of Arguim off the West Africa coast about 20°N latitude and São Jorge da Mina on the Gulf of Guinea.

The feitoria, as first seen in Europe, presupposed a going trade system with political control remaining in the hands of the nationals. In Africa and Asia, Portugal took by force or treaty the enclave where the feitoria was established; the surrounding territory, as in Europe, continued to be governed as it had been before the Portuguese entered. In Brazil, where the Indians practiced the most rudimentary form of barter and lacked a political system that maintained stable control over any area, the feitoria was both an armed post and a creator of production and trade. The development of brazilwood cutting and the creation of a market for other forest products came first.

The doação had been used to colonize the uninhabited islands of the Atlantic: the Madeiras, Azores, and Cape Verdes, as well as some smaller islands. The first such grants had been made by Prince Henry in the Madeira Islands in 1446; among the grantees was Bartomoleu Perestrelo who received the island of Porto Santo.[2] (His daughter married Christopher Columbus many years later.) Such grants were extensive territorial concessions, including both economic and political powers. The key elements in this type of grant were an outgrowth of the Reconquest, the advance of the Christian Portuguese against the Moors. Landownership went to those who won it. In the north of Portugal at the beginning of the Reconquest, many small farms were in the hands of the peasantry, whose overlords were either the king directly or other nobles or clergy—bishops, abbots of monasteries, or masters of religious orders. The mountainous and broken terrain favored such small divisions of land.

The landownership pattern changed as the Reconquest moved toward the south and east of the Tejo (Tagus) River, into the regions of Alentejo and Algarve. The nobles and churchmen who took leading parts in the wars against the Moors claimed large amounts of land as their reward, including economic and political privileges which otherwise might have been exercised by the king, or left in the hands of the local commoners.

The Portuguese kings sought to compel cultivation of idle lands. The Law of Sesmarias, enacted by King Fernando in 1375, provided for confiscation of idle lands and giving them to other owners whose tenure depended on keeping their grants in cultivation.[3] In the north of Portugal sesmarias were small; in the south they tended to become larger as the costs of putting lands into cultivation became greater. In the Atlantic islands sesmarias were still larger, for the expenses of moving from Portugal to the Azores or Madeira were very high. In Brazil the sesmaria became much larger yet, and might match the size of a large estate in Portugal.

Portugal applied in its colonies the same concepts of royal control over economics and political structure. The king granted the islands to Henry; and Henry, in turn, granted them as proprietary grants to others, with the grantees usually receiving the title of captain. The rights to manufacture sugar, for example, were usually a monopoly given to favorites who had the ability to develop them. The slave trade, gold, and other commerce belonged to the king. Foreign commerce was limited to merchants, native or foreign, who held a concession from the king. The spice trade of the East became a royal monopoly. The king regarded Brazil as his property to grant to whomever he wished and in the form he wished. He was simultaneously a great lord of lands and a great merchant—in Portugal, in the islands, in the East, and in Brazil.

Brazil offered less than the East, or even the islands in the Atlantic, in its initial prospects. As late as the time of João III, his chancellor spoke of Brazil as "barbarous, unstable and poor." But however poor the first prospects seemed to some, the king authorized feitorias, or captaincies, in Brazil as he had in Africa and India.

The first feitoria was established at Cabo Frio, where the coast turns rather abruptly toward the west, about one hundred miles from Rio de Janeiro, in 1503. Another was created in Guanabara Bay. Not much definite is known about either of them, and it is possible that Cabo Frio was an outpost fortification more than a trading center.

Brazilwood was the only product of substantial commercial value. Europe bought great quantities to make dyestuff for the expanding textile manufacture. The principal area of the trees lay between São Vicente to the south and Rio Grande to the north in amounts that were inexhaustible in colonial times, although it was necessary to go inland farther and farther to find them.

King Manuel faced the problem of finding the best solution for developing Brazil. Portugal was a small country of about a million people. Its resources were not adequate to develop simultaneously the East, Africa, and Brazil. The East glittered far more than Brazil in the Portuguese eye and attracted more merchants and people of substance. Africa below the Sahara paid for itself in slaves, gold, malagueta pepper, and numerous other products; but the always financially exhausting cost of Morocco was too much strain on the royal purse.

King Manuel adopted the traditional solution that Portugal had evolved for new territories: he established feitorias. The problem was to find men who would invest their money in Brazil rather than the fabulous East. True, the Samorin of Calicut was almost as naked as the Indians of Brazil; but the parts not covered by a loin cloth were covered with diamonds, rubies, and pearls that whetted the greed of the Europeans. And the East had a market system that facilitated trading for its products. Brazil had none of this. Whatever wealth Brazil potentially had would have to be hacked from thick forests, in which lurked great dangers from other men, from animals, and from disease. Where could the king find men who would forego the performance of India for "the promises of Brazil?" The one advantage Brazil could offer over India was a much shorter voyage—four months less than the route to the East.

After the return to Portugal of the 1501–02 expedition to Brazil, in which Vespucci sailed and about which he made a report to his Medici employer, Manuel contracted with a group of Lisbon merchants to develop Brazil. An Italian merchant in Seville reported: "The king of Portugal leased the land that Vespucci discovered," wrote the Florentine merchant Piero Rondinelli, "to certain 'New Christians' who are obligated to send six ships every year and to discover annually three hundred leagues or more and construct a fort."[4] The lessees, Fernando de Noronha (Loronha) and associates, contracted to pay the king nothing the first year, one-sixth of the value of the wood in the second, and one-quarter in the third. In 1504 Noronha was made captain of the islands off northeast Brazil which now bear his name. This was the first donatory captaincy in Brazil; it was granted because he allegedly discovered it.[5]

The existence of the brazilwood concession to Noronha is confirmed by Lunardo de Cá Masser, who wrote: "This Brazil wood is leased to Fernando della Rogna, 'New Christian' . . . who . . . sends his fleets and men every year to the said Terra Nova at his own expense . . . "[6]

The existence of the Noronha contract confirms Vespucci's statement that on his "fourth voyage" he founded a feitoria at Cabo Frio in 1503. Two vessels (of six that sailed from Portugal) were loaded with brazilwood and returned to Portugal. Twenty-four men with arms remained to man the fort-feitoria.[7] Until recently most historians have stated or assumed that Noronha's contract was renewed for another five years for an annual fee of 4,000 cruzados paid to the king. On the basis of more extensive research, John L. Vogt believes that the contract was not renewed but that the logging was thrown open, with Noronha and his associates still participating.[8]

The French, chief users of the dye wood, broke into the trade shortly after the discovery of Brazil.[9] French merchants lived in Portugal and knew of Brazil and India from the time of the first expeditions. There is no mystery about the appearance of the French cutting and shipping wood from Brazil. The first known ship was the *Espoir*, commanded by Binot Paulmier de Gonneville, in 1504–05. He first started out for the East. While trading in Lisbon, he had seen "the great wealth of spices and other rarities arriving in Lisbon on the Portuguese ships from the East Indies" and had decided to make an eastern voyage. Taking on as guides two Portuguese who had just returned from the East, he sailed for India but was forced by the weather to make Brazil instead.

His presence was illegal in Portuguese eyes; but the French, English, and others never acknowledged the validity of the papal bulls nor the Treaty of Tordesillas dividing the discoveries between the Portuguese and Spaniards. We would like to know much more about the French voyages, but enough is known to make it clear that the French sailors of Normandy, Brittany, and even from the Mediterranean were in Brazil soon after the discovery and showed great ability in making friends with the Indians. They persuaded the natives to cut wood and in some cases to fight for them against the Portuguese. The Indians distinguished between the lighter colored French with ofttimes reddish hair, calling them *mair*, and the darker Portuguese, calling them *pero*. Other terms were applied to both the French and the Portuguese by the Indians up and down the coast.

French pirates and corsairs preyed on Portuguese (and Spanish) shipping, both in European and American waters, as was the practice off European and African coasts long before the discovery of America. The line between legal corsairs and pirates was not easily drawn. The kings of both Portugal and Spain often made representations to the

lish sovereigns against the pirates (or corsairs) and
ured that the illegal practices would stop; but they
se letters of marque and reprisal were customarily
opean monarchs as a means of recovering damages
for their own merchants who had been robbed at sea. This custom
led to an endless series of attacks and robberies, each side blaming
the other. The French presence along the Brazilian coast continued
for more than a century; and boundary questions were held over to
the nineteenth century.

Paulmier de Gonneville touched down in southern Brazil, possibly
in the Santa Catarina of today, where he remained for about six
months. The Indians of this region dressed in loose garments covering
both front and back and were described as "simple, not asking anything but to live happy lives without great labor." Gonneville makes
the interesting statement that he brought home the son of Chief
Arosca, as well as another Indian, "because it is the custom of those
who go to the new lands of the Indies to lead to Christianity some of
the Indians" from "this country of the Western Indies, where for
some years past . . . the Normans and Bretons go to cut dye wood,
get cotton, monkeys, parrots, and other things."[10]

Farther north, possibly in the area of Porto Seguro, he found unfriendly Indians who killed some of his men. He described them as
"loutish, naked as the day they came from their mother's womb, men
and women, and furthermore, cruel maneaters."[11] Other Christians,
he said, had preceded him there. (Cabral or later Portuguese?) Still
farther north he found the Indians friendly, but not so his fellow
Christians. After a grueling voyage home, he was off the Isle of Jersey,
when an English pirate, assisted by a French ship, attacked him. They
threw overboard his cargo and records, which included a long report
on his voyage to Brazil. He was forced to abandon ship after losing
a number of his crew. The only thing left to history is the statement
he later made to the French officials. Gonneville's voyage was made
during the years Noronha was holding his "monopoly" of the brazilwood trade.

No complete records of the numbers of ships sent to Brazil has been found. In 1511 the *Bretoa*, which belonged to Noronha and his associates—Bartolomeu Marchione, Benedetto Morelli, Francisco Martins—sailed to Cabo Frio in February and returned to Portugal with a cargo consisting of 5,000 logs of brazilwood of 20 to 30 kilograms each. The captain had two parakeets, three parrots, and a wildcat. Members of the crew had varying numbers of monkeys and other such coveted prizes bartered from the Indians. The value of this "zoo" was assessed at 23,200 *reaes* on which the crown levied a tax of 7,000 *reaes.*

The *Bretoa* carried thirty-five slaves. How were they obtained? The Regimento (instructions) expressly forbade the Portuguese "to do any harm or injury to the natives." Either the Regimento was ignored or its terms were more elastic than they seem when read today. The slaves could have been captured by force or they could have been bought from the Indians themselves.[12]

It must be presumed that other settlements besides Cabo Frio and Rio de Janeiro existed. But were they stable enough to be called feitorias, as some authors do? The wood could not be quickly picked up and loaded. Trees had to be felled and then cut up for convenient loading. The Europeans supplied the tools and techniques to the Indians who did the main part of the work, though no doubt both the Portuguese and French crews also helped. The stone-age tools with which the Indians worked before the discovery were not capable of felling the large trees efficiently and cutting them into the requisite lengths weighing from 20 to 30 kilograms. Did the Indians themselves use the dye of brazilwood? They used a variety of dyes we know, but perhaps not from the tree. The Portuguese and French brought the steel saws and axes to cut the trees as well as wedges, hammers, and other tools.

They induced the Indians to work by bartering items that in the Indian eye were very valuable—bells, venetian glass, scissors, knives, mirrors, fishhooks, and many other things that cost the Europeans little. The Portuguese could compare the Brazilian trade with that of the East, as mentioned above, where shrewd and sophisticated merchants of India, Ceylon, Malacca, China, and other regions waited in permanent markets well supplied with expensive merchandise.

The Portuguese, French, and eventually other Europeans who came to Brazil, faced a difficult problem. They had to find a suitable port, build a trading post and fort (for the "friendly" Indians were volatile and could turn from cutting wood to fighting in an instant), keep adequate supplies of food and tools brought from Europe, barter with the Indians for native foods, plant—or induce the Indians to plant—manioc, maize, beans or other foods, and introduce European plants and animals.[13]

The French, who had no distracting Eastern trade as yet, proved very good at the kind of development needed in Brazil. Louis XII and later Francis I belligerently supported the rights of their seamen to sail anywhere in America, whether in the Portuguese or Spanish territories.

Other French ships were unquestionably along the coast shortly after Gonnevilles, but details are lacking. King Manuel protested to Francis I in 1516 about interlopers; but Francis rejected such protests. He said in an often-quoted quip that he would like for somebody to show him the clause in Adam's will that divided the world between Portugal and Spain. Thus Portugal could expect little more than diplomatic disclaimers as long as Francis I encouraged his seamen.[14]

Manuel I ordered establishment of a feitoria and colonization of Brazil in the same year that he protested to Francis I about French intervention in Brazil. He sent Christóvão Jacques in 1516 to drive the French from anywhere they might be found. Jacques founded a feitoria in Pernambuco, and possibly an early prototype of the captaincy. He also sailed south along the coast as far as Río de la Plata if we accept somewhat sketchy evidence on this point. Spanish and Portuguese rivalry for the areas along the coast continued as long as the exact dividing line could not be surveyed. Magellan coasted Brazil in 1519 at the beginning of the world-encircling voyage, which was captained by Sebastián del Cano after Magellan was killed in the Philippines.

The French did not desist voyaging to Brazil. Hugues Roger was there in 1521. Jean Parmentier, a poet from Dieppe, refers to sailing to Brazil between 1520 and 1525. The cosmographer Crespin says the Normans were in Rio de Janeiro in 1525.

Aleixo García and four companions made their spectacular journey to the Andes at about this time (1524?). Reportedly survivors of Juan Díaz de Solís's 1515–16 expedition to Río de la Plata (where Solís was killed and consumed by the Indians), they had been living in Santa Catarina for some ten years. There they had picked up the story of a "white king" of fabulous wealth somewhere to the west. Starting from the coast, the original members of the expedition recruited some 2,000 Guaraní Indians to accompany them to the Andes, where they gathered a great booty. Some of the Guaraní warriors became lost in retreating from the attacking Andean Indians, and others remained in the foothills of the Andes. García and his remaining companions were attacked by the Guaranís of Paraguay, robbed and killed. The silver and gold, if it existed, was lost. The facts of this story cannot be easily separated from the fiction; but the legend of the "white king" remained around to influence the Portuguese thoughts about the mineral wealth that might be found.

Rodrigo de Acuña, who had sailed with the fleet of Frei García Jofre de Loaysa that failed to round Cape Horn or navigate the Strait of Magellan en route to the East, took refuge in Santa Catarina on returning from the south. Some of his men deserted in Santa Catarina to join other Europeans already there. Upon reaching Bahia, he found three French ships, and here too some of his men deserted, while others were killed. Although the accounts are confusing, it is clear that the French ships were in Bahia and that a French trading post existed in Pernambuco. Other adventures of Acuña are too extensive to be included here.[15]

Two other Spanish expeditions touched Brazil in 1525 and 1526 under Diogo García and Sebastian Cabot, respectively. García, with three ships, made port in São Vicente. He found a man called only the "bacharel" and never named, leading to much surmise about his identity—whether he was the same or different from another "bacharel" mentioned by others. What this bacharel had done is more evident than his identity. He had lived around São Vicente long enough to have fathered numerous *mestiça* daughters who were married to other shipwrecked or degradado Europeans. García contracted with the bacharel or with Gonçalo da Costa to purchase Indian slaves, buy supplies, and build a brigantine. At this time João Ramalho, who had been in Brazil since about 1509 or 1510, already lived in the area where São Paulo was later founded. Of him, more later. Another contemporary, Diogo Álvares, better known by his nickname of Caramuru, lived around the Recôncavo of Bahia. He too had fathered a family of children with Paraguaçú, daughter of a chief, and played an important part in Portuguese colonization.

Sebastian Cabot touched down in Pernambuco in 1526 on a voyage that was supposed to take him to the Moluccas, but he got no further than Río de la Plata. Cabot apparently visited the feitoria in Pernambuco, the origin of which is obscure. Was it built by Christóvão Jacques in 1516, or possibly as late as 1521 or 1526? A great deal of uncertainty exists. The Spaniards reported a feitoria in 1525. The same? In any case, Cabot picked up in Santa Catarina the stories about the riches to be found southward and sailed on to Río de la Plata. There were allegedly riches enough to make "the page boy as rich as the master," and he desisted from his voyage to the East.

Numerous groups of Portuguese settlers lived along the Brazilian coast by 1526. In addition, there were Spaniards, Germans, Italians, Basques, Catalans, Genoese, Neapolitans, Levantines, and, of course, French. Such a mixture resulted from the multi-national sailors that made up the ship crews of that period.

Sugar was produced in Pernambuco by 1526. The Lisbon customs collections included Pernambuco sugar which could date from 1526 or before. Among the instructions Jacques received from the king was one to relieve from duty "Pêro Capico, captain of one of the said captaincies of the said Brazil who sent me word that the period of his captaincy had ended and that he wished to return to this kingdom . . ."[16]

King João III sent Christóvão Jacques in 1526 with a fleet of six ships to drive out the French brazilwood cutters. Jacques found three ships from Brittany in Bahia, sank them, and according to King Francis I, who lodged an ineffectual protest to the king of Portugal, executed the crews in frightful ways. Some of the Frenchmen escaped Jacques and fled inland. The others, about 300, were taken to Pernambuco where they were allegedly tortured and put to death. Of these, some were buried to their necks and served as targets for men firing *arcabuzes*. Portuguese historians say they were sent alive to Portugal. If they reached Portugal, they left no trace.[17] Colonial rivalries were for keeps in the sixteenth century.

Francis I granted letters of marque to Jean Ango of Dieppe to avenge the deaths of French crews and recover the loss in ships. João III later asserted, certainly with some exaggeration, that French attacks had cost his subjects 300 ships and 500,000 cruzados of merchandise.

At least one English voyage reached Brazil in this period. William Hawkins made three voyages to Africa and Brazil, the first in 1530. He reported that he got along well with the Indians. Other records show that by 1530, Spanish, French, and English, as well as Portuguese ships traded in Brazil. Many members of the crews were shipwrecked or left ashore as *degredados* or deserted ship and remained in Brazil by preference. Still others were forced ashore after being defeated in naval battles. They had some chance of survival on shore with the Indians but almost none if captured by their "Christian" enemies. Not all who fell into the hands of the Indians ended up on the *boucan* (the spit for drying and roasting meat commonly used by the Indians of the tropics from Brazil to the Caribbean).

The English historian Robert Southey, whose history of colonial Brazil still ranks as the best in the English language, though written a century and a half ago, was obviously incorrect when he wrote that, in the first years of the sixteenth century, "Brazil was left open like a common." He was much closer to the facts when he said that "individuals meantime being left to themselves settled in the harbors and islands along the coast; and little towns and villages were growing up."[18] On the other hand, there does not exist sufficient documentation to justify the Portuguese historian Jaime Cortesão, whose opinions Oliveira Marques accepts, in locating specifically so many feitorias, unless he acknowledges every temporary landing of ships to cut brazilwood as a feitoria.[19]

More settlements were springing up, nevertheless, as we know from evidence of the years when Cabot and García saw São Vicente. The settlers had constructed "ten or twelve houses, one of stone with tiled roof and a tower for defense against the Indians if necessary. They have native fruits, Spanish chicken and hogs, and an abundance of vegetables."[20] Who had brought from Europe the chickens and hogs and seeds for vegetables? No record tells us; but it was the custom of ships of the time to have live animals aboard for food and to transplant seeds and animals in the lands they reached. We see other signs of the situation when Cabot left for home in May 1530. He had on board some 70 Indians belonging to Gonçalo da Costa as well as to the bacharel and "other Christians who lived in the land." The Indians soon died in captivity. "Saved" by baptism into Christianity before death? No record gives us the answer.

The first settlers were of great help to the Portuguese when formal colonization began, as were some of the early French woodcutters who had established themselves along the coast.

King João III saw the need for stronger colonizing efforts. Christóvão Jacques proposed to bring a thousand colonists; but the king did not accept his offer. João de Melo da Câmara, brother of the captain-donatary of São Miguel in the Azores, wanted to settle two thousand colonists free of expense to the crown. They would be, he promised, "people of substance and very rich who could bring with them many horses, mares, cattle, and everything for the development of the land."[21]

João III chose instead Martin Afonso de Sousa as the man entrusted with the task of establishing a firm Portuguese colonization in Brazil. Sousa was a collateral kinsman of the king, descended from Afonso III. The king and Sousa had been boyhood playmates. Sousa was given three missions: to forestall Spanish colonization on the coast; to drive out the French who were already there; and to establish a colony with some of the men of the expedition "who might wish to stay there and people the land."[22]

Charles V (I of Spain), the Emperor, who was double brother-in-law of João III (each married to the other's sister), had already sent out four expeditions that touched on the Brazilian coast—Juan de

Solís, Diego García, Sebastian Cabot, and Rodrigo de Acuña. None of these had been sent directly to Brazil as colonizers, but there was basis for Spanish ownership of parts of the coast and João III became uneasy. Where the Río de la Plata led nobody yet knew, but it could possibly lead men to the riches of the "white king" already being sought. Furthermore, by 1530 Spain had much better evidence than hearsay about the riches of the Andes.

After a quarter of a century of consolidation in the Caribbean and the conquest of Mexico, the Spaniards had begun to follow an isthmus-of-Panama crossing discovered by Nuñez de Balboa (1513). They were advancing down the Pacific Coast of South America in search of the "rich empire" widely known to the Indians living from Central America southward. The explorations of Pascual de Andagoya in 1522 and those of Francisco Pizarro and Diego de Almagro, with financial aid secured by the priest Hernando de Lugue, were known or rumored in Portugal. In 1528 Pizarro and Cortés met in Spain, where Portuguese courtiers attending the Portuguese wife of Charles V, Empress Isabel, sister of João III, could hardly have missed hearing about the activities of the Spaniards.

João III was discussing with his advisers and debating with himself the best course to adopt for defense and development of Brazil. He had found out that the system in the East impoverished his own treasury and enriched his favorites. "The factors grow rich while the kings become poor" had become a well-known saying in Portugal. He hoped to change this in Brazil and perhaps have some of the luck his brother-in-law was having in Spanish America (from which Charles V was not yet getting the great revenues that João III imagined). As yet, nobody knew where the boundary was between their respective realms in America; the impression grew in Portugal that Brazil was "alongside Peru" and that Peru was perhaps within the Portuguese sphere. At least, the Portuguese were never timid in pushing their claims to the utmost limit they could imagine. One of the missions of Martin Afonso de Sousa was to examine the terrain and gather more geographical knowledge.

Spain learned of Sousa's projected expedition. The Empress Isabel, in the absence of Charles V, protested to her brother João III against voyages to the Río de la Plata and Amazon because Spain considered these to be within Spanish realms (which later knowledge verified). João sent a copy of Sousa's *regimento*, or instructions, to Spain with the assurance that no trespass was contemplated.

João III had great difficulty in financing Sousa's fleet. His treasure chest had been almost emptied in paying his many other expenses. The fleets sent to the East cost large sums. Portugal carried on constant war with the Arabs and Turks in the Persian gulf and Indian Ocean defending its merchants and feitorias. Even more expensive, and with little economic return, were the armies and navy Portugal maintained to defend Ceuta, Tangier, Arzila, and other Moroccan territories from the frequent attacks of the Moors. The thousands of men who won pensions from the king kept the royal purse empty paying obligations to men who no longer served an economic purpose.

João III thought of all such expenses, no doubt, when he instructed Sousa "to remember the people and the armada you have and the amount it cost and continues to cost." The king himself could hardly forget. His chief counselor, the Count of Castanheira (also a kinsman of the king and cousin of Sousa), reported years later that shipwrecks by midcentury had cost 3,353,150 cruzados, not including those off Guinea and Brazil.

Martim Afonso de Sousa's fleet consisted of two caravels and three larger ships with about 400 people, counting fidalgos, sailors, and men at arms of several nationalities—Spaniards, Germans, Italians— as well as Portuguese. A person called Pêro Capico was possibly the same man who was feitor in Pernambuco in 1526. Other members of the expedition had also been in Brazil before.

The king gave Sousa wide powers and restrained him with some limitations. He was not to infringe on Spanish territory; but given the existing state of geographical knowledge he could hardly avoid doing so if he sent his ships, as instructed, to the Amazon and Río de la Plata.

Nobody knew for certain where the Tordesillas line cut through South America. Alonso de la Cruz, a Spaniard, had written shortly before in his *Yslario* that the Portuguese claimed Santo Amaro and

São Vicente but, he said, "they are mistaken" because all Brazil lay "four degrees further east" than they thought; the line was consequently east of that part of the Brazilian coast.[23] The Spaniards continued to make this claim until 1750, but this did not inhibit Sousa from advancing deliberately beyond São Vicente to the Río de la Plata.

Sousa's fleet sailed from Lisbon December 3, 1530. No women accompanied the expedition, only men, a fact that led some historians to deny that it had a colonizing mission. The first known Portuguese married woman was not in São Vicente until 1538. The fleet reached Cape Santo Agostinho, in today's Pernambuco, at the end of January 1531. Before Sousa's arrival, French ships had taken the feitoria. Three of the French ships were found nearby and captured. Two were incorporated into Sousa's fleet, and the third was loaded with brazilwood and sent home.

After the defeat of the French ships, Sousa sent two caravels to reconnoitre the Amazon River, at that time confused with and called the Maranhão. He sailed south with the rest of his fleet. In the Bahia de Todos os Santos, he found Diogo Álvares, famous under his Indian name Caramuru—"a Portuguese," claimed Pêro Lopes de Sousa, Martim's brother, in his diary, the only surviving detailed record of the voyage.[24] Caramuru, whose Indian name has been translated as meaning "Big Fish" or "Man of Fire" would become the key to Portuguese success at a later date.

Pêro Lopes commented on the women. He, like all the others, found the women "very pretty" and light in complexion—as some of the mestiça daughters of Caramuru no doubt were. The European judgment of the color of the Indians varied somewhat from one observer to another; but all were comparing them with the other exotic women they knew, the Blacks of Africa. After a few days in Bahia, Sousa sailed on, leaving with Caramuru, says Pêro Lopes, "a great store of seeds to test what the soil would grow," a statement used by some to prove the colonizing mission of Sousa. This was not an isolated incident but was similar to actions taken by other early voyagers, which explains why so many European plants were found growing in America at an early date.[25]

In mid-March, Sousa left for Rio de Janeiro and met great difficulty in sailing along the Brazilian coast south and west at that season. Pêro Lopes describes in a graphic, day-by-day account the contrary winds and ocean currents that hindered the fleet. Such difficulties were constantly encountered in colonial times, and still are often an important hindrance to navigation.

Near Bahia they picked up a *batel* in which Diogo Dias, feitor of the Portuguese trading post earlier captured and sacked by the French, had escaped. The batel belonged to a caravel enroute to Sofala in East Africa. Sousa renamed the caravel and incorporated it into his fleet. The caravel carried a number of Indians who had been enslaved. Sousa freed them and set them ashore, let us hope among their own tribesmen, because otherwise he did them no favor.

He remained three months in Guanabara Bay. He established an *arraial* (a temporary fortified camp) as was the Portuguese custom, and constructed two brigantines, each with fifteen benches for rowers. He also sent four men inland to scout the surrounding country. They covered an estimated 65 leagues in the mountains and traversed a large plain of 50 leagues. A "great king" met them and helped them find their way back to Guanabara Bay. He presented them with crystal and other things the Portuguese found interesting. Nothing interested them more than his assurance that in the Paraguay River, which no Portuguese had yet seen, they would find "much gold and silver." Sousa gave the "great king" many presents for the good news.

Leaving Guanabara Bay on August 1, Sousa sailed on to Cananéia, which he reached on August 12. He remained in Cananéia forty-four days. "We never saw the sun," Pêro Lopes recorded in his diary— lightning, thunder, rain, winds, broken cables, and lost anchors. In Cananéia they found a bacharel—the same mentioned before?—who had lived in Brazil for "thirty years." If taken literally, he had been there since 1501. Whether he was a shipwreck, exile, or beachcomber is a mystery that has intrigued all who write of this period. He and half a dozen or so other men rendered great help to the new arrivals.

A man named Henrique Montes, who knew the area from the time he served in the Solís and Sebastián Cabot expeditions, was with Sousa. The Spaniards had tried in vain to induce him to return to

Spain. He met again a Francisco de Chaves, also a survivor of the Solís voyage, who had lived in Brazil long enough to learn the "lingua geral," Tupí. One of the pilots, Pedro Anes, also knew Tupí. They and other residents of Cananéia assured Sousa that it was the ideal place from which to send an expedition to the land of gold. Chaves promised to guide a party that would bring back 400 Indians loaded with gold and silver. It was the "white king" legend again. Sousa thought he was well on his way to accomplishing one of his missions, namely bringing back to the king the coveted gold and silver. He chose Pêro Lobo Pinheiro to command eighty Europeans—forty besteiros and forty espingardeiros (musketeers)—to search for the promised riches. They left Cananéia on September 1, 1531.[26]

Sousa sailed on to the Río de la Plata to seek a way to Peru. Again, Pero Lopes reports, the weather was foul. They lost a batel, anchors, and sails; it was an introduction for worse to come, much worse. Those historians who write of explorations as if mariners could sail where and when they wished should read the *Diário* of Pêro Lopes. They would understand better the force of the storms, the winds that whipped them from side to side, the contrary currents of the ocean, and the sandbanks and rocks which stood as obstacles to making port and a safe landing.

On October 12, they reached Cape Santa Maria, more than 34°S (in present-day Uruguay), driven by raking storms that wrecked the flagship and left other vessels unfit for the sea until repaired. Martim Afonso's ship was wrecked and separated from the others. He lost seven men and was fortunate to get to shore with the rest of his crew. Seven days later he joined Pêro Lopes and the battered remains of his fleet. Miraculously, it seemed to them, they found a new brigantine, built by the Spaniards who abandoned it for unknown reasons. Sousa determined, regardless of the sorry prospects that faced them, to send his brother on to explore the great river. Pêro Lopes started on November 23 with 30 men and two padrões (stone pillars) "to take possession for the king our Lord." His orders were to explore the river and return within twenty days; but he took double the time, always meeting with vicissitudes which almost ended in disaster. Before he turned back on December 12, he erected the two padrões bearing the arms of Portugal and claimed the land for his king at a spot in present-day Argentina near the town of San Pedro. He started his return down river on Friday, December 13, 1531. More difficult times and wrecks awaited him before he rejoined his brother in late December.[27]

On the last day of 1531 the reconstituted fleet sailed, reaching Cananéia on January 8 and São Vicente on January 16, 1532. They liked the looks of São Vicente: "this land seemed so good to all of us," wrote Pero Lopes, "that the Captain, my brother, decided to settle it."

Sousa had been empowered by the king to grant sesmarias with lifetime but not hereditary titles. The grantee had to work his lands within two years, though in other cases the time was set at five years or anything the king chose to require. Pêro Lopes continues: "He granted land for farms to all the men and established a town on the island of São Vicente," as well as another on the mountains at Piratininga near present-day São Paulo. "He divided the people between these two towns and appointed officials and established good order and law, which was a great comfort to the people seeing the towns established, to have laws and religious services and weddings, to live with the advantages of the arts and crafts, everybody secure in the possession of his own, able to get redress of his grievances, and all the other amenities of life secure and available."[28] At least one priest was with them, though no specific mention of this is in the records.

On the highlands Sousa was assisted by João Ramalho, the Portuguese who had been in Brazil since about 1509–10 and who had a large family of mamaluco children, several of whom were daughters of the principal chief, Tibirica. João Ramalho was appointed capitão mór of the new settlement. He would become a very important link between the Portuguese and the Indians to the end of his long life.[29] Martim Afonso de Sousa decided to remain in São Vicente to await the return of the men sent west to look for the land of gold and silver.[30]

Pêro Lopes sailed for Portugal on May 22, 1532, with the principal ships of the fleet. In Pernambuco he captured two more French ships.

He also learned that another French ship, *La Pelerine*, had captured
and fortified the Portuguese feitoria, taking on a rich cargo for Marseilles.[31] Pêro Lopes recaptured the fort and, according to French
claims, hanged the commander and twenty men, two of whom were
turned over to the Indians to be eaten. The others were supposedly
sent to Portugal as prisoners. *La Pelerine* was captured fortuitously off
Málaga, Spain, by a Portuguese fleet, and taken to Portugal. A law
suit that lasted for many years between Portugal and France is the
main source of information about the episode; the evidence given by
each side was as contradictory as is usual in such suits. Pêro Lopes,
meantime, sailed from Pernambuco in December 1532 and reached
Faro in southern Portugal in late January 1533.

Martim Afonso de Sousa remained in Sâo Vicente seeing after his
towns, starting sugar cane growing, and waiting in vain for the return
of the men sent under command of Pêro Lobo to find the mines—
they never returned. Somewhere before they reached the Paraná
River, hundreds of miles short of the Andes, they had been cut to
pieces by the Indians. So neither by the Plata nor overland did Sousa
find the riches so much coveted by João III.

The ships sent to the Amazon River also failed to find the mines.
Not much is known of the two caravels sent "to Peru" via the Amazon.
They apparently reached only a short distance up the river.

The only immediate monetary return from Sousa's voyage came
from the ship sent home with a cargo from Pernambuco in 1531. Its
commander, João de Sousa, returned again to Brazil with a letter for
Martim Afonso de Sousa, arriving in Sâo Vicente in September 1532.
The king wrote to Martim Afonso that he might return home if he
liked, or remain in Brazil.

The king also informed him that he had decided to establish a
system of captaincies in Brazil like those in the Atlantic islands. For
Martim Afonso he had reserved 100 leagues (approximately 300 miles)
frontage along the sea, and for Pêro Lopes sixty leagues. Martim
Afonso accepted the captaincy but returned to Portugal. Subsequently
he became governor-general of India, where he gained great wealth

and a malodorous reputation for the way it was won, though he remained high in the king's favor. He never returned to Brazil. Nor did Pêro Lopes, who perished in a shipwreck in the Indian Ocean in 1539.

Other men, not Martim Afonso nor Pêro Lopes, became the founders of Brazil. The scenes of the principal captaincies decreed by the king lay far to the north, where Bahia and Pernambuco led the way in establishing permanent settlements.

ENDNOTES

1. Virginia Rau, "Feitores e feitorias." See, for the general background of Portugal's preparation for overseas colonization, the introduction by Malheiro Dias in *HCP*, I, i-cxxxi. Other contributions in the same work are by Julio Dantas and António Baião. A basic work, though its conclusions are not accepted by all, is J. Lúcio de Azevedo, *Épocas de Portugal econômico*.

2. Diffie and Winius, quote in translation the Porto Santo grant, pp. 303–04.

3. On *sesmarias* see Fortunato de Almeida *Historia de Portugal*, 1st ed., I, 393, 448, with bibliography; III, 465–472, where he notes that laws similar to the sesmarias were in force before 1375. The bibliography is extensive. Consult the *Dicionário de História de Portugal*, 1979 edition, V, 542–546, with numerous references. The standard work on the origins is Virginia Rau, *Sesmarias Medievais Portuguesas*; see also Henrique da Gama Barros, *História da Administração Publica*, 2nd ed., VIII, 317–52 and 495–97. The laws are published in the *Ordenações Afonsinas*, liv.iv., tit., lxxxi, and *Ordenações Manuelinas* (1521), Filipinas (1603). For Brazil see Rui Cirne Lima, *Terras devolutas*, and Costa Pôrto, *Estudo sobre o sistema sesmarial*.

4. Quoted in Peres, *Descobrimentos*, 1st ed., 1943, p. 423, note 1, from *Raccolta Colombiana* III, II, 120–21; and in part in Marcondes de Souza, *Descobrimento do Brasil*, 2nd ed., p. 113, from the letter sent from Sevilla, 5 October, 1502. T.O. Marcondes de Souza, "A expedição de 1501–02." The most recent treatment is in Max Justo Guedes, Coordinator, *História Naval Brasileira*, vol. I, tomo I, 223–245, by Guedes.

5. Helio Vianna, *História do Brasil*, 9th ed., I, pp. 52–3; Elaine Sanceau, *Captains of Brasil*, pp. 22–3, makes the point that this Noronha was not a member of the noble family of the name. The subject has recently been examined afresh by John Leonard Vogt, see his "Fernão de Noronha," summarized in Dutra, *Guide*, numbers 133 and and 135. Vogt believes that Noronha was the "overall commander" of the 1501–02 expedition.

6. Quoted in J. F. de Almeida Prado, *Primeiros povoadores*, 4th ed., p. 39, note 4. The Jewish origin of Noronha is doubted by António Baião, *HCP*, II, 278.

7. A staunch defender of the existence of the feitoria in Cabo Frio is Manuel Xavier de Vasconcellos Pedrosa in *RIHGB*, vol. 287. Also, Sanceau, *Captains*, 23–27. Jaime Cortesão cites a report by Spanish spies in Lisbon about an expedition that he believes was a second one in 1503, but in spite of Guedes' acceptance of this, it is not entirely clear that there was more than one. It may be observed, however, that there is no great issue at stake. *HNB*, I, 223–24.

8. See ante note 5.

9. Affonso de E. Taunay (cited by LC as Escragnolle), "Documentos comerciais seiscentistas," *AMP*, vol. 12, pp. 37ff. Also, Armand Marie Pascal d'Avezac, *Considerations geographiques sur l'histoire du Bresil*, Section I.

10. *Ibid.*, paragraph 25.

11. *Ibid.*, paragraph 26.

12. Sanceau, *Captains*, pp. 25ff.; Francisco Adolfo de Varnhagen, 6th Integral Edition, I, 89.

13. The most complete description of the plants and animals, both native and those brought over by the Portuguese and other Europeans is in Gabriel Soares de Souza, *Tratado descriptivo do Brasil em 1587*, 3rd edition, cited here. Soares was owner of a sugar mill in Brazil, and one of the many who sought precious metals in the interior. His work is comparable to José Acosta's *Historia* or the Bernabé Cobo's *Nuevo Mundo* for descriptions of agriculture and livestock in the sixteenth century. A modern description is F. C. Hoehne, *Botânica e agricultura no Brasil no século XVI*. Also see Lemos Brito, *História econômica*, pp. 47–64.

14. The scant record of voyages to Brazil by the Portuguese and others is full of names and dates but much uncertainty about accuracy. In view of the great value of the brazilwood, it can be taken as certain that many ships besides the *Bretoa* made the run to Brazil. Even if some of the details are uncertain, the existing record is a confirmation of the early trade. In 1514, or possibly 1512, one or two Portuguese ships freighted by Nuno Manuel and Christóvão de Haro, and piloted by João de Lisboa, coasted Brazil and Uruguay as far as the Rio de la Plata. See Laguarda Trias, *Pre-Descubrimiento*; Peres, *Descobrimentos*, 1st ed., 429–30; Almeida Prado, *Primeiros povoadores*, pp. 44–48 and 150. There are a number of references to other voyages and to the claims of priority by Portuguese and Spaniards. Juan Dias de Solís in Spanish service sailed in 1515 to establish Spanish claims to the Plata. In 1516 he was killed and eaten by the Indians. For some years thereafter the river bore his name. See Julian Maria Rubio, in Antonio Ballesteros ed., *Historia de América*, I, 1–34. One of the ships sent by Nuno Manuel and Haro, or some other, met an unfriendly reception

by the Indians led by a semi-Indianized Pedro Galego not anxious to have other Portuguese around him. The ship was subsequently forced by winds and ocean currents to Puerto Rico where the Spaniards arrested the crew for poaching westward of the Line of Demarcation. Sent to Santo Domingo as prisoners, one of them, Estevão Frois, appealed by letter to King Manuel for help. He refers to "the twenty years or more" that the Portuguese had been in Brazil, which would have meant 1494. Some Portuguese historians accept the Frois letter as proof that Brazil had been discovered by that date; but the vagueness of the statement precludes acceptance as hard evidence. For general reading see Samuel Eliot Morison, *The European Discovery of America: The Southern Voyages*, in which he treats Solís and others. Also Pedro Calmon, *História do Brasil*, I, chapters XI and XII; Francisco Adolfo de Varnhagen, *História do Brasil*, I, 82–123: Charles E. Nowell, "The French in Sixteenth Century Brazil," and *HNB*, I, I, 247–99. For a refutation of the arguments that the Frois letter proves early discovery of Brazil see Marcondes de Souza, *O descobrimento do Brasil*, pp. 345–49.

15. Almeida Prado, *Primeiros povoadores*, pp. 63–65. On Christóvão Jacques consult *HNB*, I, I, 247–99 by La Guarda Trias. For the Aleixo Garcia story, see Charles E. Nowell, "Aleixo Garcia and the White King."

16. Almeida Prado, *Primeiros povoadores*, p. 61, note 9, cited from *HCP*, III, 60.

17. Sergio Buarque de Holanda, *História geral*, I, 92–93; Elaine Sanceau, *Captains*, 31.

18. Southey, *Brazil*, I, 31–32.

19. Oliveira Marques, *História de Portugal*, I, 343–46. This work exists in English also.

20. Almeida Prado, *Primeiros povoadores*, pp. 70–73, quoting Alonso de Santa Cruz, *Yslario*.

21. Quoted in Holanda, *História geral*, I, 93.

22. Almeida Prado, *Primeiros povoadores*, pp. 74ff., and citing Herrera from *HCP* III, 100 and 141; Jordão de Freitas "A expedição de Martim Alfonso de Sousa," in *HCP*, III, 97–164. A later treatment is in Guedes, *HNB*, vol. I, tomo II, 347–99, by Rolando A. Laguarda Trias.

23. Almeida Prado, *Primeiros povoadores*, pp. 78ff.

24. Pêro Lopes de Sousa, *Diário de Navegação* . . . (1530–32). Where not otherwise specified, the narrative is taken from Sousa.

25. Almeida Prado, *Primeiros Povoadores*, pp. 82ff.

26. *Ibid.*, pp. 84ff. Mario Rodriguez, *Colonia de Sacramento*, pp. 8ff. cites the pertinent letters of Ambassador Hurtado de Mendoza from the archives as well as Gandia, *Antecedentes*, pp. 74–78 and Eugenio de Castro, *A expedição de Martim Afonso de Sousa*.

27. At his farthest, he had reached a point some 600 to 700 miles west of the mouth of the Amazon River, the westernmost point the Line of Demarcation would have fallen.

28. Sanceau, *Captains*, pp. 79–83.

29. For a number of years some historians maintained that João Ramalho had arrived in Brazil about 1490 (before the discovery of American by Columbus) based on a reading of certain chronicles and documents. The finding of Ramalho's will cleared up this mistake. He came to Brazil about 1510. See Affonso de E. Taunay, "O testamento de João Ramalho," *AMP*, 10 (1941), 61ff. Also see Marcondes

de Souza, *Algumas achegas*, and "O conhecimento pre-colombiano do Brasil."

30. Sanceau, *Captains*, pp. 71–84.

31. On the *Pelerine* see Sanceau, *Captains*, pp. 85–91.

3

CAPTAINS OF BRAZIL

℧ he captaincy system was an extension of the experience gained in land distribution during the Reconquest from the Muslims. As established in Brazil, it was modeled on grants made in Portugal's Atlantic islands. The first captaincy in the New World was located on the islands of Fernando de Noronha in 1504, but the effective beginning dates from 1534.

Two separate legal instruments, in part alike word for word, bestowed the captaincy on the grantee. One was the doação (donation), hence the name donatário (donatary) for the owner. The other was the foral (charter), setting out in more detail the prerogatives of the donatary and the colonists. In medieval times the foral had often been granted by the donatários to the tenents, but the system had gradually evolved so that, in the reign of Manuel I and his successors, the king granted the foral directly to the people or the donatary. This was the system followed in Brazil.

A controversy has sprung up among historians, jurists, and economists about the nature of the grants. One school calls them feudal; another considers them capitalistic. This is one more tempest in a teapot. Inasmuch as no definition of either feudalism or capitalism has been devised to please everyone, the problem seems to be insoluble. Both systems have roots deep in Portuguese history. The foral and the doação were integral parts of the Portuguese land system, and the rulers of Portugal were promoters of businesses of many kinds from the era of the first king.

The original twelve Brazilian donatários received fifteen separate grants along the ocean front, bounded north and south by parallel lines running westward to the extent of the king's conquista (Line of Demarcation). For example, Martim Afonso de Sousa received one hundred leagues ocean front divided into two separate segments, one around São Vicente and the other Guanabara Bay. His brother Pêro received three segments: one to the south of São Vicente, one lying between Martim Afonso's lands, and one far to the north, in Itamaracá, along the northern border of Pernambuco. Other grants will be mentioned in context.

The personal land grant to each donatary included ten leagues of land along the coast and inland to the limit of the king's conquista, free and exempt from quitrents, fees, or taxes (foros, tributos, direitos), except the tithe of the Order of Christ. The donatary had twenty years to choose a personal estate in any area, but he then had to divide it into four or five different blocks with a minimum of two leagues between blocks. He could rent out his land, distribute it in segments for whatever quitrents and fees he chose, and if such lands were not distributed, the income belonged to his heirs. The king would not collect any taxes from the novidades of the land (new things not previously known) but the captain-donatary had to pay the Order of Christ its tithe.

Neither the captain-donatary, nor his wife, nor his heir could hold sesmarias. His other children and kinsmen were eligible, however, and he could grant "to any person of whatever social standing (qualidade) or condition," free of quitrents or taxes except the tithe to the Order of Christ, everything produced in the sesmarias permitted in the foral. He could not give more land to his kinsmen than to other persons, but he could buy back land from the other holders eight years after development. All grants were governed by the Ordenações das Sesmarias.

One half of the tithe of fish belonged to the Order of Christ, and "the king's other half of the tithe of fish" went to the captain-donatary.

The king received no tithe on the ten leagues of land personally granted to the donatary, but the Order of Christ received its tithe. The captain-donatary received a twentieth of the proceeds of the brazilwood shipped to Portugal after all expenses were paid, with the accounting made in the Casa da Mina in Lisbon. The king made clear, moreover, that while all brazilwood "is to be forever mine," the captain-donatary and the settlers could use what they needed in Brazil.

The foral also specified rules regarding slaves. For example, Vasco Fernando Coutinho could enslave Indians for use in his captaincy or for crews of his ships. He could also send twenty-four Indians annually to Lisbon to be sold as slaves without paying the custom tax. The number of slaves allowed for sale in Lisbon for other donataries varied; Duarte Coelho of Pernambuco could send thirty-six.

The captain-donatary and the vizinhos, residents of the captaincy, were exempt from the excise or sales tax, soap tax, salt tax, "or any other tax," except those imposed in the doação and the foral.

The inheritance of the captaincy was spelled out in a definite way. The eldest legitimate son was the heir, and failing a son, the eldest legitimate daughter. If there was no legitimate heir, the eldest illegitimate male (if not damnado coito), or failing a male, the eldest illegitimate female, could inherit. The donatary could, however, pass the heredity to a collateral legitimate male in preference to the illegitimate line. This was a vital change from the line of succession set in the time of King Duarte (1433–1438). At a stroke it gave to the donataries rights that the kings of Portugal had fought for centuries to take from their landlords.

The doação had to remain intact. The captain-donatary could not, under any pretext, "divide, exchange, break up, nor in any other manner alienate, neither by marriage of his son or daughter, nor give to any other person, not even to ransom his father or son or any other person from captivity, nor for anything else, however pious." "Because," the king said, "my purpose is that the captaincy and the captain remain forever inseparable." Violation of these provisions would forfeit the captaincy and it would pass at once to the next heir.

On the other hand, the captaincy was secured in the line of inheritance, even if the holder committed grave crimes, including treason. He could be tried and punished if found guilty, yet his heirs would still inherit.

The right and duty of the captain was to distribute sesmarias to "any person of whatever social class and condition providing they are Christians," without imposing quitrents or taxes (foro nem direito) except the tithe to the Order of Christ. The sesmarias were to be distributed in accordance with the laws set forth in the Ordenações. The foral repeated the provisions of the doação, prohibiting the captain from distributing sesmarias to himself, his wife, or his heir; but he could make grants to his other children and blood relatives. If one of his kinsmen inherited the captaincy, the beneficiary had to surrender his sesmarias within one year, on pain of reversion of the captaincy to the crown plus a fine of equal value to the captaincy.

Captaincies were easy to obtain. In fact, some captains were lukewarm about accepting the vast amounts of land they were offered. Often they had to be urged by the king to perform a royal service. The development of a captaincy was a very difficult task, and in several cases it proved impossible on the first try. Brazil was more difficult than Africa or the East, where the task was to establish forts and feitorias on the coast as centers to tap the trade already existing— whether in slaves, as in Africa, or in spices, silks, and other fine wares of Asia.

Brazil had no trade of consequence waiting to be tapped. Raw nature had to be developed, brazilwood being the first—but only the first step. Few Europeans went to African or Eastern feitorias; Brazil had to be "colonized" as Spain was already colonizing parts of America. The example was the ancient Greeks and Romans who moved out from their homelands to colonize the shores of the Mediterranean and a large part of western Europe. Portugal and Spain, colonized by Rome in ancient times, became colonizers in the sixteenth century.

The task of the captains was far more difficult than first met the eye. Vaz de Caminha described the area he saw as "all palm covered beach, very level and very beautiful . . . and so pleasant . . . that everything will grow there." Caminha did not remain long enough to learn that the very lushness of the coastal land hid near-unconquerable obstacles to settlement.

The beautiful green vision that greeted the Portuguese hid problems unseen and unimagined. They saw the glimmering sandy beaches, the beautiful green forests, the innumerable wild animals, the flocks of colorful birds, the abundant and tasty wild fruits, the teeming schools of fish, and the oysters, crabs, and shrimp in inexhaustible quantities. We might find it difficult to understand, before we examine the problems closely, why any of the colonies failed.

Neither Pernambuco nor any other colony was, however, an easy return to paradise. Lurking behind the beauty were dangers, diseases, and death. Settlers found Brazil a green hell to be conquered. Among the Portuguese were many unrepentant sinners who did not wish to merit reentry into paradise by changing their wicked and hedonistic lives in the new land.

The green forests were often nearly impassable mangrove swamps along the shore, which were great obstacles to landing and of little economic value. Behind these grew the forests; some contained tall tropical trees of unbelievably hard wood, and others formed a jungle so thick it could be penetrated only by hacking a path through it. Away from the breezes of ocean or river, the humid heat robbed even the most vigorous people of energy. Only those readers who have experienced the jungle can truly sense the terror and despair of the men who sought to conquer it.

Hidden in the forests and jungle along narrow paths were the Indians. Invariably the first contacts were friendly, but hostilities came soon thereafter. The exotic naked Indians were intrigued by the whites and intriguing to them. The new marvels introduced by the Europeans—knives, axes, saws, hammers, fish hooks, bells, mirrors, glass beads, colored cloth, and many other items never seen by the natives— were at first irresistible. Indians valued these products and responded with all they had to offer—game from the forest, fish, monkeys, parrots, other colorful birds, nuts and fruits, Indian corn and manioc, and, of course, their daughters. They would have even shared their most delectable dish, and did when some white man cared to share it, namely, the roasted thigh of a slain enemy.

What European men most willingly accepted and Indian fathers willingly offered were their daughters, and sometimes wives. The victorious warrior seldom had to commit rape. Throughout history women have found the victor attractive; and Indian women were not different. Unburdened by the sense of sexual restraint that European men imposed on their own daughters and wives, the Indians gave themselves without any sense of sin to the aggressive Europeans. Although the Indian man was not entirely without jealousy, and some were more jealous than others, he regarded a whipping as sufficient punishment for a wayward wife (one who had slipped behind her husband's back). But to offer a wife or one of several wives or daughters to a visitor was an act of hospitality within the code of etiquette, and the European man might give in return something he esteemed highly. The white man's jealousy, in contrast, was one of the characteristics Indian men and women were soon to discover.

The most important discovery made by the Indians was that the newcomers had come to take their lands. Lacking any sense of personal property ownership in a culture where all land belonged to the group—whether clan or tribe—for fishing, hunting, and cultivating small fields, they did not understand, at first, why the Europeans staked out boundaries, cut down their forests, claimed exclusive rights of fishing and hunting, took their wives and daughters when not offered, and enslaved them in ways contrary to their own rules of slavery. Soon Indian tribes turned on the colonists and fought them as long and hard, and as intermittently, as they had their local enemies.

War was not continual and unremitting, nor did Indians often ally with neighboring tribes against the newcomers. Rather, they fell victims of Europeans, who used them against other Indians or other Europeans. Within the first generation after European discovery, some tribes had allied with the French and others with the Portuguese. Even the temporarily "friendly" Indians turned on the Portuguese. Indeed, the Indians considered the Europeans treacherous. Blood feuds became the rule on both sides. An offense against one white by an Indian could start a war; and one white injuring an Indian could likewise initiate conflict.

The Indians could be helpful and often were. Other enemies were merely dangerous, to a degree that modern people are likely to belittle. Crocodiles swarmed in the rivers and sometimes attacked without provocation; piranha abounded in some streams and would always attack; and poison snakes and constrictors lurked along the paths and in the fields (and are still a danger in some parts of Brazil). There were also other obstacles: flying and crawling insects, many of them deadly; ants of every size, herbivorous and carnivorous, who could strip a tree or a field of its foliage within an hour or an animal or man of his flesh equally quickly; plus diseases and strange fevers of unknown origin, which could make life difficult and often short.

The extreme fertility of the tropical soil was often the enemy. Everything grew at such a rate that it startled the men from temperate climates. Wheat, oats, rye, rice, and many other crops and vegetables grew so fast that they became all stalk and no grain. Leafy vegetables as a rule did well, as did pumpkins and cucumbers, but the first optimistic reports were seldom verified. Like the Spaniards who had transferred European crops to the Caribbean forty years earlier, they found the exuberance of tropical nature could be an enemy rather than a friend.

The captaincies were huge in size compared to even the largest domains in Portugal itself. Duarte Coelho (Pernambuco) held several times the area of Portugal; even the smallest captaincy was equal to Portugal north of the Douro River.

The men who accepted the challenge generally had the kind of experience that equipped them for this undertaking. Pêro Lopes de Góis knew something of what faced him, since he had made a voyage in 1530–33. But none of the other captains had ever seen the new land. They were undertaking a task they could not fully envision.

João de Barros, Fernão Álvares de Andrade, and Aires da Cunha received 225 leagues of the northeast coast to hold in common for twenty-five years, after which they could divide it among themselves "as they think fit." The first quinhão (portion) began at the Amazon River and extended fifty leagues, and the second took the next 75 leagues. Both were called Maranhão and ended at the Rio da Bruz (now the Camocin). The third portion began at the Angra dos Negros (in which modern Rio Grande do Norte lies). In between, Antônio Cardoso de Barros held 40 leagues in Ceará. The northwestern part between the Amazon and São Luís do Maranhão lies in the rainy forest and jungle area. The remaining coast along the modern states of Maranhõ, Piauí, Ceará, Rio Grande do Norte, and Paraíba consists of long stretches of sandy mangrove beaches. Behind them lies the caatinga, the rough bush and cactus dry lands. Little of their grant offered much encouragement for settlement. They wanted to follow up the efforts of Martim Afonso who had sent Diogo Leite to explore the "Rio do Maranhõ" (Amazon) in 1531.

Neither Barros nor Andrade intended to come to Brazil—both were high officials of the crown. Aires da Cunha, a veteran of the East, represented them. Their aim was to find the precious metals that rumor put somewhere in the vast unknown. They prepared an armada of ten ships at great expense, a sum larger than any of the other donataries could afford. The Spaniards of course were uneasy. They had already discovered that the Portuguese did not intend to recognize the Line of Demarcation, since they had pushed on west of it wherever they happened to be.

The fleet sailed first to Pernambuco, where Duarte Coelho's captaincy had gotten off to a good start. He was helpful in materials and advice. He told them of the mountain of gold reported by the Indians, who always seemed to be supplied with tales designed to move whites on to some other place. Coelho also gave them interpreters and a rowing boat to help along the shore. They knew nothing of the real nature of the area they were seeking, nor about the coast abounding in sandy mangrove beaches, shallows, rocks, and unfriendly Potiguar Indians.

Almost a century passed before the Portuguese conquered this area, where ocean currents and winds often turned sailing into a fatal experience. They had made no reconnaissance of the coast. Judging from their experience, they knew little, if anything, of Diogo Leite's expedition. They went prepared, they thought, to take the land with "armed ships and with many men, horsemen and foot soldiers and artillery . . . at their own expense," to "seek and discover any gold and silver there might be," and, of course, to pay the king his fifth.

They set out north and then northwest along the sandy coast.The venture was soon over for Aires da Cunha. His ship was wrecked on the Maranhão coast, and he drowned in sight of the shore while his companions watched. Their leader was gone. The survivors established Fort Nazaré on an island they named Trinidade (São Luís do Maranhão). They remained for three years accomplishing nothing of consequence, or at least nothing is known of what they did. It is strange, and unfortunate for history, that João de Barros, one of the three partners and one of the great historians of Portuguese expansion, never wrote the account of Brazilian settlement he was supposedly preparing. They found no gold—that is certain. They might have lived well off the land, for this is one of the favorable areas along the difficult coast. We do not know how they fared, nor why they abandoned the site and sailed for home. Half the fleet was lost enroute. Three ships fell prisoners to the Spaniards in the Antilles, to which the winds and ocean currents naturally pushed them. Coelho reported that 700 of the 900 men perished.

In 1554 Luís de Melo da Silva attempted to sail into the Amazon with five ships and was wrecked. The remnants of his expedition reached Santo Domingo. The next year, 1555, two sons of João de Barros, João and Jerônimo, went on orders of King João III to make another attempt. Jerônimo left a record:

"my brother . . . and I . . . went to the Maranhão River [Amazon] . . . to explore . . . in hopes of great trade in gold [we] explored 500 leagues . . . in which we endured many trials of war with the French . . . and heathens . . . founded settlements in three places . . . for five years, all at my father's expense . . . and spent everything that he had, and did much service for the king."

The record is not clear about the service done for the king, but the failure of the expedition is obvious. João de Barros, who could have left a graphic account of all this, but did not, made one point that applies to almost all the captaincies. "The cost of this Armada," he said, "left me undone."

Antônio Cardoso de Barros, whose portion of forty leagues lay between those of João de Barros and his partners, made no effort to colonize his captaincy. The northeast coast was conquered only in the seventeenth century. Meantime it continued in the hands of the Indians and some European traders, mainly French.

The next 30 league portion toward the south, Itamaracá, approximately the modern state of Paraíba, fell to the lot of Pêro Lopes de Sousa. He also held the 40 leagues ocean front first called Santana, the extreme southern captaincy, as well as Santo Amaro, with ten leagues of ocean front between his brother's two portions. As reported in chapter two, Pêro sailed away from Brazil in 1532 never to return and died in a shipwreck in 1539. His widow, Isabel de Gamboa, inherited the captaincy. Santana offered no immediate economic incentives. It was near or across the Line of Demarcation. The Spaniards were making efforts to settle their lands in the south and to challenge them was risky. Santo Amaro, ten leagues along the coast northeast of São Vicente, shared more or less the life of that captaincy. In the early times it was difficult to develop, and Pêro held it in low esteem. He wrote to the Count of Castanheira, the king's minister and boyhood friend of the Sousa brothers, inviting him to take all or any part of the captaincy. The count was not disposed to do his boyhood friend a favor—the widow kept the captaincies.

Before Martim Afonso de Sousa left Brazil, he had founded São Vicente (now a part of the city of Santos) and Paratininga on the mountain above São Vicente (absorbed later by São Paulo). He had granted sesmarias to some settlers of São Vicente and set up a municipal organization, a fort, a church, and a town hall with its indispensable pelourinho (whipping post)—a symbol of authority.

Sousa had one great advantage over the other donataries. The king had financed his settlements. Sugar cane was soon planted. Cattle, sheep, and other domestic animals and fowls were already there from earlier European shipwrecks or were introduced in larger numbers by Sousa. The Spanish wife of Martim Afonso, Ana Pimentel, assumed control as absentee ruler.

Sousa (or Ana Pimentel) constructed an *engenho* (sugar mill) known as the "Engenho do Senhor Governador." Some historians record that Sousa founded a company of "Merchant Shippers" that engaged in importing and exporting, but not much is known of it. He later proved to be a shrewd and dishonest business man in the East as governor of India, lending credence to the belief that he could have organized a company for his captaincy. Later the mill came to be known as the Engenho dos Armadores, which also indicates a company. Still later it was known as São Jorge dos Erasmus after it became the property of Erasmus Schetz of Antwerp, to whom it contributed the wealth that enabled him to obtain the Duchy of Urgel in Flanders.

Early observers described São Vicente as "cool temperate . . . and very healthy and fresh, with good waters," having a distinct "winter" season from June to September. Fruits and vegetables abounded. Grapes grew abundantly; wine was made but did not keep well. The early optimistic reports about crops diminished when it was discovered that the fertility of the soil did not endure as well as in Bahia and Pernambuco.

São Vicente made progress despite difficulties. Other engenhos were established; other settlements were made. The close relationship of João Ramalho through his "marriage" with the daughter of Tibiriçá, a prominent chieftain on the plateau, as well as with a number of other Indian women, had produced a good "supply of mixed blood children, called mamelukes. The girls were attractive to Europeans. Both regular and common-law marriages, as well as enduring unions among the Indians, mamelukes, and Europeans, identified the settlers more and more with the local population. Some wives came from Portugal—the wife and children of Luís de Góis, for example. The population increased.

The quality of the São Vicente colonists was perhaps superior to some of the other captaincies. Some who came with Martim Afonso were of "good," even noble, families. Jorge Ferreira, a noble, became the ancestor of one of São Paulo's high ranking social families through marriage with one of the daughters of João Ramalho. Records do not exist for most of the mixed unions, however. The Adorno brothers from Italy became prominent citizens and founders of Brazilian families.

An outstanding captain was Brás Cubas of Oporto, who played a very prominent part in the defense and development of the colony. His two brothers also came to Brazil and later even his father. Cubas owned a sesmaria, served as provedor for the king, alcaide-mor and agent of Martim Afonso, and led in defense of the settlements.

In 1536 groups of Portuguese and Spanish castaways from shipwrecks, who preferred the free life to citizenship in São Vicente, fought alongside Indian allies and captured the town, making off with the municipal archives (for what purpose?—to destroy sesmaria deeds?). They were finally repelled with the aid of Chief Tibiriçá of Piratininga.

Other problems beset them. The town was moved to higher ground because the first location was subject to the ressaca, a tidal wave that sometimes invades the land during rough weather at sea. One wave carried away the town hall, the pelourinho, and the church. The people fished the church bells from the water and installed them in a rebuilt church in a new São Vicente.

Their original port having been destroyed, Brás Cubas led the work in 1543 to build a new port between the islands of São Vicente and Santo Amaro. Cubas also founded a town on his sesmaria. By 1545 Cubas had been appointed acting captain of the colony by Martim Afonso de Sousa. He granted São Vicente a new charter, founded a misericórdia (Brotherhood of Mercy), and built a new church dedicated to Our Lady of Mercy and a Hospital de Todos os Santos (named for the one in Lisbon). From the last, the modern city of Santos derived its name, absorbing the second São Vicente. A new Portugal was coming into being in the Brazilian wilderness—all the institutions, here as elsewhere along the coast, were Portuguese.

In 1548, Luís de Góis reported to the king that the captaincy had six engenhos of sugar, plus six hundred men, women, and children who owned 3,000 slaves (mostly Indians who could not stop fighting among themselves long enough to unite and drive the invaders back into the sea). Only Pernambuco was doing better. Adverse factors, partly geographical, caused the colony to fall behind. Crowded on a narrow shelf against the mountains that provided insufficient farm land and farther away from European markets than the captaincies to the north, particularly Pernambuco, São Vicente sugar could not compete. The colony did not fail, but its early momentum was not maintained.

The captaincy of São Tomé lay just to the north of Martim Afonso's strip embracing Guanabara Bay. Pêro de Góis was the only captain besides the Sousas who had seen the land before accepting his captaincy. He held a 30 league ocean front embracing northern Rio de Janeiro and southern Espírito Santo. Geographically, the area was highly favorable. It included the fertile lower Paraíba River valley. Góis knew the entire coast from Pernambuco to Rio de la Plata. As one of the settlers of São Vicente, he had held a sesmaria there. He had traveled into the sertão (the backlands). On one important trip he was sent by Martim Afonso on a vain search for the expedition that Francisco de Chaves led from Cananéia in 1531 to find the land of gold.

Indeed, Pêro de Góis was the most experienced of all the captains in Brazil. If anybody should have succeeded, he was the one since he knew what to expect of his captaincy. How different the ever verdant forests and jungles and the rushing waters of the rivers were from the high, dry, almost treeless rolling hills of Beja in the Alentejo of Portugal from which he came. Both Pêro and his brother Luís remained in São Vicente to 1536, as strong pillars of the new society. He then returned to Portugal to receive his captaincy.

When he returned to Brazil in 1536, his brother Luís and others from São Vicente joined him. They settled Vila da Rainha near the mouth of the Paraíba River and planted sugar cane brought from São Vicente. Things went well at first; but they needed more machinery. Pêro de Góis went again to Portugal in 1542, where he persuaded a rich merchant, Antônio Ferreira, to back him. He now returned confidently to Brazil only to find the captaincy in near ruin. In his absence the colonists had quarreled among themselves, as well as with the Indians, abandoned their plantations, and scattered.

Góis chose a new site on the Monage River, seven or eight leagues from the coast. "We could have as many engenhos as we like," he wrote his partner. To the king he later wrote: "I made a very good settlement, with many inhabitants and much property." In the adjacent captaincy to the north, Espírito Santo, belonging to Vasco Fernandes Coutinho, Góis found a sugarmaking expert and hired him to set up the engenho at a wage of one cruzado a day. He also cut a road to the coast capable of travel with horses and carts to supplement the river route. Two horse-driven engenhos were built near the coast, one for himself and one for the holders of sesmarias. He promised his partner in Lisbon 2,000 arrôbas (1 arrôba = 32 lbs.) of sugar a year as soon as the cane grew, and more in time.

Góis and his men worked hard. They did not yet have many slaves— but in the future they hoped to have many African Negro slaves. Meanwhile, he and an interpreter went into the interior to persuade the Indians to help. The Indians were the Goitacases, one of the groups speaking the linguas travadas. They were not of the Tupi who spoke the lingua geral. "These savages," wrote Soares de Sousa many years later, "have a whiter color than some others . . . a different language, are very barbarous . . and are great archers." They were not, moreover, "as fond of eating human flesh as are some already described." Góis succeeded in making an agreement with them. The future looked promising in mid-1545; but within a year all was once more in ruin.

Some of the tough lot of *degredados*, who had traveled with Vasco Fernandes Coutinho to settle Espírito Santo, came down the coast trading illegally with the Indians. They kidnaped an Indian chief in Góis's captaincy and collected ransom for his relief. Instead of freeing him, they turned him over to enemy Indians who roasted and ate him. The authors of this crime escaped safely and left the colonists of São Tomé to suffer the consequences. The formerly friendly Indians now raided Góis's colony repeatedly. Góis wrote to the king that "none could trust us." Soon the engenhos and the plantations were destroyed—cane fields burn easily. Góis and his people were besieged in Vila da Rainha. Twenty-five men were killed and Góis lost one eye. He grieved that he had disappointed those who had trusted him. He despaired of Brazil because there was "so little fear of God." If the king "did not impose his authority," all would be lost. The colonists could take no more. They left with Góis and took refuge in Espírito Santo with Vasco Fernandes Coutinho, his good friend, who welcomed them to his captaincy. But he too was in dire straits.

Luís de Góis with his Portuguese wife and family returned to São Vicente. Pêro sailed to Portugal. His town, his plantations, and his engenhos returned to the jungle and the Indians. When Pêro came back to Brazil in 1549, for he loved the land that constantly rejected him, it was as commander of the king's fleet cruising off the coast of Brazil. He died in his beloved Brazil on some unrecorded date.

To Vasco Fernandes Coutinho, a fidalgo who had won much fame in Morocco fighting the Moors as early as 1510 and later in India and Malacca, where he stood firm in the face of an elephant charge, went the captaincy of Espírito Santo. The fifty leagues granted to him lay north of the captaincy of Pêro de Campo Tourinho. Selling all his property in Portugal and borrowing what he could, he sailed for Brazil. His first settlement was on the mainland opposite the island on which Vitória now stands. Two other fidalgos, D. Jorge de Mascarenhas and D. Simão de Castelo Branco, who had accumulated enough merits and demerits in the East to be sent to Brazil to expiate their errors, accompanied him. Degredados were numerous among the other sixty settlers. They were, in general, a tough lot; and, as we have seen, some of them contributed to the failure of Pêro de Góis.

The land they moved to in May 1535 was good, fertile, and with ample promise of a prosperous future. They named their new home Espírito Santo because they landed on Pentecost. They called their town Nossa Senhora de Vitória (later known as Vila Velha, Old Town). Duarte Lemos, also a veteran of the East, came from Bahia in 1537 bringing more colonists. He received as his sesmaria the best island in the bay in recognition of the great help he had given in keeping the land. "I could not have done without his help," Coutinho said later. Sesmarias were distributed to others and four engenhos for sugar were soon begun. The Goitacazes Indians at once caused trouble; but they were soon driven away.

Coutinho's ambitions along the coast extended beyond agriculture. Once his settlement seemed well established, he left it in charge of Jorge de Mascarenhas and went to Portugal to find supplies "to conquer the territory of the sertão inland until he had discovered gold and silver," as Gabriel Soares de Sousa later wrote. Duarte de Lemos sailed with Coutinho to obtain royal approval of his grants, which would have been unnecessary if he had had full faith in Coutinho's doação.

Coutinho's absence from Espírito Santo proved disastrous. For whatever reasons—and reasons were never lacking on either side between Indians and Portuguese—the Indians attacked. "The Tupiniquins from one side and the Goitacazes from another . . . burned the engenhos and many plantations." They killed Jorge de Meneses, acting captain, and later his successor Castelo Branco, as well as "many other settlers." Some of the survivors took refuge on the island belonging to Duarte de Lemos, while others fled to nearby captaincies.

When Coutinho and Duarte de Lemos returned from Portugal in 1543, they found conditions in such a sad state that all seemed lost. Duarte de Lemos thought so and sailed away, leaving Coutinho to contend with the problems. The struggle for survival continued. Coutinho again left to seek aid in 1549. That same year Tomé de Sousa arrived in Bahia to establish a captaincy-general. He had special orders to look into the affairs of Espírito Santo where, the king had heard, there was anarchy. This he did in due course. The colony survived and Coutinho returned as an unwelcomed captain. He died in dire poverty in 1561. The history of the captaincy after 1549 was intertwined with that of the captaincy-general.

The captaincy of Porto Seguro, embracing the area where Cabral had landed, north of Espírito Santo, fell to the lot of Pêro do Campo

Tourinho. Gabriel Soares de Sousa called him "noble, very determined and prudent." A rich landowner of Viana do Castelo in northern Portugal, he was also famed as a navigator because of a voyage along the coast as far as Rio de la Plata. He was a man vigorous in both action and speech—too much so in speech, as we shall see.

Like Coutinho, he sold his properties in Portugal, persuaded many of his friends to do likewise, and with his family and those of his friends embarked for Brazil with about 600 people in four ships. Tourinho reached his destination in Porto Seguro late in 1534 or early 1535. He distributed sesmarias and repelled the Indians who "made very cruel war, besieging the colony many times . . . and killing many people," but after a while they were placated. Tourinho increased the number of his settlements, founding six or seven, for which he had enough people. He was a hard driver of men, impatient and outspoken about slackers. He regarded religious holidays as a waste of time. He upbraided the vicar general and the other priests and friars for declaring so many holidays. The vicar general had proclaimed as a holiday St. Martin's day, a French saint whose day was not observed in Portugal.

Father João Bezerra caused more trouble, as he did everywhere he visited and had already done in Bahia. Showing an *alvará* (royal decree) that was later found to be falsified, Father Bezerra had, at one point, persuaded the donatary of Bahia to abandon his captaincy. The donatary then took refuge in Porto Seguro. Bezerra was called "a great scoundrel" by Duarte Coelho of Pernambuco.

Tourinho had Bezerra thrashed. The latter then joined, or maybe organized, a conspiracy against him. Conspirators were not hard to find, nor were motives. Tourinho's outspoken criticism of settlers he considered lazy had made enemies. They used his own impious statements to bring about his downfall. The settlers accused him, with truth, of having said that Corpus Christi should always be on Sunday, not Thursday, to avoid losing a day of work. He spoke lightly of cardinals and the Pope, and of the "saintlets" with scorn. What prayers of his had they ever answered? The cardinals and bishops, he said, invented new saints to please their mistresses of the same names.

Tourinho was unaware of the conspiracy against him and hopeful of his captaincy when he made a glowing prophecy: "Once the engenhos are finished," he wrote to the king in July 1546, "I trust in God Your Highness will have a new kingdom here." Eleven years had elapsed since he arrived, and he was still waiting for the engenhos. Four months later his impious words caught up with him. The conspirators shipped him off to Portugal to face the Inquisition, established in 1536 and anxious to prove its reason for existence.

Tourinho did not cringe before the Inquisition, as a weaker man would have done. He pointed out the positive side of his acts. "I founded seven churches in the said captaincy and maintained them with two friars and five priests at my own expense." The trial was long, as was usual with the Inquisition. Tourinho denied all accusations, confessed to no wrongs, and condemned his enemies by name, most of whom were signatories of the charges against him. He pleaded to be allowed to return to his captaincy before it fell into ruin. Although he apparently was acquitted, he never returned to his beloved colony.

Named for the numerous islands in its best harbor, Ilhéus the captaincy situated between Porto Seguro and Bahia, was granted to José de Figueiredo, secretary of the royal treasury. He was a rich man by inheritance and position. Like João de Barros, his high position precluded leaving Portugal. He sent a Castilian, Francisco Romero, as his agent, "at his own expense," says Gabriel Soares de Sousa, in "a fleet of ships with many colonists, provided with everything needed for the new settlement" (povoação). Romero chose as his chief town, after a brief trial elsewhere, São Jorge de Ilhéus, a site which still exists. The new captaincy was well supplied by its captain and prospered initially. The usual land distribution was made, and a sugar engenho started. The Tupiniquin Indians, presumably the same Cabral found friendly, were hostile when the colonists arrived but became friendly later. The early history of the colony is obscure and does not reveal what destroyed its promise of prosperity.

The beautiful and extensive Bahia de Todos os Santos, the Recôncavo, as it is called, was granted to Francisco Pereira Coutinho.

"Whoever wishes to know who Francisco Pereira was," says Gabriel Soares de Sousa, "let him read the books about India and he will know how great he was in valor and heroic deeds." As one of Portugal's early heroes in the East, Coutinho was with Afonso de Albuquerque in the capture of Goa in 1510 and in Ormuz in 1515. He had the bizarre distinction of having commanded the first ship that brought a rhinoceros to Portugal, a gift from the king of Cambaya to King Manuel I. The king sent it to Pope Leo *X* in one of those gestures so symbolic of Portuguese royal deference to the papacy. In the East, Coutinho had gained riches and the nickname of Rusticão, the Rustic, which may have meant that he was considered tough enough for the task of settling Brazil.

Returning from the East when captaincies were being distributed and the king was having to persuade men to accept them, Coutinho solicited and received Bahia. The riches he gained in India would be spent in Brazil. His fifty leagues extended northward from the São Francisco River just far enough to encompass the Recôncavo. It seemed to be the choicest site in all Brazil: its location, the fertility of its land, and its climate promised a return to paradise. There in 1535 or 1536, this "determined captain" (esforçado) of "tireless spirit" (animo incansavel) brought his colonists. Some were married men with families and some bachelors—"all at his own expense," says Gabriel Soares de Sousa. Francisco Pereira Coutinho began the distribution of sesmarias and authorized at least two engenhos owned by "some wealthy men who went with him."

During the first few years there was peace with the Indians. Coutinho had the help of Diogo Álvares, known to the Portuguese as "O Galego" and to the Tupinamba Indians who held the region, as Caramurú. He was "married" to an Indian wife or wives, as were nine or more other whites who had lived around the bay for several years. Caramurú had perhaps as many as twenty wives. His numerous children formed a valuable bilingual liaison with the Indians.

Two of Caramurú's daughters married men in Martim Afonso de Sousa's expedition. Caramurú, who, it could be said, had much land before the colonizing groups came, received a good sesmaria, as did his son-in-law Paulo Dias Adorno, one of three Italian brothers who cast their lot with the New World. The struggle to get established was bitter; but success seemed certain.

Francisco Pereira Coutinho's captaincy did not escape, however, the troubles that affected the others: quarrelsome whites, discontented mestiços who resented the inferior position into which most were born, and Indians who turned from friendship to hostility. Duarte Coelho, captain of Pernambuco wrote to the king: "Francisco Pereira is old and sick . . . he does not know how to deal with the people." Duarte Coelho meant that Coutinho was not hard enough, a fault he himself was never accused of. The trouble came from several sources, but mainly "the priest who was the origin of the damage and the evil." The king should "send him prisoner to Portugal and he should never be allowed to return to Brazil because I know him to be a great scoundrel." The "Great Scoundrel" was Father João Bezerra who later, as we have seen, caused much trouble in Porto Seguro.

Coutinho was unable to resist all the forces against him. Attacked by the Indians, who were incited by the French according to Tourinho, and betrayed by his enemies within the colony, he was forced after a number of years of warfare and a long siege of his town to abandon Bahia. Bezerra, who had previously fled to Ilhéus, reappeared in a ship claiming to have come from Portugal with a warrant (alvará), allegedly from the king. The warrant called for the arrest of Coutinho. He surrendered and was taken to Ilhéus instead of Portugal, and from there to Porto Seguro where Tourinho treated him as an unwelcome guest.

A year later, realizing he had been deceived and hearing that the situation had quieted down in Bahia, he returned in 1547. Diogo Álvares (Caramurú), who had likewise fled, also returned. A storm blew his two ships to shore on Itaparica, a large island in the mouth of the bay. Coutinho and some of his companions were killed and consumed by the Indians. Caramurú was spared and resumed life with his large family. He was present when Tomé de Sousa arrived in Bahia in 1549 to establish the new royal government of Brazil.

The most successful captaincy was Pernambuco, or "New Lusitania" as it was called by its donatary proprietor, Duarte Coelho. Coelho had possibly been to Brazil as early as 1503 with his father Gonçalo, one of Portugal's famous navigators. Duarte sailed to the East in 1509 and remained there for many years. Back in Portugal in 1527, he was sent to serve in West Africa and Morocco and in 1531 to France. In 1533 he encountered Martim Afonso de Sousa in the Azores on Sousa's return from Brazil, and the two men sailed to Portugal together. Speculation has it that Coelho's interest in Brazil was stimulated by Sousa. In any case he applied for and received a captaincy for "the many services" he had rendered the crown in the past; "as well as for those I hope to obtain from him in the future," the king added.

The king gave Coelho sixty leagues reaching from the São Francisco River northward to the Igaraçú. This was a combination of the best land for the best man. Pernambuco proved to be the most successful of the captaincies for a number of reasons: the land was on a fertile and well-watered coastal plain; the winds tempered the hot climate of a territory lying between 8° and 11° south of the Equator; and animals and fish abounded. Perhaps the most important advantage was that it lay on the eastern hump of Brazil in the best situation for ships to and from Europe and for communication with the other settlements along the Brazilian coast.

Duarte Coelho was the chief blessing of the captaincy. Experienced in the rough life of the sea and warfare and long accustomed to command, he knew the art of tempering sternness with justice. He was also an educated man who knew how to write expressive letters to his king, and dared to do so.

The Portuguese already knew Pernambuco better than any other place on the Brazilian coast. There, possibly as early as 1516, Christóvão Jacques had established a feitoria. Sugar was produced, possibly as early as 1521. When Duarte Coelho as donatário arrived in March 1535, the fort and feitoria, then under command of Paulus Nunes, was transferred to Coelho.

No early Portuguese settler appeared to help Duarte Coelho with the Indians, as João Ramalho had helped in São Vicente or Diogo

Alvares (Caramurú) in Bahia. But several Portuguese with Indian "wives" lived around Pernambuco as a result of numerous previous contacts. They and their children served as guides and interpreters. He reinforced the feitoria that became the town of Recife, so named because of the reef running several miles parallel to the shore. Among the explanations for the name Pernambuco is that an opening in the reef called by the Indians *parana puca* (hole in the sea) became in the Portuguese pronunciation Pernambuco. Within the reef was a safe harbor that became the center of shipping and commerce.

Mixed families of Portuguese men and Indian women multiplied rapidly, and this factor explains why a few Portuguese settlers were able to cling to the rim of a land already peopled with warriors hostile to them. Among the others who came to Pernambuco was Vasco Fernandes de Lucena, member of a learned and distinguished literary family. Leaving his wife and children at home, he fathered a mestizo family and acquired a fluent knowledge of the Indian language along with the reputation among the Indians of having deadly magical powers. Such talents, which might seem trivial in serious history, were very important in the conquest. His Indian wife, during one siege, slipped into the Indian camp and influenced the women to persuade their men to stop the fighting.

North of Recife, some three miles on the left side of the Beberibe River, he established Olinda on a beautiful hill overlooking the ocean. The beauty of the site is said to have caused it to be called O Linda, the beautiful, a bit of logical history that less romantic historians deny. Olinda became the residential area of the new planter class created by the distribution of sesmarias. In time, they became bitterly jealous of the merchants of Recife, who profited from the crops of sugar produced by the senhores de engenho. Duarte Coelho brought a large number of married men with their families, including his own young wife, Brites de Albuquerque, descendant of a distinguished family. Her brother Jerônimo also came. He was a mighty warrior and conquistador—of women as well as Indians. Jerônimo set about peopling the colony with mestizo children as well as legitimate children from a Portuguese wife, whom he was later ordered to marry. Some reckon

his children at 24, others say 32. They were, of course, only the acknowledged children of his "wives." Jerônimo was past middle age
when the queen gave him one of her proteges as his legal wife; with
her, he had eleven children.

The records of the Indian wars are too scattered and confused to
permit a chronological history of events. The early writers, Gabriel
Soares de Sousa and Frei Vicente do Salvador, are sparing with their
dates. Duarte Coelho in his letters to the king did not write about the
Indian wars but rather his plans and hopes. He constantly dwelt on
his troubles, for like the other less-successful captains, he too was
often faced with problems impossible to solve.

Before arriving in Pernambuco, the Portuguese knew that sugar
cane would be their best crop. Duarte Coelho concentrated his efforts
on clearing the forests to plant cane and on building engenhos to
refine it into sugar. This process was going on all along the coast in
half a dozen captaincies simultaneously.

The fertile land produced tall cane stalks with an abundance of
sweet juice. The main problem was the expense of building and supplying the engenhos—iron rollers for grinding the cane, copper pots
for boiling the juice, dams to create lakes to move the water-driven
mills, plus the oxen and horses for grinding the cane in the simpler
mills and for all sorts of tasks around the plantations. Most essential
was an expert who knew how to make the sugar; without him all the
effort was lost. A long time elapsed from clearing land and planting
until the date that the sugar could be sold in Europe and money
returned to the planters. A period of three to five years often passed
before a single cruzado could be collected to pay for an engenho,
which could cost 10,000 cruzados or more.

Not one donatário had the wealth to place his captaincy on a paying
basis without outside capitalization, although some were considered
very wealthy men in Portugal. All had to borrow from Lisbon merchants or obtain royal aid. Duarte Coelho was no exception. In 1540
he returned home to obtain more financing. He was heavily in debt,
he told the king, and needed more money. He could produce cotton
and cut brazilwood for ready cash, but development required addi-

tional capital. To impress the king he made the oft-repeated statement: "I must conquer by inches the lands your majesty has granted me by leagues."

Duarte Coelho had other problems. Along with the solid families from Portugal had come many degredados, sent by the king to Brazil to expiate their crimes in exile rather than in jail or by death. The royal theory—that it was better to exile a man than to board him free or kill him—seems wise and was no doubt sound in the short run; but it shoved off some very undesirable and unregenerate characters on Brazil and other Portuguese colonies. Not all degredados, however, were desperate characters. Many were good citizens whose unnamed crimes might be minor under the modern concept of law. But along with the minor offenders came the murderers, inveterate thieves and robbers, vagrants of no value to themselves or society, priests not wanted at home, and other types not cut out for colony building. By coming to Brazil (or Africa, or the East) they received pardons and a chance to start life anew—if they wanted a chance; but some proved they were no better in the New World than in the old.

Duarte Coelho did not want them. Though other captains had asked the king to empty the jails because they could not get enough honest men willing to venture, many such "pioneers" frequently became troublemakers. Most of the captains regretted the quality of their settlers, and Coelho wrote to the king: "I swear as if I were on my dying day that they bring neither good nor profit to this country."

Coelho's protests were in vain. Sending undesirables to overseas territories to be rid of them appealed to the king as a good policy; and other nations followed Portugal's example later. Nevertheless, Coelho continued his protests: "such people are worse than the plague. I beg you for the love of God not to send me more such poison."

Trouble came to Coelho from the captaincy of Itamaracá, the property of Pêro Lopes de Sousa, adjoining him to the north. As we know, Pêro Lopes never returned to Brazil. Francisco Braga took charge in 1532. There is no adequate record of his government. After Pêro Lope's death in 1539, his widow, Isabel de Gamboa, inherited. Both

Portuguese and French wood cutters worked along the coast inhabited by the Potiguar Indians, fierce-fighting friends of the French. Braga got along with the Indians, however, but not with Duarte Coelho after his arrival in 1535. Whoever was to blame for the quarreling, Coelho got the upper hand and ordered Braga slashed across the face with a cutlass. Braga abandoned the colony and left it leaderless.

In February 1538, João Gonzales was named "feitor and almoxarife" (factor and customs officer). He founded the town of Conceição on Itamaracá Island. It became a refuge for those who had fled from other captaincies, as the terms of the doação permitted. Contiguous Pernambuco lost some of its less desirable citizens, which should have made Duarte Coelho happy. But contraband trade flourished in Itamaracá. Coelho complained to the king that its inhabitants made higher profits than he himself was allowed, but they paid nothing to the crown.

Itamaracá was, at times, useful to Pernambuco. In 1548–49 the Indians besieged both Igaraçu and Olinda. Hans Staden, the German who wrote one of the best first-hand accounts of life in Brazil among the Indians, was one member of a rescue party that obtained supplies in Itamaracá to attack the besieging Indians. From Staden's account, the war with the Indians apparently was not a very serious incident, although Frei Vicente claimed the life of the colony was completely paralyzed for a short time. By this date, Itamaracá still had not yet produced any sugar.

4

GOVERNMENT-GENERAL
AND THE JESUITS

PART I

Forty-eight years had passed since the discovery of Brazil and fourteen since Martim Afonso de Sousa established the captaincy of São Vicente. An official assessment of the situation in 1544 was that "Brazil has not only not produced anything for twenty years past . . . but it has cost more than eighty thousand cruzados to colonize and defend it." The assessment was unjust. Thinly settled as the colonizers were, the Portuguese had planted roots in prosperous Pernambuco in the north as well as in the firmly-established São Vicente in the south, roots that their rivals—French, English, Spaniards, and Dutch—could never dig out. Brazil was destined to be Portuguese, this seemed certain, although much hard fighting was yet to occur before the last intruders were removed.

Portugal needed to take some new initiatives for the protection of its rights in Brazil. The donataries needed help, including the doughty Duarte Coelho in Pernambuco. Only the crown could give the needed reinforcements; but the crown was in poor financial condition.

During the almost half a century since Cabral's arrival in Brazil, Portugal had been carrying a burden beyond its strength. Its multiple efforts had led to the establishment of a trade empire and fortified positions on both the east and west coasts of Africa, plus activities in India, Malay, China, Japan, and the East Indies. Simultaneously, campaigns in Morocco had led to the conquest of Safi, Arzila, and other cities to add to those held since the fifteenth century. The expense of these campaigns affirmed the prediction of Prince Pedro, brother of Henry the Navigator, that Ceuta would prove a sink hole (sumidouro) of men and resources. The crown policy of intermarriage with the Spanish monarchs also absorbed large sums of money, as had the custom of giving expensive gifts to the papacy. Altogether it required more money than was made in profits from the fabulous East. Reputedly rich, the king had grown poor from his expenditures, while his royal favorites governing India and the East, plus his factors in Antwerp and elsewhere, had become affluent.

By 1541 the overwhelming expenses of government absorbed the revenues of India before the fleets had returned. The king had borrowed more than could be repaid for years to come. He needed to retrench; Portugal dropped the goal of domination of Morocco, pursued since the conquest of Ceuta in 1415. As early as 1532, João III complained about "the great expense losses in holding these places with the fidalgos cavaleiros and the men at arms . . . who are continuously at war there."

João asked the Pope's permission to abandon some sites and to destroy the Christian churches to prevent them from falling into infidel hands. In 1534 he showed his financial statement to the municipal council of Lisbon so "that you can see clearly" the bad situation, "which you will not reveal to anyone." The fighting and sieges around Safi and other cities was continuous. In March 1541, Santa Cruz do Cabo de Gué (Aguer) fell to the Moors after a five-month siege. João reported the loss to the Pope and received a letter of condolence, along with permission to destroy the churches in cities he was forced to abandon. In December 1541, he informed Emperor Charles V of his intentions to abandon Safi, held since 1508, and Azamor, held since 1513. Both were left to the Moors in 1542. Portuguese retrenchment had not yet ended. In 1549, the king evacuated Alcácer Seguer, held since 1458, while Arzila and Tangier, both captured by the Portuguese in 1471, were returned to Moorish sovereignty in 1550.

João III had been forced, meanwhile, to acknowledge that the system of selling his spices through his own factor in the feitoria of Antwerp brought financial losses to the crown treasury, but not to the factors. He abolished the feitoria of Antwerp in 1549. His new policy toward Brazil, adopted at the same time he was cutting back elsewhere, was an attempt to redress the adverse balance.

Other circumstances brought Brazil more to the king's attention. By 1548 Portugal and all Europe knew of the silver mines of Potosí in "Peru," today Bolivia. The limited geographical knowledge of the time led to the belief that "Brazil and Peru are all one land," making it "certain" that the interior of Brazil also had mines. Francisco de Orellana's voyage down the Amazon in 1541 stimulated enthusiasm for a search. Such wealth should not be lost at a moment when Portugal so desperately needed revenues.

Brazil was to be held. The French, a constant threat along the coast where the captaincies had been established, and unchallenged from Itamaracá to the Amazon, were to be driven out. Spain too, according to Portuguese concepts of the Line of Demarcation, was encroaching on Portuguese territories. Asunción, Paraguay, founded by the Spaniards in 1537, was "clearly," in Portuguese minds, within Portuguese territory. The Spaniards were also founding towns north of Asunción. With threatening rivals to be thwarted, João III had to decide whether to let Brazil go or to occupy it more effectively.

When he received the news of the death of Francisco Pereira Coutinho of Bahia (and his consumption by the Indians) in 1548, he resolved to take over the abandoned captaincy and make it the headquarters of a new royal government of Brazil. The man appointed to be governor was Tomé de Sousa, collateral kinsman to the king and cousin both of Martim Afonso de Sousa and João III's chief counselor, the Count of Castanheira, all boyhood playmates of the king. Sousa had served the king in Morocco between 1527 and 1534, fighting the Muslim besiegers of Arzila and Safi. In India, where his cousins Pêro Lopes and Martim Afonso de Sousa served, with the latter acting as governor-general from 1542 to 1545, Tomé de Sousa's reputation was very high. Gabriel Soares de Sousa (no relative) called him a "fidalgo of honor" though illegitimate by birth. He was the natural son of the Prior of Rates. Gabriel Soares added that he was "wise, prudent . . . a valiant cavaleiro . . . of great qualities."

Sousa's fleet of six ships consisted of three naus, two caravels, and a brigantine. Respectable in size, it was small in comparison with Cabral's armada. It was smaller still alongside some India fleets, and insignificant measured by the hundreds of ships and thousands of men sent to death in a futile century of aggression against the "Infidels" of Morocco. About one thousand persons came with Sousa; the exact number is not known from existing documents. The extant sources speak of 600 soldiers, 400 degredados and various officials, skilled workmen, plus secular priests and six Jesuits, the first in America and led by Manuel da Nóbrega. The Jesuits were destined to exercise an influence that would merit a Churchillian statement to the effect that never were so few to have so much influence over so many. More came later. The original six began their mission immediately with the support of the governor, but not with the approval of most of the inhabitants.

The fleet sailed from Lisbon in February 1549 and arrived on March 29. On hand to greet Sousa was Diogo Álvares (Caramurú) with his family and friendly Indians, already so well known in Portugal that the king had sent a letter asking him to meet Sousa's fleet. The newcomers, who had never before seen Brazil were, as are all newcomers to Brazil, startled to see its beauty. Father Nóbrega commented: "The hills seem like large gardens and orchards."

Sousa disembarked his passengers and marched them ceremoniously to the ruins of the old town founded by Coutinho. In military fashion, with flags unfurled and soldiers standing with their arms and artillery at ready, they planted a cross and positioned the soldiers for defense. Who could know for certain that unfriendly Indians were not close at hand?

Sousa's Instructions (Regimento) reveal the king's purpose. "Seeing how much it is to God's service and mine to conserve and ennoble

the captaincies and settlements in Brazil," the king ordered the building of "large and strong" forts and towns in convenient places to help
the captaincies "administer justice and provide all things that are for
the benefit of my service and the affairs of my treasury." The rivals
of Portugal were Christians, of course, so the objective was to assure
that the Christianization would be carried out by the Portuguese. The
wording of the Instructions do not point clearly to a royal intent to
supplant the captaincies with a government general, but to "favor
and help." The Instructions, nevertheless, reclaimed for the crown
many of the powers granted to captains—and this they all understood,
for a copy of the Instructions was sent to each of them. There was
none who did not need help from the king, even at the price of losing
privileges. Only Duarte Coelho was prosperous enough to refuse royal
aid and keep his autonomy as granted in his charter.

The government-general was a new regime, as the new officials who
came with Sousa demonstrate. To complement the governor's power
and enhance his own, the king sent Pero Borges to serve as *ouvidor-
geral* (chief magistrate) and handle judicial matters and also António
Cardoso de Barros to serve as *provedormor da fazenda* (treasurer) to
manage fiscal matters. The latter was also donatário of the captaincy
of Ceará which he had not occupied. Both men received separate
Instructions outlining their powers distinct from, and independent of,
the governor's. The subordinates of the provedor-mor had their own
powers provided in Instructions of the *Provedores da Fazenda Real nas
Capitanias*. The new government was to be "central" but not mono-
lithic, as the existence of these officials and other provisions of the
Instructions make obvious.

Tomé de Sousa was ordered to notify the captains of his arrival
and to inform them that he was entitled to call on them for any
required assistance. He was also to punish the Indians who had "revolted" and killed Coutinho; at the same time he was also to offer
rewards to those who remained friendly. A weekly fair was to be
established for the Indians to sell their wares and to buy whatever
was available. Europeans were forbidden to go into the Indian villages
(aldeias) to trade without special license. Indians were to be protected

against seizure for sale into slavery by the ships and boats along the coast and rivers.

The holders of sesmarias who had been driven out with Coutinho were entitled to reclaim their land. If they failed to do so, the lands were lost, and new sesmarias were to be granted. The rivers and creeks were to be protected to stimulate the building of engenhos (sugar mills). The governor could grant appropriate lands for the senhores de engenho, and these were required to grind the cane of landholders who owned no mills. A fort (torre) was to be built by each senhor de engenho to protect it from the Indians.

Various kinds of skilled workmen came in 1549 to build a fort, other public buildings, and private houses. Among those listed are carpenters, brick masons, a lime maker, a "master builder" (Luís Dias), and others. Sousa's fleet brought tiles and bricks as well as tools and instruments required for the building crafts. A great supply of things attractive to the Indians—fishhooks, mirrors, beads—were included to induce them to work. Specialists in making molasses and sugar were, of course, among the new immigrants. There was also a pharmacist.

Soon Sousa chose a new site farther up the bay from the old town— present-day Salvador—with a beautiful view, cool breezes, and a defensible position some 300 feet atop a steep escarpment above the bay. Everybody was put to work to build the new town, with Governor Sousa setting a good example by working like a common laborer. Unfortunately, the example was not to take hold in Brazil—from the beginning the distinction of a privileged non-working class was fixed on the country. Within two months, a hundred houses were completed for private residences, mainly with cane-reinforced adobe walls and a thatched roof. Some fell within a few months under the impact of the characteristic heavy rains and high winds; but a start was made.

A wall of similar materials and mangrove stakes, a very hard wood, was built around the town. The public buildings were built using firmer stuff—stone, plaster, and tile—and included the town hall, an armory, a warehouse, a treasury building, a customs house, and "a well-finished prison." There was also a "cathedral," although no bishop was to arrive for three years. The town government, the *câmara*, was installed in the city hall; its first official act was the celebration of Corpus Christi on June 13. This was an occasion for solemn religious ceremonies and celebrations, with the usual mixture of the sacred and the carnival spirit so well known in Europe of the time and transmitted to Brazil.

The first *vereadores* (town councilors) were no doubt appointed by the governor rather than elected by the people. Even when elected, the number of "electors" was extremely small, the usual system in colonial Brazil, or anywhere at that time. This was only one of the ways in which the sixteenth century established the model for the political system that prevailed to the end of the colonial period. Much of the local government was in the hands of the "homens bons" (men of quality) who cast the few votes for the election of the members of the Senado de Câmara, the town council. The Ordenações do Reino laid down the structure of the municipal council and the mode of election. Municipal authority included police and jail, communal regulations, price controls, street cleaning, public morals, laying out of streets, hospitals, and numerous matters pertaining to the life of the city.

One aspect of Portuguese life that developed less in Brazil than in the mother country was the guild system for the control of crafts and merchants. Portugal itself did not have as strong a guild system as the northern nations in Europe. The *Corporações de Mesteres*, guilds of mechanical trades, known in Portugal in the fifteenth century, could not develop strongly when transplanted into a society where the self-sufficient engenho worked by slaves left little opportunity for free workers.

There were many complaints about the delay in paying wages and the hasty workmanship, but the positive aspects of development were also evident. Father Nobrega reported, in August 1549, that "they are beginning to plant cane and many other necessities of life, for the land is fertile and produces everything." He named among the plantings "citrus (cidra), oranges, lemons which produce in great quantity and figs as good" as those of Portugal. Many more, even hundreds, of plants and fruits could have been named—as Gabriel Soares does in his marvelously detailed description of Brazil's native and imported flora.

Of all the things introduced into Brazil from Europe, domestic animals must be ranked first in importance, even above sugar, for without cows, bulls, mares, horses, burros, sheep, goats, hogs, chickens, and domestic ducks, the development of the land would not have been possible, transportation almost nil, and the food supply very deficient without fats and milk. Also lacking would have been leather and bones for making instruments, and wool for clothing.

Soon after Sousa arrived, he began the distribution of livestock. Whether any animals had survived from the captaincy of Coutinho is unknown, but doubtful. They would have been too few to escape the Indians. More livestock came in from the Cape Verde Islands in the caravel, *Golga*, in 1550. In December 1550 Sousa distributed four cows and a young bull at two milreis a head. One of the buyers was Garcia d'Ávila, a retainer of the governor, or a *criado*. In 1551 the *Golga* again brought livestock from the Cape Verdes, paid for by the sale of brazilwood. In July 1552 Garcia d'Avila sold two steers (bois maninhos) for the governor's carts—perhaps the first sale of cattle by the man who would become the owner of extensive ranches and the builder of an imposing *torre*, a fort-palace that led to his title as Senhor da Torre. Already in 1552, Garcia d'Avila owned "nearly 200 cattle, plus hogs, goats, and mares." He found his lands "small and narrow because his herds were growing." So the governor gave him an additional two leagues along the sea. Later he assumed a perpetual lease on a sesmaria of six leagues belonging to the Conde de Castanheira. His descendants controlled thousands of square miles of land and thousands of cattle and other livestock along the São Franciso River.

In 1552 the municipal council set aside three leagues along the sea and two leagues beyond the Rio Vermelho as *pastos baldios*, or common pasture, for the lesser men who held no sesmarias. Setting aside small areas for the many while a few got vast holdings characterized the economic system planted in Brazil. Land was given to only a few in a system where grants were made in units of "a league of sesmaria," equal to nine square miles (about 6,000 acres); and it was the rule that most received more than a league, and some received several or many.

The king's objectives in founding the captaincy-general system were several, as expressed in Sousa's Instructions. Among them, and possibly in the royal view the chief objective, was to recover some of the powers and privileges so freely given to the donataries to induce them to undertake settlement. Had the captaincies been an unquestionable success, there might have emerged several domains in Brazil that would have been many times larger than Portugal itself. The nineteenth-century Brazilian historian Francisco de Varnhagen noted that, in establishing the captaincies, the king had granted Brazil its independence before it was colonized. But the failure, or near failure, of all but two captaincies enabled João III to take advantage of the situation and reassert royal authority.

The machinery of government and the legal tradition already existed for what the king wanted to accomplish. The governor-general's office and prerogatives were defined in the Ordenações do Reino (at that time the Ordenações of King Manuel). No specific and separate system of legislation and administration was drawn up for Brazil and the other Portuguese colonies as Spain had done in creating the Casa de Contratación (Board of Trade) and the Consejo de las Indias (Council of the Indies). Portuguese law codes applied overseas as they did in Portugal. The king dealt with the situation in a special way, since his absolute power permitted him to issue specific laws known as alvarás. He could also create in his overseas conquests the same types of offices that governed Portugal. It was in this tradition that he sent, with Sousa, officials in charge of two areas of authority—the ouvidor-mor for judicial matters and the provedor-mor for fiscal matters, each with his Regimento, or Instructions, distinct from and different from the governor's. Both offices already had long legal standing in Portugal. The title of ouvidor (or sobrejuizes) appeared in the early history of the royal house as a judge sitting on the king's highest courts, the Cúria do Rey.

The office of provedor-mor (treasurer and comptroller) was of more recent origin. The great increase of revenue in the sixteenth century made necessary an official to assist the king in supervising more closely his finances. In Brazil the provedor's duties included founding a custom's house and an accounting office in each captaincy. The numerous details of his Instructions are too extensive to enumerate here.

Many sub-officials were also placed in the captaincies. The result was a complicated administrative system staffed with poorly-paid civil servants who were expected to stretch their salaries with fees and gratifications from those served—which were equivalent to bribes. The salaries burdened the common purse, and the fees and bribes burdened the common people, still leaving the public servant underpaid. In the minds of the fee payers, they were excessive in number. There were often protests from the people, with little effect. Brazil is not the only instance of this system, but it is certainly a prime example of petty administration by an underpaid, indifferent, and inefficient swarm of officials.

According to their Instructions, both the ouvidor-mor and the provedor-mor were required to visit all the captaincies immediately to put the affairs of the king in order. In November 1549 ouvidor-mor Pêro Borges and provedor-mor Antônio Cardoso Barros sailed in the royal fleet under command of Pêro de Góis, last seen trying to make a success of his captaincy of São Tome. Góis had returned to Brazil to command the king's coastal fleet, intending to clear Brazil of the numerous and strong French ships which were cutting dye wood and trading with the Indians. He had only two caravels and one brigantine to oppose heavily armed French ships that sometimes reached 200 tons.

The inspection began from Bahia southward. By royal order, Duarte Coelho's Pernambuco was exempted. When Coelho learned the extent to which the new government planned to curtail the rights given in his donation, he reacted violently and wrote the king straightaway. The king had no appreciation, he wrote, of the work he had accomplished for the royal good. In "lands so far from Portugal," he thought, different rules should prevail. He resented the withdrawal of the rights that had been granted to induce new settlers to come after they and their families had already undergone so much expense and suffering. "Now then Senhor," he wrote very frankly to the king:

> since I, here, for my part, work and do what I should do, Your Highness, should not let them interfere (bolir) in such matters, for now is not the time to interfere but to increase the rights and privileges rather than decrease them. I beg Your Highness to read my letter and consider my purpose and to take action in these matters very promptly. Take into account also my sound and good intentions and understand that my nature and my purpose is to do right and speak the truth with everybody, and even more with Your Highness in the things of your service in which I steadily work.

He could truthfully say that "few have achieved more in the service of God and of the King their Lord than I have in the past and trust to God I may do in the future." The king obviously read Coelho's letters, pondered them, and gave orders to Tomé de Sousa not to interfere with Pernambuco.

Governor Sousa thought it bad policy. "Not to inspect [Duarte Coelho's] lands seems to me to be a great disservice to God, to your conscience, and your resources." Neither the governor nor the ouvidor inspected Pernambuco. But the provedor-mor, Antônio Cardoso, went, quarreled with Duarte Coelho, and left. Coelho had unknowingly established a tradition in Pernambuco—opposition to royal and central authority which has survived down to the present.

The captaincies not exempted by the king received the inspection ordered. Ouvidor-mor Pêro Borges and Provedor-mor Antônio Cardoso sailed south with Pêro de Gois in November 1549. Their subsequent reports showed that the royal checkup was indeed needed. Pêro Borges found criminals sitting on town councils—an indication that such councils existed in the early captaincies. In Ilhéus and Porto Seguro there were illiterate justices, which may not have made them any less wise in judgment but was certainly a handicap in keeping records in a society so prone to put everything down in writing. Many cases long before the courts needed resolution, and new arrests were made. The conflict of church-state jurisdiction came to light. Father João Bezerra, the priest who had caused such disasters in Bahia,

Ilhéus, and Porto Seguro was found living among the Indians with a civilian refugee from justice. The civilian was arrested, but not the priest. Borges reported that he did not dare arrest him. "If Your Highness so orders it," he wrote to the king, "I shall, for he does not lead a good life."

The captain-general of the fleet left the provedor and the ouvidor in São Vicente to carry on their tasks, while he sailed away to carry out his own special mission of driving out the French interlopers, that is, interlopers from the Portuguese viewpoint. The French considered themselves to have as many rights as anybody. With his two caravels and brigantine, an undercomplement of crew, and eight bombardiers who did not know how to fire their guns and had never been to sea, Pêro de Góis was undeterred. Everywhere he heard rumors of French activity. The Bay of Guanabara and Cabo Frio, favorite sites of the French, were rich in brazilwood. In Cabo Frio he found a heavily armed 200 ton galleon loading brazilwood. Góis tried to attack with one caravel and the brigantine, the other caravel having sailed out of sight. Why Góis and his two ships were not demolished is not clear. Of fifty shots fired at the galleon "high as a tower" in the water, not one hit. The wind took Gois out of range. He found the missing caravel in Espírito Santo and dismissed the captain, an act later approved by Tomé de Sousa.

When Góis reached Bahia, he again asked the governor for bombardiers and was told by Sousa that the king had written that bombardiers must be trained in Brazil, for Portugal was short of trained men also. Góis had captured two Frenchmen in Rio de Janeiro. "I did not hang them," Sousa wrote to the king, for they were very useful. "I badly needed men who do not cost me money." One was an interpreter of the Indian language and the other could make "crossbows, guns and every kind of weapon." Bahia would need them both. Indians were still inland as well as along the coast, and the French remained along the coast for another century. Góis also reported to Sousa that there were so many French ships in Guanabara Bay that "we did not dare go after them." Luís Dias wrote in 1551: "During the year 1550 five or six ships were lost, including those taken by the French."

Gold and silver were ever in the thoughts of the Portuguese, as Pero Vaz de Caminha made clear as early as 1500. And why not? Was not "this land and Peru all one?" Governor Tomé de Sousa "wanted to see what there is in this country." He received assurance from Duarte de Lemos of Porto Seguro that inland was "pure gold" because Peru was 17°S latitude "which is where this captaincy is." It would be easy to reach Peru "where the gold is" because the Indians were friendly. From Porto Seguro, Spanish "pharmacist and astrologer" Felipe Guillén,—inventor, it was said, of a type of astrolabe— wrote that recently some Indians had arrived "who lived along the great river" and told of a "bright, shiny mountain," which because of its splendor was called "the sun of the earth." Furthermore, the stones were called by the Indians "pieces of gold." They were so numerous that the Indians made troughs of them to feed their hogs— a rather doubtful detail about the inland where there were no domestic hogs. But reports of gold can distort the vision. Two years after his arrival, Sousa wrote of sending men "via the rivers inland so far they could go no further, because I greatly wish to know what there is in this land, in order to see if I can discover some good fortune for Your Highness."

Tomé de Sousa was no doubt "a very sensible man," as described by contemporaries, and it would not have been sensible to ignore these tales from the interior. Especially since Guillén had enhanced the attraction with reports of emeralds and other valuable gems. He offered to search; but he was not sent because of eye trouble (from all the glitter?), so Sousa sent Miguel Henriques, "a man worthy of any command you wish to give him." The party left in a gale to explore the Rio São Francisco, whose ample mouth seemed to promise an entry into the interior and might be the great river the Indians had described. Starting out on November 5, 1550, they had not returned seven months later. Sousa concluded that they had been lost at sea. He wrote the king fatalistically: "What I conclude is that when our Lord should want to grant another Peru to Your Highness here, He will arrange it when He wants to and as He likes." He assured the king that he was ready on royal command to make more efforts; and later he did. Meanwhile, Sousa told the king there were other sources of riches: "Last year there came to this city the caravel of Galga, of Your Highness, with cattle [from Cape Verde], which is the most noble and richest thing that can be brought to these parts."

The six Jesuits who accompanied Tomé de Sousa belonged to a new religious order founded only fifteen years before their arrival in Brazil and approved by the Pope only nine years earlier. Ignácio de Loyola recruited the original members in Paris, France. With his fellow students at the College of Santa Barbara, whose head was the Portuguese Diogo de Gouveia, he reached the conviction that they had a divine mission to create an effective organization to combat the Protestantism then growing rapidly in Europe. Among Loyola's companions were Francisco Xavier, a fellow Spaniard, and Simão Rodríguez de Azevedo, a Portuguese. Loyola, veteran of the Spanish army, conceived a missionary-teaching order with military structure and discipline headed by a man who would be called a general.

Loyola organized his first devout followers in 1534. Five years later they assumed the name Company of Jesus. Their immediate success convinced them that God had really chosen them as his own. They also convinced the papacy of their holy call. Pope Paul III approved the order by the bull of Regimini Militantis Ecclesia on September 27, 1540. Their stated mission was to go "to whatever lands we may be sent—whether to the Turks, whether to lands of other infidels, even the parts called the Indies, as well as to the heretical and schismatic countries."

Loyola became the first general of the Jesuits in 1541. They gained the approval and support of the king of Portugal even before that of the Pope. On the recommendation of Diogo de Gouveia, João III sent to Rome for six Jesuits. Only two came because more were not available so soon after the organization of the company. Others came a bit later and gained prestige for their devotion to the sick and poor in the hospitals. The people called them "apostles." Jesuit thinking emphasized foreign missions, however, even more than European activities. In 1541, Francis Xavier went to India, Japan, and China, and he had some success in each. He died off the coast of China in 1552, and later was canonized.

In 1550, four more Jesuits came to Brazil. They brought seven small orphan boys who were to learn the Tupí language and aid in the ccnversion of the Indians. The seven boys came from the orphanage of Father Domenech, a Catalan living in Lisbon who had founded the orphanage to care for and train the waifs of Lisbon in Christian ways. The boys learned Tupí rapidly from their peers and became valuable assistants in interpreting for the Jesuits and in the schools (colegios) they founded.

From 1549, when the first six Jesuits arrived, to 1604, some 28 separate groups of Jesuits reached in Brazil. The number increased in later times. Measured against the task they had set for themselves, their numbers were never more than a token of what was needed either to Christianize or to educate. There were other orders with missions and schools, who made a great contribution to the task, but the Jesuits had greater influence and prestige. Their schools were open in theory to all and free, but they could not meet the needs of a public education system. No school system did until the late nineteenth century.

There was never an attempt to educate all the people. By definition the slaves were eliminated from consideration. They had not been brought thousands of miles at great cost to be put into schools and educated at their master's expense. Only the few Indians who were Christianized and settled into aldeias were educated to some extent; and it is unlikely that they ever represented even one percent of the total number of Indians. The increasing number of unattached people—the middle stratum below the few who prospered through land grants or in business or in the military as officers—could in theory enter these schools, if there had been enough and if they could have supported themselves. But this was a proletariat on the whole and upward mobility was very limited. The increasing number of freedmen were equally unlikely to get an education. Thus, it can be said that education had a very low priority in the Portuguese colonial scheme. More will be said about the development of higher secondary schools in later centuries. It may be noted here, however, that Brazil never had a university of its own. Students who could afford it went to Portugal.

When Nóbrega and his companions reached Bahia with Tomé de

Sousa, he reported in April 1549 that they had found forty or fifty people in the Vila Velha and that "they received us with great happiness and we found a kind of church . . . which was no little comfort to us because we could say mass and hear confessions." He also wrote: "I hear very ugly things about the priests." And still again: "There are priests here," he said, "but it is the scum who come from there . . . No priest should be allowed to embark who does not lead a very exemplary life, because the others destroy everything that is done."

The Jesuits began to learn something of the Indians at the first mass held after their arrival. They were "instinctive imitators" and followed the services exactly: "they kneeled, beat themselves on the chest, and raised their eyes to Heaven." Had they had experience with some of the bad priests before Nóbrega came? Did they understand anything of the Christian service? Nóbrega soon took up the matter of putting prayers into Tupí, though he found the Indians "so brutish that they have no words" for the prayers. Father Navarro, who was a "grande lingua" (great linguist) was a great help and "edificava o gentio" (uplifted the people). He adapted words for the Christian songs and zealously helped in the Friday flagellations, "rushing now here and now there." Father Vicente Rodrigues soon began to teach reading and writing as well as later bringing up the question of "not eating human flesh, or of having more than one wife."

As leader of the Jesuits and first provincial, Manuel da Nóbrega manifested leadership qualities quickly, and he evoked praise from all who observed his life. Among his acts, he took some of the orphan boys to Pernambuco where he and his fellow Jesuit Antônio Pires were welcomed by the donatary Duarte Coelho. There was much Christianizing to do, especially among the Portuguese themselves. How could the Jesuits seriously preach monogamy and Christian virtues to the Indians who saw the contrary examples set by the colonists? The Portuguese were generally promiscuous with the Indian girls; and the secular priests also often took concubines. From the viewpoint of the church, it was horrible to contemplate that some Portuguese Christians had not received communion in twenty years.

Coelho wished the Jesuits success and gave them a building site on a hill where a church already existed. Nóbrega returned to Bahia in 1552, leaving Father Pires to build the church and establish a colégio. At this time there were still only ten Jesuits along hundreds of miles of coast—and the multitude to be converted was numberless. As rapidly as he could, Father Nóbrega sent Jesuits to all the captaincies and called for more to come from Portugal. Soon, he prayed, a bishopric would be created in Salvador, Bahia.

Ways had to be found to attract more Indians to Christianity. A "Principal Indian" who lived in Bahia had already accepted the faith. The Jesuits gave him a red beret and a pair of trousers to cover his *vergonhas* (privates). On one occasion they seated him at the table with them as a sign of respect and in order to impress the other "negroes."

The civilians did not approve of such demonstrations of equality. Nóbrega wrote to Simão: "Our Christianity" among the whites is a bad example. Impenitents for seven years, they were ardent polygamists. Nóbrega thought that a vicar general was needed. The Jesuits lacked some of the essentials of worship: oil for baptisms, confirmations, and the last sacraments, for example, because they did not regard the native oils as canonical. Father Manuel Lourenço, appointed vicar in 1549, had become established in his church by December of the same year; though it is not clear how or when he arrived in Bahia.

The governor-general was the strongest supporter of the Jesuits. Tomé de Sousa, said Nóbrega, "was chosen by God" to be governor; he is "careful and sensible," and "Our Lord will preserve him to govern this our people of Israel . . . He understands the spirit of the Company so well that he lacks only a little of being a member." Nóbrega urged sending a great number of whites of good character rather than the degraded dregs, for only good settlers could develop Brazil. The degraded continued to come, however. Although some of these were of good quality for the task to be done, others were a real plague even though they were sent in the service of the king.

Again and again Nóbrega referred to the deplorable state of the whites, whose moral life was on a low level. They took their concubines, free and slave, in profusion, and abandoned them at will, with the explanation that there were no women of marriageable social condition, meaning obviously, white women. Nóbrega recognized the justice of the complaint and called for women from Portugal "who there would not be marriageable," even if of "vidas erradas" (wayward lives). Whites in some respects were worse than Indians, or "negroes" as they were commonly called. Father Bezerra, by unjustly killing an Indian chief, brought down the vengeance of the chief's sons and various villages of Indians. Except for their nefarious banquets on human flesh, the "negroes" led a better life than the whites, and it would be wise, many thought, to return them to their villages.

How much Christianization took place before the Jesuits arrived? Some villages of Indians already Christianized before the arrival of the Jesuits had been assaulted by whites and Indians, and one of the padres (the other having died) was brought back among the slaves. The padre was freed but not the captured Indians. It seems obvious that some priests from the founding of the captaincy had taken their mission seriously. Did the Jesuits underemphasize the work of these priests as a means of validating their own work?

Nóbrega appealed frequently for support from Portugal. In the aldeias established for the Indian children, they needed workers to cultivate and to fish. A field of cotton provided a minimum of clothing to cover the naked "shameful parts." Five slaves were enough to provide for 200 children; and Nóbrega needed slaves because "slaves are very cheap here." The nakedness of the Christianized Indians brought a pain to the heart, and it was necessary to send some clothing, "at least a skirt for every woman." The nakedness of the Indians distressed Nóbrega. He was happy when he heard that, in the cooler lands of the south and interior, "the women go dressed in the Gypsy style, in dresses of cotton."

Nóbrega wrote to Portugal for tools for carpentry and for seeds in abundance. He spoke of three hundred houses surrounded with sugar cane. Brazil, he thought, must be two-thirds of the world. Temperate airs guaranteed good health and rapid convalescence. Fruits and fish were in such abundance, "no need to speak of them" (nem falar).

But it was frightening that "such a beautiful land" had been in the hands of "such an uncultured people," who were sensual, polygamous to the limit, constantly at war, and ate war prisoners and the children born of them (after proper fattening up). They did not fight for avarice and acquisition, but from the "bitter hatred" (ódio cordial) and heredity—pure Adamic ire. "If they chance on one another in the trail, they take to their clubs, stones or the teeth at once."

He found them, nevertheless, so anxious to learn the "Good Tidings" that there were within a short time "some six or seven hundred *catecumenos* (new converts receiving doctrinal instruction) ready for baptism." One mother had taken the colored stone from the pierced lip of her son so he could make the sign of the cross with more ease, and the example was taken up "miraculously" by others.

The Indians loved the music and processions. They found the trumpets fascinating and wanted nothing else but tubas and triumphal processions. Corpus Christi was celebrated in streets strewn with palm branches, with the artillery firing and "dances and artifices after the manner of Portugal."

The zeal of the Jesuits was unquenchable. "Why did not more come from Coimbra, even if with "little learning" (poucas letras), to place the Christian virtues into the hearts of the natives (géntio). Nóbrega frequently referred to the Indian mind as a "blank paper" on which "anything you wish can be written." (And the rational philosophers of the seventeenth century get credit for this concept of the mind!)

Dangers? There were plenty. Once a Christian was killed a few leagues from Bahia, which could have caused war if the Indians themselves had not brought in the murderer for punishment. Governor Tomé de Sousa had him bound to the end of a cannon and blown up in sight of the people. On the more peaceful side, Nóbrega painted a picture of preaching in the light of the moon and teaching the neophytes to say in Tupi: "Jesus, I commend my soul to thee."

The *pajés* caused a great deal of trouble preaching that the water of baptism caused death. They also asserted that baptism rendered human meat inedible. One Indian remarked to Nóbrega that "those for whom you pray die." They were the counselors of war, the augurs, and the doctors, who were generally respected and feared by the Indians. The need to compete with them forced the Jesuits to learn a great deal about materia medica and healing, not to mention the psychosomatic and psychological aspects of treating the patient.

Nóbrega frequently praised the healthy climate of Brazil, where the principal causes of death were old age and the "mal gálico" (Gallic Plague = syphilis). The humidity caused a great deal of "dropsy"— a wrong diagnosis, but the disease was real.

There were many other diseases mentioned by the Jesuits, Nóbrega among them, that seemed to belie the rhapsodies about the healthy climate. These dread diseases included *cámara de sangue* (painful and bleeding evacuation) and *bexigas* (smallpox). Native women suffered "from putrefaction of the sexual organs, a disease common among these Brazilian women, even the virgins."

Other diseases included bouba or pia, a stage of syphilis mentioned by Nóbrega, *bócio* (goiter, an endemic thyroid swelling), various varieties of parasitic diseases, dermatosis, and dysentery. Malaria was perhaps known in America before Columbus, but was also brought from Europe where it had been a scourge for many centuries. The Europeans brought smallpox, measles, leprosy, perhaps gonorrhea, tuberculosis, scarlet fever, and other skin diseases. To the list must be added diseases from Africa, including filariasis (filarial worms in the blood), trachoma, maculo (a form of diarrhea that weakens the sphincter muscle), ainhum (a disease that causes a thickening of the area at the base of the toes and leads to the loss of these organs), and perhaps yellow fever.

The swarms of mosquitoes, even if they carried no diseases, caused damaging infections. Snake bites killed many. A host of other diseases mentioned by early writers suggests something of a mystery about why they insisted on the healthfulness of Brazil. It may be observed also that reports of longevity among people whose births were not reported anywhere, at least before the Discovery, and not usually afterwards, are hard to accept. How could the pre-conquest Indians, who by most records could not count above three, have known their ages?

We know more of these things from the letters of the Jesuits and other orders than from medical reports, which were few. With the scant knowledge characteristic of the medicine of the time, such reports were not highly scientific. Also, medicines imported from Europe deteriorated rapidly. The use of native plants was so mixed with magic that their real curative powers are unknowable, though widely used and praised. Take this example: "to be in good health it is necessary to work and sweat a lot, as Father Navarro does. All the foods here are hard to digest (desgastar), but God remedied this with a plant whose smoke greatly aids the digestion, as well as other body ailments and purges the fleuma of the stomach." What marvel was this? The whites had discovered the alleged marvels of the Indian's tobacco. Luís de Góis soon introduced it into Portugal, and Father André Thevet into France; but the French Ambassador to Portugal, Jean Nicot, had the "honor" of having its essence named for him.

These matters of health were subsidiary to the salvation of the Indians. Conversion was hindered by some Indians who had backslid and returned to their tribes, defaming the padres as tyrants. One mestiço had been killed in the woods for urging the governor to take a hard line (mão dura); "perhaps by fear they will be converted more quickly than by love."

Some of the converts went back to the forests to enjoy the banquets of human meat. "They are so numerous and the land so large, and they grow constantly in number, that if they did not carry on continuous war, and did not eat one another, the country would not contain them." The Fathers worked among those condemned to death and cannibalization; but the Indians believed so strongly that death and "burial" in the stomachs of their enemies was honorable that some did not want to be rescued. Many white Christians had taken to the life of the Indians and were so "poisoned" that they wanted no other life.

Other converts were excellent aids. "I think," said Antônio Pires of one woman, that she "is a better confessor than I." The use of unordained "linguas" as confessors of Indians who did not know Portuguese led to a sharp dispute with the higher authority of the

Church. An Indian woman, wife of a chief of a village, told a group who were belittling the Christians: "Get out of here, animals, who do not recognize what is good! Do you have anything worthwhile that did not come from the Christians?" An Indian woman convert would say to would-be seducers: "I belong to God, God is my Lord, to whom you should speak if you want anything from me." Nóbrega reported there was much talk of gold and precious stones, but "the true treasure . . . the real jewels" were "the souls" that "are in the shadows and now begin to see the light."

There had been some good results. Antônio Pires reported that some of the converted Indians were so docile that "they take no account of their parents or kinsmen." He urged many others to come from Coimbra. "How you must suffer to remain so long there when there is so much for you to do here." At a time when they were furiously burning "New Christians" in Portugal, the Jesuits were making new Christians (cristãos novos) of the Indians in Brazil. But the Indians, as Vaz de Caminha noted, were not *fanados* (circumcised) and to the Portuguese this meant that they had never been Jews.

The problem of concubinage always bothered Nóbrega and the other Jesuits. It was necessary to close the eyes to concubinage of whites with baptized Indians in the hope that these unions could be sanctified in marriage.

Nóbrega, visiting some of the aldeias, found concubinage without restraints among the whites "including the Padres," who baptized the concubines first as if, by this act, they could wipe away the sin of multiple unions. There was also the bigamy of whites who also had wives in Portugal. He refused absolution to them, and time after time insisted on the need to bring women from Portugal, even those of second choice, provided with dowries. The poor among the white Christians contented themselves with the "negras." The frequent plea was: send more women! "White women are so wanted here that whatever kind will do a lot of good in this land, and they will benefit and the men here will leave their lives of sin." Also needed were "*moradores* (settlers) who cultivate and love the land" and "not those whose hearts are in Portugal."

The Fathers needed better houses for themselves and for the little Indians in the school. They also wanted "slaves from Guinea" to cultivate the farms and cotton. Later Nóbrega had to write Simão Rodrigues that slaves from Guinea intended for the colégio had died of harsh treatment enroute to Brazil. Only the cows, "doze vaquinhas," for the children had arrived. He asked that in the next remittance of slaves from Guinea three or four be reserved for the Colégio of Bahia. To pay for them, cotton could be planted, sent to Portugal for processing, and returned to Brazil in the form of clothing.

Nóbrega used almost any means to get support from Portugal. The "carta dos meninos do Colégio de Jesus da Bahia," sent to Lisbon on August 5, 1552, was no doubt mainly written by the Jesuits, with the children of the school used merely as a front. It contained the often repeated appeal for reinforcement. Among other statements in the letter: "If some tambourinest (tamborileiro) and flutist (gaiteiro) should come here, I think that there would not be a single chief who would not send his children to him for instruction." The music would be a great aid in conversion to Christianity. The missionaries with musicians could go among the Indians "safe in this way, because the negros would let their enemies (those they hate because they eat one another) into their lands and houses if they come with music and singing." "And when the children go playing and singing in the aldeias, the adults (who generally fear us and hide their children) come and dance without rest, even the old women." These women were among the chief enemies of the Jesuits because they took leading parts in the roasting and eating of enemies. They found it difficult to get the confidence of the Indians: "They do not dare trust us entirely because of the frauds and evil done to them up to now by the Christians." He often appealed for many church bells (sinos) and many saint's bells (campainhas) and musicians to go into the villages "singing and playing in all of them in the same style as the 'negros' and with the same tunes and songs, changing the words to praise the Lord."

Nóbrega pleaded largely in vain for adequate support of the Order. He resolved, "with the counsel of the other Fathers," to acquire a bit of land and "with our own hands" and the aid of the Indians and the boys (colomins) "to cultivate and grow food for the children" of the aldeias. They also went from door to door begging during the first hard years. The king had not forgotten them; but he did not always remember their needs.

Eventually some African slaves were acquired, at first only temporarily. Nóbrega explained that the three Guineas entrusted to the Jesuits would soon have served their time, and it was necessary to apply some of the money they had received in buying "native slaves." Things were looking up. They had "a boat and slaves to fish." The women had married, and the couples lived in the "farms" (roças) separate from the others in their own houses and looked after by a layman. As for the marriages, it was not merely a matter of morals, "because the females prepare the flour (farinha) and do all the main part of the work and service; the men only cultivate, fish and hunt, and little more."

Nóbrega had yearned and prayed for the arrival of a bishop to put the sinful whites to right. He was emphatic about what kind of man he wanted. The bishop must be the best type available. Because, Nóbrega stressed, if the king sent another bishop who was slow-paced, phlegmatic, and negligent, he would die of sorrow "and perhaps go to Hell for my little patience."

The bishop arrived. On June 22, 1552, Bishop Pedro Fernandes Sardinha landed in Bahia after a three-month voyage from Lisbon. Nóbrega had left Recife in January and only in March reached Bahia, demonstrating once more that travel along the coast of Brazil was often as time-consuming as from Lisbon.

Nóbrega was pleased, at first. Bishop Sardinha was, he said, "very zealous for the glory and honor" of God. He did not know at the time how soon he would regret seeing the new bishop. Within a short period Nóbrega was describing him as "disconsolate," hierarchical, and not of an age to withstand "the exposures of this country." If the bishop did not bear up, it would be better to send him elsewhere; "otherwise we shall not have a prelate nor will the country progress."

Nóbrega soon passed on his "doubts" about the bishop to the "letrados" of Portugal. He asked rhetorically: "If it is proper to hear confessions using an interpreter for the people who do not know how to speak our language, because it seems to be something new not previously used in Christianity?" We have already reported Nóbrega using such interpreters, even women. Some of those who did not know Portuguese were "the wife and children of Diogo Álvares Caramelu (Caramurú)."

Father Nóbrega had another problem. "It is the custom here," he wrote, "to permit the natives (gentios) in the churches and at mass to sit side by side with the Christians, and they are not thrown out in order not to offend them. Should the old law be maintained or should the congregations be allowed to be all mixed together?"

And there were still other questions which went back to the development of the early Church, when it came into contact with the varied religions of the Roman Empire and on its fringes—the Germans, for example. Nóbrega did not mention, and perhaps did not know, how much of what was called "Roman" Catholic in his time had been derived from acculturation.

There were so many questions. The bishop was a very strict man. The Vicar of Salvador had been imprisoned for ten days without it being known exactly why, and so had other clergy for "disobedience." On the other hand, Bishop Sardinha "was a very fine preacher and very popular with the people."

The Jesuits in Brazil "found many different types of negros." In spite of all their troubles and dangers, they were well received in many villages. "In one aldeia where we entered one afternoon," the Christianized Indian children went ahead to give the word that they were coming, "and many negros came loaded with fish, of which we ate very well." In others they were offered wild game and shrimp, so that they ate well "wherever we went". Not all Jesuits thought the conversions of the Indians would be lasting. Francisco Rodrigues thought that the fervor of the Indians was "nothing more than to have clothes to wear and be baptized."

Another question related to one of the bishop's objections was: if the Indians asked baptism "and they do not have shirts or other clothing to cover themselves," should baptism be refused? The bishop endorsed refusal, "because to go about naked is against the law of nature, and whoever does not keep this law is in mortal sin, and such person is not in condition to receive the sacraments." "On the other hand," said Nóbrega, "I do not know when so many heathen people (gentio) can be dressed, because they have gone naked for so many thousands of years, not denying that it would be good to persuade them to preach to them that they should be dressed and get them started in this way when possible?"

Other very important questions were: "Whether it is permitted to make war on these heathens and capture them . . . if they do not keep the law of nature in all ways?" What of "unjust slavery" for which the whites bore a "guilty conscience," buying (called resgatando, i.e. rescuing) Indian children from their fathers, who were never free again, but sold by one to another as if they were tools or cattle? The priests of Brazil had looked the other way (faziam a vista grossa) in these cases. He had submitted all these questions to the Colégio in Coimbra and to the Letrados of the University more than a year earlier and had received no answer.

Bishop Pedro Fernandes Sardinha was no help. "As far as the Heathens and their salvation was concerned, he cared little because he did not consider himself their bishop." Nóbrega, writing on the death of Bishop Sardinha by Indians, wrote: "Our Lord in his providence, who permitted that the [bishop] fleeing from the Heathens of this land, having little wish to die by their hands, should be eaten by them; and that I, who always desired death and ask it of Our Lord, and put myself in the situations [of danger] more than he, should be denied it."

PART II

The immense size of the land to be "unified" was comprehended by newcomers to Brazil only after they had experienced the great distances by traveling over them. Governor Tomé de Sousa was not different from other newcomers in this respect. His principal mission was to see that the existing captaincies were brought under royal control. The inspection trips made by Ouvidor-mor Pedro Borges and Provedor-mor Antônio de Barros were in obedience to the royal Instructions. We can visualize the task better if we note that one year after Sousa arrived in Salvador not one ship had come into that port from Recife, Espírito Santo, or São Vicente. The Jesuit Father Francisco Pires wrote in 1552: "sometimes a year passes and we do not have news of one another because of the weather conditions and the few vessels along the coast; and at times ships come faster from Portugal than from the other captaincies." Father Nóbrega corroborated Pires's statement when he wrote from São Vicente in 1553: "It is easier to get a message from Lisbon than from Bahia."

The reasons for infrequent communication were several. There was not much incentive to travel between captaincies, nor were ships available. The Brazilian coast offered major sailing difficulties for ships without auxiliary power. The only auxiliary power in this era was the oar—and oars were not practical for sailing ships large enough to carry much cargo. Sailing ships had to wait for the proper seasonal winds. There is a spring-fall pattern of winds, named monsoons after the Indian Ocean seasonal winds with which the Portuguese were well acquainted.

Governor Sousa was obligated by his instructions to make an inspection, whatever the sailing problems. Toward the end of 1552, he decided that Bahia was in a sufficient state of organization to permit his absence. He did not go to Pernambuco because the king had, in effect, removed the captaincy from his jurisdiction. Father Nóbrega accompanied Sousa in order to visit the Jesuits sent to establish aldeias and colégios in the other captaincies.

The first stop was Ilhéus, now a part of the state of Bahia. Sousa reported to the king that Ilhéus was "the best thing on this coast for plantations and the one that gives Your Highness the greatest income." He dismissed the alcaide-mor, nevertheless, as acting captain because he was "a New Christian under indictment by the Inquisition."

Farther south in Porto Seguro he visited the memorable Pêro Campo de Tourinho, who had survived the Inquisition's investigation of his "heresies and blasphemies." He survived Sousa's inspection also.

Nóbrega found in Porto Seguro and Ilhéus a combination of Tupiniquins mixed with Christians of bad life. King Manuel had sent priests who had made some conversions, yet they were unfortunately corrupted by the perverted whites who still lived besmirched by customs of the savages (gentiaga) in spite of the continued use of the Mass. They treated the peaceable Tupiniquins as "dogs" instead of taking advantage of their docility to teach them Christianity.

In Espirito Santo, the captain was Vasco Fernandes Coutinho. The king had included in Sousa's instructions special mention of the need to straighten out the affairs of the captaincy. When, a short time later, Coutinho took refuge in Bahia, Bishop Sardinha excommunicated him for "drinking smoke." There was no need to visit the abandoned captaincy of São Tomé on the Paraíba River. Its owner, Pêro de Góis, was now commanding the small fleet in which Sousa was sailing. Nor was there any reason to stop long in Guanabara Bay (Rio de Janeiro). No captaincy was there, but the Tamoio Indians were; and they were no friends of the Portuguese.

Sailing southwest, São Vicente was the next and last captaincy. Sousa was impressed. The port of Santos, he reported, could harbor "all the ships in the world," possibly true of the ships in that era. He admired the town of São Vicente established by his cousin Martim Afonso de Sousa, who was still donatary and living in Portugal as a very wealthy and important man after returning from India, where he had served as governor. Tomé de Sousa wanted to consolidate São Vicente and Santos, but he abstained out of deference to or fear of his influential kinsman.

São Vicente had a stone church, private homes also built of stone, a well-established Jesuit Colégio, and a stone fort provided with cannon at Bertioga. It was first commanded by the German soldier-of-fortune Hans Staden. Sousa wanted to look into the affairs of the town Martim Afonso had established on the mountain plateau above São

Vicente. The plans of Nóbrega and Sousa for this area coincided to a point, and then diverged. Father Leonardo had been sent to São Vicente where he converted many and married many living in sin. He reported that "in the country some fourteen of fifteen leagues from here," he was told "there are some Christians scattered here and there, . . . who live a life of savages." He had sent two "linguas," interpreters who knew Tupi, to the region.

One of them was Brother Correia who had been many years in Brazil and for a time had lived the life of the savages. On the last day of the journey into what was to become the nucleus of São Paulo, they met messengers from some of the inhabitants who requested them to come up the mountains and visit. These were the whites, remnants of those placed in the original settlement by Martim Afonso de Sousa. They were "nine leagues away in the sertão, on the banks of a river they call Piratininga," but Father Leonardo could not find even a trace of the town.

Tomé de Sousa gathered together some old and new settlers in a town called Santo André da Borda do Campo. It was located at the base of the plateau and reached after a sharp climb up the tough and sinuous trail to the top of the Serra do Mar—3,000 feet above sea level.

Sousa wanted to interrupt the commerce that had already begun between the Portuguese and the Spaniards who had settled Asunción in 1537. The Spanish were pushing up the Paraguay and Paraná rivers establishing towns almost directly west of São Vicente. Traders had already found a route along the Tieté River to the Paraná River and down to Iguassú, from which they could cross level country to Asunción. The amount of this trade and how long it had been established cannot be stated, but in 1552 the customs house of São Vicente had already collected 100 cruzados from Spanish traders in Paraguay. Sousa reported to the king: "I ordered with severe penalties that this road was to be avoided."

The Jesuits were determined to go inland far from the whites. "The farther away the Whites, the more prestige we have among the Indians." Given the "little constancy" and the "contumacious Heathens in their perverse customs," the Fathers resolved to go "a hundred leagues" and "construct a great building and in it gather the children of the Heathens and bring together many Indians in a large city, making them live according to the laws of reason." They wanted to move from São Paulo toward Paraguay, "a little more than a hundred leagues from the captaincy, and they say within the jurisdiction of the king of Portugal." Sousa did not see eye to eye with the desire of Nóbrega to go toward Paraguay. He thought a few "linguas" might be all right, but the time had not come to establish more Jesuit houses.

Sousa had another reason to refuse his good friend Father Manuel da Nóbrega permission to lead the Jesuits into the interior to establish a "great city" among the Indians. He thought it might attract the criminal elements of São Vicente and absorb the territory where, Sousa hoped, mines would be found. The conflict with Nóbrega grieved Sousa. "I feel this very deeply," he wrote the king. "They are taking it as a martyrdom that I am inflicting on them." He left the issue up to João III. There would be many more differences between governors and churchmen.

The seven Jesuits who came out with Governor Duarte da Costa all became important in the development of Brazil. But none was to have so much influence as young José de Anchieta, a frail Canarian already known for his learning and piety. He earned the reputation of being a true miracle worker (taumaturgo). Only twenty years old, not yet ordained, he was sent to São Vicente by Nóbrega, about Christmas time of 1553, and later to São Paulo. He became a teacher of Latin to his fellow Jesuits, several of whom were also not yet ordained. The new order had to train its people as it recruited them and sent them to the mission fields. Anchieta readily learned the Tupi language and taught the young Indians Christian doctrine. The details left to us describing the deprivation and poverty of the young pupils of the colégio and of the Jesuits themselves make it seem impossible that they could have survived in such a harsh environment of nature and people. But survive they did, and so did the new village of São Paulo.

The Jesuits often lived in poverty and begged door to door for food for themselves and their young Indian charges. Nóbrega referred often to "hunger" and the "cold" they suffered and spoke of the "marvel that the children (meninos) do not flee and return to their parents." "Now it seems to me that I am poor indeed, because before . . . I had an abundance of mutton and beef and drank wine and did not lack clothing. But now, if it is not oranges and citrons, I am seldom well fed. We live on charity" (esmolas).

Anchieta was discouraged about the mestiços of the São Paulo area. The Tibiriçá-Ramalhos, he reported, "grow every day worse in the hatred they have of us. Not being able to do anything personally against our works, they apply themselves to the ruin of the Indians, so that they destroyed entirely one aldeia, . . . inciting the Indians to kill their enemies and eat their flesh." Anchieta cited cases of "bad Christians," who corrupted the Indians already converted, belittling them as "women." Nevertheless, "the number of children who attended the school increased day by day."

Luís Gonçalves da Câmara wrote: "There is great fervor in their confessions, and many come in crying . . . asking confession and in great grief because they do not know how to confess." In spite of difficulties, he added: "They all know the catechism (doutrina) better than many Old Christians." Many were slaves living in sin, and others separated from their mates. Many disciplined themselves with such great fervor that they confound (confusão) the whites. The children were the marvels. "They learn to read and write and are very advanced; others sing and play the flute; and others, mamelucos, more apt (destros) learn grammar" (Latin). They were instructed by a young unnamed Latinist (gramático) of Coimbra, "who came here as an exile."

Not all children showed such aptitude. The "mestiço children," he alleged, were "the worst people of this land, some of them worse than the Indians themselves." The Jesuits concluded that "these are not people who can be counted on for conversion of the unfaithed." Two of them, "tempted by the spirit of fornication," had fled but been recaptured. It was thought better to treat mestiços like Indians until they could be sent to Portugal for further training, "where there are fewer obstacles and dangers of ruination than here where the women go nude and do not deny themselves to anyone, but even they themselves proposition and pursue the men, throwing themselves into the hammocks with them because they consider it an honor to sleep with Christians."

Some of the orphans of Lisbon who had been brought to learn Tupi and help in the Christian work were not exempt from the general rule governing the relations of Portuguese men and Indian girls and were caught in the web of lust.

It was often difficult to withstand the hardships and discouragement, and some wondered if it was worthwhile to try to save "barbarous people who eat one another." The victorious warriors offered their women the severed and barbecued sexual organs of their vanquished enemies as an aphrodisiac. The captured Indian who fled the honorable fate of serving as barbecue was rejected not only by those from whom he fled but also by his own people as a coward and imbecile. This explains why some captured Indians refused the efforts of the padres to release them.

Pêro Correia and João de Sousa were killed by the Indians to whom they were preaching in 1554. Anchieta took this as a sure sign that "the Lord wishes to establish his church here, for in this way He fashions the stones for its foundation." These deaths were blamed on a Castillian who led them into a trap.

The reports Nóbrega got about the secular clergy were, with rare exceptions, bad. Of ten padres de missa in São Paulo highlands, "only two or three do not have seven or eight children, as do the other" whites and Indians. These same priests had harems of "five or six Indian women . . . of bad life." One of them had not said mass for ten years, and some of the others for three or four. Some eight hundred whites were refugees from justice (homiziados), and they had formed into five "opposing gangs and every one has at least ten Indian women and some up to sixty and seventy."

As for the whites of the São Paulo region: "There are some who have mother and daughter" and "from both, children." Others had with them "two sisters, and aunts, and nieces and in the same way from one and the other, many children." In the region on which Nóbrega and Leonardo Nunes were reporting, "it is estimated that these number, between boys and girls, four thousand, and all fifteen or fourteen years or younger." Father Nunes said, however that when news arrived that the Jesuits were coming, "they fell into a state of panic . . . and all, the priests as well as the others, quitting their vices so that when we arrived they would not be found in such a state of sins." The Jesuits thought they were accomplishing something, at least. Around São Paulo for twenty or thirty leagues there was no butchery of humans, and "many times the Indians come with many presents of wild game and chickens," as well as fish and other things.

In the war that broke out in 1554, there were "in almost all the aldeias those miserable ceremonies of killing . . . even in the vila of the Portuguese" [São Vicente]. One of the enemy "was killed with the greatest festivity, in the presence of the Portuguese," who "approved and encouraged" the spectacle. The example enticed the catechumens of the padres to go on the war path in search of their succulent fellow men. Even Chief Tibiriçá had to be kept, with great difficulty, from reverting to cannibalism. There was little hope "unless a great many Christians come here who live their lives according to the will of God, subject the Indians to the yoke of slavery and oblige them to gather under the banner of Christ." "It is true," Anchieta wrote, "that our catechumens gave us in the beginning great examples of faith and probity, but as they are moved more by the hope of profit and a certain vainglory than by faith they have no firmness whatever and turn easily at the least obstacle to their vomit. After the war, they came back—even Tibiriçá—repentant, and hope was renewed.

In 1557 (or 58?) there was a "great plague which killed a great many of the enemies" who had attacked the settlements. "The dead were taken from the houses and thrown to the jaguars" that came during the night "and ate them."

In the midst of all the turmoil, Anchieta continued compiling a grammar and dictionary of Tupí. The task was difficult because the Indians "have only a few words that serve in general" to express the Christian religion. He warned those still in Portugal:

It is not enough to come out of Coimbra with ordinary fervor that will wither before you pass the Line, growing cold and leaving only desires to return to Portugal: it is necessary, Brothers, to bring your spiritual baggage full to last to the end of the journey; because without a doubt the work of the Company here is immense and it is necessary to have all virtues in everyone in order to entrust the honor of the Company to him, for at times it is necessary to go among the Indians in the midst of evil, for six or seven months without confession or mass, where it is better to be and necessary to be a saint to be a brother of the Company.

João Ramalho and his large family of mamelucos were crucial at this juncture. Although the German Ulrich Schmidel, who left valuable memoirs of his years in Brazil, certainly exaggerated greatly when he said that Ramalho could put 50,000 in the field of battle one day, we can admit the wisdom of Sousa in making Ramalho captain of the new town. He also restrained those who might have left São Vicente defenseless by seeking greater fortune in the interior.

Sousa had another motive for his restraints on Nóbrega and his would-be followers. He was convinced that Asunción lay on the Portuguese side of the Line of Demarcation. He wanted to stop the Spaniards from coming farther east, and halting their trade would be one way of pursuing his objective. Sousa was in error, however. Asunción was not on the Portuguese side by several hundred miles, a fact the development of knowledge of the geography of South America slowly revealed. But Sousa's plan foreshadowed the future Portuguese policy of taking territory first and negotiating later. He had, perhaps unwittingly, opened the way to the Paulista *bandeiras* that led Brazil's westward expansion and made territories Brazilian which were legally Spanish by demarcation.

For settlements in the mountain areas, João Ramalho was one of the keys, if not the key. He was not clearly on the Jesuit and Portuguese side. Of Ramalho, Nóbrega wrote: "He has many women. He and his sons go with sisters, and have children by them, the father as well as the sons. They go to war along with the Indians, and their celebrations (festas) are the same as those of the Indians, and they go naked like the Indians themselves." Ramalho accused the Jesuits of sexual sins like the other whites and secular priests when they refused him communion and held him excommunicated; but he failed to establish his case and eventually was brought to heel.

Even if the Jesuits described Ramalho as polygamous, incestuous, slanderous, and excommunicated, he was useful to them: "João Ramalho the oldest Portuguese in this land has many children with many kinsmen in all this sertão." But Ramalho had to be presented in a more favorable light if he was to be of greater service to the cause of Christianizing the Indians.

Ramalho's character had to be cleaned up. He had left a wife and children in Portugal. He supposed her dead, but had no proof of his wife's death. "He is very anxious to marry the mother of his children." A cynic might ask which of his wives, but for Nóbrega it was the daughter of Tibiriçá, the principal chief of the region. Nóbrega wanted an investigation made at once in Portugal to verify that Ramalho was free to marry, "because if this man were in a state of grace, he would do great good for Our Lord in this land." The situation was "of such great importance" that it had to be cleared up at once. Nóbrega advocated an appeal to the Pope to absolve Ramalho and others who were so much needed.

The "Jesuitical" reasoning in this and other instances is interesting, for it shows the burning zeal with which Nóbrega and his companions worked for the Christian salvation of the Indians and of useful Portuguese like Ramalho, some of whom like Correia became members of the Order. Nóbrega also wanted to clear up the situation of "two or three other mestiços who wish to marry Indian women from whom they have children, despite any affinity that exist between them." A practical matter was the cost of making such appeals: "This will be a great service to Our Lord. And if it costs something, it will be sent from here in sugar."

The doubtful steadfastness of the early converts was a constant problem. There was some backsliding, and some went back to enjoy the banquets of human flesh. A member of the Ramalho family, threatened by the Inquisition for his "Heathen practices," retorted: "I'll put an end to the Inquisition with my arrows." Anchieta reflected sadly: "And they are Christians, born of Christian parents. He who is basically a thorn, cannot produce grapes."

Sousa did not entirely stop the Jesuits. When he left for Bahia, Nóbrega acted at once. With other Jesuits, he spent several weeks scouting the interior in search of a suitable center for the salvation of souls. He also desired to verify the route to Paraguay, where he seemed to want to establish a Portuguese Jesuit settlement. Deciding, however, that he wished to be closer to the coast, on August 29, 1553, he founded, or ordered founded, a settlement at Piratininga where the Indian villages had drawn together. He began with 50 catechumens. The town and the colégio were moved January 25, 1554, to a site they named São Paulo. São Paulo soon absorbed Santo André. There, far removed from the difficult bishop of Bahia, the friendly but authoritative governor, and the captain of São Vicente, Father Nóbrega could develop his concept of a Christian Indian community with less interference from the secular church and royal authority.

Governor Tomé de Sousa arrived in Bahia from São Vicente on May 1, 1553, and soon thereafter, on July 13, handed over the government to his successor, Duarte de Costa. He had requested relief in order to return to Portugal to visit his wife and arrange the marriage of his daughter. But the fascination of Brazil and his realization of the immense work yet to be done beckoned him to stay. Nóbrega wanted him to remain in spite of the rebuff in São Vicente, calling Sousa "a great blessing to the land." Sousa left Brazil both gladly and sadly. When informed that his successor was sailing into the bay, he recorded: "my mouth watered at the thought of returning to Portugal, but now . . . it feels so dry that I want to spit and cannot."

5

DEFENSE AND DEVELOPMENT

PART I

Ⓣhe new governor, Duarte da Costa, proved too mild to control the centrifugal forces created by the nature of Brazil's geography, which offered multiple opportunities for individualism in a loosely knit society. He questioned why he had been chosen for such a difficult post. He had never before held a position of military or administrative importance, having been the king's chief armorer, a position inherited from his father.

Bishop Sardinha caused the governor great trouble, and so did Costa's own son. The son, a veteran of the East, was restless in the restricted environment. With his cronies he engaged in annoying the citizens and courting the girls. The bishop wanted him bridled but the governor refused. The disagreement between governor and bishop spread to the people and split Bahia into factions. The governor, the bishop, and others wrote bitter letters to the king. The king reprimanded the bishop for the bitterness of his letters. Violence broke out. Bishop Sardinha excommunicated his opponents freely and was accused of breaking open a man's skull so that his brains showed.

Even in the midst of the quarreling, Governor Costa launched a search for precious metals—one of the principal objectives of the crown from the time of discovery. As we have seen, Tomé de Sousa

115

had sent out an unsuccessful prospecting party. Governor Costa appointed the Spaniard Francisco de Bruza (or Bruzza) de Espinosa y Megare, who had previously been in Peru, to lead another expedition from Porto Seguro. Bruza started out in 1553 with twelve men, accompanied by Jesuit Father João de Aspilcueta Navarro on orders from Nóbrega. Navarro, writing on June 24, 1555, said that "more than a year and a half ago," they had penetrated 350 leagues into the interior (about 1050 miles) for three months. Later the distance was said to have been only 200 leagues. They brought the news that Peru was not "alongside" and reports of the "gold and silver" among the Indians were nothing but rumors.

While the prospecting party was away, a "revolt" of the Indians interrupted the quarrels of the colonists. Such wars between the invading Portuguese and the native owners of the country were normal, and the reasons for Indian outbreaks arose from the general situation as much as specific causes. Nóbrega, normally ready to side with the Indians rather than the colonists, pointed out in one of his letters that in this case the Indians killed people who had never injured them, including monks, priests, and women so pretty that "even the brute beasts would leave them and do them no harm." There were not very many white women in Brazil at this date, thus it seems that Nóbrega must have included Indian women in his reckoning.

The Portuguese faced an alliance between Indians normally enemies of one another. The Tupinambás, who lived around Bahia, had formed a temporary friendship with the inland Tapuyas in order to push the Portuguese out. The war began on a Sunday when the Indians attacked the engenho of Antônio Cardoso, claiming it as their own. They began stealing cattle, assaulting people traveling between settlements, killing slaves, and kidnaping and killing whites.

In the face of danger, Bishop Sardinha and the governor's son Don Álvaro made a reluctant but necessary truce. The governor appointed his hitherto troublesome and swashbuckling son to command the troops against the Indians. Álvaro led an initial force of some seventy footsoldiers and six horses. Later greatly reinforced, it was called by one modern historian, perhaps with some literary license: "The first outline of a colonial militia." All the captaincies had such militias in principle by the terms of their doações.

Álvaro da Costa conducted a successful campaign in the style that North American colonials followed later. He burned villages, recovered cattle, rescued human captives, and brought the Indians into submission. He was transformed from being the scourge of the colony into one of its heroes.

The bishop had offended too many people for too long, and the king had already decided to bring him home to Portugal. But Bishop Sardinha was never to leave Brazil. The ship bearing him home in June 1556, the *Ajuda*, suffered a wreck at the mouth of the Coruripe River in Alagoas. The Caeté Indians first helped the shipwrecks ashore in what seemed to be an act of human kindness, but their motives soon proved otherwise. They killed and ate them, including the bishop. Father Nóbrega, who had found the bishop a difficult man, envied him the good fortune of martyrdom. "To me," Nóbrega wrote, who had always desired to die at the hands of the Indians, "it has been denied." The story of the event had its messengers, one Portuguese who spoke the Indian language and two Indians.

Governor Duarte da Costa had not been able to repel the rivals of Portugal, and his successors were not able to do so for a century. The French were the main enemy. They were so numerous along the coast that the question of whether the French or the Portuguese would take over Brazil remained unanswered until the seventeenth century. In retrospect, it is difficult to understand how a nation with superior forces such as the French could muster did not prevail over the Portuguese. If reasons can be assigned for their failure, a prime one would be the lack of a consistent royal effort to establish true colonies with large numbers of French settlers rather than merely trading posts.

The one serious French effort at colonization in the sixteenth century was based on a false premise. It was led by Nicolas Durand de Villegagnon, who confused the object of colonization with religious concepts. His policies soon put him into conflict with his colonists and his backers in France.

We have noted the known battles between the Portuguese and

French during and prior to the governorship of Tomé de Sousa. We do not know how many unrecorded naval engagements there might have been. The French cut brazilwood and traded with the Indians in the whole area from Santa Catarina to the Amazon River. Their favorite haunt during the mid-sixteenth century was Guanabara Bay (Rio de Janeiro), on the edge of the brazilwood forests which extended to Rio Grande do Norte. Brazil pepper was also abundant. The French allied themselves with the Tamoio Indians, who controlled the area, and carried on a brisk trade. It has been estimated that the seven or eight ships went annually to Cabo Frio.

An incident of 1551 shows their power. A French ship blocked Gaspar Gomes in Guanabara Bay for some two and a half months, while it loaded a cargo of 60 moios (about 800 liters) of pepper and brazilwood. Four years later, Francisco do Porto Carreiro, who had succeeded Pêro de Góis as capitão-mor of the coastal fleet, wrote to João III about the French ships which plied the coastal waters freely and about the Portuguese ships they had captured.

The French succeeded in part because they did not establish fixed posts that could be attacked by the Portuguese. They could be expected to appear almost anywhere, but could be hunted systematically nowhere. So many French ships were present that it is unlikely that the Portuguese perceived initially that Villegagnon's expedition was aimed at colonization and not merely trade.

Villegagnon was a French nobleman and military man who had won distinction fighting in Algeria against the Muslims; in Hungary and Malta against the Turks (also Muslims, of course); in Italy against the forces of Emperor Charles V; and in Scotland against the English. While serving as vice-admiral of Brittany, he became dissatisfied after failing to gain the backing of King Henry II in a dispute with the governor of Brest. At this moment, he heard of the great opportunity for adventure in Brazil and determined to found a colony.

He was also a passionately religious man whose beliefs oscillated between traditional Roman Catholicism and the new ideas of the Protestant Revolution. What he believed and espoused with vigor one day he denounced the next, and then would again reembrace. He was, in this respect, in step with the France of his time. In the mid-sixteenth century millions were searching their souls to determine which of many different religious beliefs was most acceptable. There was a material aspect to the religious issue: the choice of the wrong belief in the wrong place at the wrong time could cost the believer both property and life. This situation led many to trim their religious sails according to the directions of the wind.

Some historians have treated the Villegagnon expedition as an effort to establish refuge for Protestants at a time when France's religious troubles were beginning. The circumstances of its organization show this interpretation to be false, although some of his recruits were religious dissenters. He visualized his enterprise rather as an extension of France into the New World, following the model of Spain and Portugal. The name for the proposed colony, Antarctic France (meaning only, France south of the Equator), showed his purpose. The main reason he had a number of dissenters from Catholicism in the beginning, and later recruited more, was not so much from design but rather because such people were willing to try their fortunes in a new land that they supposed free of religious wars.

The two principal accounts of the colony were written by Father André Thévét, a Catholic priest who accompanied Villegagnon, and Jean de Léry, a Protestant cleric who came out the next year with a fleet bringing additional reinforcements. Villegagnon's own writings trace a history of wavering and changing theological concepts.

His support came from both Protestant and Catholic forces in France. He gained aid from Admiral Gaspard de Coligny, the chief Protestant leader. But Coligny went to Henry II, staunch Catholic, for authorization and financial backing for the expedition. The Cardinal of Lorraine also supported Villegagnon enthusiastically, a fact indicating the primarily French rather than merely Protestant nature of the undertaking.

Villegagnon landed in Guanabara Bay on November 10, 1555. He soon came to regard himself as absolute king of his Antarctic France. King Henry II had provided him with two large, heavily gunned ships loaded with ammunition, supplies, and all the necessities for building a strong fort. Royal support enabled him to get the help of Norman and Brittany shippers, who had already profited from Brazil trade and now saw a wider and brighter horizon of commerce opening to them. That a great new world was beckoning to be conquered from the Portuguese and the natives of Brazil was obvious to all. The time seemed right to participate in a big venture.

The colonists came from various social segments. Some were Protestants, as previously stated. Others were prisoners released from the jails of Paris, Rouen, and other cities—similar to the degredados sent by the Portuguese. This method was used by European nations as late as the nineteenth century to rid themselves of people who otherwise would live as prisoners or go to the gallows. But Villegagnon was able also to recruit many skilled artisans of various trades. He brought about six hundred people in all.

After a first landing at some spot not easily identified, a settlement was made on the small island of Sergipe. It was renamed Villegagnon, where the Brazilian naval college now stands. He built a fort, named Coligny after his backer. Villegagnon know from his lifetime of military experience the value of a strong, defensible point. He chose the island because he thought it a good defense against Tamoios, friends at the moment, but who might turn against him, and against the Portuguese who were expected to discover him sooner or later.

He had other motives as he stated to Calvin in a letter of March 3, 1557—his own men could not flee to the mainland to cohabit with Indian women. The Indian women who came to the island were with their husbands and not accessible to his men.

Villegagnon was a hard taskmaster. He drove his men from sunup to sundown in the burning sun of a Brazilian summer that normally registers in the high nineties Fahrenheit (35° or more centigrade) and sometimes goes over the one hundred mark (40° and more centigrade). The reality of life on the barren islands was poles apart from the promise of a tropical paradise that had lured the men to Antarctic France. For drink they had green, stinking water from the cisterns Villegagnon had dug, not the wine to which they were accustomed. The only water came from rain on the island or was brought in from the mainland. They were reduced to eating bread of manioc flour instead of their usual wheat. They also ate fruits and some native foods, but it added up to very slim fare and was insufficient to keep them healthy. Like the Spaniards in the early settlement of the Caribbean and the Portuguese in Brazil, the French settlers suffered want, and even starvation, if not resupplied from Europe.

Villegagnon's puritanical code greatly increased his difficulties. Like the Jesuits, he was attempting to enforce a sexual code to which his European colonists were unaccustomed and the Indians understood not at all. The Europeans followed a code that freely admitted illicit sex was a sin, but forgivable. The Indians knew sex only as natural human practice, with limited restraints. Indian fathers, with no feeling of moral wrong, offered their daughters to the European in return for favors or gifts.

Villegagnon forbade absolutely any sexual relations with the Indian girls. Furthermore, he attempted to force the same abstinence on the Frenchmen already living among the Indians, who served as interpreters and intermediaries with the Indians. He could not prevent completely cohabitation between his men and the "savage she-dogs," even though he decreed the death penalty for offenders. He tried to enforce his will on long-time French dwellers who had mestiço families. The attempt to force one Norman to marry his Indian concubine by Christian ceremony after she had been baptized, or to abandon her on pain of death, led to a revolt and plot on Villegagnon's life. He was saved by his Scottish bodyguard; some of the plotters were executed. Twenty to twenty-five interpreters fled to live among the Indians. An epidemic of unknown origin killed off hundreds of Indians, some say as many as eight hundred, and the Indians blamed the French.

The strong fort manned with cannon and other guns was immune to Indian attack. Villegagnon's military thinking had proved correct in this respect—a mainland fortification might have been vulnerable.

Trade gradually won the Indians to friendship and a military alliance against their mutual enemies. On the French side were the Tamoios (Tupinambás), who warred without quarter against the

Tupiniquins, the Goitacá, and the Macapá, all of whom lived around Guanabara Bay and on its islands. Villegagnon felt no respect for the Indians except as allies. "It seems to me," he wrote to Calvin during his Protestant period, "that we have fallen among beasts (bichos) in human form."

Villegagnon visualized himself as omnipotent in both religious and political leadership. Well versed in the scriptures and religious matters, he held regular church services. The anomalous situation quickly became evident. Among his people were such Protestants as Nicolas Barre, to whom we owe much of our information about the colony, and the Catholic priest André Thévét, whose *Singularité de la France Antarctique* was the first book published about it. Religious differences could no more be reconciled in Antarctic France than in France itself. Villegagnon, nevertheless, attempted to force conformity to whatever religious views he held at the moment. At night he held regular services, where theology was argued with more heat than light.

The ships of the first expedition sailed for France on January 31, 1556. Among the passengers who had seen the earthly paradise and found that it did not resemble their visions was Father André Thévét. He published his celebrated book the next year, in 1557. Villegagnon sent an appeal for more colonists, specifically Protestant clerics. The appeal reached Calvin's headquarters in Geneva, and a number of men set out with his blessings to join the second expedition to Antarctic France also organized with Coligny's aid. Their start was inauspicious. Bad weather twice forced them back to port. They reached Brazil in February 1557.

Among the passengers were several girls and one woman, clothed naturally, thus introducing French fashions that the Indian women were not quick to follow. Several small boys accompanied the expedition to learn the Indian languages and serve as interpreters. The passengers included fourteen Protestant clergy, and one, Jean de Léry, mentioned earlier, wrote a book of enduring importance about the history of Antarctic France. His writings sometimes duplicate Thévét's, but his Protestant views were radically different. The two men did not meet, Thévét having sailed for France in January 1556 and

Léry arriving in February 1557. Guanabara Bay reminded Léry of "Lake Geneva in America."

Guanabara Bay was like Geneva in other ways. It was the scene of passionate theological discussions in which Villegagnon sought to become for Antarctic France what Calvin was for Geneva—the final word on religious doctrines. Like Calvin, Villegagnon was willing to condemn to death those who dared dissent from his opinions. Was he Catholic or Protestant at this time? If his views seem confused to us today, they seemed even more so to his Catholic and Protestant colonists. To those more interested in finding a way to survive in a new life than in discovering a sure road to another, he was a dangerous tyrant who wasted precious time in religious harangues that would have been better spent developing the economy of the colony. Furthermore, he was a constant threat to their lives, especially to the Catholics after he espoused Calvin's doctrines and wrote enthusiastically to Calvin about the arrival of the Calvinist ministers.

By mid-1557 he was disputing with the Protestant minister Pierre Richier about the admissibility of adding water to the sacramental wine. He forbade Richier to administer the sacraments or to refer to the subject in his sermons. By October the increasing bitterness caused some Protestant ministers and others to flee to the mainland to join earlier exiles who had established a settlement called La Briqueterie, where they lived and ate with the Indians. Léry found the Indians more humane than Villegagnon and his followers. The experience enabled Léry to learn some of the lingua geral (Tupí) and more about Indian customs and local plants and animals. He incorporated this knowledge into his book, *Histoire d'un voyage fait en la Terre du Brésil.*

Some of the refugees made an agreement with a Norman ship captain then loading brazilwood, pepper, cotton, monkeys, parrots, and other products to take them back to France. Five of the Protestants remained behind, however, because the ship was so worm-eaten, they feared to sail in it. Villegagnon welcomed them when they returned, but later questioned them exhaustively about their doctrinal beliefs. He executed three of them and threw their bodies into the sea.

The reports of Protestants returning to Geneva with news of Villegagnon's government dampened the spirits of those who had seen Brazil as a refuge for thousands of dissenters from Roman Catholicism. The projected sailing of seven or eight hundred new colonists was postponed. Support for Villegagnon declined. Distrusted by Catholics and Protestants alike in Antarctic France, as well as in France and Geneva, Villegagnon returned to France to defend himself. As badly as events were unfolding under him in Antarctic France, they became worse in his absence.

The French had incurred the hostility of the Maracajá Indians, who were enemies of the Tamoio allies of the Portuguese. Moreover, while the French were splitting themselves into factions over theological points entirely irrelevant to the problem of earthly survival, the Portuguese had at last awakened to the difference in the goals between the French merchant ships sailing regularly along the coast and Villegagnon's colonizing effort.

PART II

Mem de Sá, the new governor-general (1558–1572), arrived in Bahia in 1558. Vigorous and able, he arrived with instructions to drive the French and all other foreigners from Brazil. The advantage in the coming struggle seemed to lay with France, a country much larger, richer, and more populous than Portugal. Also at this juncture, João III had just died, leaving his three-year-old grandson Sebastião (1557–1578) to rule under a regency.

France, too, was suffering a number of difficulties at this time. During its war with Spain from 1556 to 1559, the government had declared bankruptcy. In 1557 King Henry II was killed in a jousting match. The death of Queen Mary Tudor and the ascension of Elizabeth changed the English government from a Catholic to a Protestant monarch, and the new queen continued the traditional alliance with

Portugal. Spain, also Catholic and opposed to the spread of Protestantism to the New World, was no friend of France and only less a rival because its new king, Philip II (1556–1598), had also declared bankruptcy in 1557.

Thus, if Portugal was not strong, neither was France at that moment. The French in Brazil could not count on much aid from their homeland. Portugal still had its Eastern and African trade and could put many ships at sea. Even with all its world-wide problems, Portugal was not weak in Brazil against the French.

The new Portuguese governor in Bahia proved to be the right man at the time needed. Governor Mem de Sá, brother of the famed poet Francisco de Sá Miranda, was a *fidalgo* of the *casa real*, a *licenciado* in law and a *desembargador* of the Casa de Suplicação (judge of the royal court of appeals). Zealously religious, he went regularly to mass. He initiated his governorship of Brazil with a spiritual retreat in the company of Father Manoel da Nóbrega. His fourteen years in office were characterized by close cooperation with churchmen, especially the Jesuits.

The second bishop in Bahia, Pedro Leitão, arrived in December 1559. He too was a strong supporter of the Jesuits and worked in harmony with Governor Mem de Sá, promoting the establishment of Indian aldeias in a reversal of the policy of his predecessor.

Mem de Sá immediately faced several crucial problems, most notably the Indians and the doubtful survival of some of the captaincies. If we were recording primarily the Indian version of the period, we would emphasize that they considered their crucial problem to be how to drive out the Portuguese. No solution had been found, and none was found by the Indians. The two groups had mutually contradictory interests; the Portuguese were taking the lands the Indians had held for all known time, and they were forcing the Indians to work for them by one process or another. The Indian danger, as the Portuguese saw it, was more important to the settlers of Bahia, Ilhéus, Porto Seguro, and other captaincies than the threat posed by the French traders along the coast or by the Villegagnon colony in Guanabara Bay. The land taken from the Indians had been liberally distributed in sesmarias, as already explained, in a somewhat hasty way in order to get it into use.

As a result of this haste, many conflicting boundaries and disputes had arisen. The governor first set himself to solve this problem since it was threatening the life of the colony. The country was seething with law suits and feuds. Mem de Sá wrote the king: "When I arrived in this city there were many law suits . . . and some feuds. I cut short the suits, reconciled the opposing parties and with other means ended the feuds, making friends of enemies."

Any relief from suits and disputes was only temporary. It could not last in a situation where land was the chief wealth. Land boundaries were conflicting, and forged or doctored titles were the rule. But for the moment, Mem de Sá's success enabled him to create a sense of cooperation among the colonists. He finished the Engenho do Rey, "the sugar mill your highness orders constructed for the settlers." It was for the use of cane growers who had no mill of their own.

His Indian policy had a double thrust: first to settle the Indians who had come to terms with the Portuguese into villages under Jesuit control and second to make war on those who had not. In carrying out the first policy he concentrated four or five or more Indian villages, into one "mission," placing over it one of the chief Indians as meirinho (police) with Jesuit supervisors, endoctrinators, and school teachers. (The Spaniards were at about the same time beginning a similar system of reducciones or congregas in New Spain.)

Many of the Portuguese colonists opposed the aldeia system. Nóbrega wrote that some wanted the Indians to live just as they had before the discovery of Brazil:

The Christians want the Indians to eat one another because they believe this makes the land more secure, and they want the Indians to kidnap one another in order that they may obtain them as slaves and tyrannize over them in every manner. And they do not want the Indians to be gathered together for indoctrination; they want them to be at hand for their own service.

Nóbrega may be considered an expert witness.

Mem de Sá carried on relentless war against the unconquered Indians. The civil population of Salvador and the engenhos around the Recôncavo supported the governor's campaigns. Neither life nor property was safe from the Indians, who made surprise attacks on the canoes plying the waters of the bay. In one such attack they captured some African slaves. Mem de Sá sent three separate expeditions against the Indians, killing and capturing many. He was convinced, as were his predecessors, that force was the only language they understood.

Other captaincies were under attack. Espírito Santo (modern capital Vitória) was near the point of total extinction. The settlers abandoned their fields and took refuge in the town, where their only food was oranges, one of the many fruits transplanted from the Old World. Francisco de Sá, the governor's son, died in action against the Indians attacking Espírito Santo. The besieged colonists of Ilhéus were unable to defend themselves. Mem de Sá, in person, led an expedition in 1559 to relieve both captaincies. The old and incapacitated Vasco Fernandes Coutinho, captain of Espírito Santo, was ready to surrender his captaincy to the crown. Taking refuge in Salvador, he was condemned by the bishop for the horrible "Indian" custom of "drinking smoke."

When Mem de Sá returned from his Indian campaigns, he received significant news concerning a previous request to allow the importation of African slaves. Not until 1550, when the crown sent a few slaves, is there notice of a group sent to Brazil. Until then the few known black slaves were brought by the donataries or by individuals. We noted earlier that Father Nóbrega had petitioned for African slaves. An alvará of March 1559 directed the governor of São Tomé, the island off the Congo coast that had become an assembly center for shipping slaves, to allow the legal export of up to 120 slaves to every senhor de engenho in Brazil, paying only one-third the usual duties rather than one-half.

In Espírito Santo, Mem de Sá learned more about the French in Guanabara Bay. "Their whole purpose," he wrote the king on June 11, 1559, "is to make themselves strong; they have a lot of people and are well armed. Their fields are only of pepper. May it please our

Lord that we be able to undo their intentions." He had learned much from the "negros who are with the French" about the fortifications on the rock at the entrance to the harbor, on Sergipe (i.e., Villegagnon Island), and on the mainland. He estimated 800 well-armed men and "many women who come from France."

The French had penetrated the interior of the Paraiba River in the direction of São Vicente, southwest of Rio de Janeiro. The inhabitants of São Vicente, the governor reported, "are very widely scattered" and they should be united into two centers—a statement indicating that Tomé de Sousa's settlements were not as strong as first estimated. "They have no arms, artillery, animals, muskets or powder, all of which should be provided."

Much of what Mem de Sá wrote was incorrect or exaggerated. Perhaps he had learned more from Jean Cointa, Seigneur de Boules, who deserted the French settlement and took refuge in São Vicente, from where he was sent to Bahia. Later he was present at the Portuguese attack on Fort Coligny on Villegagnon Island. Later still Cointa was prosecuted by the Inquisition but was not executed, as some historians report, since he subsequently was reported to be in India.

The reinforcements asked for by Mem de Sá arrived in Bahia on November 30, 1559. He sailed south on January 16, 1560, and reached Guanabara Bay on February 21. He commanded what he called "a very small armada and few people." According to his report, the ships from Portugal "brought only their crews" (gente do mar). His fleet, composed of two ships (naus) and eight smaller vessels, waited until March 15 for the contingent from São Vicente to arrive. The French forces under the command of Bois-le-Comte, a nephew of Villegagnon, numbered 120, Mem de Sá estimated, and aided by 1,500 Indians. Nóbrega said 800 Indians.

The Portuguese forced the French to abandon Villegagnon Island after two days and nights of constant attack. After some additional skirmishing on the mainland and destruction of the fort, Mem de Sá sailed on to São Vicente, permitting the French to reoccupy Villegagnon and other islands. Was the battle a draw or a Portuguese victory? The French had lost a round of fighting; but they retained a foothold in Guanabara Bay.

While in São Vicente, Mem de Sá ordered Piratininga moved to the site of the Jesuit mission of São Paulo for better protection of both village and mission from the Indians. He also sent an expedition down the Tietê River, which runs through São Paulo, to make war on the Indians, who were defeated April 4, 1561. Anchieta went along as interpreter. The Portuguese victory did not prevent an Indian attack in force on São Paulo in July 1562. The town was saved by João Ramalho's father-in-law, Indian Chief Tibiriçá, who died December 25 of that year.

The hope of gold and silver was never far from Portuguese thoughts. Mem de Sá took advantage of his time in São Vicente to send Brás Cubas and Luis Martins, a miner from Portugal, on a search that covered some 300 leagues (about 900 miles) without finding anything of value until they reached Jaraguá on their return. They found some green stones that "looked like emeralds," but were probably tourmalines. On a second try, Martins found small deposits of gold in six different places about 30 leagues from Santos.

On his return to Bahia where he arrived in August 1560, Mem de Sá stopped again at Espírito Santo. Vasco Fernandes Coutinho had renounced his captaincy and the colonists were on the point of evacuating. Governor Sá appointed Belchior de Azevedo to govern. Later both Espírito Santo and Ilhéus were sold with royal consent to other donataries: Ilhéus to Lucas Giraldes, a prominent Genoese merchant resident in Lisbon, and Porto Seguro to the Duke of Aveiro.

Wars with the Indians had hardly ended in one place before breaking out elsewhere. So many took place that it is impossible to distinguish one from another. Porto Seguro was suddenly threatened with invasion in 1560 from Indians from the interior speaking the linguas travadas. The war against them may have been the same as Adorno's entrada. The new invaders were the Aimorés. They appeared first along the Caravelas River south of Porto Seguro and were considered savages even by other Indians. Their name, according to one version, was given to them by the Tupí speakers; it was their word for a very spiny fish that laid poisonous eggs. Whether this interpretation of their name was correct or not, they were enemies of all the other Indians, preferring human meat to any other. They built neither villages nor straw huts (tujupares) nor slept in hammocks but on a bed of leaves on the ground. They did not cultivate any crop whatever. They customarily traveled in small bands and could neither swim nor build canoes, but were great runners. The best way to escape them was to take to the water. Their cannibalism did not have ceremonial aspects and was not for vengeance but for food. "One day they are in one place and the next in another . . . they attack all the other Indians like highwaymen." The forces sent by Mem de Sá repelled them from Porto Seguro in late 1560 and 1561.

Relatively speaking, conditions had become peaceful in some places. Jesuit Father Ruí Pereira wrote in 1560:

> This country is so pacified that not only can the whites go safely many leagues inland, but our own Indian who traveled among his enemies was not molested, reporting that they said 'this man is a friend of the whites and if we do him any harm, they will kill us' . . . This conversion was largely brought about because the governor came to understand and to acknowledge that without instilling fear in them nothing can be done.

The governor found the business of administration a complex task. He wanted, among his other objectives, to stimulate trade, still small, and believed that "the shippers (armadores) are the nerve center of Brazil."

Mem de Sá continued to distribute sesmarias in large numbers, or at least as many as could be granted when the units were about 6,000 acres in size. Sesmarias were not absolutely equal in size, varying somewhat with the terrain. Several of two leagues each were distributed. Mem de Sá himself held a sesmaria with an engenho that became famous as Sergipe do Conde. It came down by inheritance to the Count of Linhares, Fernando de Noronha, who married Sá's daughter. Later the Jesuits owned it.

The size of the grants (two leagues is about the size of Manhattan Island) guaranteed that land ownership would be the privilege of the few. It was denied to almost the entire population, whether White, Black, or Indian.

The French and Indians of the Guanabara Bay and São Paulo area continued to demand Mem de Sá's attention. The temporary capture of Villegagnon's fort in 1560 and the short peace with the Indians repelled at São Paulo in 1562 were battles won in a long war. The French, dispersed around Guanabara Bay and along the coast to Cabo Frio, remained in effective control of the area in alliance with their friends, the Tamoios. French trade in dye wood, pepper, cotton, and other products continued. The Portuguese could not enter the bay or land along the coast between the bay and Cabo Frio without risking attack.

The difficulties of the Portuguese were increased by a temporary alliance formed among the Indians themselves, somewhat exaggeratedly called the "Confederation of the Tamoios." But whether united among themselves, or as separate groups, the Indians were a constant threat. To make peace with them was essential. The Jesuits became the spearhead of the peace attempt. In April 1563, Fathers Nóbrega and Anchieta went to Iperoig, near Ubatuba on the coast between Rió de Janeiro and São Vicente; there the Tamoio chiefs had their temporary headquarters. The two Portuguese made themselves hostages to Indians who might kill and eat them. Nóbrega returned to São Vicente on June 21, leaving Anchieta alone. Anchieta spent his days talking with the Indians in Tupí and composing a long Latin poem of six thousand verses dedicated to the Virgin. He composed it in sands on the beach, committing it to memory for writing down later. He learned Tupí well enough to formulate its grammar, the first of a hitherto unwritten language. It was published in 1595. If Anchieta did not win their friendship, he won at least a temporary neutrality that kept them from assisting their kinsmen when the Portuguese returned to attack the French between Guanabara Bay and Cabo Frio.

Mem de Sá was too preoccupied with the problems involved in making Brazil viable, and the support he received from Portugal was too little to enable him to deal with the French as he would have liked. Portugal had its own troubles. The infant King Sebastião and his mother the queen regent faced many difficulties besides Brazil. The extension of Portuguese power in the East and the defense of positions in Morocco required forces far beyond those needed in Brazil. When Constantino de Braganza became Viceroy of India in 1558, he sailed from Portugal with 2,000 men at arms. He deployed more than a hundred ships and some 3,000 men in his attack on Damão in 1558–59. In 1560, he commanded an armada of about ninety ships in the capture of Jaffnapatam, Ceylon.

In Morocco, from March 4 to May 7, 1562, an army led by Xarife Mulei Abdala, estimated by the Portuguese at 150,000, besieged Portuguese-held Mazagão. Its defense aroused great patriotic and religious fervor in Portugal and required large reinforcements. When the Muslim army retreated, the Portuguese hailed it as a great victory and the Pope ordered a pontifical mass said at the Council of Trent.

The priorities of official policy in Portugal, and in the minds of the Portuguese people, plainly held the defense of Brazil against the French secondary to fighting the Muslims in North Africa. It was much easier and quicker to win honors in Morocco than in Brazil or the East. A man could fight in Morocco and return home in less time than it took to travel to Brazil. Africa held a traditional attraction for Portugal. In the same year Cardinal Henry became regent, 1562, he received a recommendation that Portugal should send an expedition to discover the route to Timbuktu. Meanwhile Brazil begged in vain for adequate reinforcements.

Mem de Sá had other serious problems in addition to inadequate home support. A disastrous smallpox epidemic struck both São Vicente and Bahia in 1563–64, leaving the governor with minimal forces to attack the French and Tamoios. He sent his nephew, Estácio de Sá, in December 1563 with a fleet called "bem pequena" (very small). When Estácio de Sá stopped over in Espírito Santo to gather reinforcements, he was able to gain the assistance of Chief Arariboia of the Temininós tribe. On arriving in Guanabara Bay on February 6, 1564, Estácio reconnoitered the enemy and decided that an attack on the larger French and Tamoio forces was not feasible. He made a temporary settlement just inside the bay and later on Villegagnon, but soon sailed on to São Vicente to gather more forces. After months in São Vicente, he returned to Guanabara Bay accompanied by Nóbrega and Anchieta who, as we have seen, had been able to win the partial neutrality of the Tamoios.

Once more in the bay, Estácio de Sá founded a town, São Sebastião do Rio de Janeiro, on March 1, 1565, just inside Sugar Loaf along the area now known as Praia Vermelha. He granted an area of six leagues square for the new town, allotting one and a half leagues to the câmara (municipal council). He also set up an embryo municipal government, appointing a *juis ordinario* and an *alcaide-mor* as well as other officials. He distributed sesmarias to his chief followers. With some reinforcements from Mem de Sá, Estácio de Sá held on for two years.

At this juncture, across the Atlantic, the French attacked Madeira in October 1566. They held it for fifteen days, sacking and burning Funchal and surrounding areas and raping and killing hundreds. Unable to protect its nearby territory, Portugal could spare little for Brazil. In fact, it required a great effort in 1566 to send three galleons (galeões) commanded by Christóvão de Barros. Mem de Sá joined these with six caravels and two other ships (navios) and went to the aid of his nephew.

The governor-general left Bahia in late 1566 and arrived in Rio on January 18, 1567, accompanied by both Bishop Pedro Leitão and Father Nóbrega. The attack on the French began soon thereafter. Estácio de Sa, wounded by a poisoned arrow, died February 20. The Portuguese gained enough of the mainland by March 1, 1567, to move the site of the town to Morro do Castelo (literally, Castle Hill) for its second founding. Mem de Sá distributed more sesmarias and introduced more cattle. Salvador Correia de Sá became governor and capitáo-mor on March 4, 1567, though Mem de Sá also remained in Rio to 1568.

The Jesuits founded their first church in Rio de Janeiro. Later a second Jesuit church became the cathedral. A Jesuit colégio, the third in Brazil, was also established, with Nobrega becoming the first rector.

For their support, they received a league and a half sesmaria, extended to a much larger sesmaria spreading toward the Organ Mountains. The charitable society known as the Misericórdia was also founded at this time. The same year, 1568, the king approved a Jesuit colégio in São Paulo for fifty padres.

Martim Afonso Arariboia, the Temiminós Indian chief named for his famous godfather, had served the Portuguese so well that he received a large sesmaria across the bay on March 16, 1568. He is honored as the founder of the city of Niterói. His incorporation into the new Portuguese society was nearly complete after he was named a knight of the Order of Christ. The defense of Rio de Janeiro against attacking Indians owed much to Arariboia's dedication to the Portuguese cause.

The French had lost another battle, but not yet Brazil. They continued to live around Guanabara Bay, along the coast to Cabo Frio, and in various other places from Espírito Santo northward not under Portuguese control. Many French ships were captured and many Frenchmen killed, but the profits from cutting brazilwood and growing pepper, combined with a variety of other products, kept them coming back.

Spain also showed an interest in occupying lands it considered to be on its side of the Line of Demarcation. On May 15, 1568, Philip II granted to Hernández de Serpa an area in the Guianas, an ill-defined region north of the Amazon River. Portugal had not yet occupied the coast north of Paraíba to the Amazon, but neither had it relinquished title to anything that might lie on its side of the line. Again, international factors and Spanish domestic problems helped save the vast area for Portugal.

The revolt of the Netherlands in 1567 and the long and bitter wars that followed were in progress in 1569 when the Moriscos—Christianized Moslems and their descendants—in Spain rebelled. There was no complete peace for Spain on any front during the rest of the sixteenth and seventeenth centuries. Spain became also the chief force in the Christian alliance against the rising Turkish danger, almost the whole alliance in fact. In 1570 Don Juan of Austria, half brother of Philip II, led the Christian forces to victory in the naval battle of Lepanto, giving the Christian nations a breathing spell.

Spain made an attempt, without success, between 1570 and 1573 to settle the Brazilian coast south of São Vicente. Portugal, left almost unopposed, eventually occupied all the territory on its side of the line, plus hundreds of thousands of square miles on Spain's side, but not during Mem de Sá's governorship.

Mem de Sá had governed well and had not neglected to acquire personal wealth as well, a course of conduct not considered illegal or immoral in this era. He felt entitled to rest from his constant problems of governing Brazil, and he asked the crown to permit his return to Portugal.

The new governor, Luís Fernandes de Vasconcelos, enroute to Brazil, met a tragic fate when attacked by a French fleet. The war with France in Brazil, an undeclared war, touched Portugal as well as its colonies. Appointed in February 1570, Vasconcellos sailed with seven vessels, one of them, the *Santiago*, with about forty Jesuits aboard. Attacked off the Canary Islands in July by the French "Huguenot Pirate" Jacques Sore, the *Santiago* was captured. The French killed most of the Jesuits, including Provincial Inácio de Azevedo. Vasconcelos sailed on to within sight of Brazil but missed his course in the critical area off northeast Brazil. He sailed to the Antilles and then attempted to return to Portugal.

His luck had not improved, however. He met another fleet of pirates, this time English and French combined under the command of Jean Capdeville. He and another thirteen Jesuits were killed. Only two Jesuits escaped both incidents.

Mem de Sá, scanning the sea for his replacement, was forced to remain in Brazil. Portugal attributed the attacks to "Lutherans and Calvinists" at the service of Charles IX of France; it threatened war and prepared a fleet of some thirty vessels. France also prepared, but no declaration of war followed; the conflicts continued on an unofficial but no less real basis. France's fourth religious war in ten years began in 1572 following the St. Bartholomew Massacre of the Protestants on August 23 and 24, leaving no time or forces for pursuing the conquest of Brazil. It was an age when religious passions outweighed other considerations. On hearing about St. Bartholomew, Portugal dispatched a special ambassador to Charles IX to congratulate him on the destruction of the Protestants. But the common religious tie did not bring the de facto war at sea between Portugal and France to an end.

During the period from 1549 to the end of Mem de Sá's term in 1572, an increasing number of African slaves were introduced into Brazil. Portugal began to face the moral problem of slavery in all its overseas possessions except Africa. The question did not arise seriously in connection with slaves from Africa; only faint and individual voices questioned the age-old custom of enslaving the Black people south of the Sahara. But a dichotomy of feelings existed about enslavement of people from the East and the Indians in Brazil; not even the Jesuits and other clergy were entirely clear in their thinking about Indian slavery.

Father Nóbrega and his companions advocated a policy that placed the Indians in their care—a relatively few of the Indians, that is. But there were thousands of Indians, nobody can say how many, all actual or potential enemies, who might, and often did, attack without warning. What should be done with the captives? More difficult to answer was the question raised by cannibalism. The Indians fought and enslaved one another, or ate their captives. Sometimes captured, Indians were bound to a tree by their captors and fattened up for a feast day.

What should be done with such Indians when they were discovered and rescued? These came to be known as the "cord" Indians. To rescue them was reckoned as a Christian act. And after rescue, what? The rescue was almost always by force. The customs of the times entitled the captor to ownership, not merely in Brazil or Portugal, but in many other areas of the world as well. In Brazil the churchmen wished to incorporate the captives into the aldeias. Mem de Sá and other governors after him were importuned by both sides, clerics and civilians. Both groups sent their appeals straight to the king, who was, at the same time, receiving similar questions from the East. Everywhere the conduct of the Portuguese colonists and warriors was provoking trouble for Portugal.

King Sebastião, in 1570, was influenced by the Jesuits and the Mesa da Consciência. In March he issued a decree forbidding the enslavement of Brazilian Indians. It was backed by the papal bull Veritas Ipsa, which declared the Indians sons of Adam and members of the human race. This document, issued by Pope Paul III in May 1537, declared the Indians free and subject to slavery only under the rules of "just war."

"Just war!"

All the zeal and devotion of the Jesuits, not all of whom were as devoted as Nóbrega and Anchieta, could not find a solution to the "Indian problem." But Nóbrega and Anchieta were not blind sentimentalists about the Indians. Both concluded after experiencing the life of the Indian that only through force could they be civilized. The Jesuit Francisco Mandoro, after five months in Salvador, Bahia, which he described as having some two hundred settlers who lived mostly on their estates, found the Indians so far from being Christianized that they never on their own accord said the Ave Maria—a very serious omission in his eyes.

His evidence about the Jesuits themselves was less favorable. In the colégio of Salvador where there were forty Jesuits (sujeitos), they did nothing, he said, but "take care of their temporal affairs." Most were unhappy and wanted to return to Portugal. Regarding the results from the colégio, he believed that "learning is making no progress."

Complaints about the Indians were repeated over and over. The law of 1570 did not solve the Indian problem; it was the subject of much subsequent legislation. The same year, Sebastião forbade the enslavement of Japanese because, he said, it hindered their Christianization. He did not mention, as he could have, that the Japanese were hardly subjects for enslavement.

The last years of Mem de Sá's administration were occupied with the problems of economic development and defense. He issued a law in the king's name requiring the colonists whose wealth was reckoned at four hundred milreis or more to donate an arquebus, a pike, a lance, or a helmet for the militia. Another provision of the law of May 16, 1570, exempted from taxation all engenhos built within ten years, their only tax being the 10% duty on sugar entering Portugal.

Repeated attacks by the French convinced the Portuguese that their ships were unsafe unless accompanied by strong armed fleets—a fact Spain discovered as early as 1522. In November 1571, the king decreed a new system. The earlier policy had been based to some extent on relationships developed during the middle ages. As noted earlier, Portugal encouraged foreign traders and granted many charters of privilege to English, Flemish, French, Italian, and other merchants, receiving in turn similar privileges for Portuguese merchants in foreign ports. The earliest expansion of Portugal in Africa, Asia, and Brazil included foreign merchants and numerous other foreigners. Portugal did not arbitrarily exclude foreigners or foreign ships. Although Brazil was not thrown entirely open to world trade, there were many ways that foreigners could send ships to Brazil.

Circumstances forced Portugal to adopt a more restrictive policy. The threat from French, English, Spanish, and Dutch ships menaced Portugal's hold on Brazil. The first clearly restrictive law stated that no one could ship merchandise to Brazil, or to any other overseas territory of Portugal, in foreign ships—only Portuguese ships were permitted. A prescribed sailing period was set, August 1 to March 31 from Portugal. A minimum of four ships had to sail in convoy, and one had to be a large armed vessel. After reaching the equator, the ships could separate, each sailing to its destined port. On the return voyage, they would again combine into one fleet, joining any other Portuguese vessels they might meet.

The merchants criticized this law on the grounds that it limited their opportunities to take advantage of profitable situations. They alleged that the dangers envisaged by the law were almost nil, and it could be relaxed.

A good measure of what Portugal had to protect in Brazil is found in Pêro de Magalhaes Gândavo's *Tratado da Terra do Brazil*, written in approximately 1570. Gândavo reported sixty sugar engenhos in the captaincies from Itamaracá southward along the coast to São Vicente:

Captaincy	Settlers (vizinhos)	Engenhos
Itamaracá	100	0 (2 in construction)
Pernambuco	1000	23 (3 or 4 incomplete)
Bahia	1100	18
Ilhéus	200	8
Porto Seguro	220	5
Espírito Santo	200	1
Rio de Janeiro	140	1
São Vicente	500	4

He reckoned total annual production at about 70,000 arrôbas, or only slightly above 1,000 arrôbas per mill. Production was rising rapidly, as we shall see later.

The exact dates of Gândavo's sojourn in Brazil is unknown, but from the internal evidence of his document, it can be placed about 1565 at the earliest. He returned to Portugal probably before 1570, although some of his information relates to 1572 and 1573. His observations, therefore, cover the last years of Mem de Sá's government. Gândavo gathered most of his material while still in Brazil, "where for some years I found myself and collected this brief information; and in fact most of the things that I write I saw and experienced."

He has been accused of being a Brazilophile, and he indeed was. But so were most of the early writers who lived in Brazil, a fact that has not changed in the twentieth century. He saw Brazil in a rapid growth period: "it is growing more prosperous every day." Furthermore, "after the fertile lands that are now unproductive for lack of settlers are peopled, they will certainly create large fortunes like those now existing in the lands owned by the settlers of this country."

Gândavo had a model to cite: "And it is also hoped that this province will in time flourish like the Antilles of Castile. Brazil must also have mineral wealth yet undiscovered." His description covers the part of the coast then settled, "three hundred and fifty leagues" (about 1,050 miles). "There are eight captaincies, all have very safe ports where any ship, however large, can enter. There are no settlements of Portuguese in the interior because of the Indians . . . and also because for supplies and trade with the kingdom [Portugal] it is necessary to live by the sea."

He described the captaincies one by one and enumerated their main products. Of the engenhos he reported: "some grind with oxen, and these are called trapiches; they produce less sugar than the others. But most of the engenhos in Brazil grind with water power. Each of these engenhos, taking one with another, produce 3,000 arrôbas a year." The production he cited must have applied to water-driven engenhos only.

In Pernambuco, 1,000 vizinhos (colonists) with their 23 engenhos produced some 50,000 arrôbas a year, more than any other captaincy, but "the production is not consistent, depending on the weather." For the work force, "there are many Indian slaves, which comprises the principal wealth. From here they are taken to all the other captaincies where they are bought, for in this captaincy there are many and cheaper than anywhere else along the coast." More ships came there from Portugal than to any other captaincy.

Bahia, site of the government-general and the bishopric was "the most heavily settled with Portuguese of all Brazil." It had eighteen engenhos and more under construction, "although the settlers lean (se lanção) more toward cotton than to sugar cane because it produces better in this soil." In addition to the bishopric and the Jesuit college, "where they teach Latin and casa de consciencia . . . there are five churches inland among the free Indians where some padres live to Christianize them and perform marriages among the Indians so they will not live in concubinage." Salvador, Bahia, he described as located on a "very large, beautiful bay, three leagues wide and navigable fifteen leagues inland . . . with very fertile land that produces an infinite amount of cotton." All the transportation between plantations in the bay was by boats.

Ilhéus, thirty leagues south of Bahia at about 14 3/4° south latitude, belonged to Francisco Giraldes, an Italian merchant resident in Portugal, who had "put in a captain" to govern it. Its population numbered "about 200 vizinhos. . .eight engenhos [and] a Jesuit monastery just now under construction." The Aimoré Indians were a great menace to the captaincy.

Porto Seguro, farther south, and where Cabral had landed, belonged to the Duke of Aveiro, "who had appointed his own captain." It had about 220 vizinhos, five engenhos, and a Jesuit monastery. The Aimoré Indians threatened it, however. Espírito Santo with 200 vizinhos had only one engenho but it produced "the best sugar in all Brazil," and a great deal of cotton and brazilwood. Proof that sugar was not indispensable is revealed by his statement that the settlers were living "very richly" from the produce of their estates. They were so well supplied that, in 1560 and 1565, the forces attacking the French in Rio de Janeiro were sent "all the foods necessary" for their maintenance.

Rio de Janeiro, lying on the Tropic of Capricorn, sixty leagues south of Espírito Santo, had a population that numbered about 140 vizinhos. "This is the most fertile land in all Brazil," Gândavo stated, with abundant water and brazilwood. Here was the Jesuit monastery founded by Father Manuel da Nóbrega (whom Gândavo does not mention) and endowed with extensive lands.

Some 70 leagues farther west and a little south of Rio de Janeiro, was São Vicente, the property of Pêro Lopes de Sousa, son of Martim Afonso. He was not resident, however, but "appointed a captain" to govern. Both the principal coastal towns, São Vicente and Santos, had Jesuit colleges. Inland ten leagues on the mountain plateau was São Paulo, where the Jesuit monastery had been founded in 1554, the ninth Gândavo mentioned. He described São Paulo as populated mainly by "Mamelucos, children of Portuguese by Indian women." The Jesuits were gathering "great spiritual fruits" in the salvation of the Indians and were developing the lands. "They also restore to freedom many Indians" unjustly enslaved—but it should be noted that only the "unjustly" enslaved were freed. Indian enslavement was compatible with the morals of the time if done as the law prescribed.

The captaincy of São Vicente, which included São Paulo, had some 500 vizinhos and four engenhos. Gândavo saw it as very fertile land "from which the settlers produce much foodstuffs and wealth; and all enjoy an abundance." He had a very optimistic view of Brazil:

All the settlers (moradores) of this coast of Brazil have sesmarias . . . and the first thing they want is slaves . . . because without them they cannot develop (sustentar) the land, and one of the reasons why Brazil does not flourish more is because the slaves rise up and flee inland, and they flee every day. And if the Indians were not so flighty and changeable (fugitivos e mudaveis) there would be nothing with which to compare the riches of Brazil.

The most profitable products were "sugar, cotton and bread of Brazil" (manioc). "There is very little money," he added, "and they exchange one thing for another." The principal livestock was cattle, and there was "an abundance in all the captaincies." Goats and sheep were few but increasing—the goats more than the sheep, "and they give birth to two and three" at a time. "Mares and horses are still expensive because they are few." They had been, according to Gândavo, originally bought from Cabo Verde, but others may have come from Portugal or elsewhere. He also mentioned "a lot of hog raising, and many chickens, hens, and native ducks. Amber, which washed up on the shore, had made many people rich; "they send their slaves to the beach" to gather it.

The only cloth manufactured in Brazil in Gândavo's time was cotton, "everything else comes from the kingdom." Of the African slaves he remarked: "There are also many slaves from Guinea, and these are easier to keep than the Indians because they never flee, nor do they have anywhere to go." Whoever came to live in Brazil, "however poor they may be, if they can acquire two pairs or half a dozen slaves, which one with another can cost a little more or less up to ten cruzados," could live well. "Some fish and hunt for him and others grow food . . . And little by little they become rich and live decently . . . because the Indian slaves get food for themselves and for their masters, who thus have no expense for provisions for their slaves or for themselves."

Gândavo did not foresee, perhaps, that life was still on a simple base that would change considerably in a few years. In his time "most of the beds are hammocks . . . a custom taken from the Indians." He saw the settlers as "more generous" (mais largas) than the people of the kingdom both in eating and dressing. They loved to help one another and "give to the poor who are beginning to appear (vivir) in this land," but no poor went from door to door begging in this kingdom.

Gândavo noted, as did others, the effects of the winds in coastal communication. The winds along the coast from Rio Grande do Norte to São Vicente blew generally toward the south and southeast from March to August (winter) and toward the north and northeast from September to February, but there were variations during these periods. The water currents, said Gândavo, "flow the same directions as the winds, and because of this, it is not possible to navigate from one captaincy to the others if you do not wait for the monsoons . . . and many times voyages are slow, and when the ships sail out of season they run many risks and end up most of the time in the part from which they left."

He, like many others who reported on sixteenth-century Brazil, described a very healthy climate, except when a wind blew from the interior that was "very dangerous and sickening." When it blew for several days, "many people die, Portuguese as well as Indians." Fortunately, Gândavo claimed, God had willed that this did not often happen. Apart from the wind, "this land is very healthy and has good air where people feel well and live many years. Especially the old are in better condition and seem to revive."

What did people eat? They ate "in the place of wheat bread, farinha de pão" [literally, wood flour, manioc]. It was a meal made from the manioc root with a consistency and hardness resembling sawdust, but edible and nourishing. It was prepared in two ways, soft for immediate consumption and dry for preservation for a later time. The dry form was called "farinha de guerra," or war bread, because it could be kept for weeks of campaigning. They also ate aipim, a root somewhat similar to the manioc, sweet potatoes, from which cake could be made, and maize (Indian corn), which was native and grew in all the captaincies. There was "an abundance of cow's milk," a great deal of rice, favas [bread] beans, and a variety of vegetables "that make Brazil a land of abundance" (que fartão muito a terra). He reinforced his description by mentioning the "abundance of shell fish and fish all along the coast. "With these provisions (mantimentos) the settlers of Brazil sustain themselves without using up anything of their wealth" (fazendas).

Gândavo mentioned also the principal game both the Indians and Portuguese caught in traps of various kinds or shot with guns or bow and arrow—deer, wild hogs, tapirs, rabbits, pacas, armadillo, wild fowls (galinhas de mato), "which the Indians shoot with arrows," and other plentiful game.

Fruits were numerous and varied: pineapple, "better tasting than any fruit" of Portugal, cashew, and "bananas, which in the Indian language are called pacovas." "With this fruit most of the slaves" were fed. He mentioned also guava, similar to nespers, and peppers. Of the fruits and vegetables that Gândavo classified as European in origin, he mentioned cucumbers, many kinds of figs, pomegranates, grapes, lemons, and oranges in "an infinite amount."

Gândavo was greatly impressed with the "multitude of barbarous people that nature planted throughout Brazil . . . enemies of one another, with hatred and discord among them." "If it were not so," he said, "the Portuguese could not live in this land nor would it be possible to conquer so many people." By Gândavo's time, the Portuguese had driven inland and conquered or killed many Indians, but some powerful groups still had to be faced in 1570, a situation lasting for another two centuries. The Portuguese opinion of the Indians can be summed up in a saying that arose from the lack of letters f, l, and r in the Tupi language: that the Indians were without fe, lei, or rei— meaning they had neither faith, law, nor king—an exaggeration containing a large kernel of truth.

The custom of going without clothing continued long after the European discovery of Brazil, even among the Indians who were settled in the aldeias. They fought their battles in the same nakedness: "It thus seems a very strange thing to see two or three thousand naked men on opposing sides whistling, shouting and shooting at one another with bows and arrows." They never thought of losing in battle, only winning. "No life is spared of those captured in battle, they kill them all and eat them."

Gândavo's opinion of the Indians was shared by most Europeans, if not all:

Finally, these Indians are very inhuman and cruel, not moved by any pity. They live like brute animals, without any order or discipline of mankind. They are very dishonest and given to all kinds of sensuality, and prone to all the vices as if they did not have human reason, yet men and women are very discreet in their coupling (ajuntamento) and demonstrate in this some sense of privacy (vergonha).

Gândavo added more interesting details about Indian customs too long to quote here.

Most of what is left out here emphasized the negative, but he also mentioned some things of which he approved. "These Indians have this virtue; that whatever they eat, however little there is of it, they invite everybody present to share with them." This quality was so rare among whites that Gândavo thought it worth including in his description of the Indians. We have no Indian view of the whites because they lacked a written language of their own, nor are we blessed with accounts written after they had learned Portuguese.

Gândavo was optimistic about the success of the Jesuits in curbing enslavement—too optimistic as later history revealed. One of the improvements he noted was that when Indians were brought in from the forest, or from other captaincies, they were taken to the customs house and questioned to ascertain their origins and status, "because nobody may sell them except their own parents or those who captured them in just war." This procedure was in accord with King Sebastião's law of 1570, but it was not easily enforced.

Gândavo's generally rose-colored picture of Brazil still had some flaws. "This whole land of Brazil is covered with ants, small and large," which damaged grape vines and orange trees, "and if it were not for those ants there would be many vineyards." On the other hand, he thought vineyards were not needed because a steady supply of wine came from Portugal. Other insects bothered the settlers, among them "innumerable mosquitoes, principally along the rivers among the trees called mangroves." They were unbearable; "nobody can stand them," he remarked, but neither he nor anybody else connected them with the fevers that annually killed thousands of people.

Gañdavo was not dismayed by the recurring plagues, however. "I would love to treat the things of this province more in detail," but he reserved fuller treatment for another book in which he planned to show that Brazil was the remedy for all the poor of Portugal. In Brazil, he asserted, "Everybody lives richly and without suffering the lack of necessities." We do not have Gañdavo's intended fuller description, but the extant account is an excellent summary of the condition of the country near the end of Mem de Sá's term of office.

Mem de Sá was never to realize his hopes of returning to his Portuguese home. On March 2, 1572, after fourteen years of a service that left Brazil much further advanced than he had found it, Sá died in Salvador, Bahia. He left many problems unsolved, but that can be blamed in large part on the lack of support from his home country. Portugal had to contend with innumerable burdens, which kept this small nation from meeting adequately its worldwide obligations.

Mem de Sá accumulated a considerable estate in Brazil. There were no moral barriers in Portugal, Brazil, or any other country in the sixteenth century, to prevent public officials from taking advantage of opportunities for self-enrichment; in fact, the contrary was true. Poorly paid from the public treasury, they were presumed to accept tips, favors, and acquire property as compensation for their low salaries.

His sugar mills, the largest engenho in Brazil in 1572, was later known as Sergipe do Conde. (Later it became the property of the Jesuits Colegio de Santo Antão de Lisboa.) The work on Mem de Sá's property was done by 21 African slaves, each worth sixteen milreis to forty milreis, plus 90 more "slaves of the country," namely Indians, worth six to ten milreis each. There were also five Indians of Pernambuco, 20 moços (boys), 58 Indian women valued at from two milreis to seven milreis each, and still another lot of 26 women "brought in by Domingos Ribeiro." Every worker had an assigned task. The engenho thus had 111 workers, plus an additional population of 109 before some fled. It had two thousand clay forms and produced 167 loaves of sugar.

The Casa Grande, or lord's mansion, was described as "a fortress in which Simão de Sá lives." It was built of stone and cement and surrounded by "a tiled bulwark with a picket stockade." There were also the houses for the priest, the factor, and the molasses skimmer (escumeiro), as well as two "large straw houses for the Negroes of Guinea." The principal buildings were those of the engenho.

The furniture of the Casa Grande was limited to four chairs with backs, and a smaller one without. No mention was made of beds, tables, household furnishings, or other adornments. They were added a few years later when sugar produced great wealth. In this earlier period riches were measured in the tools of trade and slaves.

At the time Gândavo wrote, runaway Indian slaves were already a problem. The African slaves were less likely to run away at this time because numerous cannibal Indians were close around the engenhos. Later when the Indians had been driven back or were less numerous, the African slaves also fled. The varied origins of the African slaves and their different languages rendered more difficult communication between them and thus inhibited any organized planning for flight. In later periods the knowledge of at least some Portuguese gave African slaves a better basis for communication and planning escapes. The enmities between tribes carried over from Africa and often kept them apart in Brazil. The Portuguese knew how to use African enmities to their advantage as a system of control.

6

ADMINISTRATIVE DIVISION AND REUNION

𝕿 he death of Mem de Sá and his intended successor left the government in the hands of an interim governor, the provedor-mor da fazenda, Fernão da Silva. The crown divided the government into northern and southern administrative units in 1572. Valid reasons existed for this division. Communications between the northern and the southern regions were difficult for two important reasons: the existence of variable monsoon winds along the coast and the impracticality of travel by land because unfriendly Indians held most of the interior.

The northern government extended from Ilhéus to Pernambuco, with Salvador, Bahia, its capital. Luís de Brito de Almeida became governor (1573–78) and received a sesmaria of twelve leagues. The southern portion included the captaincies from Porto Seguro to São Vicente, and Rio de Janeiro was its capital. The first governor was Christóvão de Barros, 1572–74, followed by Antônio de Salema, 1574–78.

The governors faced the tasks of conquering more territory from the Indians and defending the coast from the French and their Indians allies. Friction between the Portuguese and the Potiguars led to wars that continued to the end of the century. The breakdown of an old alliance was especially serious because the coastal-dwelling Potiguares were allied with the French.

Meanwhile the attempt to explore the interior, capture Indians, and find minerals continued. Two entradas, started from Porto Seguro in 1572 and 1573 under command of Sebastião Fernando des Tourinho, brought better knowledge of the interior but no mineral discoveries. He explored portions of the Jequitinhonha, Araçuaí, and Doce rivers. In 1574 Antônio Adôrno, a mameluco fidalgo descended on his father's side from the Italian family that had arrived a generation earlier and who was well-versed in Indian lore and language, ascended the Rio das Caravelas. The other entradas, commanded by Sebastião Álvares and João Coelho de Souza respectively, were made in 1574. João Coelho was the brother of Gabriel Soares de Souza. On his death Coelho allegedly sent the secret location of the mines he had discovered to his brother. If so, his secret was too well disguised, since Gabriel Soares never found the mines and died later in the attempt.

Governor Luís de Brito de Almeida of the northern captaincies inherited a running battle with the Potiguares in the interior, formerly allies, who lived north of Itamaracá and Pernambuco. They were a source of legal slaves until an incident caused an outbreak of war. On a slaving raid in 1572, a mameluco had captured the daughter of Chief Ininguaçú. The corregidor, Antônio de Salema, later governor of the south with his capital in Rio de Janeiro, ordered the girl restored to her father. Diogo Dias, a fazendeiro with a casa forte on the frontier of Itamaracá, refused to release her.

The chief then allied himself with other Potiguares of the coast who were friends of the French. The combined forces of the Potiguares and French attacked, feigned retreat, and, as described by Frei Vicente, caught Diogo Dias in an ambush. Charging "with a roar that shook the earth," they slaughtered the Portuguese to the last man. It is not clear who might have told Frei Vicente the story of the battle of the Brazilian Alamo, but the state of hostility was a bitter fact in 1574, when Ouvidor–geral Fernão da Silva attempted a punitive campaign. He invaded the interior as far as the Paraiba River with all the forces he could raise in Itamaracá and Pernambuco, but he found no Potiguares. They had slipped away and were in hiding. He took possession of the river in the name of Portugal, although it is not clear why he needed to do so, since Portugal claimed the entire country. He returned to Bahia without unsheathing his sword and was the butt of some mild ridicule. The Indians returned to their tactics of harassment. Governor Luís de Brito prepared a fleet of ten small vessels to sail his troops to Itamaracá for a fresh campaign. It was dispersed by adverse winds before reaching its destination—the problem of the variable monsoons was an ever-present problem for the Portuguese. The governor was again in Bahia in September 1575.

He arrived in time to send his forces under the command of ouvidor Cosme Rangel, including many Indian allies, against fugitive African slaves who had formed one of the first known quilombos. The campaign was a success, but the problem of fugitive slaves continued. The formation of a settlement of fugitives set a bad example, in the eyes of owners, for other restive slaves. The fugitives were also a danger to towns, engenhos, and travelers on the road. This problem lasted throughout the colonial period and until the emancipation of Brazilian slaves in 1888.

Still another Indian campaign began in 1574 in the region between Salvador and the São Francisco River, which reaches the sea about half way between Recife and Salvdor. Although this coast was part of the captaincy of Bahia and had been known from almost the first years of discovery, the Indians were still largely hostile, making overland communication between Salvador and Recife impractical. Furthermore, the French often came to the region of the Rio Real, north of Salvador, to cut dye wood and trade with the Indians.

The Portuguese had an opportunity to make peace with these Indians in 1574, when they sent messengers to Salvador asking for missionaries to establish churches in their territory. Governor Luís de Brito de Almeida gladly sent two Jesuits accompanied by 20 soldiers in 1575. They established three churches, and some important chiefs soon adhered. Soon thereafter, some of the Portuguese settlers in Bahia began claiming as slaves certain Indians who had, they said, fled from them in 1568. Two other Jesuits attempted a reconciliation, but in vain. The governor marched with reinforcements in November 1575. He defeated the Indians and brought around 1,200 to Bahia, where most died of measles and smallpox.

Christovão de Barros governed in Rio de Janeiro from 1572 to 1574. His main preoccupations were the continued fortification of the city since the French danger was still ever-present, and the building of an engenho for those cane-growers who had received sesmarias but had no mill of their own. These two tasks were the business of all the governors of colonial Brazil and provide twin themes in its history.

When Governor Antônio de Salema took over the southern captaincies in 1574, he stopped over in Salvador and drew up with the northern governor ten new articles to add to the 1570 law regulating Indian affairs. Dated January 6, these articles were designed to protect the Indians while, at the same time, guaranteeing the colonists their availability as laborers. The compromise that these articles implied was never genuinely accomplished. This fact was amply clear when Salema reached Rio de Janeiro to face the problem of the French, who continued to occupy the region of Cabo Frio in alliance with the Tamoio Indians. Gabriel Soares says they loaded a thousand quintals of wood annually. With forces drawn from Porto Seguro and São Vicente, Governor Salema, by a clever stratagem of betrayal, attacked and defeated the French and Tamoios, slaughtering a large number and enslaving more.

The accounts differ about the actual numbers. Some sources list 2,000 killed and 4,000 enslaved; others, following Gabriel Soares, claim 8,000 to 10,000 prisoners. Aside from the savagery on both sides, one surprising fact was the almost invariable success of the Portuguese against the French, who persisted in returning to risk life and fortune in order to cut and ship dye wood. Obviously the textile factories of France consumed large amounts.

The policy of the Portuguese crown was to keep the church structure in step with the progress of colonization. In 1575 Rio de Janeiro was designated a prelacy by the papacy after a royal request—the usual arrangement between church and state. The Portuguese colonists objected strenuously because they saw the prelacy as a threat to their loose lives and their abuse of the Indians. A period of conflict began. The first prelate, Father Bartolomeu Simões Pereira, died in 1598, with the symptoms of his illness pointing to poison. Other similar conflicts occurred frequently during the whole colonial period, raising a question about how the church was able to survive in the face of persistent hostility from the colonists.

The years between 1575 and 1581 were a busy and progressive time in Brazil. A royal decree of 1573 exempting Brazil sugar from import duties in Portugal for three years stimulated the desire of the settlers for more land. New immigrants from Portugal opened up more lands, built more engenhos, and increased the cultivation of other crops for sale in Europe and Africa. Many African slaves were imported. Various religious orders opened new schools and missions. Portugal's relations with the other parts of its empire and with European nations also influenced Brazil's development. Documents revealing the full details of this period have not yet been studied, as is true for great segments of Brazilian history, but enough is known to reveal the significant events.

In 1575, Paulo Dias de Nováis, grandson of the famous discoverer of the Cape of Good Hope, received Angola as a captaincy and feitoria. Angola became at once a source of slaves for Brazil, and for Spanish America as well. In 1576 it exported some 12,000 people as slaves, and from 1575 to 1591 an estimated 52,000 Africans. What proportion of these slaves came to Brazil cannot be known exactly, but the Angolan male became the preferred worker. He was competent as a farmer and cattleman and often skilled in various manual arts. He was more obedient than the Africans of Guinea in West Africa. Furthermore, when Africans from diverse regions with completely different languages were mixed together, the group was less likely to revolt or flee. Angolans influenced Brazilian Portuguese because of their large numbers, adding words from their own speech which differed from those of other West Africans.

Another portent of Brazil's future came from the southern Spanish settlements. The uncertainty of the exact location of the demarcation line made both Spaniards and Portuguese reluctant to admit the other's claim to any territory that might conceivably be conquered. The result was that conflicting claims overlapped hundred of miles. Spanish maps placed the line only slightly west of the city of São Paulo, not far, in fact, from where correct measurements would have placed it. Portuguese claims reached to the Paraná River.

The Spanish settlements had been advanced from Paraguay, first settled in 1537, up the Paraná River to the Tieté River by 1553 and to the Piquirí by 1557, a location near the great cataracts known as the Sete Quedas (the Seven Falls) where the Ciudad Real de Guairá was founded. In 1576, moving north and east to the confluence of the rivers Ivaí and Corumbataí, they founded Vila Rica del Espíritu Santo, west of São Paulo. The two towns formed the basis of the province of Guaíra and location of the future Spanish Jesuit settlements. This region was still hundreds of miles west of the line of demarcation and the Spaniards were within their legal rights.

Whether the Portuguese were alarmed by these Spanish settlements is not certain. There is no record of protest soon after the event. The Portuguese were not indifferent to the Spanish danger anywhere, however, and at the first opportunity they made a move to occupy the disputed region. The Spaniards had also moved down river in 1573 and founded Santa Fé, Argentina.

The same papal breve that created the prelacy in Rio in 1575 left the boundaries undefined. The separate ecclesiastical administration for the southern captaincies strengthened, nevertheless, the Portuguese claim on doubtful areas. Although the division of Brazil into two separate civil jurisdictions was soon reversed, the ecclesiastical administrations continued, and still other divisions were made as settlements spread.

The brief experiment with a divided Brazil had not solved the problems as hoped, and in 1578 the single captaincy-general was restored. The first governor-general, the first in fact to hold this title, was Lourenço da Veiga. He was given the right of vice-patronage; he could nominate men to clerical positions in Brazil just as the king could do for all the territories in his realm.

Lourenço da Veiga governed Brazil until his death in 1581. The crown had recognized by this date that the number of officials, based on the Portuguese scheme of administration, was excessive. Da Veiga was charged with the task of eliminating some positions and combining the functions of others. He also increased the subsidy to the Jesuits, a further indication of the favorable attitude of the Portuguese crown toward them.

The reunion of Brazil did nothing to eliminate the geographical problems created by the monsoons. Communication between Bahia and Rio de Janeiro continued to be difficult. In recognition of this fact, the new governor of Rio de Janeiro, Salvador Correia de Sá, a member of the family that had conquered the city from the French, received extra responsibilities. He governed from 1578 to 1598.

Another event in 1578 fixed a dividing line in Brazilian and Portuguese history. King Sebastião of Portugal was disastrously defeated and killed while fighting the Moors in Morocco. The defeat was a greater shock to Portugal than to Brazil; yet it touched Brazil in several ways as well.

Cardinal Henry, brother of João III and uncle of the dead Sebastião, succeeded to the throne. A crushed nation, its leading men dead or captured, was forced to face the future with an old and sick king whose main distinction had been his service as head of the Inquisition and regent during Sebastião's youth. Since no Portuguese had clear title to succeed him, there was some discussion about seeking a papal absolution from his priestly vows so that he could marry and perhaps produce an heir. Vain talk. The cardinal was already failing in health and ruled for only a year and a half, a period during which the question of succession to the throne took precedence over other pressing problems.

For thousands of Portuguese the most urgent problem was the ransom of their kinsmen or friends captured in Morocco. At a time when the country had already been drained of money to finance the war, it was necessary to find additional funds to pay the ransom. For those who did not have the money, the captivity became permanent.

In 1579, to add to Portugal's other disasters, the plague struck. It had been ten years since the Great Plague of 1569 had killed an estimated 70,000 to 80,000 in Lisbon alone, plus large numbers throughout the kingdom. On this date the victims numbered 40,000 in Lisbon and 25,000 in Évora, a much smaller city. Such numbers are probably exaggerated. How could a city of 100,000 lose four-fifths of its population in 1569 and half again in 1579? But exaggerations or not, the reported figures serve to show the destructive nature of epidemics out of control.

Thoughts of Brazil were probably not weighing heavily on the minds of the Portugese in the midst of such misfortunes. The French settled and were cutting dye wood around the Rio Real, south of the Rio São Francisco. In 1579, during the governorship of Lourenço da Veiga, eleven French ships were forced out of Rio de Janeiro harbor. Hakluyt reported four French ships in Rio de Janeiro on May 18, 1580. He also stated that French ships were awaited with fear in Santos harbor in February 1580. The French had well drawn maps of their settlement in Brazil, and their ships were so numerous along the coast that no exact count was possible.

The English, who had only occasionally appeared in Brazil, now made more incursions. John Whitehall, living in Santos, changed his name to João Leitão and married the daughter of José Adôrno (Joffo Dore). In 1578 he wrote to a friend in England, Richard Staper, urging him to send a ship to Santos and suggesting the items to include in the cargo. A ship, the *Minion* out of London, came in response and remained in Santos from February to June 1581; it was denounced by the prelate of Rio de Janeiro, Bartolomeu Simões Pereira, as a vessel owned by heretics.

The French activity and the renewed English interest in Brazil coincided with Portugal's dynastic crisis. The involvement of other nations in Brazil predated the assumption of the Portuguese throne by Philip II of Spain. This phase of Portuguese-Brazilian history under the rule of Spanish kings was in no way as dramatic in the colony as what is known in Portugal as the era of their Babylonian Captivity (1580–1640). That other nations coveted Brazilian riches was natural, regardless of who ruled.

The difficulty of regulating the work of slaves and keeping them from running away became more acute. Their numbers increased in unison with the growth of sugar production, tobacco, cacao, and other crops. The conquest of Angola in 1574–75 had led to an immediate increase in the availability of slaves. The actual number brought to Brazil is unknown, but Gandâvo's earlier observation that African slaves were more easily guarded than Indians, because they did not flee into the interior so readily, lost its validity. By 1579 the situation had changed.

The worst enemies of the settlers, wrote Father Pero Rodrigues in 1579, were "the rebels from Guinea, who are in the mountains, from which they come to make attacks and cause a lot of trouble." He predicted that "a time could come when they will dare to attack and destroy estates, as their relatives do on the island of São Tomé," which was an island lying on the equator off of the coast of West Africa. The Jesuits defended the use of Indian archers in their aldeias to protect them from African slaves, explaining that "the Negroes of Guinea are numerous" and the Indians feared them.

The situation was different with respect to the still unconquered Indians, especially those allied with the French along the coast from Paraiba to Maranhão. Governor da Veiga was organizing an expedition against them when the court accepted an offer in 1579 from Frutuoso Barbosa, a rich landholder in Pernambuco, to establish a new captaincy at his own expense in return for appointment as capitâo-mor for ten years with the right to receive all revenues. It can be conjectured that the court was happy to make such a grant at this time because it was hard pressed as a result of military defeat, the ensuing plague, and the failure of the India fleet to arrive home after two years at sea. Barbosa was named "Captain at sea and on land" on January 25, 1579, and sailed in four ships in 1580 with the families of settlers, soldiers, and perhaps some Carmelites. Barbosa lost one ship to corsairs off the Cape Verde Islands and the remaining three were caught in a storm off Pernambuco and driven to the West Indies, from where he returned to Portugal. He would try again later.

The problem of dynastic succession was thrust on Portugal on January 31, 1580, when King Henry died. Even on his deathbed, he had been urged to name this or that candidate as his successsor. Three persons held the best claims, although there were others who were hopeful. The Duchess of Braganza, granddaughter of King Manuel I was a legitimate heir, but her case was weakened because she was a woman. King Henry had suggested to her that if she would withdraw her claim on the throne, he would name her husband King of Brazil and permanent administrator of the Order of Christ. If the duchess had not refused the offer, Brazil would have had its own king in 1580.

Antônio, Prior of Crato, was also a candidate. Experienced in administration and on the battlefield, he was also a grandson of King Manuel I. But he was the illegitimate son of Infante Luis. Illegitimacy did not seem to be a great disadvantage. For example, João I, founder of the Aviz dynasty, had been illegitimate. But Antônio did not have a great following among the nobility and was not favored by Henry. An attempt to prove his legitimacy failed.

The third leading candidate, another grandson of Manuel I, was Philip of Spain, son of the Infanta Isabel, who had married Charles V. Isabel's rare beauty and golden hair can be seen in the portrait by Titian that hangs in the Prado Museum in Madrid. Aside from his unquestioned legitimacy, Philip had a strong army on the frontier and powerful supporters among the Portuguese nobles, plus a purse to persuade the reluctant. The principal objection was that he was a foreigner, not a Portuguese.

A Cortes met in Lisbon on March 10, 1579, and took an oath to accept the candidate named by King Henry. Philip refused to accept this solution, claiming he was the sole heir. The Portuguese have accused Philip's supporters of treason to Portugal, but his case must have seemed stronger to many Portuguese than the competing claims of a female and an illegitimate male.

The Cortes met again in Almerim on January 11, 1580. Philip could count on receiving the vote of many nobles and clergy. But Lisbon and other towns opposed him, swearing to die rather than accept him as king. On January 18, King Henry declared Philip to be his only legitimate successor, but when he died on January 31, the issue was still unsettled.

A council of five, previously named by Henry, assumed the powers of government. In March, Philip's representatives presented his case to the Cortes, which adjourned without a decision. The various contenders continued to press their claims and seek supporters. The Duchess and Duke of Braganza sought aid in France and England since both nations were interested in defeating Philip. Antônio also sought French and English aid. On June 12, the news spread that Philip's forces had invaded Portugal.

In the midst of much confusion and near armed conflict, Antônio declared himself "defender" of Portugal and marched on Lisbon. Some troops sent to fight against him changed their minds and joined him instead. The Duke of Braganza declared for Antônio. The council of five was indecisive and did nothing. Antônio, unopposed, entered Lisbon and was accepted as king by the Câmara. Street demonstrators acclaimed him, but many nobles, gentry, magistrates, and even city councilmen fled. On June 28 Antônio captured Setubal, 40 kilometers south of Lisbon on the Sado River, where the council had been sitting. The council fled to Algarve. Antônio gained supporters in Cascais, at the mouth of the Tagus, and in Coimbra, Braganza, Oporto, Braga, and many other towns. The "people" were with him. But he had no effective army.

The rumors of invasion that had been spread to justify Antônio's rising were premature, but correct. Philip had been in Badajoz, on the frontier, awaiting the right moment; Antônio's move on Lisbon seemed propitious. Philip marched his troops into Elvas, across the border from Badajoz on June 18, and then began a general campaign. Within a few days his forces had spread across Portugal to Alcácer do Sal, another town on the Sado River and farther upriver from Setúbal, without firing a shot.

His fleet took the Algarve when Portimão fell on July 14. On July 17 in Castro Marim, on the Guadiana River separating Spain from Portugal, the council of five, proclaimed Philip II king of Portugal. Their decision came too late to have much impact. The army of the Duke of Alua reached Setúbal, which surrendered with almost no fighting in July. As a result of the lack of control over Spanish soldiers, and against Philip's specific orders, the town was partially sacked.

The custom of sacking conquered territory was too ingrained in military practice to be easily denied to soldiers—often they got little or no other pay. Philip was proclaimed king on July 18. The fortress of Setúbal soon surrendered.

The Spanish troops marched north toward Lisbon. In early August the Spanish fleet reached Cascais and captured it with less fighting than expected. Diogo Meneses, the Portuguese commander, was beheaded. This was not the first, nor the last, act that widened the gulf of misunderstanding—never to be narrowed—separating Spaniards from Portuguese. Antônio, his cause lost, sought an accommodation, but the Spaniards were not interested. The fort of São Julião guarding the entrance to the Tagus, commanded by Tristão Vaz da Veiga, the brother of the governor of Brazil, surrendered without a fight and for a bribe. The amount of the bribe varies with the historian who relates the story. Fortunato de Almeida puts it at 3,000 cruzados; Frei Vicente claims 4,000 escudos. The humiliation of having a traitorous brother was allegedly a factor in the death of Lourenço; he died in Brazil in June 1581.

Antônio was badly defeated at Alcântara in the west of Lisbon where the port terminal now stands. He fled north attempting to gather support, but the excesses of his followers in Aveiro and other towns turned his potential supporters against him. Driven from Oporto he hid for some time despite the 80,000 ducats Philip offered for his capture, dead or alive. On January 6, 1581, he fled by ship to France.

Philip convoked a Cortes which met in Tomar; there on April 16, 1581, he was acclaimed king. An amnesty was granted to all but a list of his most outstanding opponents. Some of those opposing him were subsequently found in his service in Brazil.

The Cortes of Tomar fashioned a constitution to govern Portugal under the Spanish kings in the future. In view of the complete control Philip had in Portugal, it seems somewhat strange that he accepted its restrictions, unless we credit him with the sincere intention, which the Portuguese never do, of reconciling Portugal to the Spanish family. Among its main provisions effecting Brazil were:

(1) All viceroys or governors, or officials with similar powers, would be Portuguese or members of the royal family, such as a brother, son, or nephew.

(2) The same rule would be observed with regard to all offices, high or low, at sea or on land then existing or to exist in the future; and garrisons and personnel of forts would be Portuguese.

(3) The trade of India, Guinea, and other areas discovered, or to be discovered, would not be taken from the Portuguese, nor would any change whatever be made in former practices; only Portuguese officials would be employed in ships and commerce.

(4) Philip agreed to use not only Portuguese resources but those of his other possessions to defend Portugal and its overseas territories.

Portuguese and Brazilian historians have tended to attribute all the misfortunes in either country after 1580 to the three Spanish Philips who ruled from 1580 to 1640. Portuguese historians are especially bitter and certain about the evils of the Philips. But aside from the fact that we can never know what might have happened if events had transpired otherwise, the evil consequences in Brazil are not easily seen.

One view often cited is that Portugal and Brazil became the victims of Spain's enemies. But the enemies were present before 1580 as we have shown. They had been created much earlier by commercial rivalries, even with nations supposedly allied to Portugal such as England; these enemies were not the invention of the Spanish kings of Portugal. Brazil accepted Philip II with only minor protest and some equivocating on the part of officials who wanted to be sure they chose the winning side. A modern Brazilian historian has summarized the situation: "Brazil continued to be effectively a colony of Portugal . . . It manifested absolutely indifference to the dynastic question."

Changes occurred in Brazil and the other Portuguese territories, but they were not directly traceable to the Spanish kings. The stipulations of the Cortes of Tomar bound them more effectively than any Portuguese king had ever been bound. The Cortes had, in fact, used the occasion to nail down the substance of many previous petitions that Portuguese kings had frequently evaded. Portugal, Brazil, and the colonies in Africa and the East soon adjusted because nothing essential in their lives had changed; trade, clerical privileges, land ownership, and daily life went on as before.

Changes took place in the course of development, but they cannot rightly be laid at the door of the Philips. A deep resentment of a "foreign" king remained, nevertheless, and was manifest whenever something happened requiring a scapegoat. The Brazilians did not feel this way as much as the "people" of Portugal; the king was too far away across the Atlantic Ocean to make a tremendous difference to the Brazilians.

In Bahia, Governor Lourenço da Veiga died in June 1581, soon after learning of the change of dynasties. Ouvidor Cosme Rangel assumed power with the cooperation of the bishop and municipal councilors. Later, having quarreled with the bishop and some of the councilors who withdrew from Salvador and lived in the country, he ruled alone. The news of Philip's accession was recorded on November 11, 1581, without any indication of protest. The São Paulo câmara did not even make note of the change.

The most immediate and obvious long-run effect of the union of the two crowns was the legal spread of Portuguese trade into Spanish areas. The same year Philip became king of Portugal, an expedition went down river from Asunción and Santa Fé to refound Buenos Aires on June 11, 1580. This event was connected to the general rivalry of the Spaniards and Portuguese in South America, but it was not related directly to the change of dynasty in Portugal. The new Buenos Aires was founded at a propitious moment for the extension of Brazilian trade to the west coast of South America. Buenos Aires connected Brazil with a usable and legal route to Chilean gold and Peruvian silver.

Many Spaniards were found in Brazil after this date, but more Portuguese made their way to Buenos Aires and the Pacific coast, rendering the theoretical Line of Demarcation even less visible than previously. As a result, hundreds of thousands of square miles of territory lying on that side of the line indisputably Spanish fell eventually to Portugal.

Philip II continued the deliberate policy of driving the French from Brazil. He followed the same strategy in Florida and other parts of the Atlantic coast now in United States territory. After 1580 it became the responsibility of the crown to keep foreigners out of Brazil. At this juncture two serious rivals, who were not new but now much stronger, England and Holland, rose to challenge the monopoly of colonization claimed since 1494 by Spain and Portugal.

7

FOREIGN RIVALS
AND INTERNAL DEVELOPMENT

ngland had only begun, by 1580, to make serious efforts in America, and mainly in the Caribbean against Spain, although John Hawkins had visited the coast of Brazil three times between 1530 and 1532. There were other voyages later, but England never pursued the Brazilian trade before 1580 like France. Internal problems and better prospects in the Caribbean explain England's late interest in Brazil.

Holland was a new nation coming into being in 1580 when Spain and Portugal were joined under one crown. Known only as the "low countries," these seventeen provinces with distinct characteristics had long existed in the areas now known as Holland, Luxemburg, and parts of Belgium and France. By dint of hard fighting, they gained "liberties" that they enjoyed from the fourteenth century onward. The dukes of Burgundy had been forced to respect their semi-autonomy in the fifteenth century. They grew rich exporting fish and importing wool, flax, dyes, and other raw materials, which were then used to manufacture other products sold throughout Europe. They traded via Spain and Portugal with the New World and the East.

The "Lowlanders" had been experienced sea-going people for centuries, confining their voyages largely to northern European waters. The great discoveries gave them a larger market for their products.

They had become part of Spain's possessions through the marriage of Juana, daughter of Ferdinand and Isabella, to Philip, the son of Holy Roman Emperor Maximilian. One of the sons of this union was Charles, who inherited the title Duke of Burgundy; he became king of Spain in 1516 and was elected Holy Roman Emperor in 1519. Philip II was the son of Charles, inheriting both the Duchy of Burgundy and the kingdom of Spain.

The only point of union between the lowland provinces was their overlord. Though they spoke various dialects of German and French, they also sent representatives to an Estates General from time to time and had something of a sense of confederation against outsiders. Quarrels among themselves over economic matters were frequent, and no feeling of nationhood existed. When Protestantism spread widely in the seven Dutch-Flemish speaking areas in the northern provinces, a new reason arose for continued feelings of separation from the ten southern provinces remaining mainly Catholic.

The religious question had not yet become critical at the time Philip inherited the duchy from Charles V. Charles had been raised among them and spoke Flemish natively, having learned Spanish only after becoming king of Spain. The outbreak of religious wars in France in 1560 caused many French Calvinists to flee to the lowlands. Coincidentally, Philip II sent in Spanish soldiers and officials. Alarmed, the nobles of the seventeen provinces formed a league in 1566 to check "foreign" influences. Its members comprised both Catholics and Protestants. They petitioned Philip to keep out the Inquisition. When Philip's agents rejected the petition, violence broke out. Fanatical Calvinists pillaged Catholic churches and destroyed many beautiful art works in their fight against "popery." Social and economic grievances became intertwined with religious differences to nourish a general anti-Spanish and anti-Catholic revolt. The Inquisition and the Spanish troops killed thousands. New taxes violated their "liberties." The estates of many nobles were confiscated, among the losers was William of Orange (The Silent), who had been Philip's "Stadtholder" (representative) in the County of Holland. Acting as a sovereign, he rose against the Spaniards, rallying the seventeen provinces, Catholic and Protestant, to form a union in 1576 strong enough to drive out the Spaniards. International complications now arose.

Elizabeth of England, fearing the English Catholic supporters of Mary Queen of Scots, then a prisoner in England where she had fled after being driven out of Scotland by the Presbyterians, gave surreptitious aid to the lowland rebels. A schism between the Catholics, living mainly in the south of the lowlands, and the Protestants, living mainly in the north, led to the Union of Utrecht, an association of the seven mainly Protestant provinces in 1579. They declared their independence from Spain in 1581. Philip II thus had to face a political, economic, and religious revolt of his rich and vigorous lowland subjects at the juncture of assuming the kingship of Portugal and its worldwide trading empire.

Portugal had long maintained trade dating back to the twelfth century with the low countries and England. After the discovery of Brazil its products reached the low countries quite legally, and Brazil received their exports through Portugal. Records do not show how early the first direct trade with Brazil began. The customs records of England, the Low Countries, and German ports such as Hamburg show brazilwood and brazil pepper but do not reveal the direct provenance of these products. The ship *São João* captured and hauled into England in 1581 had a cargo of 428 boxes of sugar, of which 350 boxes belonged to German and Dutch merchants and the remainder to the captain and the crew. The Union of Utrecht confirmed to the Portuguese the previously existing right to enter freely, reside, and trade.

The struggle of Antônio, Prior of Crato, for the throne illustrates the extraneous influences affecting Brazil. Driven from Portugal, Antônio still had a following in the Azores who held Terceira for him. When Antônio refused the support of Elizabeth of England, he obtained aid from Catherine de Medici, queen mother of France, who renounced her own pretended rights to the Portuguese throne and recognized Antônio as king. She agreed to furnish him with an army and navy, and he pledged to cede Brazil to her. The forces sent to the Azores under command of her cousin Filipe Strozzi suffered defeat, and he was killed. Antônio escaped to France. He tried to mount a campaign in 1583—again without success. Thus did Brazil escape falling officially into French hands.

Meantime, the Brazilian resistance to the French along the coast and the further advance into new territories continued, with no perceptible difference after Philip's succession to the Portuguese throne. The case of Frutuoso Barbosa and the conquest of Paraíba do Norte illustrate the situation. Having failed in his first attempt in 1579, he returned to Portugal in 1580 and organized a second expedition, the unsettled conditions of the country not withstanding. In Pernambuco he obtained the aid of the captain and the *ouvidor*, Simão Rodrigues Cardoso, who marched overland while Barbosa sailed for Paraíba. Finding eight French ships, he burned five, or, according to some versions, their crews burned them and fled to take refuge among the Indians. He nevertheless carelessly allowed himself to be ambushed by the French and their Indian allies; he lost forty men, among them his son. Forced to retire, he left the French in a stronger position and more of a threat to Itamaracá, where three engenhos had been burned in his absence.

The fear of the foreigners was constant and led to the improvement of fortifications in Rio de Janeiro, Santos, and other ports. The English appeared again in 1582-83, but not as a result of a planned effort to raid and trade in Brazil. Edward Fenton sailed from England with two ships on May 1, 1582, with the intention of going to the East via the Straits of Magellan. After spending some months along the African coast, he crossed the Atlantic to Santa Catarina. He captured a ship from the Spanish fleet with sixteen to twenty men aboard commanded by Diego Flores Valdes; it was also enroute to the Straits of Magellan.

Fenton sailed into Santos where he remained from January 19 to 24, 1583, allegedly to make repairs. While in Santos, he was attacked by three ships of Flores's fleet under command of Andrés Aquino. One Spanish ship was sunk in an all-night battle. Fenton then sailed north and was probably somewhere between Paraíba and Ceará before returning to England. While along the coast, "he spread the news," says Frei Vicente, "that the Catholic king was dead and that Dom Antônio ruled in the kingdom of Portugal, promising great things in the name of the queen of England." Flores ordered the construction of a fort in Santos, designed by Bautista, an Italian architect brought along for the purpose.

Three French ships entered the harbor of Rio de Janeiro in 1583 also proclaiming Antônio as king of Portugal. But after seeing the defense prepared by Governor Salvador Correia de Sá, they withdrew.

Another English ship, the *Royal Merchant*, reached Olinda, Pernambuco, in January 1583, when Fenton was in Santos. It remained six months and traded with the local residents. When it sailed, three men were left in Pernambuco to carry on. When Flores reached Pernambuco, he took them captive and confiscated merchandise evaluated at £4,446. The three prisoners were sent to Spain and then to Portugal before finally reaching England with much difficulty and expense. Before the fate of the men was known in England, another ship, the *São João da Viana*, had been leased by English merchants and sent to Brazil under command of Francisco da Rocha. Its cargo valued at £1,877 was also presumably confiscated. It seems clear that English merchants were using Portuguese ships and attempting to sail under the protection of the long-lasting treaties between Portugal and England.

Brazil had been without a governor since the death of Lourenço da Veiga in June 1581. The interim government was first placed in the hands of the Câmara of Salvador and the bishop and later the Ouvidor-geral Cosme Rangel de Macedo. The unsatisfactory relationship between these authorities was noted earlier. The new governor, Manuel Telles Barreto arrived on May 9, 1583, coincidental with the presence of the Spanish fleet under Valdes, which made port in June for repairs and supplies. The third failure to take Paraíba had impressed upon both Barreto and Flores the necessity of dealing with the continued French danger in Brazil. They agreed to organize another expedition.

While the preparations were in progress, Flores and his men were entertained by the governor, the bishop, and principally a senhor de engenho, Sebastião de Faria. Flores was his guest for eight months. If the visit seems long, it may be recalled that the costs were not great since all the food came from a large estate worked by slaves. Governor Barreto appropriated 10,000 cruzados of the crown's money to spend on the expedition. He also sent his treasurer and the chief judge (ouvidor) to Pernambuco to raise men in that location and in Itamaracá.

The French danger was greater than ever because they supported Antônio who had promised Brazil to Maria de Médici. It is not known, however, if reports of this promise had reached Brazil. With the seven ships remaining plus the two Barreto had brought to Brazil, Flores sailed for Pernambuco early in 1584. Contrary monsoon winds held them back, and twenty days were required to sail the short distance. In Pernambuco they combined forces with Captain Filipe de Moura and the same Frutuoso Barbosa who had led a force overland to the Paraíba River and burned five French ships.

Flores built a fort and left Captain Francisco Castejon (or Castrejon) with a garrison of 110 Spanish and 50 Portuguese soldiers. This arrangement was in keeping with the provision signed by Philip II in the Côrtes of Tomar, namely to use all the forces of his realm to protect Portuguese dominions. Flores also left in Paraíba a Portuguese nau and two smaller ships. Frutuoso Barbosa was recognized as donatário in accordance with the original agreement with the crown made previous to the Spanish period. Flores sailed for Spain on May 1, 1584. The name São Filipe, later changed to Filipeia, was given to the new site.

The relations between the Portuguese and Spaniards were bad, and so too were the relations of these new settlers with the pacified Indians. A battle between the two groups resulted in the deaths of about 50 whites and hundreds of Indians. The whites fled to Olinda. The French and the Potiguares besieged the fort. Reinforcements from Pernambuco burned two ships whose crews were helping the besiegers. A second, larger expedition led by Martim Leitão, with 200 horses, 300 foot solders, and hundreds of Indians and Blacks, marched in relief, but after much hard fighting returned to Pernambuco.

Captain Castejon abandoned the fort and returned to Itamaracá in mid-1585. Not a house remained in Filipeia. Paraíba seemed to defy all efforts at conquest. By this date hundreds of Europeans and perhaps thousands of Indians and Blacks had died. Both sides suffered ruinous losses in ships and arms. The French and their Potiguar allies still held Paraíba, only 75 miles north from Olinda.

Victory for the Portuguese came soon thereafter, and it emerged from the very source of this last defeat. The Potiguar Indians had been aided in the recent battles by chief Piragiba of the Tupiniquins, who had been driven from his own lands and was seeking revenge. After the retreat of the Portuguese, fighting among the Indians broke out. The Tupiniquins subsequently all themselves with the Portuguese, who returned to the Paraiba valley in November 1585. Renewed fighting in 1586, with Piragiba and the Portuguese as allies, cleared the valley for settlement. A new royal colony was founded, and the cultivation of cane and the production of sugar soon began. The coast toward Ceará and Maranhão remained in Indian and French possession; its conquest, equally difficult, came later.

The Portuguese pushed their settlements southward during this period. They opened a new trade area to the Rio de la Plata and thence to Peru. The settlement of Buenos Aires in 1580, at the time Philip II was becoming king of Portugal, opened up new legal trade opportunities that made easier relations between the Spaniards and Portuguese.

Inasmuch as all legal trade was only with crown permission and license, it did not automatically follow that Portuguese America and Spanish America could trade with one another without getting the required licenses. Within Spanish America itself—for example, between Mexico and Peru—trade was regulated according to the interests of the crown and of the particular merchants involved. The same was true between Brazil and the Rio de la Plata. There was, however, much greater tolerance of the Spaniards in Brazil after 1580. They were helping defend the country and the Portuguese in La Plata and Peru.

Until 1585 the northern limit of the La Plata trade seems to have been São Vicente. Frei Francisco de Vitória, the bishop of Tucumán in northwest Argentina, expanded the market. Shipped in from Spain via Panamá and Peru over mountain passes reaching as high as 15,000 feet, merchandise arriving in Argentina became prohibitively expensive. Meanwhile the market for Argentine products was very limited, except for items that could transport themselves—such as mules and carts.

The bishop of Tucumán viewed Brazil and the new union of the two crowns as the answer to his prayers. He saw both São Vicente and Salvador, Bahia, as rich sources of trade. Frei Francisco de Vitória was a Portuguese by birth. So was the dean of the cathedral, Francisco de Salcedo of Faro in the Algarve, who was sent Brazil as head of a trading mission in 1585.

Bishop Vitoria obtained a license from the Audiéncia of Charcas to import African slaves from Brazil for his own service. He sent Salcedo to Buenos Aires supplied with 30,000 pesos of gold and silver. A small ship was freighted, sailing to Buenos Aires on October 20, 1585. Once in São Vicente, Dean Salcedo bought another ship for 1,000 ducats. When they reached Salvador, Bahia, Governor Manuel Teles Barreto and the priest received them warmly; "with such joy that it cannot be explained" says the *Relacion del viaje del Brasil*.

The Portuguese were pleased by the request to send missionaries to Argentina—and with the prospect of trade. The dean and his party remained six months in Bahia. Frei Vicente referred to the mission, reporting that the bishop of Tucumán had sent them "to bring back students for ordination, or articles pertaining to the church." He added: "henceforth there was not a year in which some ships with royal permission, or passing ships, did not take flour (farinha) which is much appreciated there."

"Six fathers of the Company of Jesus, the eldest being Father Armiño, a man of fifty," went with Salcedo. Each received 30,000 maravedis for vestments and sacred utensils. They also took "many books and relics of the saints." In addition, they had such items as church bells, iron, steel, copper cauldrons, and "peroles" to make sugar, plus "Negroes for the service of the very reverend bishop." The ships loaded piece goods worth more than 150,000 pesos from his lordship (Sua Senhoria) and other individuals. Diego de Palma sent "very fine presents of slaves and other things . . . to the very reverend [bishop] of Tucumán."

The idea of sending Jesuits to Rio de la Plata had not originated with the bishop of Tucumán. The Bahia Jesuits had obtained a permission to this effect on November 1, 1584—hence their pleasure on the arrival of the mission from Tucuman.

The trade prospects for the future were bright, but the end of this mission was disastrous. The two ships were captured by the English. The still undeclared, but very real, state of war between Spain and England spilled over to America. Spain was trying to dethrone Elizabeth and place Mary Queen of Scots on the English throne, while England was helping Philip's rebellious Dutch subjects. In 1585 Spain had temporarily closed all ports in its realms to the Dutch and confiscated their ships sailing anywhere in the Spanish dominions. When the Dutch moved to close the port of Antwerp, Elizabeth sent 6,000 troops to aid them. In September 1585, Francis Drake raided the Spanish coast, looting and sacking the island of Santiago in the Cape Verde Islands. He continued to harass the Spaniards along the Florida coast, before returning to England in 1586.

In 1586 Robert Withrington and Christopher Lister were armed with Letters of Marque from Antônio, Prior of Crato, and sailed from England for the Pacific Ocean via the strait of Magellan. The bad luck of Father Salcedo's party was that these English ships reached the Rio de la Plata in the spring of 1587 just in time to intercept and capture them. Accounts vary about how badly Withrington despoiled the Spanish party. "He did not leave them even a shirt," according to one account; but another states that they escaped with many valuables acquired in Brazil. In any case, the Jesuits reached Asunción on August 11, 1588; this date marks the opening of those Jesuit activities which had so much impact on Brazil a few years later. Trade between Brazil, Rio de la Plata, and Peru, part legal and part contraband, continued thereafter, facilitating Portuguese encroachment on lands west of the line of demarcation.

Withrington and Lister, impressed with the possibilities of riches in Brazil, desisted from trying to make the Pacific and sailed instead to Salvador, Bahia, which they reached on April 22, 1587. Not strong enough to capture the city, they contented themselves, without much success Father Vicente claimed, to find something of value around Recôncavo and Itaparica Island, the big island in the mouth of the bay. They forced or persuaded the owner of an urca resident in Salvador, who was married to a Portuguese woman, to join them when they sailed for England in June 1587.

The English ships that caused so much fear among the colonists in Brazil were a sign of the turbulent situation existing in Europe. England and Holland had become the enemies of Spain because of their challenge on the economic front, an issue quite apart from the Dutch revolt against Spain. It can be assumed that England and Holland would have become economic rivals of Spain (and Portugal) irrespective of the religious schism. Although both were Protestant, they became rivals and enemies after 1648, once Spain was no longer their main enemy.

Mary Queen of Scots' claim to the English throne brought issues to a head between Spain and England. Philip II concluded that he could not put down the Dutch rebellion so long as England interfered. If he could put Mary on the English throne, he would gain a new ally. Elizabeth, conversely, did not feel safe with Mary alive. There had been many plots, and she knew others were afoot. To end them, she ordered Mary executed in February 1587 and then prepared to defend against the attack expected from Philip.

Philip planned to send an armada to pick up an army stationed in Holland and then to sail to England. His preparations suffered a serious delay when Drake attacked Cádiz on April 19, 1587, and burned more than a hundred ships with their provisions and military supplies. He took and held temporarily Cape St. Vincent in Portugal. Stung but not yet convinced of the impossibility of success, Philip continued preparations and in May 1588 sent to sea from Lisbon the largest fleet known to history to that date.

The Invincible Armada, as history has derisively dubbed it, encountered disaster from the beginning. Too long delayed, much of its provisions were already spoiled. Drake's raid had destroyed seasoned barrel staves and forced the use of green staves that sprung leaks and wasted water and wine. A heavy storm struck the fleet as it sailed from Lisbon. When at last it reached the English Channel in late July, the English fleet, composed of about two hundred smaller but faster ships, harried the Spaniards. The English sailed fire-ships against the Spanish. The final defeat of the armada came when a storm, a "Protestant Wind," swept the remaining ships northward. There was no alternative to sailing around Scotland and Ireland and returning to Spain.

Although still a formidable sea power, Spain could no longer hope to hold England back at sea. The Dutch fought with renewed hope of eventual success and independence. Overseas territories, including Brazil, became more vulnerable to foreign attacks and even more dependent on foreign markets for both exports and imports.

The preoccupation with foreign harassment did not prevent the growth of Brazil during the ten to fourteen years separating the account left by Gándavo and those by three other authors—Father Fernão Cardim, Gabriel Soares, and Father José Anchieta—which bring us up to the mid-1580s.

Cardim arrived in Brazil in May 1583 with Governor Manuel Telles Barreto as secretary to the Jesuit Visitador, Christóvão de Goueia, whom he accompanied on visits to Jesuit colégios and aldeias throughout Brazil. He remained in Brazil in various capacities until sent to Rome in 1598. On returning to Brazil in September 1601 in the *São Vicente*, a Flemish urca, he and fifteen other Jesuits fell captives to the English captain Francis Cook. Cardim and three fellow Jesuits were taken to England while eleven others were landed on the Portuguese coast. His manuscripts were taken from him. He remained in England until 1603, returning to Brazil in 1604. A portion of what he possessed, maybe all, was published in English in *Purchas His Pilgrims* (London, 1625). Other parts were published subsequently in Portuguese.

Cardim's work is so full of information that anything less than recounting the whole is unsatisfactory. For practical reasons we must reduce to the essentials his description of "this rich land, principally in livestock and sugar." He described the native animals, snakes, land

and sea birds, trees of all varieties, flowering bushes, vegetables, herbs, edible roots, bamboo cane, fish (both the edible and poisonous), sea monsters (in which colonial people and Indians believed—but which refuse to show themselves to modern scientists), shell fish, alligators, water mammals, and the rivers. He also mentioned the animals, trees, herbs, and fruits that had been transferred from Europe. Among his notes were these remarks:

> Dogs have multiplied immensely in this land . . . they are very greatly appreciated by the Portuguese . . . and by the Indians who hold them in higher esteem than any other possession because of the help they are in hunting . . . the [Indian] women carry them around on their backs . . . and raise them like children, giving them the breast to nurse.

In Cardim's view the Portuguese had transported Portugal to Brazil. "This Brazil is now another Portugal . . . although the houses are not very comfortable because they are built of mud walls (taipas) and straw, though now they are beginning to build of stone and mortar, with tiled roof." Clothing for most people was very simple "because the country does not produce any cloth by cotton." It was especially true in Rio de Janeiro, "for lack of ships to bring merchandise and cloth." In the other captaincies, he stated: "The men go well dressed and display many silks and velvets. And so, it has become Portugal, as I said, because of the many conveniences that come from there." The same entertainments enjoyed in Portugal had also become a part of Brazil's life.

Cardim's information shows how much Brazil had grown since Gándavo's time. Bahia now had 36 engenhos, twice as many as Gándavo reported, and they made "the best sugar along the entire coast." His figures are lower, however, than other reports from the same period. Anchieta listed 40 engenhos in Bahia in 1584 and 46 in 1585, while Gabriel Soares reported 40 at about the same time. Cardim found in Bahia 3,000 Portuguese settlers, 8,000 Christian Indians, and 3,000 to 4,000 "slaves of Guinea." The cathedral had the customary quota of canons (cônegos) and other clergy plus ten or twelve parishes, "not speaking of many churches and chapels that some rich senhores have on their estates." The Jesuits had their "new colégio almost finished . . . built entirely of stone and oyster-shell lime, as good as the stone of Portugal." The church was full of relics, ornaments of velvet, silver, gold, jewels, paintings, and statues, plus "three of the heads of the eleven thousand virgins." Normally there were about sixty Jesuits present who had about 3,000 cruzados of income and lands which left them well-fed with "meat and fish produced here; and there is never a lack of a glass of wine from Portugal." In the colégio they taught theology, morals, liberal arts, humanities, and reading and writing. They had a library; but he did not list the books.

Some devoted themselves to the conversion of the Indians. Cardim remarked, as did all newcomers, on the absence of clothing, "the nude women (something for us very new) with their hands raised to Heaven, saying in Portuguese "Praised by Jesus Christ!' " Many other things struck him: "Something else that surprised me not a little bit was that we would leave the house, some forty of us, without anything to eat and without money; nevertheless, no matter where we went, or at whatever time of day, we were all entertained and given everything needed to eat—meat, fish, shellfish, with such abundance that the Lisbon waterfront was not missed." They did not need to take their beds with them. "We always had with us the hammocks that are used as beds here."

Father Cardim's experiences illustrate some of Brazil's difficulties, notably the fickle monsoons mentioned by every observer who traveled the coast in ships. Leaving Bahia on August 18, 1583, with the Padre Visitador and many others bound for Pernambuco to the north, they battled contrary winds for one day and then "put back into Bahia." Venturing out again "against the same adverse winds," they dropped anchor in Camamu, "lands belonging to the colégio of Bahia," eighteen leagues to the south. They remained there eight days awaiting favorable winds. They were in dangerous territory; the area was still controlled by the Aimorés, "so barbarous they live like brute animals, without towns and without houses."

After sailing again, they were forced into Ilhéus, still farther south and about thirty leagues from Bahia, where they waited another eight days for favorable winds. Ilhéus belonged to Francisco Giraldes. Besides the Jesuit quarters, Ilhéus had fifty settlers (vizinhos) and three engenhos. The area grew cotton and had an abundance of food, including cows, hogs, and chickens. There was no aldeia of Indians because it was "too hard pressed by the Aimorés," and did not extend much more than half a league inland (this more than eighty years after the discovery and forty after establishment of the captaincy). But fruits abounded, including those transplanted from Europe: "The woods are full of oranges and lemons of all kinds."

They started north again on September 21, but winds were still contrary. The ship ended up in Porto Seguro, sixty leagues south of Bahia. They received another warm welcome from the four Jesuits and the other colonists. Porto Seguro had forty settlers and one engenho. They were "hard pressed by the Aimorés." The people were very poor; a type of grass grew in the area that killed the cows. The settlers had formerly produced cotton and manioc farinha, but these two products were now in short supply and "the land is becoming depopulated."

Santa Cruz, where Cabral landed, was four leagues away. It also had forty settlers, who were "a bit better off than Porto Seguro." Cardim painted a sad picture of a land about which Vaz de Caminha had given such a glowing account; but that account was written before the arrival of the Aimorés.

They left Santa Cruz on October 20, still at the mercy of the weather. But luck had found them and the winds were favorable. A "camboeiro" blew them sixty leagues north in one day and night to Bahia again, their starting point. They "resolved not to go . . . to Pernambuco at this time," because other matters arose which kept them in Bahia until June of the following year.

The matters that required the attention of the Padre Visitador were the same that concerned the inhabitants of Brazil everywhere in 1583. He drew up a compendium of "the doubts that arise here, mainly about the marriage and baptism of Indians and slaves of Guinea." He believed the fathers understood much better than law officials about how to deal with such cases.

But still critical was the problem of the monsoons which often set back all plans. A general meeting of the Jesuits was to be held in Bahia beginning December 8. Letters informing the various centers had been sent out long in advance. When the date came, the attendance was poor "because the majority did not receive the letters on time, nor could come for lack of [favorable] monsoons and ships."

Cardim thought the Jesuits should be proud of what they had taught the Indians and Blacks. In the aldeia of Espírito Santo in Bahia, they enjoyed a pastoril given by the Indians "in the Brazilian language, Portuguese and Castilian; they have a lot of flair (graça) in speaking foreign languages, especially Castilian." The Indians were very devout after conversion: "They cry copious tears and confess very trivial things," insisting on absolution and communion. "I was greatly consoled by confessing Indians, men and women, through an interpreter; they are very innocent minded and live much less sinful lives than the Portuguese."

Cardim reported on visits to three aldeias in Bahia. "In each of these aldeias there is a school of reading and writing where the fathers teach the Indian children; and to some of the more clever they also teach counting, singing and playing the flute and other instruments." All the Indians in the aldeias, adults and children, "hear mass early every day before going to their tasks; . . . they have an extraordinary love for, faith in, and respect for the fathers."

The Padre Visitador, Cardim, and their companions also visited some estates and engenhos of the Portuguese because "it was necessary to conciliate the anger of some of them against the Company." They were, as was the usual custom, entertained everywhere. When visiting the large fazendas, they slept in "luxurious beds with mattresses." During one visit they were served by the priest himself on "porcelains and silver." Even those fazendeiros who received them less cordially because they were not devoted to the Jesuits still did more for them than their best friends in Portugal. "It was startling to see the great prestige the company has here." All the fazendas had a chapel; some senhores de engenho had chaplains who were paid forty or fifty milreis a year, plus housing and food at the table of the lord. The regular procedure was that "we confessed the Portuguese," and there was one father "who knew the language of the slaves of Guinea." Cardim mentioned again that there were thirty-six engenhos in Bahia. "We visited almost all, besides many fazendas that were something to see."

He never ceased to marvel at the "great ease" the estate owners showed in entertainment: "Because at whatever the hour of night or day they served . . . all kinds of meats, chickens, turkeys, ducks, rabbits, ... and other things, all of which they produce, with every kind of fish and shell fish, of which they always have a supply because they have certain slaves who are fishermen." The rich senhores de engenho seemed to live "like counts and spend freely."

Around every engenho there were normally "six, eight or more homes of whites, and at least sixty slaves . . . but on most of them 100 to 200 slaves of Guinea and Indians." The trapiches required sixty oxen. The work day began at midnight and ended at three or four in the afternoon. "The work is intolerable, the workmen always on the run, and as a result many slaves die, and the expense [of buying more slaves] is the main reason they are in debt." Expert personnel, frequently freemen, was always expensive. Every engenho had to have a steward, carpenter, blacksmith, and a master sugar-maker plus his assistants. "The master sugar-makers are the real senhores de engenho, because in their hands is the end result and the reputation of the engenho. For this reason they are treated with much consideration; and the senhores feed them and pay them a hundred milreis and sometimes more a year."

A good view of sugar production emerges from Father Cardim's observations. He reported "four or five thousand arrôbas" annually, which was worth 5,000 cruzados in Pernambuco and three times as much in Portugal. No duties were collect in Portugal for the first ten years and only half the duty thereafter. It proved impossible to enforce this law. Before ten years had elapsed, mill owners rebuilt their engenho and called it "new" in order to regain the ten-year exemption.

The lives of the landlords shocked Father Cardim. "The weights on their consciousnesses are heavy; the sins they commit are numberless. Almost all live in concubinage because of the many opportunities they have. This sweet is loaded with the sins that they all commit. Great is the patience of God, who suffers so much." Perhaps Father Cardim was likewise tempted by the "sweet" and suffered also. But he had little evidence for asserting that the senhores de engenho, and other men, felt guilty enough to forswear their "many opportunities."

Father Cardim was well satisfied with the results of the mission. More than "three thousand souls" were baptized and many more were married sacramentally, thus "rescuing them from concubinage." The principal saint's days were occasions for processions. Brazil was not only blessed with three of the heads of the Eleven Thousand Virgins, but had many other relics. The most valued was a piece of the Holy Cross on which Jesus had died, embedded in a gold-plated silver cross given by the empress of Germany "with the consent of the Pope."

The time finally came to leave Bahia and to try for Pernambuco as in the previous year. It was the end of June, "the season of the southern monsoon had come again." The monsoon was not on schedule, as it often was not, and on the second day, when twelve leagues from Bahia, they met "contrary winds" that forced them to lay over for eleven days. The days were taken up with religious devotion, singing, music, fishing, and good food.

On July 2, they sailed on, arriving in Pernambuco on the fourteenth. As usual they were met with the utmost in welcomes, including "hammocks and horses, in which we went to the . . . colégio." The next day's religious services included a sermon "in the Angolan language given by a brother fourteen years old . . . who repeated it in Portuguese with such devotion that there was not anybody who could restrain his tears." A day later there was a sermon in the "lingua brasilica." The fazendas where they were entertained were "larger and richer than those in Bahia." They enjoyed "great banquets and extraordinary delicacies" and slept on mattresses of crimson damask with gold fringe, and quilts from India." Cardim noted one exception: "The Padre Visitador used his hammock as was his custom."

They made the usual round of visits. "We saw most of the 66 engenhos of Pernambuco, and other fazendas." Some of the engenhos were worth 40,000 cruzados and more. Drought had struck the Northeast, however, including even the normally wet areas. Hunger in the sertão had driven the Indians to take refuge with the whites along the coast, and some were taken captive.

Pernambuco was richer and more heavily populated than Bahia. It had 2,000 settlers and great numbers of Guinea slaves, "amounting to close to 2,000," but "the Indians are now few in number." The number of engenhos listed by Cardim agrees with Father Anchieta's figures, but not his estimate of the number of slaves. Anchieta estimated "up to 10,000 slaves of Guinea and Angola, and of Indians up to 2,000."

Pernambuco produced around 200,000 arrôbas of sugar annually. More cane was produced than the 66 mills could grind. Approximately forty ships visited Pernambuco annually, but they did have enough cargo space to take all the sugar.

The wealth of some men impressed Cardim. He estimated their fortunes at forty, fifty, and even eighty thousand cruzados. "Some of them are heavily in debt because of the large losses they suffer in their Guinea slaves, a great many of whom die, and because of the excesses of extravagant expenses in the way they live. They dress themselves and their wives and children in all kinds of velvet damask and other silks, and in this they go to great extremes."

Gabriel Soares de Sousa claimed the donatary had an annual income of 10,000 cruzados. Olinda, the capital city, had seventy settlers and the captaincy many more. Around some of the engenhos there were twenty or thirty settlers, plus still others who lived around the edges. For defense, a force of 3,000 foot soldiers and 400 horses could be recruited—and up to 5,000 Black and Indian slaves could be added. More than a thousand men received incomes of 1,000 cruzados annually; some earned up to 10,000 cruzados a year. Forty or fifty ships a year entered the port bringing merchandise from Europe and exporting sugar and brazilwood, a forest resource which had been leased out by the king at 20,000 cruzados annually for ten years.

Such wealth brought a life style displeasing to Father Cardim. "The women are grand ladies and not very devout, nor did they go to mass, prayers or confessions." Some of the men owned three or four horses costing 200 to 300 cruzados each. The normal order was festivals and display. On the occasion of weddings, they dressed themselves and their horses in velvets and silks, each man in a different color. Bull fights were very common. They were especially fond of banquets where ten or twelve senhores got together. Normally they bought 50,000 cruzados of wine a year from Portugal, and in some years 80,000 cruzados. "In Pernambuco there is more pomposity than in Lisbon." Pernambuco had 21 Jesuits "who live well although the cost of living is three times what it is in Portugal."

The time came for the Padre Visitador and his party to hazard the vagaries of the monsoon and return to Bahia. This time the winds were right. They sailed from Pernambuco on October 16 and reached Bahia four days later. The next day, October 21, was the festival of the Eleven Thousand Virgins. That called for a procession in which the three heads were paraded in a lavishly decorated float built to look like a ship. Father Cardim had a great love of festivals and described them in interesting detail.

The Padre Visitador still had more visits to make. His party left Bahia November 14 and reached Espírito Santo, located 120 leagues south of Bahia, seven days later. There followed the usual banquets, masses, confessions, and communions. The Jesuits had two aldeias with 3,000 Christian Indians situated about three leagues from the town, plus other aldeias along the coast with 2,000 additional Indians who were partly Christian and partly "pagan."

Cardim stated that becoming Christian did not free the Indians from slavery: "The Portuguese have a great many slaves among the Christian Indians." Espírito Santo had six engenhos and was rich in cotton and livestock. It also had large forests of valuable trees, both native and European. Vitória, the capital, had more than 150 settlers. Cardim did not list the exact number of Jesuits, but he seems to indicate that seven were present.

When they left for Rio de Janeiro, they were caught in a terrible storm and had to run with "bare masts." But "God in his goodness delivered us," and on December 20, 1584, they reached Rio. The Jesuits of the colégio and Governor Salvador Correia de Sá received them with customary joy and salvos of artillery. The display of a relic of São Sebastião, embedded in silver and carried in a great procession on the bay, plus the presence of Martim Afonso Arariboia, the Temiminó chief who had extended indispensable help in conquering the region and who, as a result, had received a sesmaria on land where Niterói now stands, added prestige to the occasion. Cardim's enthusiastic account of the great reception did not fail to mention the nuzinhas—the naked little girls, who were painted in "pleasing colors," wore rattles on their legs and arms, and sported feather headdresses.

The two Jesuit aldeias held 3,000 Christian Indians. Livestock was abundant; the wood was of great value; native spices and fruit trees abounded; and wheat bore 60 grains for each grain planted. Three engenhos were in operation. "In sum, a very fertile land." Cardim found the bay so beautiful it "seemed painted by the supreme painter and architect of the world, God our Lord." Not even the hardest doubter of the divine presence could deny the justice of Cardim's view of Guanabara Bay. Rio de Janeiro's citizens (vizinhos) numbered 150, and they owned "many Indian slaves." The Jesuits held the choicest location in the city and were building a beautiful new building. "Coimbra has no advantage over this." There were 28 fathers and brothers at this location.

The next step on the peregrination was São Vicente. They left before the end of the northeast monsoon in January; the short voyage required six days. The Jesuits from Piratininga, São Paulo, wanted the Padre Visitador present by January 25 to join in celebrating the founding of the colégio. The road was so steep and rough that, in places, they had to crawl on hands and feet. Here there were no horses and hammocks for them. Once in Piratininga, they remained almost to the end of February 1585. The Padre Visitador left a number of relics for the fathers in Piratininga, among them a piece of the Holy Cross.

When Padre Visitador returned to São Vicente, Cardim remained behind at the colegio in São Paulo for a few days "preaching, and

confessing the people." Cardim left amidst their tears. He found São
Paulo a very healthy place, enjoying "great cold and frosts . . . full of
old people who were more than centenarians." Of these, there were
four, he alleged, whose life span totaled 500 years. The people dressed
simply in rough woolen clothing. The settlers numbered "about 120
with many Indian slaves," who were ministered to by six or seven
Jesuits. They wanted no parish priest. Cattle abounded and there
were vineyards more extensive than he had seen in any one place in
Portugal. Cardim exclaimed: "This land looks like a new Portugal."

The captaincy of São Vicente had four vilas, including Piratininga.
The vila of São Vicente had earlier been rich but was now poor
"because the land is exhausted and there is a shortage on Indians to
cultivate it . . . the town is losing people." Its population numbered
about 80 settlers and normally six Jesuits. Santos had about the same
number of settlers, and Itanhaém about 50. The Padre Visitador had
agreed to move the Jesuits in São Vicente to Santos.

When they returned to Rio de Janeiro in April, the Padre Visitador
found orders directing him to go to Bahia to receive twelve new Jesuits
coming from Europe. The voyage to Bahia took 32 days at sea. "Our
lord willed us to suffer to make us understand how difficult is navigation along this coast." Their ship almost sank in sight of Bahia.
Cardim thought the Lord had spared them for the good of Brazil. He
had not, however, done as well for the twelve Jesuits enroute from
Europe. They had been captured in late January by "heretical corsairs," and among the dead was Father Cardim's young brother Lourenço. "I was very envious of him," stated Cardim, because his brother
had gone to Heaven ahead of him.

Cardim described Brazil at about the same time as Gabriel Soares
de Sousa. Bahia, Sousa reported, had more than a hundred residents
whose annual income ranged from 1,000 to 5,000 cruzados. Their
estates he evaluated at "20,000 to 50,000 cruzados, or more." They
also had many horses, servants, slaves, and an excess of clothing,
especially the women. "They dress only in silks . . . at great expense,
above all the people of lesser station, because any peon wears shoes
and doublets of satin or damask." The wives splashed their finery

"adorned in jewelry of gold." The houses were furnished with silver table service.

Eight or ten ships regularly, and sometimes as many as fifteen or twenty, loaded sugar and cotton. Two thousand Portuguese, four thousand Africans from Guinea, and six thousand Indians were available for defense against enemies.

Bahia had 40 engenhos, counting four under construction, of which 21 were powered by water and 15 by oxen. The annual export exceeded 120,000 arrôbas of sugar plus large quantities of preserved fruit. The Recôncavo was served by 14,000 boats for sugar transport, with about 100 of them large enough to carry a small cannon. Sousa listed 62 churches in Bahia, and three monasteries which were "well built, clean and well provided with ornaments." He agreed with Cardim about the abundance of horses, cattle, goats, sheep, hogs, chickens ("fatter and larger than those of Portugal"), and other animals.

He left the most complete list of the fruit trees and food products which had been introduced at an earlier date from Europe, including the edible snail. His description of pacovas (native banana) in comparison with the bananas introduced from Guinea and São Tomé is the best available. Sousa reported on the bad as well as the good. He made a gruesome list of insects, especially ticks, flies, and mosquitoes; several kinds were not merely annoying but deadly. The mosquitoes swarmed over the naked Indians, "especially when they are dirty, as is their custom." The most devastating insects were the ants, large and small, and the termites. The ants destroyed the crops and fruit trees, while the termites ate the houses. The most destructive was the large saúvas, "the plague of Brazil." He described with masochistic admiration their destructive industriousness.

Cardim and Sousa wrote during the term in office of Governor Manuel Telles Barreto, who died in 1587. Cardim's letter quoted above was signed in Bahia on October 16, 1585. His next known letter was written May 1, 1590. It is brief but informative. Communications had been difficult because "the sea was infested with the French and the English." In Bahia, "there are so many rumors going round about the English and the French who were swarming at sea" that ships feared to sail. When the Padre Visitador and his companions were enroute home, his ship was captured off Portugal in September 1589. The French sailors subjected them to gross mistreatment and then put them into a small boat about eighty leagues off the coast of Spain. They were fortunate that "God gave them a good wind," making the Cantabrian coast in two days and a half, thence across Spain to Portugal.

The turn of events in Europe thus influenced the life of Brazil greatly. Its political administration continued Portuguese, but its economic life was increasingly affected by the English and Dutch, particularly the Dutch. The threat of French conquest also became greater. It seems a logical inference, even if one not susceptible to documentary proof, that Brazil's economic opportunities were broadened as result of the increased involvement of England and Holland in overseas territories. Meanwhile, much of the life of Brazil proceeded along its own course almost as if the major political developments in Europe were merely distant events of only passing interest.

8

INDIANS, INTERNAL EXPANSION, AND THE INQUISITION

n the death of Governor-General Barreto in 1587, Francisco Giraldes was appointed his successor. Giraldes, donatary of Ilhéus, descended from an Italian merchant family living in Portugal. An interim government took power pending his arrival. With Giraldes came a new official, the sargento-mor, who was in charge of fortifications and artillery. It is noteworthy that this fleet sailed in the midst of the final preparation of the huge Armada sent against England.

The events that overtook the ship on which Giraldes sailed are likewise noteworthy, although not unusual. For forty days it drifted about haphazardly (a matroca) between Madeira and the Guinea coast, unable to reach the Equator. The ship was then pushed by winds to the West Indies, the usual plight of ships that could not catch the winds to Brazil. After a year the ship made it back to Portugal without ever having landed anywhere in America, arriving at the same time as the India fleet with which it had originally sailed was returning from the East.

Giraldes died before trying again. One result of the Giraldes fiasco was that the interim government ruled for four years, longer than many of the governors. During this period the crown farmed out the brazilwood contract for 13,600 milreis a year, a sum it was not always able to collect.

The most significant act of the interim government was the conquest of Sergipe in 1589. Although lying between Pernambuco and Bahia, the two most important captaincies, the area had defied settlement. Since the São Francisco River flowed through its rich forests and fertile land, Sergipe was highly valued by the Portuguese. The Indians still held it, however. After the disaster that had been suffered by the Portuguese in Rio Real, the Indians were even less tractable.

The need to clear the route overland was urgent given the strong French presence, the highly risky sea route, and the monsoons that could cause months of delay. The Portuguese considered the situation intolerable. They want to act, but a new law of August 22, 1587, had forbidden attacks on the Indians. The interim government, nevertheless, obtained permission to make a "just" war. Christóvão de Barros, assuming the active leadership, began a campaign against Chief Baepeba and an estimated 20,000 Indians in late 1589. The number of Indians, even if the estimate was highly exaggerated (as seems probable), greatly outnumbered the Portuguese and their allies. The Jesuits sent 400 of their own Indians on the campaign.

The Portuguese won two decisive victories on December 23, and January 1, 1590. They killed by their count, 1,600 and captured 4,000, who were distributed as slaves. An unknown number fled to the interior. A town and a fort, São Christóvão, were established on the Sergipe River. Some of the heroes of the day were made "cavaleiros" as was the custom on the battlefields of Morocco, where Barros himself had won his honors.

Barros also distributed sesmarias, and what sesmarias! He gave his son António Cardoso de Barros "all the lands from the Sergipe river to the Rio São Francisco." Sergipe del Rey, as they named the new captaincy, was suitable for pasturage, and cattle and other livestock were rapidly introduced. Later the *Livro da Razão do Estado* recorded: "This captaincy has more than two hundred white settlers (moradores) whose herds are separated from one another; and they are so avaricious for land that there are settlers who have thirty leagues of sesmaria in different areas." António Cardoso de Barros held as his sesmaria the land along the coast between the Sergipe River to the São Francisco River and inland more than eight leagues (approximately 24 miles). Garcia d'Ávila extended his already large holdings.

Soon Sergipe supplied oxen for the engenhos in Bahia and even in Pernambuco. The wars against the Indians continued in the area north of the São Francisco River, now Alagoas, belonging then to the captaincy of Pernambuco. The usual grants of sesmarias followed the conquest: For example, Diogo de Mello received five leagues along the sea and seven inland, equivalent to about thirty-five square miles, lying along both sides of the São Miguel River.

The land route from Bahia to Pernambuco was now open and fairly safe. The French lost their footholds on the Sergipe and Real rivers, where they had traded with the Indians and engaged in dyewood logging.

The early 1590s witnessed a number of developments important to Brazilian life: a new governor arrived; new efforts were made to penetrate the interior to find mines; more foreign attacks kept the coastal dwellers alarmed; trade with other nations increased; slave imports from Africa increased; Indians continued to be a menace in some regions and were enslaved when the occasion arose; the Inquisition came to Brazil for the first time; and a Conselho da Fazenda was organized in Portugal with authority over the governments of Brazil and other overseas territories.

Governor Francisco de Sousa arrived in June 1591 and ruled until 1602. During his long and generally popular term, he won the nickname "das manhas," the cunning, for his ability to accomplish his goals.

Portugal undertook a limited reorganization of its colonial structure. The growth of an empire encompassing the world had not been accompanied by a special home organization similar to Spain's Casa de Contratación (1503) or the Consejo de Indias (1524). Philip II created a Conselho da Fazenda in November 1591 with authority over both home and colonial matters. It differed from the Spanish system because the special colonial offices were entirely separate from the home government; for example, the Council of Indies was distinct from the Council of Castile and other similar councils that ruled Spanish realms. The new Conselho da Fazenda may be viewed as one of the few visible influences that the rule of Spanish kings in Portugal had on Brazil. The new council absorbed functions previously held by different officials, such as vedores of Portugal itself, India, and Africa.

The Vedor da Fazenda with the aid of four councilors presided over four divisions. The first was Portugal, and the second included India, Mina, Guinea, Brazil, São Tomé, and Cabo Verde. Others dealt with Military Orders, the Atlantic islands, Morocco, litigation, and the like. All revenues thereafter went through the Conselho. This simplified matters somewhat but still did not prevent conflicts of jurisdiction. It failed to provide Brazil with a single home office to look toward for solutions to its problems. Later reorganizations attempted to redefine responsibilities, but Portugal never achieved centralization in dealing with overseas governments.

In the same fleet with the governor came Gabriel Soares de Sousa, who had had—and continued to have—a picturesque career. From his brother, who had died in the interior while searching for mines, he inherited maps that showed the way to hidden deposits. In 1584 he went to the royal court to petition the Portuguese council of Philip II for a license to search for the mines. He requested suitable rewards for anything he found. His long stay in Spain gave him time to prepare the detailed and informative report cited above, later called the *Tratado Descriptivo do Brasil em 1587*.

He received the title "Capitão Mor e Governador da Conquista e Descobrimento do Rio de São Francisco" and extensive political and economic powers. He was granted the right to reward his principal assistants (some his own kinsmen) with membership in the Order of Christ, plus other honors. He created a climate of great expectation among his followers and obviously within the court, since he was granted such extensive powers. He sailed from Lisbon on April 7, 1591, with 360 men, including four Carmelites.

Gabriel Soares de Sousa's activities in this respect helped subsequent adventurers in reaching the headwaters of the São Francisco

River. At that time, and much later, it was thought to flow directly from the west and to be the source of gold, silver, and gems. The source was supposedly Peru. Much later it was discovered that, in fact, the river flowed from the south, deep in the state of Minas Gerais, for a thousand miles before turning sharply southeast about three hundred miles from the coast. Time, a century of time, proved correct the belief that precious metals and a great variety of gems, including diamonds, were hidden in its tributaries and adjoining hills.

Sousa made a great contribution to the exploration of the interior of Brazil, but he failed to profit from his dreams. His ship was wrecked in June at the mouth of the Vasa Barris River, just north of the Sergipe, where the Portuguese had defeated the French and Indians the year before. Thanks to this recent conquest, most of the members of his expedition were saved and reached Salvador, Bahia.

The newly arrived governor, Francisco de Sousa, carried out with enthusiasm the order from the king to assist this expedition, for he too was a fervent believer in the mines. Reorganized after the wreck, the expedition followed the Paraguaçú River leading out of the Recôncavo and reached the caatinga, a dry cactus-covered country that characterizes a large part of Brazil's northeast area. His orders were drawn up by a government that had not the slightest concept of the true nature of the land. He was directed to form settlements every fifty leagues. His first settlement was made near the João Amaro of today. Progress was slow and tough. He lost men to intermittent fever, and his animals fell prey to the bite of bats, to snakes, and hungry jaguars. He struggled forward and had to fight off unconquered Indians

Fifty leagues further into the interior, after trying to cross the mountains, Gabriel Soares de Sousa died. The party retreated to Bahia. Governor Francisco de Sousa, "The Cunning," took all the records and maps. Perhaps at this time he conceived the plan later attempted near the end of his governorship—to find the mines himself. We shall later meet him as Gabriel Soares's successor and with even greater privileges.

Upon his death Gabriel Soares was granted one wish that few men get. His will, written in 1584, requested burial in the São Bento Convent, and he wrote his own epitaph. It may be seen to this day on the stone in the floor: AQUÍ JAZ UM PECADOR - Here Lies a Sinner.

Brazil's problems with foreign raiders persisted. Another English corsair (the Spaniards and Portuguese say pirate) raided Brazil in 1591. Bound for the Pacific Ocean to seek the treasure fleets, as Drake had done, Thomas Cavendish stopped over in Santos on Christmas Day. He remained for two months, gathering everything of value and burning some engenhos. Sailing on, he failed to make the Straits of Magellan and turned back north. His second attack on Santos failed, as did his raid on Espírito Santo. Cavendish turned his fleet toward England and died before reaching home.

Anthony Knivet, who was with Cavendish, was captured and lived some years in Brazil, writing a good account of his experiences. The amount of gold mined in Santos impressed him. His description of the life of Indians hunters reveals the roughness and horrors of that occupation. Attacks such as those of Cavendish plus the fear of other raids led Governor Francisco de Sousa to devote much attention to rebuilding old fortifications and constructing new ones to protect the main port cities.

In the hope of gaining better protection, the government attempted to correct fiscal abuses and to prevent fraud, hoping to use the additional funds for defense. Desembargador Baltazar Ferraz had received orders in February 1591, before the arrival of Governor Francisco de Sousa, to tour the ports and examine the records for the previous fifteen years. In October 1592 a Consulado was created and financed with an increase of 3% in the import and export duties on goods in the trade with Portugal. The objective was to provide an armada of twelve warships to convoy commerce. The tax was collected, but the fleet was never created. Baltazar Ferraz never made an inspection of Brazilian port records, nor is there any indication that Governor Francisco de Sousa, after his arrival in June 1591, ordered him to do so.

Ships from Hamburg sailed directly to Brazil as early as 1587.

Eleven ships sailed from Hamburg to Brazil in 1590, and nineteen between 1590 and 1602. If these figures are not rigorously exact, they are more likely too low than too high. The usual practice was for the Hanseatic merchants to form secret partnerships with Portuguese merchants in order to avoid the law. The advantage of such secret partnerships to the Portuguese was their access to the greater cargo capacity of ships known as "urcas," which were used by northern merchants.

The Portuguese government regarded this practice as dangerous because foreigners could gather information about Brazil. The fear was justified. Foreigners did learn more about the geography and other matters that enabled them to encroach on the Portuguese monopoly. Since the Portuguese were Roman Catholics, they also feared the Germans, Dutch and English because many were Protestants. The fear of the "New Christians," the Jews who had converted to Christianity either voluntarily or through force, constantly haunted the Portuguese. Most of these Jews lived in Portugal, or in Holland where many had fled. Some reconverted to Judaism after reaching the freedom of Holland.

The defeat of the Armada in 1588 had intensified existing fears because England and Holland became more aggressive. The port cities in France which sent ships to Brazil were also heavily Protestant, and consequently every French seaman was suspect. All such ships were labeled "pirates," though the exact division between pirates and privateers was difficult to draw.

Philip II delayed in taking measures to stop the close trade relations of Portugal and Brazil with the Dutch and the other northern areas. By 1590, however, it was clear that the rebellious Dutch considered themselves the enemies of Spain everywhere in the world. The Dutch were learning more about the trade of the East as well as Brazil. Meanwhile, the burgeoning Dutch merchants no longer remained content to confine their trade to legal Portuguese channels.

The second law prohibiting foreign ships in Brazil was enacted February 9, 1591. It prohibited foreign ships, except those with a special license, from going to Portugal and its dominations, especially

Brazil. The new legislation attempted to reinforce the law of 1571 that had originally forbidden ships to freight directly to Brazil and other overseas provinces.

In prior decades the Dutch had participated in financing engenhos in Brazil, usually through Portuguese merchants. Many were said to be New Christians from Viana do Castelo and Oporto. In 1594 there were only three or four sugar refineries in Holland. By 1621, however, the number had increased to 29, of which 25 were located in Amsterdam.

In 1594 Philip II permitted Dutch "kulks and other hollander shippes" to sail to Brazil annually in two fleets of twenty ships of 200 tons and up. This act notwithstanding, the king later ordered the seizure of Dutch ships in Portugal and Spain.

The success of the Dutch in the East was demonstrated in 1597, when Cornelius Houtman returned to Holland from a voyage to the Orient with three of the four vessels taken on the outward sailing. Nevertheless, the long tradition of Dutch-Portuguese trade was not entirely broken. Brazil continued to see Dutch ships.

A special Inquisitional Court arrived in Bahia in June 1591 in the same fleet with Governor Francisco de Sousa. Its mission was to search out those "New Christians" and Old Christians guilty of certain sins considered especially evil but who had escaped the normal routine of confession and penance.

The forced conversion of the Jews and Moslems in Portugal had created a problem different from the one in Spain, although it had the same aim, political and religious unity. After the general pogrom of 1391 in Spain, there had appeared a phenomenon unique in the history of the Jews—a tendency to convert to Christianity. The new converts (converso) made their way into government service, business, and even the church. The educational tradition long existing among the Jews and Moslems was valuable to monarchs engaged in creating a new type of state, a state less dependent on the nobility, a class not generally known for higher education and not generally inclined toward bureaucratic paperwork. Men with more education were needed.

The new converts met this requirement, and the new state met their desire for upward mobility. It was no secret that many government employees, members of the professional classes in general, priests, monks, and nuns were "New Christians." There was prejudice against them but they remained largely unmolested until 1478.

The tendency to overlook signs of Judaism among New Christians was reversed when the Inquisition began operation in Spain in 1478. This special court was specifically brought into existence to ferret out deviations from orthodoxy. Its influence was initially confined to various parts of Spain and to Spanish overseas territories; eventually it affected Portugal.

Portugal had never experienced the kind of pogrom that occurred in Spain in 1391. Although Jews and Moslems were not considered equal to Christians, they had the protection of the laws, even when discrimination existed. They had the protection of the kings. A certain number of Spanish Jewish conversos, also known as marranos, migrated to Portugal, but the total number is uncertain. Records have survived of only those few who became well known because of their prominence or, at times, their troubles.

The prevailing situation in Portugal changed after Spain expelled its Jews in 1492. A decree was signed March 31, shortly after the fall of Granada. The Jews living in Granada were granted four months to convert to Christianity or leave Spain. Some converted, but most fled, leaving behind all they possessed that was not portable; sometimes these goods were stolen from them. The number of deported Jews is unknown, but it is variously estimated by different historians at between 100,000 and 500,000.

Some Jews went to North Africa where Muslims attacked and killed many of them. Some survivors returned to Spain to accept Christian baptism. Others went to Italy, where some died of starvation in Genoa and others succumbed to the plague in Naples.

Portugal, with contiguous borders, offered a quicker refuge for Spanish Jews. João II took the pragmatic view; he collected a head tax of eight cruzados from those allowed into Portugal. They could enter only at certain designated frontier points. He promised transportation for them out of Portugal at the cost of passage within a period of eight months, the maximum time they were allowed to remain in Portugal.

João demonstrated his pragmatic views in several ways. He permitted six hundred of the richer families to pay 60,000 cruzados for the right to remain permanently. Then he distributed these families around Portugal to designated cities. Some skilled workmen also received the permanent right of residence, and paid only half the normal entrance tax. On royal orders, thirty families were sent to Oporto and given houses near a synagogue.

The king's treatment of the Jews was inconsistent; benevolence was mixed with brutality. Those who came over the border clandestinely were punished when caught. If they escaped detection, they lived in constant fear of discovery.

Although no exact count of the number of Jews entering Portugal has ever been made—nor can be from existing records—guesses have been plentiful. The nineteenth-century Portuguese historian Alexandre Herculano, anti-clerical and pro-semitic, guessed that 260,000 of an estimated 800,000 expelled from Spain entered Portugal. His numbers are regarded as far too high by modern historians. Damião de Góis, a sixteenth-century historian, said 20,000 families. If we assume five to a family, it would mean 100,000 individuals. Barnaldez, a contemporary chronicler, estimated 93,000. Fortunato de Almeida, a twentieth-century pro-clerical historian, regarded even the latter figure as greatly exaggerated, since it would have been about 10% of the total population of Portugal in the late fifteenth century.

When João II died in October 1595, Manuel I ascended the throne (1495–1521) and freed the enslaved Spanish Jews. The Christian "owners" of enslaved Jews and Muslims resented the loss of their slaves, some of whom had been bought and others given to them by João II. But King Manuel's tolerant policy abruptly ended. He proposed marriage to Isabella, daughter of Ferdinand and Isabella of Spain, but she refused to enter Portugal until the Jews were expelled. On December 5, 1496, Manuel decreed that all the freed Muslims and Jews should be expelled within ten months, or by October 1497.

Some of his counselors pointed out that Jews were permitted to live in the Papal States. He insisted, nevertheless, on conversion or expulsion.

The inhumanity of the following months has been stressed by Christian writers. The Muslims received less harsh treatment because of the fear of the Muslim states in Africa, or at least some observers so interpreted the king's policy. The Jews received orders to go to designated ports in Portugal, but no ships awaited them. Later, Lisbon was specified as the only port of embarkation; but again no ships were provided. They thus faced death or conversion. If they converted, they were promised that no close inquiry would be made into their religious practices for twenty years. The date was later extended to 1534, but the "New Christians" lived in a precarious situation. Since there was no system of instruction in the Christian religion and no investigations, most, if not all, supposedly remained steadfast in their Jewish beliefs.

Opportunities in Portugal's overseas dominions gave relief to some New Christians. Portugal needed people in the East, Africa, and Brazil. The crown's policies were, however, inconsistent. While some suffered discrimination and persecution, others received economic privileges that increased their wealth and social standing and enabled them to marry into Old Christian families. A mix of peoples (neither race" nor "religion" can properly be used) came into being that defied any accurate definition; but the law called them "New Christian" however little the Jewish part of their ancestry.

Some were exiled to Brazil. Many Brazilian historians speak freely of the very large number of New Christians in the settlement of Bahia and Pernambuco, as well as other captaincies. But with the exception of a few prominent people "alleged" to be New Christians, concrete data is lacking. Brazil was a new land with new opportunities for the intelligent and industrious, and New Christians found it easier to overcome discrimination in Brazil than in Portugal. A portion eventually made their way into the La Plata region, and from there into Peru. Some remained in Brazil and became so thoroughly merged into the population that nobody can say for certain who they were.

It was the uncertainty about the degree of Christian in the New Christians that angered and often baffled the Inquisition. Many who were known as New Christians were half, or a fourth, or less.

The Inquisition never established a permanent court in Brazil. The Bishop of Bahia, endowed with inquisitorial powers, was assisted by "familiares" whose Old Christian lineage was unchallenged. They were invested with the powers to search out and denounce sin and heresy or the repudiation of Catholicism in any way. Judaizers—even more than Protestants—were considered the greatest danger to society.

By 1591 the feeling against the New Christians and Protestants had risen nearly to an exploding point because the Dutch had proved unconquerable and because many merchants in Holland were formerly Portuguese New Christians. The Dutch were a danger to Portuguese control of Brazil. The time had come, in the eyes of the Inquisition, guardian of the morals and doctrinal purity of the Portuguese, to inquire into the extent of the threat to Catholic Christianity and Christian morals in Brazil. The appointed Inquisitor, Heitor Furtado de Mendonça, and his two assistants came out in the ship with new Governor Francisco de Sousa, landing in Bahia on June 9, 1591.

The historiography of the New Christians—what historians have written about them—has become an inseparable part of their history. The older historians, João Lúcio de Azevedo and others of his era, believed that crypto-Judaism was a fact. They explained the Inquisition as a logical, legal, and justified moral way of dealing with this phenomenon and wholly within the prevailing norms of Iberian society. The inquisitorial procedures, such as secret denunciations, the use of torture to induce confessions, elaborate and thorough questioning of witnesses as well as the accused while they suffered in jail for long periods before being indicted formally of anything (and sometimes never formally brought to trial) were, this school of historians alleged, the normal procedure in the civil courts of the period.

But later historians have pointed out that the civil courts, cruel as they were in comparison with present-day procedures, gave the accused much more protection than was given by the Inquisition. The fact that Jews, or their ancestors, had been forcibly baptized but never properly instructed in Catholicism did not make them less subject to the laws of the Inquisition. The Brazilian New Christian, sometimes a century removed from the forced conversion of 1497, and sometimes, if not usually, with only a half, one quarter, or less Jewish ancestry, were to be examined in 1591 for signs of what the Inquisition defined as Jewish practices.

Other interpretations of the Inquisition see different reasons for searching out the New Christians. Jewish students of the subject such as Kayserling, Baer, and Roth and non-Jews such as Baião, Amador de los Rios, and Mendes dos Remédios deny the moral value of forced conversion, but they believe most of the New Christians were in fact Judaizers, who secretly and heroically resisted Christian persecution for centuries.

New views on this matter have recently been presented by historians Saraiva and Netanyahu. António José Saraiva, in *A Inquisição Portuguesa*, argued that most of the New Christians were true Christians and that the concept of crypto-Jews was created by the Inquisition as an excuse to attack a segment of an economic class, the New Christian bourgeoisie. Saraiva saw religion as merely a pretext for declaring war on a social class.

Netanyahu, in *The Marranos of Spain*, offered much the same view. He stated that the objective of the Inquisition was "not to eradicate a Jewish heresy from the midst of Marrano group, but to eradicate the Marranos from the midst of the Spanish people." Portugal, with a much larger percentage of New Christians than Spain, was in a different position. This school of thought has maintained that the New Christians were in the process of assimilation. A large number of mixed marriages had occurred until the Inquisition was introduced into Spain and later Portugal. Thus, in this view, the Inquisition created Marronism by closing the door of Christianity forever to converted Jews. Therefore a distinct class, which did not have the guidance of its own religious leaders, the rabbis, was also shut off from the guidance of the Christian priests.

The New Christian became an undigested element in a society that admitted only unity in religion and government. In a situation where not even the slightest element of non-conformity was allowed, the briefest conversations about practices alleged to be "Jewish," even by those who no longer knew the religious origins of such practices, became, to the Inquisitors, a proper subject of inquiry. The Inquisition could function only if there were "guilty" persons to ferret out.

In 1591 the Inquisition arrived in Brazil to look for Judaizers and other types of sinners. It seems doubtful that a special court of the Inquisition would have been formed if the "Jewish problem" had not been the main objective of the inquiry. To pinpoint the "guilty," the Inquisition relied on confessions, denunciations, and witnesses.

The Inquisition began functioning in Bahia on July 28, 1591, setting a period of 30 days for all living within a league of Salvador to come forward and confess their sins or denounce others. In order to assist the memory of the people, it published a *Carta Manitória* that listed the sins to be confessed or denounced, including witchcraft, immoral sex acts, blasphemy, and numerous other sins, as well as Protestantism and Judaizing. The text of the Carta distributed in Brazil has not been found, but it can be presumed to be substantially the same as that used in Portugal.

In order to assist the people in the detection of Judaism, the Carta contained a special list of things that constituted Judaism. Among other things, it listed: observation of Saturday as a Holy Day and refraining from work; ritual killing of animals and chickens; testing the blade of a knife on the fingernail; covering the earth with blood; refusing to eat pork, hares, and other foods forbidden by dietary laws; observation of Jewish holidays; saying Jewish prayers; turning toward a wall and nodding the head while praying; use of the Teffelin; omission of the words Gloria Patri e Filio et Spiritu Santo when ending prayers; use of Jewish customs in burial; Jewish methods of blessing children without making the sign of the cross; circumcision; and a long, detailed list of the signs of Judaization, such as cleaning the house on Friday, lighting candles, changing to clean clothing and preparing food before sundown Friday, and other behavior deemed Jewish.

The Inquisition's *Carta Manitoria* spread fear throughout the population. Who had not committed some of the listed sins, not merely of Judaization but especially of sex? Should they confess and hope for mercy? If not, would they not be denounced? Who had not blasphemed? What normal single man had not engaged in intercourse with single women? Was that a sin? The Inquisition said yes. There were still other questions about sexual sins that might catch anyone, male or female.

Several families of New Christians were uncovered. Heitor Antunes and his wife Ana Reis had come over with Governor Mem de Sá in 1557. Heitor had prospered and had a family of four girls and three boys. He died, but his wife and children lived on. His granddaughter Ana Alcoforado, half New Christian, confessed to having emptied the water pitcher after the death of a slave. The Inquisition informed her that this act showed that she was a Judaizer and sent her to Lisbon for trial. She remained in prison from August 1601 to January 1605, when she was amnestied by papal action. In all, 155 were freed in 1605 after years of imprisonment.

Many of the accused were almost certainly telling the truth when they said they had not known their acts were Jewish until the *Carta Manitória* so informed them. Maria Lopes confessed that before baking a lamb or a pig she customarily took a certain gland from the back. She also confessed to having sent for a fresh jar of water after the death of her son, who was a priest. Ana Reis, now 80 years old, confessed to a number of allegedly Jewish practices, but said that she had learned them from her Old Christian grandmother and that she had always believed in Jesus. The Inquisition sent her to Lisbon in 1593 and she died in prison. They burned her body.

A secret synagogue supposedly existed in Matoim, Bahia, and rumors of denunciations kept the colony in a state of panic. In Matoim, it was revealed, there were many cases of marriage between New Christians and Old Christians. Investigators heard that another synagogue allegedly existed in the house of António Tomás, who had returned to Oporto, Portugal. João Nunes was accused of keeping a crucifix in his toilet; others were said to whip crucifixes. Nunes appeared before the Inquisition elegantly dressed and accompanied by a number of slaves. He was accused of taking another man's wife and using his influence to have the man jailed and also of suborning Jesuits and judges. Sent to Portugal for trial, he was acquitted and returned to Brazil.

In 1593 the Inquisition moved on to Pernambuco, where it functioned until 1595. A synagogue was rumored to exist in Camaragibe. The same Carta was circulated, and the same confessions and denunciations were heard. Diogo Dias Fernandes and his wife Branca Dias were the first Marranos identified by name. An alleged synagogue on the estate of Bento Dias Santiago was said to be a center for the reunion of Judaizers. Diogo Dias Fernandes and his wife Branca, as well as three of their daughters, were all dead by 1593. The Inquisition seized another daughter, the crippled Beatriz Fernandes, and sent her to Lisbon. In an Auto-da-Fé held on January 31, 1599, she was sentenced to perpetual prison.

Baltasar da Fonseca and his family were accused of not believing in the saints. Years later, after Pernambuco fell to the Dutch (1530–54), a man with this name openly accepted Judaism, which was permitted in Dutch-held Brazil. Ambrósio Fernandes Brandão, who became the owner of three engenhos, was accused of Judaization but was never brought before the Inquisition. He is now identified as the author of *Diálogo das Grandezas do Brasil*. Bento Teixeira, identified as the author of the poem "Prosopopeia," was seized in 1595, sent to Lisbon, and sentenced to prison. He was allowed to live outside the walls, through the influence of Jorge de Albuquerque Coelho, until his death in 1600.

The Inquisitor Furtado de Mendonça returned to Portugal in late 1595, and the inquisitorial function reverted to the Bishop of Bahia. Other cases came before him. A second visitation of the Inquisition arrived in Brazil in 1618 and a third in 1646.

The results of the Inquisition in Bahia and Pernambuco, if discovering and extirpating Judaizers was its main objective, were not great. Considering the large numbers of New Christians who supposedly came to Brazil, the number of people accused was small, and the evidence against them was weak. The rumors about Jews seems to have exceeded their numbers. If, as Saraiva and Netanyahu have held, the aim was to eliminate the Marranos as a class, the Inquisition failed in Brazil. Few were discovered and most were not conspicuous by their wealth or influence.

French and English ships continued to appear along the Brazilian coast during the years the Inquisition was sitting in Bahia and Pernambuco. They contributed to the alarm about heretics and pirates, often considered to be identical. In 1594, as previously mentioned, the French Commander Jacques Riffault appeared on the northeastern coast with three ships. He lost two ships in the treacherous entrance to the Maranhão, which was not yet colonized. Riffault left some of his men in Maranhão, an event of great importance since later the French attempted to establish a settlement in the area in 1613.

In 1595 two French ships, with smallpox aboard, put in at Bahia. The same year, a French commander, Pain de Mil (various spellings), attempted to take Sergipe but failed. He was taken prisoner with his crew of 116 men. Transferred to Salvador, Bahia, they were apparently all hanged.

Also in 1595, James Lancaster, allied with the French under Venner, arrived in Recife at the end of March. The population fled to Olinda about three miles north, and the English and French forces began the sack of Recife. They captured the *Nau da India* and its cargo, and needing more ships for the booty of the sacking, freighted three Dutch ships that were in the harbor. While Lancaster was in Recife, Captain Jean Lenoir of Dieppe sailed in. Lenoir had aided Lancaster the year before and was rewarded with part of the spoils. After 31 days in the area, that included some severe fighting, they sailed away in either eleven or fifteen ships—the various accounts are not clear. All but one of them reached England or France. Still another fleet of thirteen French vessels was repulsed in Ilhéus in 1597 and later the same year or early 1598 in Cabedello, Paraíba.

Meanwhile, the Inquisition was sitting in Olinda. While the English and French were along the coast, some citizens who had been appointed temporary captains aboard foreign ships were closely questioned about whether they had attended Protestant services or listened to Protestant doctrines. All denied contamination.

The persistent presence of the French along the coast beyond Paraíba do Norte reminded the Portuguese constantly of the danger of a permanent foreign occupation. The French and their Indian allies, although repelled in Paraíba in 1597, remained in the region of Rio Grande do Norte. They represented an ever-present danger. Consequently, in 1597 the Portuguese made another effort to occupy the coast beyond Paraíba. They organized a combined overland/sea force, commanded by Capitão-mor Manuel Mascarenhas Homem, the resident representative of the donatary of Pernambuco, and assisted by Capitão-mor Feliciano Coelho Paraiba. Two experienced campaigners against the Indians, Alexandre de Moura and Jerónimo de Albuquerque (half Indian), accompanied the expedition.

They moved out late in 1597 and soon met an enemy more deadly than the French and Indian forces—an epidemic of smallpox. Unfortunately for all, but fortunately for the Portuguese forces, the French and Indians also suffered the same epidemic. Persisting in spite of the epidemic, the Portuguese and their Indian allies reached the Potengi River at the turn of the year 1598 and established a town named Natal (Christmas) and a fort, Reis Magos (Three Kings).

Albuquerque remained in charge, aided by the Potiguares, who had become friends again, and Jesuit Father Francisco Pinto. Rio Grande do Norte became a royal captaincy in 1599. This same year a Dutch fleet under Olivier van Noort attempted a landing in Rio de Janeiro but failed. Another Dutch fleet of seven vessels commanded by captains Hartman and Broer fared better. They remained 55 days in the Recôncavo of Bahia wreaking havoc and taking a rich booty.

The century closed with Brazil under frequent attack from foreigners, and the possession of the northeast coast remained in dispute. Possession of the great interior west and south of São Paulo was also disputed by Spaniards and Portuguese.

9

EARLY BANDEIRAS
AND THE NORTHEAST COAST

Following the settlement of the areas around Piratininga and
São Paulo, the Portuguese looked eagerly west and south,
curious to know what was there. Previously Father Nóbrega
had been restrained by Tomé de Sousa from making advances toward
the interior. The advances came, in due course, in the expeditions
known as bandeiras. Bandeiras were groups or companies of men who
joined under a commander and a flag (a bandeira) to push into the
sertão.

Their chief motives were to find precious metals and capture Indians. Some were official and organized by governors; others were
private, organized by individuals. Some degree of government support, or compliance, was usually necessary for the private bandeiras.
They were generally different from the expeditions, usually known as
entradas, going out from Bahia and other northern captaincies; the
latter were more often, but not invariably, initiated by the governors.
In essence they had the same objectives.

These early Portuguese movements west and southwest from São
Paulo brought them into contact with Spanish colonists who had
preceded them. The Spaniards first moved into Paraguay in 1537.
From Paraguay they began moving up the Paraguay and Paraná rivers
and their confluents, where in 1554 they made a small settlement at
Ontiveros on a site above the Sete Quedas Falls on the Paraná River.

207

This settlement, renamed Ciudad Real del Guaíra, was moved about three leagues north in 1557 to the confluence of the Paraná and Piquirí rivers. Still another settlement called Vila Rica del Espíritu Santo was founded in 1576 where the Ivaí and Corumbatí rivers meet. The towns lying west of the city of São Paulo formed the basis of the future Spanish province of Guaíra.

In 1588 the Spanish Jesuits from Asunción settled in the Guaíra region with the aim of grouping the Indians into aldeias. Thirteen missions were founded, with boundaries reaching east to the Tibagi River, north to the Paranapanema, west to the Paraná, and south to the Iguaçú. The Jesuits and the Spanish settlers competed for the Indians; the settlers wanted to put them under encomienda. The Jesuits won against the Spaniards, but their missions later fell victim to the attacks of the bandeirantes.

Though Governor Tomé de Sousa had forbidden trade with the Spaniards, it continued nevertheless. The records do not show how frequently this prohibition was violated, but the first recorded dates are only a few years later. It is clear that the Paulistas never took seriously laws designed to keep them away from the riches of the interior. The bandeirantes were sons and grandsons of João Ramalho and other Portuguese who, like him, had large families of mixed-blood children—the so-called mamelucos.

The Paulistas had not prospered and become rich like many of the senhores de engenho along the coast. The fertile lands, forests, and grasslands eventually yielded enormous wealth, but in the late sixteenth and seventeenth centuries there was no large market for their produce. The steep escarpment that separated São Paulo from the coast stymied the development of profitable products. The Paulistas had enough to eat, but lived a simple life. Yet they aspired to more; therefore they sought to become traders in the only line of merchandise the richer colonists were willing to buy from them—Indian slaves.

Everybody wanted to get into Indian-catching. "The city councillors of 1572 . . . were on the road to the forests and left their offices," according to a contemporary document quoted by Afonso d'E. Taunay in his history of the bandeirantes.

Except three or four principal holidays, few people are in the town, but always either on their estates or in the forests and plains hunting for Indians, which is the way they spend their lives . . . All their lives, from the time they leave school to their old age is nothing but going out to bring in Indians and sell them. With this they dress in silk shirts, drink wine and buy everything they have. In the whole town of São Paulo there are not more than one or two who do not go out to capture Indians, or send their sons out, or other members of their family, as if they were going to mines of gold and silver including even the judges and clergy of the town.

São Paulo in 1583 was a town of 120 white families. We may count this roughly as 600 people. By the end of the century it had 3,500 "almas" or souls, presuming this figure meant only whites. It was still poor, and at a much later date it boasted only one conventional-style bed, which was requisitioned by the city fathers on one occasion when an ouvidor visited. The citizens usually slept in "Carijó Indian hammocks."

The common language of the people was Tupi. Manioc meal was the basic food. The Indians already "civilized" formed the bulk of the forces hunting down other Indians, who were often members of the same linguistic tribes. The language spoken by the Indians was unimportant to their enslavers.

The groups of hunters who went out were organized into bandeiras. Bandeira was a military term dating back to at least the early sixteenth century. Having no set size, some bandeiras in the seventeenth century were composed of hundreds of men. It achieved a legal existence among the Paulistas when the câmara of São Paulo in 1581 prescribed a form of organization. A meirinho and a clerk were a prerequisite for its activities. The aim was to prevent disorder and the "devastation" of the captives that had apparently characterized the previous bandeiras.

The first organized bandeira, according to some scholars, was by the capitão-mor of São Vicente, Jerónimo Leitão, in 1585. Choosing an exact date to mark the beginning of "bandeiras" is difficult however, since under whatever name, the Paulistas had been hunters of men—and remained so after this date.

Sebastião Marinho set out in 1590 for the region of the Tocantíns and Goiás. These regions lie far to the north of São Paulo. Governor Salvador Correia de Sá had campaigned frequently to clear the Indians from the Rio de Janeiro to São Paulo route, but they were not precisely bandeiras. None of his campaigns nor others mounted more than a century later eliminated the Indians as obstacles to Portuguese expansion.

In the campaign of 1590, the son of Salvador, Martim de Sá, took along Anthony Knivet, an Englishman who had been captured when Cavendish raided Santos. His memoirs reveal the tough and brutal life of the hunters of Indians. In 1594, Captain Jorge Correia of São Vicente led an expedition southward toward the Carijós and Tupinães, groups which habitually harried communications between the Spanish settlements and the coast of Santa Catarina. A bandeira in 1595 may have been a continuation of the Correia expedition.

Sometimes the Indians turned the tables on their assailants. In 1596 they attacked São Paulo and it was repelled only with assistance from Santos. More important was a bandeira, apparently also in 1596, known as the "War of the Paraíba River" and led by João Pereira de Sousa Botafogo. The Paraíba runs between the Serra do Mar and the Serra da Mantiqueira. Not all the participants returned until 1600, the year Governor Francisco de Sousa, who had requested appointment as governor of the south and the mines, sent out his first expedition to search for precious metals.

With the Indians largely cleared out of the Paraíba do Sul River, it became the preferred route to the interior. Two problems remained however: the river was swift-flowing and little suited to transportation and the passes over the Serra da Mantiqueira were sharp and precipitous. The Paraíba flows east and slightly north from São Paulo and empties into the Atlantic north of Cabo Frio. One of the passes known as the Garganta do Embaú led northward toward the upper confluents of the São Francisco River, where gold was eventually discovered. Another route through Moji Mirím led to Goiás, and still another via Atibaia and Bragança to southern Minas Gerais. The crossing where the Tieté River broke through the Mantiqueira Mountains became the route to the Paraná River and onward to Mato Grosso and other areas where Spain had made its settlements.

In 1601, Andre Leão, on an expedition authorized by Governor Francisco de Sousa, followed the Tieté River and crossed the Mantiqueira Mountains to the headwaters of the São Francisco River. He found no mines. In 1602, Nicolau Barreto, who was also authorized by the governor to prospect for metals, descended the Tieté and Paraná Rivers as far Guairá, or, according to some accounts, he followed the route of the São Francisco. Still others say that he went to Peru, but this claim is unlikely. He returned in two years without having discovered the precious metals he sought. When the captured Indians were sold in São Paulo two years later, following custom, a third were reserved for the crown.

The Spaniards in Paraguay protested to the king about the raids, but he failed to halt them. Diogo de Quadros in 1606, Manuel de Preto in 1606–7, and Belchior Dias Carneiro in 1607 all took the route toward the south and west hunting for Indians in regions far beyond the line of demarcation. Finding mines was always one objective of these expeditions, but the capture of Indians was more certain of yielding a profit. The long range outcome was to gain immense territories for Portugal.

The creation of the Relação of Bahia in 1609 bound the diverse regions of Brazil into one system. Previously the administration of justice had been mainly in the hands of the ouvidores of the various captaincies. All appeals ultimately went to Lisbon. The system entailed great expense for those appealing to Lisbon and thus favored the richer citizens. With an appeals court in Bahia serving all Brazil, it was hoped that justice would be closer and ipso facto closer to reality.

One important characteristic of Portuguese law was its lack of a constitutional basis. The king was the law and his decrees could change any ruling made in the past, without reference to a restraining precedent. Portugal had law codes called Ordenações drawn up at various times, and the Ordenações Filipinas (1603) was the code in force at the time the Relação was established in 1609. Yet the king could legislate beyond any existing codes or the laws contained in them. The king's word was the law.

The Portuguese renewed efforts to formulate a satisfactory Indian policy. A law of July 30, 1609, declared the Indians entirely free and imposed severe penalties for infractions of the laws. No Indians were to be captured or held as slaves. This represents one instance where a connection can be seen between Portuguese policy and the Spanish kings. The same year a new ordinance of 1609 issued by Philip III for the Spanish American colonies sought to prevent the abuse of Indians. This 1609 law respecting the Indians of Brazil was one aspect of the effort to get better control over the people.

The cement that tied Brazilian society together was composed of two main elements: loyalty to the king and loyalty to the church and the king as head of the church embodied both. In advocating the concept that he derived his rights from God for the just rule of the people, the king had three principal arms of operation: the church, the law, and the hereditary nobility. In actual practice the three could be embodied in one man—a noble who was a churchman, educated in law, and holding a position of power by royal appointment. Usually, however, the three operated separately to serve the king. A noble was military commander; a priest was appointed guardian of divine morality; and a lawyer served the ideal of justice. In theory, none could have any superior loyalty.

In practice this loyalty could be diluted. The churchman looked to the Pope as the supreme representative of his religion. The noble, at times, thought of his class as equal in importance to the crown. Both noble and churchmen were also bound by traditional ties to their extended family. The one important class that had no superior loyalty in theory, was the legal class, the *letrado*. A lawyer's career, after training in the university, depended on service to the state, represented by the king. This class could, and often did, dilute the rigidity of the law with family preference.

Unless a lawyer was educated in the law at the one university serving the entire realm, Coimbra, he had no hope of securing royal preference. This was generally true of churchmen as well, if they were to rise in the hierarchy. Only a small number of nobles who chose the military profession were exceptions to this rule. For the commoner, the one sure way to rise was through education in civil or canon law, or both, at the University of Coimbra. To say a person is "É legal" remains the highest accolade that can be bestowed in Brazil down to the present.

The Relação represented the crowns effort to implant in Brazil an institution that embodied the supreme and divine-right claim to power. The first efforts to create a Relação in Brazil similar in function to those existing in Portugal illustrates the inherent difficulties of overseas administration. In line with other reforms then in progress, Philip II decided to create a high court in Brazil. The state of justice in Brazil was not good, and some thought a high court could remedy the prevailing evils. The ouvidor geral, a one-judge court attempting to give coherence to all the ouvidores in Brazil, could not cope with the problems. The creation of a Relação for Brazil was in line with Portuguese legal developments and with the need for more officials to handle the increasing problems of the empire.

The Relação planned in 1588 consisted of ten desembargadores, or high judges. Appointing the judges and then making the court function were two different matters, however. Men were appointed, but most never got to Brazil. Geography posed the first problem in reaching their destination. Most of the ten judges embarked with the newly-appointed governor, Francisco Giraldes. The governor was forced by winds and currents to land in Santo Domingo in Hispaniola, and he returned to Portugal without having coming close to his destination. Four of the ten judges finally did arrive in Brazil.

Various other proposals for legal reform in Brazil were discussed in Portugal. No action had been taken by 1590 and the matter of creating a court for Brazil was temporarily shelved. A new king, Philip III, came to the throne in 1598, and a new council, the Conselho da India, was created in 1604 (lasting only to 1614 when abolished). The discussion of a Relação for Brazil was renewed. Meanwhile complaints about the corruption of justice in Brazil continued to reach the court.

When finally constituted, the presiding officer was the governor-general in Bahia. He was without voice or vote, but he could send judges on special assignments, a right which enhanced his powers. The Regimento of 1588, with minor modifications, served as the model for the Relação instituted in 1609. Many opposed its establishment because, they argued, "Brazil is not capable of supporting so many lawyers." Such beliefs are not rare in our own country and in our own time.

The arrival of the Relação in Bahia and the proclamation of the new Indian law coincided. The purpose of the new legislation was to restate clearly the crown's intention of making the Indians free and of enforcing the law, which had not been done to date. All Indians, whether still hinterland pagans or living in aldeias and other settled areas, were free and had to be paid wages for their labor. The Jesuits were permitted to bring Indians into the aldeias, but they too had to pay wages. A special official to protect Indians was to be appointed by the governor in conjunction with the chancellor of the Relação.

All Indians illegally captured in the past were declared free; all legal documents or judicial decisions attesting to their enslavement were declared null and void. No violations were to be tolerated and no appeals were to go to the crown. The Relação was instructed to enforce the law with annual inspections.

The law met the same resistance that all previous attempts to protect the Indians had met. The Portuguese regarded it as a burden placed on them by a Spanish king, who, in their hearts, was not acceptable. The municipal council of Filipeío in Paraíba declared that the law was "made and formulated in the kingdom of Castile" and was not applicable to Brazil. Prior the this date many in Brazil had advocated the model of the Encomienda and the Repartimiento of the Spanish Indies. But they rejected the Spanish model when it did not suit them.

When the Relação presented the new law to the municipal council of Bahia on June 28, 1610, the members broke out in riotous opposition. The Jesuits were immediately blamed, and crowds surrounded the Jesuit college and the governor's residence.The protesters demanded that the Jesuits sign a document condemning the law, which they refused to do. They did agree, however, that legally captured Indians should remain in captivity. The Jesuits also pledged not to employ Indians in their personal service in the aldeias.

Faced with such a rebellion and threats of more violence against the Jesuits and himself, Governor Diogo de Meneses (1608–12) sent a strongly worded letter to the crown advocating modification of the law. Many other protests also went to the court. Consequently, the law was changed by a new statute in September 1611; it restated the condition of freedom accorded the Indians, but permitted capture in "just" wars as defined by a council composed of the governor, the bishop and other religious officials, and the Relação.

The net result was a return to the pre-1609 situation in spite of the elaborate machinery of protection provided in the modified law. The Europeans regarded the work of the Indians as necessary to their welfare. White men had not come to a new world to work as laborers. Englishmen in Virginia were, at this very time, driven to work for themselves because the Indians of North America were much less submissive to field labor than those in Brazil. African slave labor eventually took hold in North American plantations as it was already doing in Brazil.

Meanwhile, a new factor in Indian relations arose in 1607, when the Spanish Jesuits, whose first efforts in Guaíra had been weak and ineffective, organized the Province of Paraguay. It embraced territories now in southern Bolivia, northern Argentina, and southern Brazil. New missions were founded in Guaíra in 1610 at Loreto and Inácio, and others later as far south as the Tapé and Uruguay rivers and north into Itatí in southern Mato Grosso.

The missions offered tempting targets to the bandeirantes. The sedentary and unarmed Indians were much more numerous than the unconquered tribes. Furthermore, grouped into relatively compact settlements, the mission Indians were captured more easily than Indians scattered over thousands of miles of territory. The mission Indians also possessed skills as farmers and artisans which made them more valuable as slaves. For a few years the Spanish Jesuits, despite the danger, defied the raiders and continued to found more missions.

Raids occurred regularly, the 1609 law to the contrary. They were organized by Clemente Álvares in 1610, Christóvão de Aguiar and Bras Gonçalves in 1610, Pedro Vaz de Barros in 1611, Sebastião Preto in 1612, and Lázaro da Costa in 1615. Records show eight raids between 1606 and 1615. Manuel Preto, an outstanding bandeirante for years, led raids in 1619 into the Guaíra region against the missions.

Some researchers list other raids, but because authors emphasize different leaders, it is not always possible to differentiate between the bandeiras. In 1622 António Castanho da Silva died on a raid into Peru. Manuel Preto, accompanied by António Raposo Tavares, who became one of the most famous bandeirantes, attacked the Jesuit missions of Guaíra in 1623.

Meanwhile in the north, the settlement of Natal, Rio Grande do Norte, on Christmas day 1598, left the one thousand mile coastline to the Amazon River still in control of the Indians and their French friends. The constant threat from the French, Dutch, and English made it imperative to extend Portuguese authority over this coast— or risk losing it.

Pero Coelho de Soares, brother-in-law of Frutuoso Barbosa, offered to undertake the conquest. In 1603 starting out from Paraíba, he reached the Jaguaribe River in Ceará. The next year he met the opposition of combined Indian and French forces. The Portuguese reached as far as the Parnaíba River but were forced to return. A major and costly blunder created bad relations with previously friendly Indians. The Portuguese forced a number of the Tabajaras and Potiguares to return with them to Paraíba and Pernambuco, where the Indians were compelled to work in the sugar engenhos.

When Pero Coelho de Soares renewed his efforts to advance in 1606, he met an enemy more terrible than men—one of the droughts that periodically devastated the northeast and decimated the population. The remnants of his expedition retreated to Rio Grande do Norte.

The Jesuits came forward to help in the conquest, as they had on many occasions in the past. The Fathers Francisco Pinto and Luís Figueira went out in 1607 attempting to pacify the Indians. They took with them some Indians "unjustly" imprisoned on previous expeditions. When they reached Serra de Ibiapaba in 1608, the Tacarijus Indians attacked and killed Father Pinto, forcing his companion to retreat.

Under Martim Soares Moreno, a young lieutenant who had participated in the previous expeditions and made the effort to learn the language of the Indians, the Portuguese made another advance. Moreno gained the friendship of Potiguar Chief Jacauna and, with his aid, repelled a landing of French traders. In 1611 a fort was built at the mouth of the Ceará River, near the fort later called São Sebastião. During the advance toward the Maranhão River (the true Maranhão, not the Amazon), another fort was established near Camocim by the second Jerónimo de Albuquerque in 1613. Thereafter the coastline to Pernambuco was in Portuguese possession. The French were still present, however, and about to make their strongest effort since the era of Villegagnon to establish themselves in Brazil.

The Portuguese had not succeeded in their first efforts to settle the northwest-northeast coast in the sixteenth century. Earlier the French had been in Maranhão, and Jacques Riffault had attempted to establish a settlement on the island of Santana in 1594, resulting in the loss of two of his three ships to heavy seas. An important result of these shipwrecks was that a few Frenchmen began to live among the Indians. The French presence made it more difficult for the Portuguese to conquer these Indians. One Frenchman, Charles de Vaux, returned to France and became a propagandist for the colonization of Maranhão.

The task was immediately taken up with enthusiasm by Daniel de la Touche, Seigneur de La Ravardiere, who earlier had participated in an expedition to the Guiana coast. In 1610, before the Portuguese had occupied part of Ceará or advanced to the area of Maranhão, he obtained from the French government a concession of 100 leagues around a fort established south of the Equator. He enrolled in his effort François de Rassilly, Seigneur des Aumels, and Nicolas de Harlay de Sancy, Baron de la Molle and of GrosBois. Both were named Lieutenant Generals of the King in the West Indies and Lands of

Brazil by Marie de Médici, Regent of France for her infant son Louis XIII. With three ships and personnel including a number of nobles, they sailed for Brazil in 1612. Four Capuchin monks accompanied them; two wrote histories of the expedition that rank among the best first-hand accounts of colonizing efforts in Brazil. They established a fort called Saint Louis, in honor of Louis IX, the saintly medieval king of France in the thirteenth century. A town founded with the aid of the Tupinambá Indians received the same name and is the São Luís of today. As previously noted, the Portuguese received news of the French effort and sent Jerónimo de Albuquerque to make a settlement nearby at Camocim.

The French threatened the Portuguese in 1614. Governor General Gaspar de Sousa sent Albuquerque and Sargentomor Diogo de Campos Moreno of the State of Brazil with troops composed of Portuguese, Indians, and "Brazilians"—meaning in this case anybody who was neither Portuguese born or Indian—to establish Fort Santa Maria on a site called Guaxenduba on Baía de São José, opposite the French settlement. They successfully repulsed a French attack. Finally, La Ravardiere and Diogo de Campos signed a truce; they agreed to consult Madrid and Paris and to await the decision of their respective governments regarding the legal ownership of Maranhão.

The government of Philip III refused categorically the French claims and ordered reinforcements. Meanwhile, Albuquerque had built a fort, São José de Itapari, on the Island of Maranhao. Alexandre de Moura brought additional forces from Pernambuco, occupied strategic positions, and prepared to attack the French. La Ravardiere protested this breach of the truce, but recognizing his vulnerability to attack by Portuguese troops, he agreed to withdraw to Europe in November 1615. Maranhão became Portuguese.

The Amazon still remained outside Portuguese control. Although its true and almost unbelievable dimensions, one-third of South America and half of Brazil as presently constituted, remained almost unknown, its value was not doubted by anyone.

Perhaps seen by Vespucci in 1499 and by Diego de Lepe and Vicente Yáñez Pinzón in 1500, all Portuguese efforts to make settlements in the region had failed. The Spaniard Francisco de Orellana had sailed down the river in 1540/41. The fantastic character Lope de Aguirre (who had murdered the original commander of the expedition, Pedro de Ursua) repeated the down-river venture in 1559–60, reaching Venezuela where he met his death by execution in 1561. His insolent letters to the king would rank high on any list of denunciatory literature.

Before the Portuguese renewed their efforts in the Amazon in the seventeenth century, English, French, and Dutch traders and would-be colonizers had already found the Amazon. The great interest of Sir Walter Raleigh in the mythical inland lake, where the "El Dorado" covered himself in gold and then bathed in the lake to wash off the gold as a means of making an offering to his Gods, had stimulated English interest. In 1613 James I of England conceded the area from the Essequibo River in modern British Guiana to the Amazon, equivalent to roughly 700 miles and larger than the whole of the British Isles, to a few Gentleman Adventurers.

England, France, and Holland did not recognize the division between Spain and Portugal made in the Treaty of Tordesillas in 1494. Dutch traders and settlers were already in the Amazon with settlements on the Jenipapo River (Paru today) trading tobacco, cotton, woods, and urucu (annatto—a reddish-yellow dye). There are other reports of a few English and Irish visitors. As on previous occasions, the Portuguese faced a real threat to their claims to Brazil. The most interesting fact is that such a small country triumphed over stronger nations. The foreign observer who tries to explain this outcome should take into account the character of the Portuguese and Brazilian people.

After the victory in Maranhão, the Portuguese pushed on to the Amazon to meet and forestall any foreign incursions. Alexandre de Moura, who brought the reinforcements that forced the French surrender, had orders to advance to the Amazon, and he sent Francisco Caldeira de Castelo Branco along the coast. Castelo Branco entered the Pará River (southern branch of the Amazon as it enters the Atlantic), and built a fort, Forte do Presépio, near the point where the Guamá River flows into the Pará, in January 1616. This became in time the city of Belém, capital of the new captaincy of Pará, which was originally called Feliz Lusitania (Felicitious Lusitania)—a name too romantic to endure.

The early history of the new captaincy was sufficiently sad to justify changing its first overly optimistic name. Relations with the local Indians, at first felicitious, soon turned sour, and the new colony faced several years of war with the Tupinambás. Quarrels among the Portuguese settlers were equally threatening. In 1618 Castello Branco was accused of harboring a criminal, his nephew, who had committed a murder, and he was deposed by the colonists.

Reinforcements came from both Maranhão and Lisbon in time to strengthen the town against Indian attacks. A strong attack was repelled in January 1619. The early life of Pará continued quite agitated and endangered for several years, but it resisted in the long run the enmity of the Indians, the factionalism of the Portuguese, and the danger from foreigners.

Around the time the Portuguese arrived and founded Belém in 1616, Pedro Teixeira captured a Dutch ship. Soon the Portuguese learned that the upriver settlement of Dutch consisted of about 250 to 300 people, with women and children, not merely men, present to demonstrate its colonizing intent. The English and Irish were also there. In 1623 Captain Luís Aranha de Vasconcelos captured Dutch settlements named Orange and Nassau near the mouth of the Xingú River. In their place the Portuguese placed the settlement of Gurupá. On the left bank of the Amazon in 1625, Capitão-mor Bento Maciel Parente destroyed the English settlements and established Nossa Senhora do Desterro.

Both the English and the Dutch later returned in spite of their bad experiences. But their settlements were destroyed again, the Dutch in 1629 and the English in 1631–32. They came back to Cabo do Norte in 1639 and 1646 but could not hold out. Meanwhile, the Dutch had made permanent settlements in the Guianas and in New York, and the English had established themselves in Virginia in 1607 and in New England in 1620.

The Dutch were determined to make more serious efforts to settle in Bahia and Pernambuco.

10

DUTCH SETTLEMENT, 1624–1641

he most serious challenge to Portugal's possession of Brazil
came from the Dutch invasions of Bahia and Pernambuco.
The United Provinces grew rapidly after revolting against
Spain. Holding successfully the mouth of the Scheldt River, they
choked off the trade of the Spanish Lowlands, which later became
mainly Belgium; its leading commercial port was Antwerp. By 1600
the Dutch had an estimated 16,000 ships, more than any other nation
by far and perhaps more than all northern Europe combined. When
the Dutch East India Company was organized in 1602, the Dutch
were on their way to half a century of commercial expansion in Europe
and of immense power everywhere in the world that European ships
regularly traded. The English, who eventually overtook and overcame
the Dutch, directed their main efforts outside Brazil.

The Dutch pursued trade in Brazil, legal and illegal, plus what they
considered privateering, but which their opponents called piracy.
They—as well as the English, Irish, and French—invested great sums
of money and lives in the effort to occupy valuable positions in the
Amazon. Although the Dutch signed a 12-year truce with Spain in
1609, it applied mainly in Holland, and had no major effect on Dutch
policies at sea. Dutch ships continued to sail beyond the Cape of Good
Hope to the East and to haunt American waters, including Brazil.
They explored North America and in 1614 settled New Amsterdam
(later renamed New York when the English captured it in 1664).

A Dutch fleet under Admiral Joris Van Spilberg, with six vessels of the Dutch East Indian Company bound for the Moluccas via Magellan, reached the Ilha Grande between Rio de Janeiro and São Vicente on October 20, 1614. The fleet was short of provisions and water, and many of the crew were suffering·badly from scurvy. Ilha Grande was undefended and looked unoccupied, and van Spilberg disembarked his sick crewmen and began gathering supplies and water. Ten days later five canoes of armed Portuguese and Indians attacked three Dutch sloops and massacred their crews.

Other fighting followed but Spilberg stayed in the Ilha Grande the remainder of 1614 and into 1615. His crew was unable to man the ships, thus he appealed to the authorities in São Vicente for assistance. He was refused, although the laws concerning forced arrivals of foreign ships prescribed conditions that should have made his appeal legal. He consequently disembarked forces under his personal command and occupied parts of São Vicente, including the engenho belonging to the Schetz family of Antwerp.

While the Dutch were organizing their Dutch West Indian Company to build up their trade and engage in privateering or trade (the word used depends on which side is writing the history) suggestions were made for a company to preserve the trade for Portugal. The authors of this proposal were Portuguese Jews resident in Holland who had escaped persecution. According to the Brazilian historian Varnhagen, "the injustices and persecutions they had suffered had still not killed the love of their homeland." They submitted a proposal January 7, 1621, that included a provision giving them the right to trade in the colonies. Similar rights had been granted in 1601 for a payment of 200,000 cruzados, but the agreement had been annuled in 1610 without return of the payment. The new proposal bore no fruit, but it resembled somewhat the Brazil Company of 1649, in which Portuguese New Christians had a minor participation.

The chief advocate of the formation of a company for New World trade and colonization, later named the West India Company, was Willem Usselincx, a Calvinist emigrant from Catholic Antwerp to Holland. He wrote numerous pamphlets advancing the idea that the

Dutch should establish agricultural colonies in the New World to provide Holland with an export market. Usselincx believed the animal and vegetal products of the New World were more important sources of wealth than precious metals. Brazil, in particular, supplied sugar, tobacco, hides, and other vegetable products the Dutch could use as the basis for rich trade.

His main function was to convince the Dutch of the best method of capturing the Brazil trade—hence his advocacy of a company to persuade, or force, Spain to admit Dutch trade. He calculated the minimum yield of Brazilian sugar at 4,800,000 guilders profit. Brazil and other American colonies could be won over to Dutch friendship by fair treatment, he said. Others considered him naive and foresaw the necessity of force.

The Dutch West India Company was chartered June 3, 1621. It did not spring up miraculously like a rabbit from a magician's hat; it came from the planning of men who saw what they thought must be done when the twelve-year truce ended. Planning, not coincidence, led to the organization of the company. The members of the company were in general the same who sat in the Estates-General. The principal terms of the charter gave the company a twenty-four year monopoly over trade in the Americas and part of Africa—or, in other words, in areas where the Dutch East India Company did not operate. Brazil was not the only objective. Nonetheless the operations of the company in other areas subsequently affected Brazil as well.

The Dutch already knew Brazil well. Brazilian sugar, refined in Holland as early as 1594, was processed in 29 refineries in 1621, of which 25 were in Amsterdam. Neither Brazil nor Holland could lightly surrender their growing trade connection. The truce had facilitated the trade. A memorial presented to the Estates-General of the Netherlands in 1622 stated that 40,000 to 50,000 boxes of sugar had entered annually from Brazil during the truce years. The renewal of war between Holland and Spain threatened this trade.

In September 1622 it was suggested that "nothing would be more advantageous to the Company than the conquest of the kingdom Brazil." In April 1623 Jan Andries Moerbeeck repeated the suggestion.

Moerbeeck's pamphlet entitled "Why the West India Company should attempt to Conquer Brazil from the king of Spain, without delay" was published in 1624.

The first move against Brazil on a grand scale came on May 10, 1624, with an attack on Salvador, Bahia, capital of the colony, by the largest fleet ever to cross the Equator to that date. Salvador fell with little fighting, and most of the inhabitants fled in panic. Only the governor, a few of his faithful subjects, and some New Christians, it is said, were in the city to surrender. The flight of the people was the force that, in the long run, defeated the Dutch.

The reaction in Spain to the capture of Salvador was instantaneous and powerful. If it remained in Dutch possession, all Brazil might fall and Spanish dominion in La Plata would be insecure. The entire Caribbean area could be threatened from a secure base in Brazil. Psychologically, to lose Bahia would be a blow revealing the weakness of Spain. Religion and sentiment aroused the people against the heretic Dutch. Brazil had become the richest and most productive of all the Portuguese colonies. The vital interests of the crown, the merchants, and the noble classes were at stake.

When the news of the fall of Salvador reached Lisbon, and was rushed on to Madrid, the government burst into a fever of activity seldom seen. Spaniards and Portuguese organized a powerful fleet, even more powerful than the Dutch fleet that captured Salvador. Large numbers of nobles volunteered for service, so many that their expedition bears the name of "Jornada dos Vassalos." The Dutch fleet was composed of twenty-six ships with 509 cannon, 1,600 mariners, and 1,700 soldiers. The Spanish-Portuguese fleet consisted of seventy ships (of which fifty-two were warships) and 12,000 men under Don Fadrique de Toledo y Osorio. The Dutch received reports from spies of the organization of the Spanish-Portuguese fleet, and they were aware of the need to send reinforcements. Three fleets were readied but the weather in the North Sea, the worst in years, prevented their sailing. For months they remained in harbor; meanwhile the Spanish-Portuguese fleet was outfitting. The latter sailed, without the impediment suffered by the Dutch forces, to relieve Bahia.

More than bad weather helped the Bahians and hindered the Dutch. They had captured Salvador with ease but found themselves masters of the city only. Unable to gather food from surrounding farm lands, they soon became besieged. It is ironic that the Bahians of the Recôncavo, who had several times previously held Salvador and watched their estates ravished by foreigners, were now able to deny the enemy food and supplies. After the panic had subsided, the inhabitants reorganized and began guerrilla war against the Dutch.

The Dutch felt secure, nevertheless, since they were counting on the promised fleet of reinforcements (the one held up in Dutch ports by the ice and winds). They dispatched a fleet to Angola to seize the source of Portuguese slaves, which were the indispensable ingredient of a successful tropical plantation system. The mission failed; the Portuguese in Angola defended themselves successfully. The Dutch had a bit of good fortune when they captured a small Spanish fleet that sailed into Bahia ignorant of the occupation. They benefited also from dissension among the Bahia defenders. But their own ranks were the victims of even worse leadership. The Dutch commanders were two brothers (one died of drunkenness) who were no match for the Portuguese-Brazilian defenders. After holding Salvador almost a year, the Dutch surrendered to the Spanish-Portuguese fleet of Don Fadrique de Toledo in April 1625. The Dutch relief fleet arrived a short time later, but it was too late to save the situation and too weak to recapture the city.

The invaders took considerable quantities of sugar and other products, however, and shipped them to the Dutch West India Company. The loss of Salvador and other Dutch areas were serious but not fatal. In 1627, the Spanish-Portuguese fleet having returned to Europe, the Dutch commander Piet Heyn sailed into the Recôncavo. He made no attempt to capture the city but gathered a rich haul of sugar, tobacco, and other products. The Herrin XIX, as the governors of the Dutch West India Company were known, had reasons for optimism. The greatest stroke of luck in the history of the company was the capture of a Spanish treasure fleet laden with silver, gold, 1,000 pearls, two million hides, silk, musk, amber, and other products estimated at 12 million guilders in Matanzas Bay, Cuba, in September 1628. The stockholders received a 75% dividend; but Heyn and his men were given a niggardly portion, and he resigned to enter the service of the Estates-General.

The Portuguese lost many ships at sea from the attacks of foreign vessels. A report in 1626 listed 120 ships with sixty thousand boxes of sugar, brazilwood, hides, cotton, amber, and slaves evaluated at more than five million cruzados lost during the three previous years. In 1626 alone twenty ships disappeared after attacks by pirates and corsairs from Holland and Algeria. Many of the captured passengers were taken to Algiers and ransomed at great expense. The lost cargoes were sold in England, the Mediterranean, and other ports in competition with the Portuguese. Matias de Albuquerque reported toward the end of 1627 on the "diminishing benefits from Brazil" and urged improved coastal defenses. The defenses were not sufficient to prevent a second Dutch attack in force, however.

The capture of the Spanish treasure fleet was the biggest but not the only haul made by the Dutch. They captured many cargoes bound for Portugal. Their coffers could now be opened for another major attempt in Brazil. The chosen target was Pernambuco.

Before this blow fell, the court gave its attention to pressing internal matters. A perennial problem was the maintenance of royal prerogative and respect for royal legislation. The creation of the Relação in 1609 had been intended as a solution to these problems. The Dutch occupation of Salvador revealed the degree to which the Relação had not lived up to expectations.

General dissatisfaction with the Relação led to its suppression in 1626. Part of the reason was the low reputation of the lawyer class, the venality of judges, and the opposition of powerful men of the colony. Friction with the governor, in particular the suspension of laws in order to raise troops, contributed to its unpopularity. Some individuals came to its aid, often in unsigned petitions, because they believed it was the only defense against the excesses of the bishops, the donatários, and the "powerful of the land." Opponents alleged that the Relação was too costly.

When the Relação was abolished, the ouvidor geral was reinstated as the highest judicial official. Appeals had to be made to Portugal. Most of the judges of the Relação were returned to Portugal and were given similar or higher positions. The Relação had proved its worth, nevertheless. Years later, when the crisis of the Dutch occupation was nearing its end in 1652, the Relação was restored.

The Portuguese were certain that new Dutch attacks would come. One obvious place was Pernambuco, because the Dutch knew the area well. They had been there often as legal traders or raiders. Moreover, Holland had twenty-nine sugar refineries using Brazilian raw sugar. Dutch merchants resided in Recife and elsewhere in Brazil, and there were Dutch miners and engineers. Pernambuco was the leading sugar producer in Brazil and indeed of the entire world. Its senhores de engenho were famed for their extravagant and ostentatious way of life, often spending even more than their rich plantations produced. Pernambuco and its immediate neighbors boasted 120 engenhos, and despite the great loss of ships, the cargoes reaching markets were enough to maintain the prosperity of the colony.

The Dutch fleet arrived February 16, 1630, and occupied Recife and Olinda with ease. But, as in the case of Salvador six years earlier, the conquest of the outlying zone proved a major task. The Brazilian forces knew how to take advantage of terrain unknown to the mercenary armies of the Dutch, who were subjected to ceaseless harassment.

There was nothing unusual about the use of mercenaries at that time. Europe had no national armies, nor any armies serving the nation as patriots with the exception of the Spanish forces. Armies were raised by military leaders who hired themselves out to states who paid the right price, and they shifted from one side to another according to their selfish interests. Holland, a small country with few people, customarily hired mercenary forces. The economic base of Europe was so low that men joined armies with the hope of loot and living off the country. The forces serving the Dutch in Brazil were mercenaries. Facing them were men fighting for a cause, though patriotism was often less than one hundred percent pure.

Every engenho with its people formed an obstacle and the tropical terrain baffled the mercenary soldiers. Dutch communications between Olinda and Recife, a distance of only about three miles along the coast, could be maintained only with an armed escort and was not always safe. Matias de Albuquerque was able to establish an armed camp, the Arraial do Bom Jesus, only three miles from Recife and Olinda, where he held out to 1635. Several other armed camps kept the Dutch in check. The forces serving the Dutch constantly had to be changed and reinforced.

The home governments of Portugal and Spain could not match the Dutch strength. Their great effort in 1625 was the peak of their power. Nevertheless, the Spanish court made strenuous efforts to organize a fleet to relieve Pernambuco. The effort was in vain. Both Spain and Portugal had suffered so many losses after 1625 that neither would make the extra effort necessary. Madrid complained that the Portuguese would not help defend their own colony. Lisbon responded that the Dutch would not have attacked Brazil if Portugal was not ruled by Spanish kings. While they bickered, the Dutch dug in. After the fall of Arraial do Bom Jesus, Paraíba, and the fort of Nazaré in 1635, the Dutch forces appeared to be winning, and the Brazilians were forced to retreat to the south of Pernambuco.

Spain, more deeply involved than ever in the Thirty Years War by 1635, could only watch and argue with Lisbon while Dutch reinforcements slowly wore down Albuquerque's well-conceived and well-executed defenses which suffered from insufficient supplies. After the initial enthusiasm, the help of the local citizens (moradores) diminished, leaving Albuquerque without adequate manpower. The defenders were drawn from every element of Brazilian society. Albuquerque himself had a Brazilian ancestry. There were Portuguese born in Portugal, Portuguese born in Brazil (called mazombos), Blacks, both African-born and Creolos, plus Indians and every conceivable mixture.

This conflict became truly a "Brazilian" rather than a Portuguese war. It was a guerrilla force that could hit, retreat, disperse, and reform quickly—and then hit again in some other place while the slow-moving mercenary forces were thrashing about in confusion. In frontal battles, the Dutch forces usually won, but in the art of war as practiced in Brazil, they were losers in the end. The details of the five-year campaign are fascinating for those who delight in military history, but they are too long to be described here.

The arrival of Johan Mauritz of Nassau-Siegen (Count Maurice of Nassau) in 1637 with fresh forces and the titles "Governor, Captain and Admiral" seemed to seal the fate of northeast Brazil. Its destiny was to be Dutch, or was it? In fact, the rule of Count Maurice of Nassau was merely an interlude in Brazilian history. Only 33 years old at the time of his arrival, a descendant of the House of Orange and a veteran of Europe's Thirty Year's War with the rank of colonel, Maurice was a man of unusual military and organizational ability. He was also the typical "Renaissance Man" with an intensive love of the arts and sciences. He represented his nation in the century of its greatest artistic and scientific achievements. The most tolerant intellectual and religious atmosphere in Europe prevailed in Holland (albeit with some countercurrents).

Maurice came to Brazil to establish a new Holland, not merely to conduct a war he thought was all but won. With him came Frans Post and Albert Eckhout, two Dutch painters whose work left us the best views of the country and the people, plus Georg Marcgraf (Marcgrave) and Willem Piso, two scientists of diversified talents. They made extensive studies of the land and its flora, fauna, and geography. Regrettably their work did not survive in its entirety, but what is extant constitutes a unique source of scientific knowledge of northeast Brazil in the mid-seventeenth century.

Maurice immediately moved to drive the Brazilian forces out of Pernambuco in 1637. He sent a force to capture El Mina in Africa (whose garrison strangely surrendered a strong position with little fighting). He wanted to extend his rule north to Ceará and south toward Bahia. The siege of Bahia in 1638 was a failure, however, at a high cost in lives of men and officers. A short time later, he faced another major challenge from Spanish-Portuguese arms.

During the years after 1630, when the Dutch occupied Pernambuco,

Spain suffered a number of devastating blows on both land and sea. The Herrin XIX assured Count Maurice that Spain was in such bad condition it would not consider sending a fleet to Brazil. The Herrin XIX proved wrong, however. The Count-Duke of Olivares, minister of Philip IV, and the king himself were determined to recover all Brazil. Their complaint was about the dilatory nature of Portugal's contribution to the effort to reconquer its own colony. This characterized the usual relationship between the partners in the dual monarchy.

On September 6, 1638, an armada, painfully assembled, received orders to sail from the Tagus River. The commander was Dom Fernão de Mascarenhas, Conde da Torre, who was unfitted for the task but who was forced to assume it because of his high title and because nobody wanted it. The armada looked formidable—forty-six under sail including twenty-six galleons, with 5,000 soldiers plus ship crews. Meanwhile, Maurice appealed frantically to the directors of the company for reinforcements.

The Conde da Torre sailed, but only after a long delay in the Cape Verde Islands where he lost 3,000 men who died of disease. He reached the Pernambuco coast on January 10, 1639, leading the Dutch to expect an immediate attack. Instead, he sailed to Salvador in the hope of getting supplies and more men. But Bahia was also in a bad state.

During 1639 both sides made preparations for the forthcoming showdown. The Dutch received some reinforcements under Arciszewski; but jealousy, or some other undisclosed reason, caused Maurice to send him back to Holland. In Salvador, pillage and rape by soldiers who da Torre could not control made his appeals for help fall on deaf ears much of the time. Governor Salvador Correia de Sá e Benevides of Rio de Janeiro gathered forces to help. Neither side was in shape to wage a first-class battle. Nevertheless, the reinforcements that came to the Conde da Torre from the Azores, Rio de Janeiro, and Buenos Aires enabled him to nearly double the strength of his forces. On November 18 and 19, he put to sea eighteen Spanish and twelve Portuguese galleons and other ships totaling eighty-seven with some five or six thousand troops (which rumors had inflated to as many as 12,000).

Neither luck nor the Lord was with the Spanish-Portuguese fleet. Strong winds from the north initially held them back. In January 1640 winds from the south suddenly sprang up and drove them past Recife to Paraíba. Da Torre worked back to Itamaracá where the Dutch fleet of forty-one ships gained some advantage in a running fight lasting five days. But the Spanish–Portuguese fleet failed to land its soldiers. Some of the Dutch commanders were later court-martialled for cowardice, and one was executed. It was not a great victory for anyone; but inasmuch as Conde de la Torre had not taken Recife, the Dutch came out ahead.

Luís Barbalho, one of the Portuguese commanders, volunteered to go ashore at Cape São Roque with 1,200 to 1,300 men and make his way back through the hinterland to Salvador. The Conde de la Torre returned to Salvador in a small ship. Luís Barbalho joined the forces sent by Torre overland from Bahia under André Vidal, João Barbalho, the Indian chieftan Camarâo, and others—about 2,000 soldiers—in an epic and cruel march of 1,200 miles through the Dutch-held territory. In a bitter exchange of correspondence with Barbalho, Count Maurice refused quarter to captured soldiers, quoting intercepted orders Barbalho had given before the fleet sailed.

The Spanish-Portuguese forces were greatly aided by the moradores in fighting their way through Dutch territory—a warning to the Dutch of the questionable loyalty of the people they had temporarily conquered. Nassau deported about 60 Carmelites, Benedictines, and Franciscans on charges of disloyalty to Dutch Brazil. A Dutch fleet under Admirals Jol and Lichthart arrived in March 1640 and sailed to the Recôncavo, where they destroyed 27 engenhos. They were discouraged from assaulting Salvador, however, by the arrival of Barbalho and his men from the long march.

Reinforcements from Europe arrived for Bahia in June 1640 under the command of Dom Jorge de Mascarenhas, Marquis of Montalvão, who was first to bear the title of Viceroy of Brazil. The war of attrition, destruction, and killing without quarter was devastating both Portuguese-held and Dutch-held Brazil. The Catholic clergy of Pernambuco petitioned Count Maurice to countermand his drastic orders. The origin of this petition is attributed to Montalvão by Barlaeus and by Portuguese writers to Count Maurice. A correspondence of recriminations followed, but eventually an agreement was signed by the junta that succeeded Montalvão to cease the horrors and destruction of war.

When Count Maurice corresponded with Montalvão, he learned that a revolt in Portugal in December 1640 had restored the Portuguese line of kings on the throne. The Duke of Braganza had assumed power with the title João IV. The news seemed good for the Dutch cause, and Count Maurice held spectacular celebrations in Recife with prizes for the winners of various contests. One of the principal winners was João Fernandes Vieira—of whom more later. The count thought he was celebrating the victory of the Dutch in Brazil, and he soon began to extend his field of action.

The revolt against the Spanish king should not have surprised anyone, given the attitude of the Portuguese towards the Spaniards. And yet it is evident, from the complete lack of any plan of defense against an uprising, that Philip IV and his governing regent—the Duchess of Mântua, granddaughter of Philip II, and cousin of Philip IV—were taken by surprise. The plotters were few in number, perhaps explaining the success of their surprise. They coaxed along the logical pretender to the throne, the Duke of Braganza, who was willing but worried and hesitant. His wife Luisa of Guzmán, daughter of the Duke of Medina Sidonia, one of the highest nobles of Spain, urged him to revolt because it was better, she said, to die fighting than to live serving.

The stress between the two nations became more evident after the Dutch occupation of Pernambuco in 1630. Dutch, English, and French attacks on all parts of the Spanish-Portuguese empire required more defense than was available. Spain's conflict with France in the Thirty-Years War and the still exhausting struggle with the Dutch also brought Spain closer to collapse. Spain thought Portugal indifferent to the defense of its own empire, and Portugal resented and resisted every tax suggested by Spain to raise money for imperial defense.

The small band that invaded the palace on December 1, 1640, seized the regent and proclaimed João IV. Some of the clergy distinguished themselves in the brief struggle. The people of the city, unaware of events, remained indoors until aroused by bands of the rebels, who spread the news of the new king. Crowds then gathered and showed their enthusiastic support. The archbishops of Lisbon and Braga, and at first the Inquisitor General (who declined), were named regents until the king could travel to Lisbon from Vila Viçosa, his estate in east Portugal. He arrived December 6. The entire nation accepted him with the minimum of resistance. Portugal had a new king; but the war of independence still had to be won. It continued until 1668.

The immediate task of João IV was to keep his throne. The task was not simple, even considering the complications facing Spain. He could list these problems: a war of independence from Spain, requiring the immediate raising of an army and the gathering of a fleet; the need to establish relations with England, France, Holland, Sweden, Denmark, Rome, and other nations and to win their recognition of his sovereignty; the question of how to respond to Dutch possession of part of Brazil; the organization of both a home and overseas government; and the defense of his possessions in the East from Dutch and English attacks.

The support of the people for the new king was understandable. They had never accepted the Spanish kings in their hearts. The folklore and literature of the period carried the theme of the "captivity" of Portugal by Spain. The Jesuit support of the anti-Spanish cause placed them on the winning side and gave them strong influence with João IV. They became his powerful collaborators, and thereby benefited.

What of the Portuguese governors and people in Brazil? The reaction was a little more cautious, but not long delayed. As historians have somewhat unkindly remarked, the principal concern of officials was to keep their posts. They were aided in making quick decisions by the obvious views of the people—the old king has been deposed, long live the new king. Viceroy Montalvão may have had divided loyalties since he was half Spanish; but he hesitated little in proclaiming João IV.

The bulk of the army the viceroy commanded was composed of

Neapolitan and Spanish troops with no loyalty to Portugal or Brazil. The emissary of the new king to Bahia, carrying instructions to supplant Montalvão with a junta if he hesitated, was the Jesuit Francisco Vilhena. Montalvão was able to disarm the troops whom he feared might remain faithful to Spain. Father António Vieira was sent to Lisbon to report on Montalvão's actions and Father Provincial Manuel Fernandes went to Rio de Janeiro.

Montalvão's quick actions did not save him. Vilhena either mistakenly or deliberately misinterpreted his orders and formed a junta, on April 16, 1641, that deposed Montalvão and sent him to Lisbon as a prisoner. The junta in Bahia ruled until the next year, when a new governor, António Teles, arrived with instructions to depose and punish the junta.

The situation for the governor of Rio de Janeiro, Salvador Correia de Sá, was even more difficult. Son of a Spanish mother, husband of a Spanish wife, closely identified with the Spaniards in many ways, he must have had qualms about an easy change of allegiance. But he saw the will of the people and quickly followed it. Rio celebrated the new king with festivals, fireworks, vivas, and salvos of cannon shots.

The situation in São Paulo was yet more complicated. The sixty years of Spanish rule had witnessed a great growth of trade to the La Plata and Peru and the intermingling of Spanish and Portuguese people in São Paulo, Buenos Aires, Lima, and other areas. So many people of Spanish origin were in São Paulo that they composed one of two leading factions based nominally on families ties. The Camargos represented the Spanish faction and the Pires (or Garcias) the Portuguese.

Amador Bueno da Ribeira was a leader of the Camargo faction, although his mother was Portuguese. Amador was among the leaders of the revolt that drove the Jesuits out of São Paulo in 1640. As *juiz ordinário*, he had represented the activities of the Jesuits who were preaching Sebastianism—the belief that King Sebastião, though dead, would rise again to lead the Portuguese. Amador Bueno held this belief to be "disrespectful to El-Rei, our Lord Philip IV." The Câmara of São Vicente accused the Jesuits of spreading the belief that "we have another living king." As early as 1634 in Bahia, Father António

Vieira had preached that the encoberto, the "Hidden One", Sebastião, would return.

Amador's position on the Jesuits, Sebastianism, and Philip IV seemed to indicate that he was a leader who would likely keep faith with the Spanish king. The opposite proved true. When proclaimed king of São Paulo by the Camargo faction, he quickly repudiated the position and acclaimed João IV as king of Portugal and Brazil.

The news from Portugal prompted a Dutch response in Brazil. Some favored a quick peace which would enable the Dutch to pull in their extended forces and economize. Others favored a continuation of the war outside Europe and further conquests. The Portuguese proposed a ten-year truce and the return of Brazil, with compensation to the Dutch. Initially, the Dutch rejected the proposal outright. On the other hand, Dutch leaders realized that a truce with Portugal would enable them to concentrate their forces against Spain.

After prolonged negotiations, a truce was worked out for a ten-year period and signed in June 1641. The truce was to begin in Europe at once. Peace would be declared in Brazil and other areas of the world as soon as proper notice of the truce was transmitted. The Dutch granted military and naval aid to the Portuguese against Spain and agreed to carry on mutual trade and peaceful relations. Negotiations for a permanent treaty were scheduled to begin in eight months. Delays in ratification gave the Dutch an excuse to continue hostilities into 1642. Count Maurice and Viceroy Montalvão were already in negotiations for humanizing the war before the June 1641 truce. When Montalvão was deposed and returned to Lisbon, the junta that succeeded and the new governor-general, Antônio Teles da Silva, eventually came to an agreement with the Dutch.

When João IV came to the throne in December 1640, circumstances forced him to alter many aspects of Portuguese legislation. Portugal needed to obtain aid from other nations to deter Spanish reconquest. Therefore, Portugal granted economic concessions to foreign nations in exchange for their support.

The English were in the best situation to make an advantageous treaty with Portugal. Long-standing trade and generally friendly relations dating back to the thirteenth century, specifically the Treaty of Windsor of 1386, enabled a considerable number of English merchants in Portugal to trade directly with Brazil. Portugal sent a mission to England in February 1641 to obtain English support. At the moment England and Spain were at peace. Charles I, deeply embroiled in a civil war with his own subjects, found much difficulty in arriving at an understanding with Portugal. In the midst of the negotiations, England learned about the favorable terms for commerce and shipping granted the Dutch.

The discussions were prolonged into early 1642, and a treaty was signed on January 29. Four English families were allowed to establish themselves in Pernambuco, Bahia, and Rio de Janeiro. English goods enjoyed reduced taxes: a total of 23%—10% tithe, 10% sisa, and 3% consular fees.

In July a treaty was signed with Sweden calling for peace, friendship, and commercial relations. Sweden also sent military supplies to Portugal. Thus Portugal strengthened its defenses to resist Spanish efforts at reconquest.

The Portuguese in 1641 had few resources to meet mounting problems. The ten-year truce with the Dutch did not stop Dutch attacks. The Dutch East India Company continued to whittle away portions of the Portuguese empire. Portugal had almost no navy and only the remnants of a merchant fleet.

The Conselho Ultramarino was organized in 1642 to govern overseas affairs. Its first president was the Marques de Montalvão, who had been removed from his post as Viceroy of Brazil in 1641 and then rehabilitated on arrival in Portugal. Salvador Correia de Sá e Benevides was one of the councilors. The Conselho's function was to centralize overseas government, but it never achieved authority equivalent to the Council of the Indies that governed, under the king, the Spanish colonies in America.

The policy of the government prohibited commerce with foreign colonies in America. Buenos Aires was the exception. Commerce was encouraged after the establishment of Buenos Aires in 1580 as a route for tapping the Peruvian silver and gold. The separation of Portugal from Spain in 1640 diminished the Rio de la Plata trade for a time, but it later expanded. Not so the commerce with other adjoining or nearby territories under foreign control. Trade with the Maynas on the upper Amazon and the Rio Negro frontier was prohibited—likewise with French Guiana. Some contraband existed, however.

Before 1641 Portuguese merchants could count on the cooperation of the numerous Portuguese who had established businesses in Buenos Aires. The war between Portugal and Spain (1640–1668) made such trade illegal. Nevertheless, in 1643, King João IV asked his advisers for recommendations about how to reopen commerce with the Plata region. Salvador Correia de Sá e Benevides proposed two simultaneous expeditions: one by sea to capture Buenos Aires and the other overland by the Paulistas to attack the Spanish colonies through Paraguay. Success, he said, would facilitate the desired commerce, give Brazil a great area for cattle grazing, and capture the silver trade of Buenos Aires, or even Potosí.

In 1644 António Pais Veigas also suggested attacks on Buenos Aires as one way to capture silver and pay the expenses of an expedition to reconquer Angola, which had been a Dutch possession since 1641. The danger of carrying the war to a Spanish possession was not considered too great since Spain was too weak to send a fleet to protect Buenos Aires.

COUNT MAURICE AND THE NORTHEAST

In the midst of war and administrative problems, Count Maurice devoted much of his energy to building up the Dutch colony in Brazil. The abandoned sugar engenhos were sold at auction and on credit to new owners. The merchants, encouraged by the apparent strength of the Dutch position, lent money to the senhores de engenho to restore their properties, replant cane, and buy slaves. Count Maurice also formed a municipal council, the Escabinos (Schepenen), and appointed officials to look after the interests of the company and to govern in the captured provinces - Alagoas, Paraíba, Itamaracá, and Rio Grande do Norte. He also named a high council and established courts of justice.

Part of his policy of reconciling the Brazilians to Dutch rule was the holding of regular audiences where he listened to grievances. He personally assisted many of the needy, and he punished severely acts against the Brazilians. Three soldiers, for example, were executed for stealing a cow (a normal act in time of war). For his charitable acts, he was compared to Santo António whose reputation among the people was that of the saint.

He limited interest charged on personal loans without security to 18% and on loans secured by personal or real property to 12%. He voided usurious loans made on engenhos and lavradores by loan sharks, Dutch merchants, and Jews. He protested against the high fees and tips (propinas) exacted by functionaries of the courts of justice for performing their duties.

His religious policies with respect to the Catholics won him much support. He permitted Catholic worship, but forbade the entrance of new clerics into Dutch Brazil as long as the existing number was deemed sufficient. He made an exception of some French Capuchins. The Calvinist ministers (predikants) thought him too tolerant and brought pressure on him to limit the freedom of Catholics. Frei Manuel Calado, whose description of Pernambuco under the Dutch is the best written from the Portuguese view, recorded that Count Maurice told him mass could be held behind closed doors within the city limits of Recife. The Protestant ministers were sometimes successful in their protests, however. When Maranhão was captured in 1641, religious freedom was denied.

Count Maurice generally practiced tolerance and understanding toward the Portuguese. In his "political testament" of May 6, 1644, he wrote: "The Portuguese will be submissive if they are treated with courtesy and benevolence . . . I know from my own experience that the Portuguese is a person who values courtesy and good treatment more than he does worldly goods."

Count Maurice's political tact was illustrated in 1640 when he called an assembly of Luso-Brazilians to obtain support against the guerrillas still operating in the countryside. For nine days he listened to requests and complaints against the officials, high and low, and he acted favorably in many instances. This was a rare, perhaps unique, action by a governor in Brazil. He won the good will of large numbers of the Portuguese-Brazilian population. When in 1642 it was rumored that he might be removed from office, a protest was sent to Holland signed by many of the leading citizens: "If he should leave this state, very shortly all that his presence has accomplished and made to bloom will be lost."

The most complete knowledge we have of Brazil in this period comes from the reports prepared by Adriaen van der Dusen on Count Maurice's orders in 1638–39. No other reports of the seventeenth century are equally informative.

The existence of a monocultural economy, in this instance cane sugar, led to serious food deficiencies. The sugar producers, intent only on profits, were not zealous in growing manioc, "the bread of the country." Count Maurice noted that shortages of manioc caused high prices and all suffered, "especially the poor." He issued an edital on January 18, 1638, ordering all landlords to plant two hundred hills of manioc for each slave. Other orders with the same objectives were issued later in 1638, 1639, and 1640. In the last, he noted the noncompliance with his previous orders. He commanded that "no senhor de engenho or cane farmers (lavradores) of whatever class or nation shall begin to mill sugar in the forthcoming cutting season that begins the first August unless he has first planted 300 hills of manioc for each black working person (peça de trabalho), man or woman, he owns." He set an example for emulation when he planted at his own residence 852 orange trees, 50 lemon trees, 80 limões doces, 80 pomegranates, 66 figs, and 700 coconut palms—plus native trees such as the mamão, jenipapo, manga, caju, and many others.

Count Maurice also understood the need of "circuses" as well as bread. The people, the rich as well as the poor, needed diversion from the routine of life. In 1641, he organized "Grandes Cavalhadas" and invited "all the young men and good horsemen who owned fine horses in the entire captaincy of Pernambuco." The principal citizens were seated in the grandstands (palanques e teatros); the common people sat wherever they could find a spot. There were jogos de canas, orangeade to drink, and "even a comedy in the French language, with great ostentation, though few or none of the Portuguese understood the words."

Very entertaining was the trick of the "boi voador", the flying bull, to celebrate the opening of the new bridge across the river. The credulous people flocked to Recife to see the Dutch "miracle." After showing a live bull atop a building, the bull was withdrawn. Then a bull's hide stuffed with straw was drawn through the air in ropes—an event recorded by Frei Manuel de Calado.

Recife, rather than Olinda, became the capital city of the Dutch. Count Maurice made great improvements. The street and squares were renamed and paved with stones in the Dutch fashion. To protect the new pavements, he forbade sugar cane carts of more than 300 kilos (about 660 pounds) to drive in the town. Cane was thereafter transported in boats on the river.

In 1642 Count Maurice constructed a large building, named by him Vrijburg, which was located at the confluence of the Capibaribe and Beberibe rivers. It was an example of how the city could develop if others followed suit. The next year another building, called Boa Vista, was erected near the center of the town. Vrijburg had an extensive orchard described by Frei Calado. It contained fruit trees of every kind that grew in Brazil and many brought in from other parts of the world. A zoological garden had "every type of bird and animal to be found." Calado made a long list. "There was not an unusual thing (coisa curiosa) in Brazil that was not to be found there."

He also assembled a museum containing everything characteristic of Brazil, such as bows, arrows, spears, Indian feather work, and fine furniture made of Jacarandá wood and ivory—"all elegantly worked and all made in Brazil" with ornamental carvings of tropical plants, palm leaves, cashew, and pineapple. The artists he brought to Brazil, Frans Post and Albert Eckhout, did many fine paintings showing the varied types of people of Brazil. They compiled a vast collection of paintings of animals and plants of northeast Brazil and Africa. Much of this survives today in European museums. Until the nineteenth century there were no scientific observations of Brazil superior to those made at Count Maurice's direction.

Other artists who accompanied Count Maurice were Zacharias

Wagener, Pierre Gondreville, and Cornelis Sebastiaansz Golijath, a cartographer who made valuable maps and drawings of Recife and forts in Bahia. Among the scientists were George Marcgraf (Marcgrave), who made astronomical and meteorological studies. He constructed the first observatory known in the New World and was the first to observe and describe solar eclipses in the New World. He also made a topographical map of the coast between Rio Grande do Norte and Sergipe, finished in 1643 and published in 1647 by Barlaeus. Willem Piso, physician to Count Maurice, made studies of the diseases of Brazil; they were not outdated until the nineteenth century—and still have relevance. Many of the officials who came during the Dutch occupation and some of the predikants, though not ranked as artists or scientists, nevertheless were men of talent and learning who made observations and published works that preserve for us much knowledge of Brazil.

Recife became one of the most important cities in the western hemisphere under the stimulating guidance of Count Maurice. It was both the political capital and economic center of Dutch Brazil. Its significance in the Dutch mind was so great that a map, made by Father Carrafa and published by Johannes Blaeu, measured the meridians of longitude from Recife. The population of about six thousand was very heterogeneous. French merchants and soldiers were numerous. They built a French Calvinist church. Some of the French were Catholics, however, openly or secretly. Several wrote letters and accounts of their observations in Brazil. Some Frenchmen also served in the Portuguese armed forces, reversing the traditional role of their countrymen in Brazilian warfare.

The English were also present. Captain Goodlad commanded a company of English soldiers. Others listed as English were Colonel James Henderson, Majors Sedenum van Poynets, and Philip Andrews. Still another English soldier of special interest was Cuthbert Pudsey, who wrote an account of his experiences; it is still unpublished and now resides in the Biblioteca Nacional of Rio de Janeiro. Samuel Bachiler, a Church of England minister, preached in both Recife and Paraíba.

There were also Scots present. Many were retail merchants and peddlers—the same role they had in New Amsterdam (New York) during this period. They made large sales in the countryside. The Scots encountered considerable Dutch prejudice because they were transients who took their profits home to Scotland and left, the Dutch thought, no profit to Brazil. This viewpoint has a familiar ring; it is an attitude many people continue to express about the effect of foreign capital in the modern era.

Large numbers of Germans also served in the mercenary army, including the commander-in-chief from 1647 to 1654, Sigismund von Schoppe. The Polish Colonel Crestofle d'Artischau Arciszewski was a brilliant field commander whose disagreements with Count Maurice led to his disgrace and return to Europe. Danes, Swedes, and other foreigners served also. As noted earlier, armies were not based on national patriotism but paid service. Count Maurice and all the higher officers were mercenaries.

The Jews numbered about one thousand by some estimates and more according to others. They were a large percentage of the total population. Both Askenazi and Sephardic Jews migrated to Dutch Brazil, where the religious atmosphere was less hostile than anywhere except Holland itself. Sephardic Jews were more numerous than the Askenazi, and the former adjusted more easily to the country. Some came with the conquest. They enjoyed the same religious rights as other inhabitants of the Netherlands and Dutch Brazil. The Sephardim spoke Portuguese as well as Dutch, giving them a considerable advantage as intermediaries between the conquering Dutch and the Portuguese-speaking population. They worked principally as brokers, sugar merchants, slave traders, money lenders, and tax collectors. They prospered and thereby engendered the envy of competitors in these same fields.

Catholics and Calvinists agreed on one point—Jews should not be allowed freedom of worship. The Jews had two synagogues in Recife and others in Paraíba and Penedo. The Catholics protested against the "favors the Israelites enjoy, having open synagogues, which even the Moors and Turks find scandalous." The Calvinists in 1640 protested against the "boldness" of the Jews: "so great that they not only meet publicly in the market here in Recife but also are planning to build a synagogue." The ministers wanted them stopped. Pressure on the Jews was constant and in 1645 they appealed to the Estates-General of Holland for protection.

There is no way to measure the relative extent of Jewish participation in the economic activities of the colony, but the jealousy was widespread. As a modern Brazilian scholar, J.A. Gonsalves de Melo, writes: "This animosity became a real antisemitic campaign." The Jewish population can be differentiated by noting that some were New Christians who first came to Brazil and then returned to Judaism; some were New Christians who did not return to Judaism; and some were New Christians who escaped to Holland, where they returned to Judaism and later emigrated to Dutch Brazil. Charles Boxer remarks about the Askenazim and Sephardim: "Both kinds of Jews were disliked and despised by their 'Old Christian' neighbors, whether Catholic Portuguese or Calvinist Dutch; but the numbers and influence of the Jewish community, though relatively considerable, have been exaggerated by contemporary pamphleteers and modern historians." As early as 1637 they were denounced as "people inclined to deceit and welshing (falencias) . . . and despised by all the nations of the world." Some of the jealousy arose because of their enjoyment of economic rights denied in Holland—for example, the right to engage in retail trade.

In 1641, alleging that "Jews from all the corners of the world are moving here," the city council (escabinos) of Recife asserted that the Jews dominated everything "to such an extent that the Christians are mere spectators of the business of the Jews." They advocated barring Jews from "maintaining stores or selling retail." Sometimes Jews suffered physical attacks in the streets—in one case, a Jew accused of blasphemy was stoned. Another, not one of the economically successful, committed suicide when unable to pay his debts. He was refused burial and his body was exposed on the gallows. They lived mainly on one street, known as Jodenstraat, street of the Jews. Their cemetery was located outside the city.

Some of the prominent Sephardic Jews of Amsterdam moved to

Brazil. Rabbi Isaac Aboad Fonseca was there from 1642 to 1654. Others were the physician Abraham Mercado and a young medical student, Isaac de Castro, who was burned by the Inquisition in Lisbon in 1647. Rabbi Fonseca wrote the first Jewish literary work in Brazil, *Zekher asiti laniflaet El* (I made a memorial unto God's miracles), in 1646. Prejudice against New Christians, especially those of the second or later generation who had been born Christians and later reverted to Judaism (the men being circumcised as adults), was stronger than against the Jews themselves. Most left Brazil when the Dutch surrendered in 1654. Some returned to Holland, some went to the West Indies, and some to New Amsterdam (New York) to form the first Jewish group in North America.

Marriages between foreign men and Luso-Brazilian women was much more common than between foreign women and Luso-Brazilian men. There were, of course, a great many more European men than women in the colony, and foreign women were often married before arrival. Father Calado says about twenty women married foreigners, which seems a very small percentage of mixed marriages; but some prominent present-day names with Dutch, or other foreign origin, date from this period. Father Calado did not consider them married in reality because the ceremony was Protestant. Foreigners married Indian or Negro women in some instances. No documents exist to show how much concubinage and rape occurred during war conditions.

11

DUTCH RETREAT, 1641–1654

onditions seemed to favor the Dutch in 1641, and many believed that they had established themselves permanently in Brazil. This was not so, however. Relations between the Dutch and the Luso-Brazilians were never easy. Culture and religion were different, even if not always antagonistic. Although many moradores accepted the new situation, and some cooperated and prospered, the division between the two peoples was visible and, in the main, unbreachable. The Dutch West India Company did not view Brazil as an extension of Holland but as a commercial operation. Brazil in 1630—when the Dutch arrived—was a firmly established Portuguese and Catholic society not pushed aside easily by a foreign company.

The interests of the senhores de engenho and the other landholders at times coincided with those of the Dutch, Jewish, and other foreign merchants, but in the long run they were not the same. These groups depended on one another but had no mutual affection. The landowners owed great sums to the government and to merchants for loans made to restore plantations and buy slaves after the devastating war. This indebtedness was a constant strain on both sides. Fires in 1640, floods and epidemics among the slaves in 1641 and 1642, a drought in 1644, and then a fall in the price of sugar from 28 schellingen in March 1642 to 21 schellingen in February 1645, a figure below the cost of production, were factors increasing the debts of the producers on loans taken at high interest rates.

The Dutch period has been characterized as the "Sugar Wars," not merely in the sense that both sides fought for control of sugar producing areas, but also because sugar sustained both sides. The area of Brazil outside Dutch occupation was able, despite the Dutch blockade to produce, export, and sell the sugar that was the main resource of both Brazil and the mother country. The Dutch occupation was also sustained and depended on the production and export of sugar from Pernambuco. Hence the destructive nature of the wars— continuous efforts by both sides to obliterate the sugar production of the other. In the long run, the Brazilian-Portuguese were more effective in this scorched-earth policy.

From 1630 to 1641 the Portuguese armies, composed of Spanish and Italian as well as Portuguese soldiers, had been mainly under Portuguese command. That is to say, soldiers that Spain could recruit as long as Spanish kings ruled Portugal. From 1641 forward, when Portugal was fighting for independence from Spain, the war against the Dutch in Brazil was fought mainly by Brazilians. They were the Portuguese living in Brazil, Indians, mamelucos, Blacks, or any mixtures of these groups. Only the top commanders were usually (but not always) Portuguese officers.

Religious differences added to the conflict. The sermons of the priests and friars aroused the Catholic population. Meanwhile, Protestant ministers remained firm in their hatred of the Catholics. The prohibition against the entrance of new priests and friars to replace those who had died reduced the number steadily and threatened eventual extinction of all ordained Catholic priests who could administer the sacraments. The moradores complained that there was no one to teach grammar and Latin and that "many were dying in all the captaincies without confession."

The restoration of the Portuguese line of kings in Portugal in December 1640 revived the hopes of those who wanted the Dutch expelled. In 1641, or possibly 1642, a number of the chief moradores who had cooperated with the Dutch sent a letter to João IV congratulating him on his ascension to the throne and asking him not to forget Brazil. Among the signers were the future leaders of the revolt that came in 1645.

The Portuguese and Brazilians accused the Dutch of violating the truce of 1641. The terms had allowed a year for the official transmission of the news to all parts of the Portuguese possessions. Count Maurice believed he saw an opportunity to take advantage of trends favoring the Dutch. He seized Maranhão in Brazil and both Angola and the island of São Tomé in Africa. Still other acts by the Dutch in Angola and elsewhere strengthened the moradores in their resolve to revolt.

An Indian uprising against the Dutch in Ceará in 1643, the recall of Count Maurice in 1644, the plotting of André Vidal de Negreiros on orders from Governor-general António Teles da Silva, and a promise made in secret by João IV to Frei Estevão de Jesus of Pernambuco were all factors leading up to the decision to revolt against Dutch rule.

The plan was to invite the principal Dutch civil and military officials to a banquet held in the home of one of the conspiradores, and then arrest them. The plan leaked to the Dutch, however. Organized by Antônio Dias Cardoso, a veteran of the guerrilla wars during the first years of Dutch occupation, the Luso-Brazilian forces later defeated the Dutch under Hendrik van Haus at Outeiro das Taboças (Hill of the Bamboos) on August 3.

The rebels received little aid from the king of Portugal, who feared to sacrifice the support of the Dutch in his war against Spain. Indeed, two terços of infantry under Martín Soares Moreno and André Vidal de Negreiros were sent from Salvador, ostensibly to help crush the revolt. But they joined the revolt instead. The Luso-Brazilians inflicted more defeats on the Dutch, who found themselves besieged in Recife. An impasse followed in which the Dutch dominated the sea and thus could provision the city, but they could not clear the rebels from the countryside.

At this juncture the Dutch seemed militarily much stronger. Father António Vieira made an assessment of the situation in the *Papel Forte*:

In Brazil they have more than sixty ships, some of great force; we have seven, if indeed we have them still. They are free from the power of Spain; we have the whole power of Spain to contend with. They have no enemy in Europe; we have no friend . . . . Finally, the Dutch have their industry, their diligence, their desire to gain, their unanimity, and their love of the common weal; we have our disunion, our envy, our presumption, our negligence, and our perpetual attention to individual interests.

But the Dutch had serious problems of their own. The West India Company was heavily in debt. Furthermore, the political structure of the United Provinces belied the name. Amsterdam dominated, or sought to dominate, the other provinces; but there was often so much dissension that no action could be taken, or action was long delayed. Some of the Dutch were much more interested in maintaining peace with Portugal in order to obtain free access to the salt of Setubal, which was used in curing their fish catches. They were reluctant to support the company in Brazil.

The stalemate in Pernambuco dragged on several years before the Estates General resolved to reinforce Dutch Brazil. It sent an army of 5,000 mercenaries in 1648 under German General Sigismund von Schoppe. Believed large enough to defeat easily the numerically inferior local forces, it suffered instead a disastrous defeat by 2,200 men commanded by Francisco Barreto on April 19, 1648, at a hill called Guararapes. Repeating the same mistake that had cost them the first battle, the Dutch were again badly defeated at Guararapes on February 19, 1649. The war was again at a stalemate.

Father Antônio Vieira who advocated at one time trading Brazil for Dutch aid against Spain, thought the best policy for Portugal was the organization of commercial companies on the model of the English and Dutch companies. One company would operate in the East, and one in the West, meaning Brazil. The capital would be raised from Swedish, French, and Portuguese investors. He proposed that the merchants who traded with Brazil, among them the New Christians, should be required to invest. Vieira also proposed that the Jews who had escaped from Portugal, the Sephardim, and lived in Holland or other countries should be invited to invest. His opponents considered

Vieira's suggestion of admitting foreign capital an affront to national pride. His proposed incorporation of Portuguese New Christians and foreign Jews was denounced as a betrayal of Christianity. João IV did not accept Vieira's ideas, nor did the Inquisition, which protested that its very existence depended on the revenues received from the property confiscated from those convicted of Judaizing. To exempt them from confiscation, as Vieira proposed, would be ungodly.

An opinion presented to the king on December 5, 1648, discussed the relative positions of Portugal and Holland. It advocated the formation of a commercial company as "the only solution under God" to supply Brazil. Some thirty to forty warships plus another forty armed ships belonging to individuals were expected to make the Dutch consider peace. Meanwhile, in Brazil both sides were in a desperate economic and military condition. Both the Luso-Brazilian besiegers of Recife and the besieged Dutch suffered hunger and short supplies.

King João IV finally came round to the side of those advocating a company. Disregarding the Inquisition, on February 6, 1649, he prohibited the seizure of the property of New Christians condemned by the Inquisition and permitted the investment of such property in the new company. An alvará of March 10 approved the articles of incorporation of the Companhia Geral do Comércio do Brazil.

The principal investors were the wealthiest men of Portugal. The Botelho family, for example, subscribed 40,000 cruzados. The total raised was 1,255,000 cruzados. How much came from New Christians? Charles R. Boxer writes: "All the leading foreign merchants in Portugal were urged to subscribe liberally to the Company, on pain of not being allowed to participate in the trade with any of the Portuguese colonies. It is uncertain how far these foreign merchants did participate, but the bulk of the money subscribed (1,255,000) cruzados came from the leading New-Christian merchants of Lisbon."

The duties and privileges of the company were set forth in fifty-two articles. All Portuguese territories were eligible to invest, with a minimum set at twenty cruzados. A directory was limited to those who invested 5,000 cruzados. The shares could not be sequestered— this provision was a protection against the Inquisition. The company had a primary obligation and a unique privilege; the obligation was to maintain a fleet of thirty-six warships to convoy the merchant ships, and the privilege was a monopoly over the export of wine, olive oil, codfish, and wheat flour to Brazil. Later a brazilwood monopoly was given to the company. The company could levy taxes on sugar, tobacco, cotton, hides, and other products at prescribed rates. The products imported into Brazil were to be sold at fixed prices. To protect the monopoly, the king prohibited the manufacture of honey, wine, and brandy.

The company was obligated to send two fleets annually to Brazil protected by sixteen warships. The first fleet sailed from Lisbon in November 1649 and included 48 merchantmen, with 32 armed, plus an escort of 18 men-of-war. Of these, ten were English ships on charter. The first port of call was Salvador. From there, a portion of the fleet was scheduled to go to Rio de Janeiro to escort twenty merchantmen awaiting protection.

Four months later on March 7, 1650, the convoy anchored in Bahia. Along the route there was a skirmish with the Dutch near Recife, with perhaps one ship lost. The citizens of Salvador were not in all respects happy to see the Portuguese fleet. On the one hand, it was good to have fresh supplies and the means of sending home their sugar and other crops. But on this occasion, as on most similar occasions, the sailors and soldiers, long at sea, acted in a brutish and licentious way. The people declared they preferred another Dutch invasion to rescue by such friends.

On the return trip the Bahia fleet of about seventy vessels made Lisbon in January 1651 in good condition with 40,000 caixas of sugar, plus tobacco and other goods. The Rio de Janeiro convoy, on the other hand, was attacked on entering the Tagus by an English fleet. Why this attack by an old ally, an affirmed enemy of Spain and strong rivals of the Dutch? The intricacies of international politics explain. After the execution of Charles I of England, his sons were welcomed in Portugal by João IV.

The Commonwealth government under Oliver Cromwell took exception and for most of 1650 the English and Portuguese were at war.

Portugal was forced to sign a harsh treaty. Admiral Blake blockaded the Tagus from May to October, and during this interval, in September, he caught the Rio de Janeiro fleet that had sailed without convoy. Only nine of its ships reached Portugal safely. The Portuguese had to shift their chartering activities to other sources than English ships until a firmer peace was established.

The Brazil Company should have been a success, but it operated in a period of enormous difficulties. Many of the company's problems were internal. The Inquisition bitterly opposed the royal policy of protecting New Christians. Others alleged that the company did not maintain fleets as large as prescribed, that the amounts of monopolized products taken to Brazil were not enough to meet the demand, that it charged unjustly high prices, and that Brazilian produce spoiled because the company did not supply enough shipping. Two examples of the irritations blamed on the company can be cited: at times mass could not be said in Rio de Janeiro because there was no wine and Espírito Santo had insufficient oil.

Part of the difficulties arose from the marketing system. The company sold wholesale. Retailers marked up the prices and created scarcities that drove prices in the black market even higher. The company reaped the blame. In Brazil the production of wine and brandy, contrary to law, hurt the company. The company earned small or no profits, only dividends of 15% were paid.

João IV put great hopes in the company as the salvation of Brazil and worked hard at finding remedies for its troubles. Beset with criticism, João IV attempted to remedy its worse abuses and faults. The most pressing complaint related to the failure to supply the market with adequate quantities of monopoly articles. The venality of company employees and officials was believed to be the cause of scarcity and high prices. João appointed a commission of inquiry which recommended abolition of the monopoly because it injured the company itself. Complaints and suggested remedies mounted up. After João IV died in 1656, the Conselho da Fazenda recommended to Queen-Regent Luisa the incorporation of the company into the state. An alvará of May 9, 1658, abolished the monopoly and reduced the fleet sailings to one a year, guarded by only ten warships. Navigation to Brazil was freed, but the return voyage of all ships had to be with the company fleet. A tax on sugar compensated the company for the loss of monopoly rights. The intended solutions failed. The tax on sugar came at a time when foreign competition was increasing. The system of free shipping did not meet the Brazilian demand for supplies, and complaints about shortages continued.

The crown made another effort on November 15, 1662, and took over the administration. The next year, the company became the Junta do Commércio, or a tribunal of commerce with general duties not confined to Brazil. It continued control of the naval fleet for the annual convoy.

The Dutch still retained the possibility of victory in Dutch Brazil until 1652 when the first of three Dutch-English wars began. The war was not the sole cause of the failure to hold Brazil, but it was important. The basis of Dutch wealth and power was their shipping and banking. Too small in territory to develop a manufacturing or military power, they relied on their seaborne resources. They shipped not merely the merchandise that flowed between them and other countries, but also goods between England, France, Portugal, and other territories. In 1651, under the rule of the Commonwealth (Charles I having been beheaded in 1649), England passed the first Navigation Act, requiring all imports or exports to be shipped either in English vessels or those of the country of origin. The law applied to all countries, not Holland alone, but it affected that nation the most, and Holland fought back against this serious threat to its economy.

In 1653 João IV, taking advantage of Dutch involvement with England, put a large fleet at sea to sail to the relief of Pernambuco. Under command of Pedro Jaques de Magalhães, the fleet closed the port of Recife. On January 26, 1654, Recife surrendered, and the Dutch period in Brazil, except for sporadic efforts in the Amazon, came to an end.

For three years after the Dutch retreat from Brazil, negotiations between Portugal and Holland continued in an effort to settle their differences. Tiring of the delays, the Dutch sent Admiral Opdam with a demand that the Portuguese return Brazil, Angola, and São Tomé within two weeks and also pay an indemnity of 600,000 florins, 13,000 boxes of sugar, one thousand cows, 300 horses, 600 sheep, and other considerations of value.

The Portuguese refused and within a month the Dutch fleet withdrew, after presenting a declaration of war on Portugal. Joined by Admiral Ruiter, who took command, the Dutch fleet blockaded Portugal from Setúbal to the Berlengas Islands until winter drove them back. They appeared again, however, the next summer. After three months, complications with Denmark and Sweden forced the Dutch to sail home.

The restoration of the Stuart kings in England in 1660 led to renewed peace with Portugal and the marriage in 1662 of Charles II to Catherine of Braganza, daughter of João IV and sister of Afonso VI. Under English influence Portugal and Holland signed a peace treaty in August 1661. Portugal agreed to pay four million cruzados indemnity to Holland over a period of sixteen years at the rate of 250,000 a year in specie, sugar, tobacco, or salt. Portugal also agreed to restore Dutch artillery captured in Brazil and to allow the Dutch to trade between Brazil and Portugal. The Praia do Flamengo in Rio de Janeiro drew its name from the Dutch merchants established there. The failure to fix firmly the effective data of the treaty enabled the Dutch "legally" to carry on the war in the East and capture Quilon, Canganor, Cananor, and Cochin and to hold them thereafter. Ceylon had already fallen in 1658.

A portion of the four millions due as an indemnity was raised by assessing a tax on Brazil. The tax amounted to 140,000 cruzados annually. The distribution of the assessment among the captaincies provides a good indication of the relative wealth of Brazilian areas: Bahia was assessed 80,000, and the remaining captaincies 60,000 each. The tax, supposedly expiring at the end of sixteen years, continued to be assessed even after independence, and it was still in the imperial Brazilian budget of 1830.

12

BANDEIRAS, 1625–1650

ecause Brazil was not unified under a governor-general, men who might have been used to war against the Dutch went instead, in the usual way, to hunt for Indians. Bandeiras put out from São Paulo and other areas. The number of slaving raids increased greatly in the seventeenth century and were aimed initially at the Spanish Jesuit missions. Captured Indians sold readily in São Paulo, Santos, Rio de Janeiro, and further north in Bahia and Pernambuco. In Rio the price of a working-age Indian was twenty milreis in 1628, one fifth the sum for a Black of the same age. Because so many were shipped out, they were sometimes scarce in São Paulo.

The demand in the northern captaincies increased during the Dutch occupation because the African market was closed or partly blocked to the Portuguese. Nonetheless, most of the Indians who worked in the north and northeast were from the local areas rather than the south. When the Dutch occupied Salvador in 1624–25, the câmara of Salvador appealed to São Paulo for Indians.

After 1628 the attacks of the bandeirantes became regular and systematic. Guaíra was the nearest and easiest source of Indians. In 1629 a bandeira led by Manuel Preto, Antonio Raposo Tavares, Pedro Vaz de Barros, Salvador Pires de Medeiros, and other Paulistas—the largest bandeira yet organized with 900 mamelukes and 2,000 Indian auxiliaries led by 69 Paulistas—moved out from São Paulo in four companies. It destroyed a number of Indian reductions and the Spanish towns of Villa Rica on the Ivaí River and Ciudad Real near the mouth of the Pequirí. Several thousand captured Indians were taken to São Paulo for sale. The Jesuits fled to the Paraná River with their remaining flock. Two Spanish Jesuits accompanied the bandeirantes to São Paulo to protest to their fellow Portuguese Jesuits and to Portuguese authorities. Their protests were in vain. They later carried their case to Madrid and got permission to arm their Indians. The Spanish Jesuits moved their remaining Indians southward to the Uruguay and Tape rivers and west of the Paraná to Itatí (Itatím) in present-day South Mato Grosso.

The bandeirantes pursued the Spanish Jesuits as they retreated south. In 1635 Luís Dias Leme made an exploratory raid, known as the bandeira of Aracambi, going by sea to Rio Grande do Sul. He remained for eight months, possibly as a reconnaissance for the raid the next year. António Raposo Tavares led a raid in 1636 with 120 whites and Mamelukes, plus 1,000 Indian allies. This bandeira attacked in the Jacuí River region of Rio Grande do Sul, returning to São Paulo with their captives. Francisco Bueno started out on the Taquarí River in 1637 in the Tape region, attacking the missions on the Uruguay River and returning in 1639 to São Paulo with a large number of captives. After 1635 the raids extended to the reductions of San Pedro and San Pablo, Concepción, Santiago de Xerez near los Gualachos, San Joseph, Angeles, Santa Maria Maior, and other affluents of the Aquidauana.

In 1637 Francisco Bueno led almost one hundred Paulistas including members of the Cunha, Bueno, and Prêto families in a bandeira. Another bandeira into the Ibicuí River moved out in 1638 under Fernão Dias Pais, later to win the sobriquet "the Emerald Hunter"; he was accompanied by his brother Pascoal Leite Pais. They met an unpleasant surprise, suffering a reverse in 1638 in Casapaguaçú. It was inflicted by the combined forces of the Jesuits and Governor Pedro de Lugo y Navarra of Paraguay.

The attacks made on the missions by the bandeirantes had the approval of Bishop Bernardo de Cárdenas, who was an enemy of the

Jesuits while serving as acting governor of Paraguay in 1640. Such an attitude was not typical of the Spanish authorities, however. By 1641 the region along the Tape and Uruguay rivers had been raided, and all the reductions of Indians captured. The missionaries were forced back to the banks of the Uruguay and Paraná Rivers. Here the Jesuits were able to repel the bandeirantes Jerónimo Pedroso and Manuel Pires. The bandeirante Francisco Bueno reached the Paraguay River in 1644 and died there. After these defeats the bandeirantes sought easier conquests nearer São Paulo to the west and north; but their raiding for Indians and searching for metals never ceased.

The bandeirantes did not earn big profits from their raids except in the attacks on the Jesuit reductions, where large numbers of Indians were captured with comparative ease. Hunting unreduced Indians scattered over wide areas, who were often more knowledgeable about the geography than the bandeirantes and ready to fight back for months or years, often yielded few captives to be divided among hundreds of hunters.

The low price of Indian slaves in comparison with Africans made the bandeiras a marginal economic enterprise. Only the great demand in São Paulo, and the relative poverty of most of the hunters justified the continuance of the bandeiras. For many men, the choice was either going on bandeiras or doing nothing.

The Portuguese revolution against the Spanish line of kings in December 1640 created a less favorable situation for the bandeirantes. Once the change was known in Brazil and Spanish America, the continuance of the Spanish governors' complacent policy toward the Paulistas was no longer possible. Coming close on the heals of the defeats suffered in their southward drives, the bandeirantes found it safer to direct their attention farther from Spanish centers of power. They went no longer toward Paraguay but north and west of São Paulo in their Indian raids and searches for precious metals and gems. They nevertheless opened southern Brazil to Portuguese occupation later in the century.

The progress of the war against the Dutch in the Northeast affected rather directly the activities of the bandeirantes. When the Dutch controlled parts of the African coast, from about 1641 to 1648, and the supply of African slaves was partially curtailed, Indians were more marketable. After the reconquest of Angola in 1648 by Salvador Correia de Sá, the market for Indians decreased. When the Dutch shifted their purchases of sugar to the Caribbean islands after 1654, the decline of Brazilian sugar production lessened still more the demand for Indian slaves. But the market never dried up completely so long as there were Indians who could be captured and enslaved.

When the Spanish Jesuits had successfully appealed to Philip IV to permit the arming of their Indians, they had also carried an appeal to the pope. The result was the publication in Brazil of the breve *Veritas Ipsa* of 1537 favoring the granting of freedom to the Indians. It had been directed a century earlier at the Indians under Spanish control in the Caribbean and continental Spanish America.

The papal decision to circulate *Veritas Ipsa* in Brazil, where it arrived in 1640, came about only in part because of the problems the Spanish Jesuits were having with the bandeirantes. Conflicts between civilians and churchmen over the Indians were constant in colonial society. Although they were faithful Catholics who were loyal to the king and ready to die in the fight against heretics and foreigners, the citizens of Brazil viewed the Indian question in terms quite different from the issues of religious faith and patriotism. They saw nothing incongruous in opposing, with violence if necessary, any effort to deprive them of their "right" to capture and enslave the Indians.

When the prelacy of Rio de Janeiro had been created in 1575, for example, the people reacted quickly against the presence of a religious authority that threatened their hold on the Indians. The first prelate, Father Bartolomeu Simões Pereira, was harried by his parishioners and died in 1598 in circumstances that suggested poison. The second prelate held his office only two years; persecuted and maltreated by the people, he was deposed by the Relação of Bahia. A third nominee refused to serve.

When the Prelate Father Matéus da Costa Aborim took the side of the Indians, levying spiritual penalties against those who, in his view, abused them, he was bitterly opposed and died from poison in

1629. The next two nominees refused the post, and the third, Father Lourenço de Mendonça, who continued the protective attitude toward the Indians, met strong resistance. His opponents exploded a barrel of gunpowder in his residence, but failed to kill him. He was forced to return to Portugal. His successor, Father Antônio de Mariz Loureiro, was compelled on a visit to São Paulo to take refuge in the convent of São Francisco. He returned to Rio de Janeiro to meet stronger threats. He fled to Espírito Santo where he was poisoned, escaping with his life but not his sanity; he had lost his mind.

The clergy were part of the royal administration and, in effect, official. The problem rose in part from the low quality of the clergy in Brazil. They were drawn, as one modern Catholic historian writes, "from the dregs of the kingdom." How little papal support of the clergy in the fight against civilians mattered is illustrated by the case of Father Manuel de Sousa Almada, who served from 1658 to 1670. After the customary friction with the people, his residence was bombarded with a cannon. When the case came before the Relação of Bahia, the attackers were absolved and the prelate had to pay the costs.

Not all churchmen suffered as much as those we have sketched. But in general, the churchmen were at loggerheads with civilians over the Indians.

In Santos the Jesuits were forced as a result of *Veritas Ipsa* to barricade themselves in their church. When the Superior showed the sacrament to the people, they dropped to their knees in worship but continued to shout "throw out the padres, kill them." The vicar was forced to hand over the breve, and the people lifted the siege. Civilians put their souls in the hands of the Carmelites and Franciscans, who did not enforce the Pope's breve. The Santistas awaited news of actions in other cities, especially São Paulo.

The reaction in São Paulo to the papal breve was at first mild, even though the captaincy's economic life was closely tied to the enslavement of Indians. The Portuguese party, the Pires, was pro-Jesuit. But political power was then in the hands of the Spanish party, the Camargos. Gradually the Camargos won the people to the anti-Jesuit side.

The Jesuits were driven out of São Paulo in July. They took refuge in Santos but were expelled the next month. The Vicar of São Paulo placed an interdict on the city and forbade the people to receive the sacraments.

The Camargos and Pires factions remained on opposite sides of the issue. Fernão de Camargo, known as the Tigre, killed Pedro Taques of the Pires. Taques had attempted to prevent people from entering churches belonging to religious orders that continued to give the sacraments irrespective of the Jesuit vicar's interdict. The Jesuits were not allowed to return to São Paulo until 1653, when the Pires faction again controlled the câmara and the Camargos had relaxed their anti-Jesuit stand.

When Pope Urban's breve reached Rio de Janeiro in April 1640, the governor was Salvador Correia de Sá e Benevides. The economic situation in Rio was very different than in São Paulo and Santos-São Vicente. Rio had other sources of wealth and mostly African slaves. Nevertheless, the reaction of the people toward the Jesuits was violent: "kill them, kill them, kick out the Jesuits." Governor Sá was in a strong position vis-á-vis the Jesuits and the people, which enabled him to quell the incipient rebellion. He accompanied Father Diaz Taño, the bearer of the breve, with an armed guard to the Jesuit Colégio. He called himself a "slave and brother of the Company of Jesus." Sá was "the largest landowner and slave holder in Brazil." This wealth gave him dominance over the câmara, which usually did his bidding. He arranged a compromise between the Jesuits and the people. The câmara nullified the breve, in effect, which calmed the anti-Jesuit outburst.

The conflict between civilians and churchmen for control of the Indians continued in the north and Amazon region as well. It dated from the beginning of settlement. The rivalry was sharpened when Frei Christóvão de Lisboa arrived to enforce the royal alvará of May 15, 1624, for the protection of the Indians. There was never a time thereafter when the conflict was not more or less acute.

In 1626 Pedro Teixeira led an expedition up the Amazon as far as the Tapajós. Such expeditions were designated as "Tropas de Resgates" (rescue parties) in order to circumvent the laws that forbade enslaving Indians except for "just" causes. The hunters alleged they were seizing only Indians already enslaved by others. Teixeira repeated the expedition in 1628 with Pedro da Costa Favela as his partner. Such predatory raids gave the Portuguese a better view of the river and its immensity.

The Carmelites had reached the region as early as 1627 and the Jesuits by 1636. The Jesuit Luís de Figueira, between 1639 and 1643, and Antônio Vieira, at various periods, supplied the chief inspiration for the missionary and pioneer work. The Amazon was visualized as becoming for the Portuguese Jesuits what Paraguay was for Spaniards. It offered the clergy the prospect of a rich harvest of heathen souls. The Amazon also had for clergy and laymen alike an abundance of forest products, which had the potential of enriching them.

Teixeira began his most famous Amazon exploit in 1637-39. The event that inspired his expedition was the arrival in Belém of two Spanish Franciscan missionaries who had come down the Amazon and its confluents from the Spanish missions established on the east side of the Andes. In the Portuguese view, their arrival was considered a Spanish reaffirmation of their rights to lands west of the Line of Demarcation, and hence the entire Amazon basin. The capitão-mor of Pará, Jacomé Raimundo de Noronha, decided to make a counter move to check the Spanish claim. At this time Spaniards and Portuguese were still under one crown, but they were very conscious of their different nationalities. The man that Noronha chose to lead the upriver expedition was Pedro Teixeira. This was not a . . . (missing)

*Professor Diffie's manuscript ended suddenly in mid-sentence with the word "missing" in parentheses as shown above. The additional material was never found either by him or the editor. The narrative below [in brackets] was graciously furnished by Dauril Alden in the summer of 1985.

[Captain Teixeira's party, which numbered about 2,000 people, including 1,200 Indian bowmen and paddlers, and one of the Franciscans and four Spanish soldiers who had appeared in Belém, set out from the mouth of the Tocantins river in late October 1637 in more than forty great canoes. They paddled up the Amazon, Solimões, and Napo rivers; by July 1638 they reached the spot from which the Spanish friars had begun their downriver journey. There Teixeira left most of his men and continued over the Andes to Quito, where he was received with a mixture of amazement and alarm. Subsequently the viceroy of Peru, rejecting suggestions that the Portuguese "intruders" be jailed for their daring, ordered them back to Belém. They were accompanied by two Jesuits, four Mercedarian friars, and one Francisco, who went to keep watch on the suspicious Portuguese.

When Teixeira reached the left bank of the Napo (August 16, 1639), he complied with his secret instructions from captain-major Noronha and formally took possession of the entire valley for Portugal and established an outpost, Tabatinga, to mark Brazil's westernmost boundary in defiance of the Treaty of Tordesillas (1494). That act became the basis for Portugal's (and later Brazil's) claim to all of Amazonia. Two years after Teixeira's return to Belém, one of his Jesuit companions, Cristobal de Acuña, rector of the college of Cuenca in Quito (modern Ecuador), published his seminal analysis of the economic resources of the Amazon—the famous *New Discovery of . . . the Amazons* (Madrid, 1641), which the Spanish government hastily suppressed because it revealed how easy it would be to enter the undefended backdoor of the viceroyalty of Peru.]

The middle of the seventeenth century marked a transition in the objectives of the bandeiras. The large bandeiras designed to gather Indian slaves, facilitated by Spanish Jesuit missions that gathered Indians into groupings convenient for capture, generally ended for lack of easy prey. The missions were either too far away or were defended. The interior Indians were difficult to capture, were fewer in number, and often had the means and will to defend themselves. The bandeirante had to hunt out Indians in the western and north-western hinterlands (sertões) of São Paulo, Minas Gerais, Bahia, Pernambuco, Goiás and Mato Grosso. Indians along the Amazon River and its confluents were hunted, by expeditions (called tropos de resgotes) originating from Belém and other towns near the mouth of the river.

In the case of the bandeiras out of São Paulo, the distances were so great, three or four times farther than the sites of the destroyed Jesuit missions, that they became unprofitable. The costs of organizing a bandeira could not be recovered unless the bandeirantes also found silver, gold, or valuable gems.

Various events changed the character of the bandeiras. The revolt of Portugal from Spain in 1640 altered the legal situation. The boundaries largely disregarded from 1580 to 1640 became important to Spain, which was more determined to stop incursions into its territories. Portugal's relations with the Dutch also changed after 1641. The Dutch captured and held Angola and São Tomé, two centers of slave capture and trade. After Angola was recaptured in 1648 by the Portuguese under Salvador Correia de Sá e Benevides, African slaves became more easily and cheaply available to the sugar-producing captaincies in the north, and the demand for Indians declined. Although African slaves sold at prices three to five times higher than Indians, they were preferred because Africans were better workers on plantations. The recapture of Recife in 1654 removed another obstacle to the growth of the African slave trade.

Royal policy also affected the bandeiras. João was hard pressed to find money to carry on his war of independence from Spain, and he feared that the Dutch might try to recapture Pernambuco. Hoping to find a new form of wealth, he offered rewards and honors to those discovering precious minerals and stones in Brazil. In 1652 he revived the Código Mineiro, which had remained largely a dead letter since its promulgation in 1603. According to the law in the sixteenth century, gold, silver, and other metals in Portugal and its possessions were considered royal property (as were all subsoil products), and the discoverer needed a special permit from the *provedor* of metals to work mines or alluvial deposits legally. The duty of the provedor was to mark off a plot of sixty varas long by eight varas in width (about 70 by 9½ yards). The discoverer was allowed two months from the time of his concession to begin continuous work, or he forfeited his rights. He owed the Crown one-fifth, known as the Fifth, at the time of refinement and founding of the metal, unless he could prove that the ore was too lean to justify the Fifth. At times the Crown took a quinhão (a portion) of the mine, up to one-fourth, paying the expense of working it. A perpetual and hereditary title was granted when a given miner complied with all the provisions of the law.

The regimentos of 1603 and 1618 enlarged the size of plots; two plots could be allotted to one owner. One was eighty varas by forty, and the other in the same vein could be seventy by thirty if separated by two plots of seventy varas each. The discoverer of a vein could extract all the metal it contained if no one else staked a claim. If another claimant appeared, the original discoverer had the right to mark off eighty varas wherever he chose. Once the choice was made, it was final. The new claimant had only two days to stake a claim— as did the third, fourth, or any other additional claimants.

The Regimento of mines contained sixty articles (or paragraphs) defining the rules, mining methods, regulations, and various kinds of mining conditions. All were based on experience in New Spain and Peru—one example of a direct Spanish influence in Brazil.

The revised regimento of 1618 made a few changes in the law. The powers of the provedor were increased to afford closer supervision of the mines. The total size of the plots were nearly doubled. The original discoverer received a prize of twenty cruzados. One owner was allowed only three mines—anybody in any category whether Portuguese, Indian, or foreign if they had a residence permit. The law was on the books in 1603 and 1618, but was not followed.

The Código Mineiro was a dead letter in Brazil until 1652, when it was registered in the southern captaincies. Even then it was not fully applied. The law had not been drawn up to fit the terrain and conditions in Brazil. Particularly, the Regimento presumed a provedor with extraordinary knowledge of minerals and mining. In small areas such as Portugal the rules were practical and workable. But Brazil was huge, a hundred times the size of Portugal, and the prospective mines were spread over distances that defied imagination. The provedor could do little more than collect the Fifth, if he could get that. The effective execution of his duties was impossible.

There seemed little reason for revision during the first half of the seventeenth century since the history of mining in Brazil had been a story of hopes aroused and subsequently dashed. But João IV was desperate for new income, and the mining code was one possible way of stimulating the search for precious metals. The bandeirantes, their hope of income from slave capture greatly diminished, began looking for mines with greater purpose.

13

KING PEDRO II AND BRAZILIAN TRADE, 1665–1680

he death of João IV in November 1656 left as heir to the throne his thirteen-year-old son who was incompetent to rule. To conserve the monarchical tradition, he assumed the throne, nevertheless, under the regency of his mother, Queen Regent Luísa de Guzmán, who had been so influential in promoting the revolution that had placed João IV on the throne in 1640. The new king, Afonso VI, surrounded himself with low-class companions. When the queen and her ministers objected, he assumed active rule in June 1662. For the office of *escrivão da puridade*, equivalent to prime minister, Afonso fortunately named an able man, the Conde de Castelo Melhor. The queen-mother retired with great solemnity to a monastery. Meanwhile, Afonso's sister, Catherine of Braganza, was betrothed to Charles II of England in a treaty of June 1661 that permitted her to continue Roman Catholic worship. She received a dowry of two million cruzados. Tangiers in Morocco and Bombay in India went to England. The English also received commercial rights in Goa, Cochin, and Diu in India and in Bahia, Pernambuco, and Rio de Janeiro in Brazil. All these matters affected Brazil directly by tying its future to Portugal's other territories and the English alliance. This was the price Portugal had to pay for help in the war of independence from Spain.

In the midst of the Spanish war, Portuguese leaders opened negotiations for the marriage of Afonso VI, though he was unfit for marriage. Not a man any girl would choose on her own, he had no interest in giving up his sordid companions for the company of a woman. Affairs of state outweighed the facts of biology and any consideration for the happiness of any prospective bride. Afonso was married by proxy in Rochelle, France, to Maria Francisca Isabel of Savoy, who arrived in Portugal in August 1666.

After a great dinner for the new queen, which Afonso VI refused to attend, the time came for the king to join the queen in her bedroom. He balked, even though Maria Francisca was famed as *formosíssima* (extremely beautiful). The king was amiable and attentive, but he continued to refuse to perform the marriage function.

The situation produced gossip, scandal, and intrigue that affected the proper governance of the empire. The futile king, unable to treat his queen with her merited respect, saw her treated with disdain by others in the court, among them Castelo Melhor. In this situation she found a defending knight in Pedro, younger brother of the king, with whom gossip had linked the queen from the day of her arrival in Portugal.

Pedro accused Castelo Melhor of attempting to poison him and then persuaded Afonso VI to dismiss the minister. Castelo Melhor retired from the court. So did the queen, taking refuge in a convent and demanding nullification of the marriage "because Your Majesty knows very well that I am not in reality married with him." The final result of this malodorous situation was the withdrawal of Afonso VI in favor of his brother Pedro in November 1667. The annulment proceedings confirmed the king's impotence and the queen's virginity in detailed testimony. Annulment was granted in March 1668.

Pedro assumed power in January 1668 with the title Prince Regent. He retained that title until the death of Afonso VI in 1683. He did not wait long to marry his brother's former wife, a decision supported by the Cortes and the general feeling of the people. They married on April 2, 1668. Meanwhile, Afonso VI remained imprisoned in his quarters, an armed and a dangerous prisoner feared by his guards.

The nearly half century that Pedro II was in charge of Portuguese affairs as prince regent and later king was precisely the time when Brazil needed strong leadership. Among the problems were threats from the unconquered Indians still living on the periphery of Portuguese towns; the rivalry of churchmen and civilians over control of the Indians; the difficulties of governing the coast; the pervasive corruption of governors and other officials; the threat of the French from the north and the Spaniards from across the Andes; the unsettled frontiers with the Spaniards in the south and west; the problem of supplying Brazil with slaves from Africa; and finally the dangers Africans presented when they fled captivity and formed communities of their own on the outskirts of towns or in the interior. All these matters required a firm hand on the helm if the ship of state was to sail before winds favorable to Brazil and Portugal.

The system of government rendered inevitable a certain amount of what is today considered corruption in public officials. Poorly paid, the governors and others had a right to use their offices to make money on the side. The question was only about the amount of money and the methods considered acceptable.

The câmaras of Bahia and Rio de Janeiro complained to Pedro soon after he assumed the position of Prince Regent. The officials, the câmaras said, engaged in commerce to the detriment of private merchants and the interests of the crown. The governors allegedly manipulated elections to town councils and favored their friends in setting sugar prices and freight rates. Such complaints were not new. In 1670 Pedro instructed Governor-General Afonso Furtado de Mendonça and the governor of Pernambuco to conduct an investigation with the aim of reforming the system. On February 27, Pedro issued an order making all royal officials personally responsible for acts in their residéncias. He was especially concerned about abuses in the collection of tithes. The continued preoccupation with this subject reveals just how difficult it was to bring about effective reforms.

The stimulation of trade was also on Pedro's mind. Brazil was losing much of its sugar markets to Caribbean islands belonging to the English, Dutch, and Spaniards. The existing legislation, forced on Portugal by treaties signed to gain English and Dutch support against

Spain, was unfavorable to the Portuguese. Foreign ships made Brazil ports in all seasons, buying and selling at market prices. When Portuguese merchants subsequently sailed into port, they sometimes discovered that the local demand had already been filled and thus cargoes did not always find buyers—or they were forced to sell at unprofitable prices.

In March 1671 Pedro ordered the Companhia Geral to send two fleets a year to Brazil as requested by Bahia and Rio de Janeiro. One fleet went to Rio and the other fleet to Bahia and Pernambuco, with each sailing separately. In January 1672, "in order to restore the commerce which has dwindled considerably," Pedro opened Brazilian trade to vessels sailing outside the fleet system, a policy similar to Spain's register ships. He also permitted six fleets a year — two each to Rio de Janeiro, Bahia, and Pernambuco. He opened the trade system even more in March 1673, when he permitted Brazilians to trade directly with East Africa and India for spices, slaves, and other goods. This trade was limited, naturally, to subjects of Portugal.

While he was trying to reform the system of fleets, Pedro was also gathering information that might be used to reform political administration as well. On January 23, 1677, he issued the Regimento Novo, which was made effective with the arrival of Governor-General Roque de Costa Barreto. The governor was instructed to recommend general measures for strengthening the fiscal administration and improving defenses. Foreigners were to be more strictly supervised to prevent the abuse of privileges previously granted. Foreign ships were, nevertheless, to be treated in accordance with international courtesy when they entered Brazil ports under necessity. They were not allowed to trade, however, "because of the harm it can cause to the trade of my subjects."

Foreign ships with license to trade had to furnish authorities with any information requested about their cargoes. Pedro did not want to repudiate such privileges, but he also did not want this trade to harm his subjects. He made an exception for Spanish ships; they could trade in Brazilian ports if they carried silver or gold and paid the royal duties on goods received in exchange. This privilege was ex-

tended in 1679 in the instructions given to Governor Manuel Lobo
of Rio de Janeiro. Spanish ships could trade in other goods if they
were not from Europe or the West Indies.

Pedro was bent on widening Spanish trade. Governor Lobo was to
take the initiative if the Spaniards did not. Lobo also had instructions
to make a settlement in the Rio de la Plata.

The church, as a part of Portuguese administration, played a role
in Pedro's plans. Exercising the privileges previously won from the
Pope, the king secured papal bulls on December 16, 1676, designating
Bahia as an archbishop and Rio de Janeiro and Pernambuco as bish-
oprics. The bull for Rio contained a significant extension of boundaries. It included an area to the Rio de la Plata "along the coast and
inland," which the Portuguese viewed as a confirmation of their rights
to a large territory claimed by the Spaniards.

14

EAST-WEST COAST, 1650-1701

PART I

The attention previously focused on the Dutch in Brazil may have led readers to believe that Brazilian history from 1624 to 1654 was like a one-ring circus, whereas it was actually closer to a five-ring affair. Some Brazilian historians have described this era as a period when all Brazil came to the aid of Pernambuco, thereby creating a feeling of national purpose. This belief is not tenable. Other regions of Brazil, and even Portugal itself, went about their own affairs, at times ignoring the Dutch occupation. These disparate activities did, nevertheless, start to bring Brazil into a semblance of unity toward the end of the seventeenth century, and they greatly extended the areas under Portuguese sovereignty.

While the Luso-Brazilians fought to expel the Dutch from the Northeast, others were hundreds of miles away pushing further into the Amazon or the western interior, while some were moving southward toward the mouth of the Plata River. Today it can be seen that their explorations added to Brazil half of its present territory—including the vast Amazon basin; the state known as Minas Gerais because of its gold and other minerals; the southern states of Parana, Santa Catarina, and Rio Grande do Sul; and the lands west and north from São Paulo.

271

The Portuguese king, beset by many problems was compelled to make several decisions after midcentury that affected Brazil's welfare. One concerned the high court of the Relação. Some elements in colonial society that had earlier opposed the Relação now reassessed their position. The câmara of Salvador petitioned in 1642 for its restoration. The long war with the Dutch in Pernambuco and the northeast made appeals to Lisbon difficult. On September 12, 1652, the king issued a new Regimento, which became effective when the judges took their oaths of office in Salvador in March 1653.

When the king was considering the reestablishment of the Relação in Bahia, he decided on two important measures for the East-West Coast. He established a new political structure and attempted to solve the Indian problem. Pará, Maranhão, and Ceará had been governed as one jurisdiction since 1621. The difficulties of travel along the coast made this arrangement unsatisfactory. Thus, the king divided Pará and Maranhão into separate captaincies, each with its own capitão-mor.

With the end of the Dutch rule in Recife in 1654 came a reversal of the king's decision to split the government. Maranhão and Pará were reunited under Governor André Vidal de Negreiros, leaving Ceará to be governed from Recife. The immigration of a number of families from the Azores islands increased after the Dutch defeat. Sugar, cotton, and tobacco had been the principal Brazilian exports, but following the losses suffered in the East, more emphasis was placed on efforts to grow cinnamon and cloves, plus the native forest products such as nuts and cacao.

The perennial question plaguing the East-West coast and the Amazon was Indian policy. The colonists wanted to enslave them. The governors wanted the so-called "free" Indians in the king's aldeias, for their own personal and public projects. The religious orders wanted to place them in their aldeias for work as well as religious instruction. The king decided in 1652 to address the region between Ceará and the Amazon. He sent Father António Vieira, who arrived in January 1653, as Superior of the Jesuits.

Deciding that he could not carry out his wishes in Maranhão, Vieira went immediately to Pará where the Jesuits had signed an agreement not to interfere in Indian affairs, slave or free. It was the price the Jesuits paid to obtain the consent of the câmara to build a colégio, Santo Alexandre. On arriving in Pará in October 1653, he was forced to confirm the promise not to interfere in Indian affairs. He then signed on as chaplain for an expedition to the Tocantíns in search of Indians. Seeing first hand the meaning of the "rescue" or "ransom" expeditions conducted to capture Indians, he wrote the court that such abuses could be stopped only if the Jesuits were given exclusive control over Indian affairs, following the model of Paraguay.

The civilians who held workers and slaves fought against the Jesuits' position. In January 1654 a petition signed by many moradores complained that the Jesuits constantly preached to the Indians about their "legal freedom," provoking uprisings in which whites were killed.

The moradores complained that they could not even bring their children to the city to worship at Christmas because of the absence of slaves to row their canoes. Many widows, married women, and girls, they claimed, lived in poverty. Father Vieira sought to show that their poverty resulted in part from other causes. Nevertheless, he told them that a expedition would go to the Tocantins and Araguaya rivers, "from which could be brought many slaves for the brotherhood of the church and the service of the people." The city councils and Vieira sent their respective views to Lisbon.

The city council of São Luís rose in revolt in May 1661 and forced Father Vieira to release the administration of the Indians. The governor gave Vieira no help and perhaps was glad to see his powers diminished. In June the citizens of Belém invaded the Colégio Santo Alexandre, seizing Father Vieira and his fellow Jesuits prisoners and sending them to São Luís. They were later transferred to Lisbon, without the governor lifting an eyebrow to help them. Other Jesuits in the aldeias endured the same fate.

Once in Portugal, Father Vieira drew up a list of twenty-five articles rebutting all the charges made against him. Unfortunately, this effort to defend his conduct in Brazil fell on deaf ears when the weak-willed Afonso VI assumed complete power in 1662. The king's advisors were not in sympathy with Vieira, who was sent into exile in Coimbra and Oporto and later was arrested by the Inquisition on charges stemming from his authorship of the *Quinto Império*. Only in 1681, when old and broken, was he allowed to return to Brazil.

His work had long since been reversed. A new governor, Ruí Vaz de Sequeira, took office in March 1662 and declared that he had no orders to contradict the expulsion of the Jesuits. In September 1663 a new provision of the law gave the municipal councils the right to appoint the commanders of expeditions sent to capture the Indians, the right to decide where such bandeiras were sent, and lastly the distribution of the captives. The law limited the power of the clerics to spiritual matters. It excluded the governors, capitães-mores, commanders of expeditions, and any clerics from any share in the captives.

Indian attacks on the frontier settlements of Bahia, and sometimes on settlements nearer the coast, continued throughout the Dutch invasion and thereafter. To recapitulate, serious Indian attacks occurred in 1612, 1621, and 1630s. A campaign from Bahia planned against the Indians in 1640 was not carried out because of the Dutch-Brazilian war in Pernambuco. In 1654 Gaspar Dias Adorno led a reprisal campaign. Other campaigns in 1655 and later years reduced to submission some of the "friendly" tribes that had revolted. But an effort to establish a fort in the mountains of Orobo failed because so many soldiers died of sickness.

The destructive warfare with the Indians called for additional efforts. Officials in Bahia decided to call on the famed Paulistas, whose fighting ranks consisted mainly of mamalucos (mamelukes). In 1668 they went on an expedition led by Domingos Barbosa Calheiros. His efforts did not save many of the inland settlements, and their inhabitants fled to the Recôncavo, causing serious economic problems and food shortages.

Other expeditions penetrated Brazil's vast interior. In 1668 Lourenço Castanho, "O Velho," led a bandeira to the Cataguases in southern Minas Gerais, where gold fields were discovered later. In 1671 Luís Castanho de Almeida searched the interior for Indians and minerals. Crown backing for such expeditions is indicated by a decree naming Fernão Dias Pais as Governor of Sesmarias with the purpose of encouraging settlement.

Having failed to eliminate the Indian danger, Governor Alexandre de Sousa Freire (1667–73), in concert with the Relação of Bahia, declared a "just war" in March 1669, calling again on help from the Paulistas.

The situation was complicated by a rebellion in Sergipe de El-Rey, which necessitated the calling out of troops to suppress the rebels in what became a prolonged campaign. Sergipe de El-Rey was calmed only after the arrival of Viscount Barbacena (1670–75), who imprisoned those he regarded as the instigators and pardoned the rest.

Two Paulista leaders Estevão Ribeiro Baião Parente and Bras Rodrigues Arzão organized several inland parties out of Bahia. Such parties were active well into the eighteenth century in regions as far apart as Ceará and Minas Gerais. The first campaign of Parente with his son João Amaro and Arzão in 1670–71 was not successful. The second in 1672–73 captured 1,500 Indians but half died on the return to Salvador. These campaigns led to a number of inland settlements. Among them was Santo António da Conquista, later renamed João Amaro. The bloody task of subduing Indians was only one motive for the drives; every expedition sought precious metals.

King Pedro II sent Rodrigo de Castelo Blanco, a Spaniard with mining experience, to investigate reports of silver in Itabiana. After a year of prospecting and assaying, he found nothing of value, thus contradicting the reports previously made by João Vieira. Later he was appointed provedor-mor and general administrator of the mines of Paranaguá and Sabarabuçú. These activities were a part of Portugal's efforts to expand west and south.

The Paulistas undertook a third campaign in May 1673 against the Maracás, penetrating 200 leagues (600 miles) through mountain and desert terrain and capturing more than one thousand Indians. A fourth Paulista campaign begun in December 1673 and commanded by Captain Manuel de Inojoso lasted almost a year and captured 400 Indians.

The number of scarcely known expeditions (or those mentioned by historians only in a fleeting way) is perhaps even more impressive than the better known accounts of some of the famous bandeirantes. Manuel de Campos Bicudo, who in company with his son António Pires de Campos, led a bandeira to Goiás in 1671, made a total of 24 bandeiras during his lifetime. He was capitão-mor on 21, according to Pedro Taques. He is credited with reaching the Serra dos Martírios.

Matias Cardoso de Almeida, who accompanied Fernão Dias Pais on an extended bandeira, staked out the route to the cattle-growing region of Bahia along the north Bank of the São Francisco River. Manuel de Borba Gato, also with Pais, explored the sertão of the Rio das Velhas. Garcia Rodrigues Pais opened a route frequently used between Rio de Janeiro and Minas Gerais.

In 1675 Captain Manuel de Inojoso, who had distinguished himself in previous campaigns and discovered the Quitose River, was sent to learn more of the river's course. He found pastures suitable for cattle on a route 100 leagues south of Cachoeira (on the Recôncavo) in an area occupied by the Maracás. The territory was barren of food, and they ate only fish and leaves of trees. The expedition took four and a half months in the sertão, reaching Salvador in October 1675. He lost 326 men, some his own slaves. The hope of discovering rich mines faded once more when an examination of the collected stones revealed negative results.

Manuel de Campos Bicudo, mentioned previously, led a party to northern Mato Grosso in 1674. Bartolomeu Bueno de Silva (known by his nickname Anhanguera—the Old Devil) reached Goiás in 1676. His son won similar fame in the eighteenth century.

The most famous of the bandeirantes of this period was Fernão Dias Pais, the Governor of Sesmarias. In July 1674 he left São Paulo with a bandeira and spent seven years in the interior. He hoped to find precious metals and emeralds. He explored principally the head-waters of the Rio das Velhas, going downstream northward to the São Francisco River as far as the Serra Frio—where there actually existed the much sought after gold later discovered by other Paulistas. A number of well-known bandeirantes of the time accompanied him: Matias Cardozo de Almeida; Manuel de Borba Gato, who was his son-in-law; his own son, Garcia Rodrigues Pais; plus thirty other Paulistas and their Indian followers. They discovered no precious metals or precious stones of any worth, but contributed notably to knowledge of the area. They made observations of the terrain indispensable to those who subsequently discovered the mines.

Starting out from São Paulo shortly before Pais, Pascoal Pais de Araujo reached the Tocantins River. Another Portuguese, Domingos Afonso—known at times as Mafrense because he came from Mafra in Portugal and known at other times by his adopted name Sertão—settled in the interior on the São Francisco, where he became the owner of a fazenda de crear (a ranch). He discovered the mountain passes leading from the interior of Bahia and Pernambuco to the plains of the Piauí and Canindé rivers in about 1674. He established 39 cattle ranches. Another explorer of the Piauí region was Domingos Jorge Velho, a Paulista, who had been called to help in the fight against the Quilombo of Palmares and the Indians.

From 1661 to 1680 the "Indian Problem" along the East-West coast and the Amazon was solved more or less on the terms desired by the civilians, meaning that they could enslave Indians. On the first of April 1680, however, a new law declared the Indians free and provided punishment for any who captured them. It gave lands to the Indians, even some previously distributed as sesmarias, declaring that as "original and natural owners of the land," they should always have preference.

The enforcement of the new law was entrusted to a *Junta de Missões* composed of the chief authorities of the captaincies. Father Vieira, having triumphed once more, sailed for Brazil, where he lived the remainder of his life—to 1697. When news of the law reached Brazil, the captaincies of Maranhão and Pará sent representatives to Portugal to protest. Without Indians, they claimed they faced economic ruin.

The Crown sought a policy that would render Indian slavery unnecessary. The area was considered too poor to buy large numbers of Africans at prevailing prices. The Companhia do Comércio do Estado do Maranhão was organized in 1682. (The jurisdiction of the Companhia Geral do Comércio organized in 1649 had not been extended to Maranhão and Pará.) The new company was designed specifically to stimulate the weak economy of the north and to supply it with African slaves at more reasonable prices.

The charter granted to the company gave it a 20-year monopoly, during which time it could import a total of 10,000 African slaves at the rate of 500 a year for a fixed price paid in installments. It was also given a monopoly encompassing all imports and all direct trade with Portugal. At least one ship was to sail yearly from both São Luís and Belém. Among its other obligations was to stimulate the production of cacao, vanilla, cloves, and tobacco, which it could buy at fixed prices from producers. In order to produce and supply manioc to the African slaves, the company could employ Indian workers at the going wage.

If clove, cinnamon, pepper, and other spices from the East, which had once enriched merchants and nobles of Portugal could be grown in Brazil, Portugal's rivals might be thwarted. Looking backward we may wonder why the idea had not born fruit earlier and why it did not enjoy greater success at this time—and later. By 1683 cinnamon was growing in the Jesuit retreat called Quinta do Tanque in Bahia. The seedling first introduced was already a tree and others had been planted. Ten or a dozen India pepper plants had also been successfully introduced. Father Diego Altamirano, a Jesuit like Vieira, but Spanish and a provincial of Buenos Aires, saw the plants as part of a Portuguese design to take over Spanish territory. Whether the Portuguese envisioned spices as a part of their plan for expansion, as Altamirano alleged, cannot be proven from the documents, but he was not mistaken in his understanding of Portuguese policy.

Governor Francisco de Sá Meneses met difficulties immediately from the date the monopoly was imposed. The colonists opposed the exemptions granted to the Jesuits and Franciscans. Other complaints soon followed. The most graphic description of the situation comes from the pen of the historian João Francisco Lisboa, who classified the company as an "unfortunate organization" whose administrators failed in their obligations and "exceeded all bounds in robbery and vexations." He claimed that they falsified the weights and measures;

sold materials and foods of the worst quality, even rotten; and controlled the supply in order to sell at prices above those fixed by the charter. A cargo of slaves, for example, price-fixed at one hundred milréis per person on installment payments was sold at increases of ten or twenty milréis per slave—and strictly for cash. The company alleged that the slaves were imported as the personal property of administrator Jensen. The company prevented the colonists from sending their produce to Portugal, or caused difficulties, and it impeded remittances of monies from overseas sales of the colonists' crops. The monopoly accepted only cloves and cloth in payment for its products, refusing to buy sugar, tobacco, and hides. The colonists could sell only to designated merchants who were either poorly-disguised agents of the company or its favorites. Ships did not normally arrive on schedule. Furthermore, the administrators ran an Indian village that produced manioc and other products sold in competition with the colonists. The monopolists received preference in the loading of produce on the outgoing ships. The outcry against the injustice of the system began early, and a revolt was soon in the making.

The rebellion began Easter Week in 1684. The governor of Maranhão was absent from São Luís, which facilitated the uprising. Under the leadership of Manuel Beckman, a senhor de engenho, the colonists seized the capitão-mor of São Luís, expelled the Jesuits, declared the absent governor deposed, and announced that the company was dissolved. Pará did not join Maranhão in the revolt. Nevertheless, Beckman organized a government and sent his brother Tomás to Lisbon to explain to the king the reasons for his actions. He also sent the Jesuits to Lisbon, where they were well positioned to present their case to the court, and, of course, to offer another viewpoint about the causes of the revolt.

The initial enthusiasm of the colonists soon waned when it became apparent they could do little to further their cause and improve the economic situation. The king did not approve of the revolt against his governor and other officials. A new governor, Gomes Freire de Andrada, who proved his metal over a long period of Brazilian history, arrived in São Luís in 1685. He landed without meeting any resistance from the rebels and ordered the leaders arrested and tried. Manuel Beckman and Jorge Sampaio were hanged; the others received prison sentences or were exiled. The governor examined the situation and advised the king to abolish the company, which he did. Beckman had changed the status of the company for the benefit of his fellow colonists, but at the cost of his life. The Jesuits returned.

With the Beckman revolution crushed and the Jesuits restored, the recent law placing control of the "descended" Indians in the hands of the civilians was abolished. Later, the law of 1655 that had given the Jesuits power over the Indians was renewed. But this provoked renewed protests and was modified. Several moves and countermoves left intact the same policy: Indians continued to be captured in the forests and enslaved.

The Crown sought a broader solution of the Indian problem in the Amazon Valley. The Regimento das Missões of 1686 was a constitution for the government of the missions. Its objectives were to convert the Indians to Christianity, to change Indian nomads into settled village life, to teach the Portuguese language as well as mechanical trades, to require the Indians to work steadily whether in trade or agriculture, and to adapt them to monogamous marriage and family life. Royal decrees between 1687 and 1714 delineated the areas to be entrusted to the various orders: to the Franciscans in the Province of Santo Antonio went the missions of the Cabo do Norte Marajó Island, and other areas north of the Amazon River; to the Jesuits went the Tocantíns, Xingú, Tapajós, and Madeira rivers; to the Carmelites went the Negro, Branco, and Solimões rivers; to the Franciscans da Piedade went the lower Amazon including Garupá at its center; and to the Mercedarians went the Urubú, Aniba, and Uatuma rivers plus some stretches of the lower Amazon.

In order to comprehend the significance of these royal grants, it is necessary to keep in mind that the churchmen operated as a branch of the government. The missionaries felt the rivalry of the civilians at every turn; the control of Indian labor was too essential to permit an easy division between civilians and churchmen. The net effect of their activities was to eliminate many of the Indians or to incorporate them, or their mixed descendants, into a third segment of workers. These laborers maintained a status in society between slaves (Indian or African) on the bottom and whites, or near-whites, at the top.

Another perennial question facing the Portuguese in the late seventeenth century was foreign intervention in the Amazon, particularly the persistent desire of the French to extend their Guiana territories southward to the north bank of the Amazon. In 1684 Francisco da Mota Falcão proposed to the king the establishment of four forts to guard the frontiers north of Cabo do Norte. By 1685 he had finished the forts of Paru, Toere, and Santo António de Macapá—in the region where the former Cumau had existed—plus Araguari. Later that year Ferrolles, the French military chief in Cayenne, appeared before Fort Araguari and claimed that French boundaries extended to the Amazon. When the Portuguese counterclaimed that the boundary was the Vicente Pinzón River, or the Oiapoc, the French commander retired.

After a voyage to France, Ferrolles returned to Cayenne in 1691 to serve as governor. In 1694 he wrote the French court that the river the Portuguese called the Oiapoc was, in fact, the Amazon, and it was the boundary between Brazil and Cayenne. He cut a road through to the Paru River, which flows to the north bank of the Amazon. In December 1695 a French fleet under de Gennes appeared in Rio de Janeiro harbor; whether it was part of a threatening move on Brazil is not clear. In any case, once the road to the Paru had been opened, Ferrolles set out with seventy soldiers and their Indian allies, falling on the fort on the Paru River without notice. He then captured Toere and Macapá, where he left about half of his forces as a garrison. Meanwhile, the fort at Araguari had already been destroyed by the Pororoca.

Louis XIV dispatched an ambassador to Lisbon in September to claim the area on grounds of possession and boundary claims. During the interim the Portuguese recaptured Macapá on July 10, 1697. Manuel da Mota Sequeira offered to build four new forts along the Amazon to guard it from foreign intrusion. The forts were built on the Paru, Rio Negro, Pauxis, and Tapajós rivers. Another was built in 1696 to protect Belém. Negotiations contiued in Lisbon, and in March 1700 a provisional treaty provided that the question of "the lands situated between Cayenne and the north margin of the Amazon would be again taken up" in future discussions.

On June 15, 1701, Portugal signed two treaties with France. Later, the outbreak of the War of Spanish Succession led Portugal to revive its old alliance with England in 1703.

PART II

THE AMAZON AND THE INDIANS IN THE 1660'S

Two reports from the 1660s have survived describing conditions in Maranhão and Pará (the Amazon) during the term of Governor Sequeira. One was written by Manuel da Vide Souto-Maior, the procurador sent to the court by the governor, and the other by auditor, Maurício de Heriarte.

Souto-Maior estimated the vizinhos or moradores in Belém at five hundred and those in São Luís at more than a thousand. He believed both areas were capable of sustaining much greater population and production if the threat of Indian attacks diminished and the supply of slaves increased. Heriarte's population estimates were smaller.

The reports of Souto-Maior reveal that the dízimos in Maranhâo during one year were about 50,000 cruzados and those in Pará about 41,000. Fishing rights in Marajó brought in 21,000 cruzados and salt production another 2,000—with the quinto on "descended" Indians yielding additional monies. Just under 100,000 of this sum was used locally, leaving an annual surplus of 16,000 cruzados for dispatch to the homeland.

According to Maurício de Heriarte, a companion of Pedro Teixeira in the expedition to Quito in 1637–39, São Luís de Maranhão had six hundred moradores. He commented on the beauty of the site and the agreeable climate, one and one half degrees south of the Equator.

Heriarte noted with pride the expulsion of the Dutch who had occupied the city in 1642.

The island of São Luís once reportedly had eighteen villages of
Indians, but when Heriarte arrived, there were only three. The inhabitants worked for the Portuguese for two to six varas of cotton
cloth a month; cloth was the common medium of exchange in this
region because specie rarely circulated. Abundant woods for all purposes, including shipbuilding, constituted a large part of the local
wealth. Fruits of many kinds were in evidence; some varieties were
native and others imported from Europe. Good water was abundant
and teemed with fish. The moradores raised all types of domestic
animals.

Heriarte recorded four convents, a cathedral, a misericordia, and
sixteen confradias (brotherhoods). Besides the governor, there existed
a sargento-mor, an ouvidor-geral, a provedor, and three companies
of regular infantry. Two main forts guarded the city.

On the island two engenhos and six stills for brandy processed the
sugar cane. Farmers grew an abundant crop of tobacco of good
quality. Heriarte listed a large number of plants cultivated or wild,
among them indigo which the colonists did not know how to process.
An ample supply of salt came from four pans.

North of São Luís another town, a separate captaincy, Santo António de Alcântara, with about 120 settlers worked six engenhos and
"had plenty of everything." Three rivers flowed into its bay and held
a great supply of fish, especially peixe-boi (manatel) and xerobim.
The Mearim River had three engenhos and an abundance of products,
"beautiful" pastures, good woods, and, inland, some Indians.

About fifteen leagues south of São Luís two other rivers had been
settled. The Itapicuru had about 100 settlers and six engenhos, plus
good supplies of crops, fruits, animals, and pastures. A fort with twelve
guns guarded the entrance. Farther up the river a small fort with forty
soldiers guarded the settlers against the raids of the *Índios de corso*
(raiding Indians). At times the Indians came in to trade with the
settlers, paying in various products or with "slaves." The Moni River
had even better lands, with three engenhos plus an abundance of

game, fruits, pastures, and wood for shipbuilding. Six leagues farther south the Perea River contained extensive salt pans, guarded by a fort with artillery.

All the rivers and settlements elicited optimistic descriptions from Heriarte. In some areas iron ore was abundant but not worked, forcing the settlers to import iron products "at very high prices." Heriarte described in considerable detail other rivers and regions he believed had potential for development.

Heriarte mentioned several Indian groups, among them the Tabajaras and Potiguaras, who had migrated from the areas controlled by the Dutch. They had been forced out subsequently because of their collaboration with the invaders. All the Indians in Maranhão and along the Amazon were described similarly: "These Indians . . . are false, cowards, traitors, cannibals, cruel. Their God is gluttony, lasciviousness. They are murderers, liars, perfidious, people of little trust and no charity whatever, without knowledge of the Faith." Their only adornment was painting and feathers. Two Jesuits worked among them.

Heriarte added other traits that permit us to understand the general opinion of the Indians held by the Portuguese. "They always go naked and their women are unchaste." The Indians "had little honor and are malicious and vain . . . and enemies of work." Owing to the illiteracy of the Indians, we unfortunately have no comparable reports on their opinions of the Europeans.

This description of the Indians could be extended for several pages. The Indians made war on one another "for little more than nothing, even when close neighbors and kinsmen, the losers being enslaved; and the dead are eaten, (roasted or boiled), as if they were hogs. The slaves are kept for work, or sold to other tribes, and sometimes during their drunken bouts and feasts they kill the slaves and eat them." These were called "cord Indians" because they were literally tied up. The offspring of Indian slaves who had been married to women in the tribe were also eaten on occasions, "like suckling pigs," because they were the children of their enemies. Adulterous women could be sold into slavery, if they committed adultery against the will of the husband. Heriarte had already remarked, however, that "for any small thing that they are offered, they give their wives and daughters (for the use of) anyone who asks."

Heriarte added:

The Jesuit Fathers have been able to change a lot of these (bad customs) and have indoctrinated them so that now they do not commonly do these things, and if they do them, the Fathers punish them. The Indios de corso (nomadic-wild), do not have aldeias or houses in which they live, but on the contrary roam the woods sustaining themselves with hunting, wild fruits and fishing— they are not settled in one place . . . . The human meat they eat is that of their kinsmen, who are killed when they are sick and cannot walk and are thus buried in the bellies of their kinsmen.

Heriarte described the region between São Luís and Pará as "good and fertile" with extensive pasture areas for cattle and good water. He thought wheat would grow if planted. If the Indians were removed or enslaved, the region would be very habitable because of its good climate. Gurupi had a population of about 120 settlers and two engenhos (with a potential for many more), plus an abundance of manioc, corn, and other foods. Formerly every river and inlet had been heavily populated with Indians, but they had fled inland. In Jaguapipora the inhabitants worked the salt pans of the Maracanã River (also then called Guatapu) on behalf of the king. Heriarte thought the whole region from Pará to Ceará was capable of producing gold.

Belém, capital city of Pará, about 75 miles up the Pará River, is located at a site where four other rivers flow into the tributary. Heriarte estimated the presence of about 400 moradores, and the majority worked their granjarias or roças (farms or clearings). Oranges, lemons, and other fruits abounded, although the climate was somewhat hot since the location was about one degree south of the Equator. There were four religious houses: belonging to the Franciscans, Carmelites, Mercedarians, and Jesuits. The city was defended by a fort and three companies of infantry. Its officials were the capitão-mor, ouvidor, provedor, almoxarife, and escrivão real, all paid from the revenues of the crown. Seven engenhos produced sugar.

Tobacco was another money crop. Cotton and cloves abounded, although the latter was not processed as in the East and was thus of less commercial value. A type of bark similar to cinnamon was exported to Portugal. The annatto tree (urucu, achiote) produced a red-yellow dye used for coloring butter and other foods. Cacao was plentiful but the technique for processing it was apparently unknown, which is surprising because cacao was one of the principal crops of the Spanish Indies.

When the Portuguese settled this region, Heriarte asserted that there had been more than six hundred Indian villages of Tupinambás and Tapuyas in the surrounding territory. Soon after settlement they rose against the Portuguese under Capitão-mor Francisco Caldeira de Castelo Branco and killed 220 men. A much greater number of Indians were killed, and the others retreated inland, leaving only fifteen villages. The Indians worked for two varas of cotton cloth a month "which is the custom in all this land." Many Indian slaves brought from the interior labored in the tobacco fields and other cultivated lands. "All these Indians have the same characteristics as those of São Luís de Maranhão." The Indians on the islands of the river, the Marajó (then called Joanes) and the others, were "very warlike" and had not been subdued despite many Portuguese campaigns against them.

Thirty leagues upriver from Belém was the Captaincy of Cametá (designated by Heriarte as a senhorio or manor) at the mouth of the Tocantíns River (at that time also known as Rio das Pedras). Although the area could have sustained many people, few Portuguese lived there. It had only one engenho of sugar but produced the best tobacco. The Jesuits were indoctrinating the "infinite" number of Indians along the Tocantins, most unconquered. "It is commonly said that this river and the Rio de Janeiro both flow out of the Lago Dourado," the El Dorado so long sought by Spaniards and Portuguese and even romantic explorers in the twentieth century. The river teemed with fish. The colonists kept turtles in large corrals for eating and making butter. He also described with great enthusiasm the capybaras, antas (tapir), and other animals; he marveled at the size of the snakes. The possibilities for pastures and farming seemed great because of the fertile land along the river. He frequently mentioned the superstitions and savage customs of the cannibalistic Indians.

From Cametá to Garupá was eighty leagues according to Heriarte. To reach Garupá, it was necessary to leave the Tocantíns and thread the relatively narrow straits (relative to the Amazon vastness) past the town of Breves and Cá-Te-Espero ("I await you here") to enter the main stream of the Amazon flowing north of Marajó Island toward the Atlantic. Only by traveling these straits with map in hand can one understand the intricacy of transportation in those times, or even in modern times. A Jesuit father, Sotto Maior, lost his life trying to indoctrinate the Indians on the river Heriarte called the Pacajá. He was, as usual, enthusiastic about the potential of the area for development.

Garupá was located on the south bank of the main Amazon and across the river from a very large island of the same name. It had a few inhabitants, a fort, and a small garrison of regular soldiers paid by the crown. The purpose of the garrison was to keep out the foreigners (English, Dutch, French) who came to trade with the Indians, hunt the peixe-boi (manatel), and grow tobacco along the Tucujú. The difficulty of the task was emphasized by Heriarte: "This river, it seems to me, is the largest in the world," an absolutely correct appraisal. Food products abounded, but the good pastures for livestock were not much used by the settlers. The Jesuits pursued their missionary work among the Indians, and several aldeias were under their supervision.

On the north side of the river lay the captaincy granted to Bento Maciel Parente in the 1620s. It was unsettled and had only one trading post. "They say there are mines," but nobody had searched. Maciel's attempt to settle the area allegedly had been thwarted by the "sickly and sterile" land.

Heriarte like most chroniclers of the Amazon, dwelled on the pororoca, the tremendous shock of waters caused by the outflowing river and the incoming tides, "meeting with such force and thunderous noise that it seems it would turn the land upside down; and everything that it finds in its way or meets, it tears to bits." The Indians in the Garupá region "are warlike and do not care to trade with the Portuguese except by force when troops go to ransom the slaves that the Indians have acquired in their many wars with one another." He classified them as "the most belligerent . . . great traitors and murderers."

The forest and its products always interested Heriarte, and he cited the riches of natural products and the abundance of river life. The river he called Parnaíba (Xingú nowadays), a dozen leagues upriver from Garupá and fifty leagues further up the Gorupatuba, was "peopled by barbarous Indians." It had less inhabitants than formerly because the Indians had fled up the affluents of the Amazon after Bento Maciel sent Pedro Teixiera to war on them. The Jesuits had aldeias among them, nevertheless. He thought this area was less attractive than others along the Amazon, but that up along the Gorupatuba River the land was better.

The Tapajós River, one of the large affluents on the south side of the Amazon, was another forty leagues (120 miles) upstream. Few unconquered Indians lived in this area, having fled earlier in order to avoid Portuguese raids. The party came across "the largest aldeia and settlement known to us in this area up to now. It can put 60,000 bowmen (sic) in the field when they go to war. . . . Their arrows are covered with a juice of a plant that makes them poisonous . . . once wounded by these arrows there is no chance of living."

Contrary to Heriarte's usual reports about the absence of any signs of an indigenous religion among the Indians, he found tribes in this region which adored certain idols and to which they tithed ten percent of their produce. The idol was called *Potaba de Aura*, "which in their language is the name of the Devil." He described a weekly ceremony where they drank corn liquor and during which the Devil appeared among them like an earthquake. (Both the earthquake effect and the number of Indians cited seem highly doubtful to this historian.) Heriarte reported that the bones of the dead were ground up and put into a liquid "and their kinsmen and others drink it." The Jesuit missionaries "go to indoctrinate them, from time to time."

Ocean-going ships came this far up river and traded with the Indians for vases and items made from the fine-grained mud found in the river. When dried, it was like an "extremely hard green stone." The mud gives the clear water of the river a green coloring to this day, and it gave the river its name. Since the Indians warred frequently, "they have many slaves; and others they sell to the Portuguese for iron tools" in order to work their crops.

From the north bank of the Amazon flowed the Trombetas River (where Óbidos now stands), so named because of the horns the Indians blew in their ceremonies. Aside from his usual classification of the Indians as "drunks" and generally a "shameless" lot, Heriarte cited the great supply of fine clay used for making pottery. Wild rice as well as the usual manioc was plentiful.

Fifty leagues farther up the Tapinambaranas River was a lightly populated area. The Indians spoke the lingua geral rather than the varied tongues spoken by the others. They dominated the region and collected tribute. They were newcomers, however, having been driven from the northeastern Atlantic coastal areas about 1600. Although the most barbarous of Indians, and the most cannibalistic, they acted as a supply point for Portuguese going farther up the Amazon. No missionaries were among this tribe.

The Madeira River flowed into the Amazon from the south another 70 leagues upstream. The south bank was not inhabited but the north was heavily populated with two main tribes living in innumerable aldeias. Pottery, oars, and slaves constituted their main trade. Wild rice and many other fruits and foods made it a land Heriarte described with enthusiasm. He thought wheat and many other crops could be grown, including grapes for wine "for there are few of the ants called *ladras* (thieves) that steal the seed." This was the first time Heriarte mentioned the ant problem, so often called the great enemy of agriculture.

Besides the usual description of its produce and the evil nature of its people, he mentioned a "very fragrant clay" from which the inhabitants made *Igacavas* (today Igacaba, Tupí word for pots) in many sizes, including funeral urns. They traded these clay products for cotton, thread, corn, tobacco, and many other items. They also had large amounts of *pedra de bazar de camelães*, better and bigger than in India.

The Rio Negro enters the Amazon some 35 leagues further up along the north bank. Heriarte confused it with the Orinoco. "A tremendous ocean tide invades this . . . river." His confusion of the confluents of the Amazon and the Orinoco was natural, since in the rainy season they do connect in places. The difference in high and low water at Manaus on the Negro is sometimes more than sixty feet. He praised the lands along the Negro and north bank of the Amazon; there were extensive pasture lands, abundant fruits, fish, and "enormous turtles." The availability of suitable woods and the depth of the river gave the area much potential for shipbuilding.

Heriarte admired the manual arts of the Indians. Their tools were the bones of animals "with which they make anything," including idols "to whom they give honor and reverence." The canoes were larger than those on the Amazon. The large population was governed by "one Lord." He made one surprising statement: "This river (Negro) does not have mosquitoes, as do the others on the Amazon, nor other types of destructive insects (praga ruim)." He looked to the future: "Populating this river with Portuguese you can build an Império and dominate the whole of the Amazon and other rivers . . . It is capable of maintaining commerce by sea and land with the Indies of Castile and with Peru, and with all Europe." His optimistic report may have influenced the settlement of Manaus a few years later.

Another 70 leagues up the Amazon was the province of the Agoas Indians, usually called the Areias because of the extensive sand banks and islands of sand in the river. The region produced food in quantity, but "these Indians have no iron tools because they are so far from the Portuguese." He was optimistic about the region because of the great variety of woods and other products.

Heriarte gave the usual evaluation of the Indians—"pusilanimous and cowardly." They shot arrows and threw spears with poisoned tips. The Indians did not use cinnamon but gathered cacao to make "wine" for their drunken bouts. Meat was not eaten because it was forbidden by their religion, "except human meat." They produced cakes of salt from a plant called capinasu that resembled saltpeter. The Indians slept at night in small houses on beds of straw, rather than in hammocks, because the mosquitoes were so numerous and large.

The region above the Agoas was a section of the Amazon known as the Solimões, "low lands and many lakes." This region allegedly contained the famed "Amazons", but Heriarte reported that "the said Amazons are not found there" and he thought they did not exist. His opinion of the Indian character was the same as in other regions. He nevertheless praised their skills in handicraft. They went naked but wore hats made of palm straw. On the Rio do Ouro, so–called because · of the small nuggets of gold, lived the Iguanaes Indians, "somewhat white and with good features." They raised large numbers of chickens (native or from contact with Portuguese?). The Portuguese did not find gold but there were large amounts of canafístula, cacao, and other products.

From the section of the river Heriarte called the Solimões, it was 20 leagues upriver to the "province of the Carapunas," where the flow was very swift. Many Indians aldeias with difficult access were situated on the steep river banks. The area was well suited to cattle and other livestock. The Indians produced cotton and pottery and traded with other tribes. They herded large turtles into corrals in the river. In general they were naked except a few who wore shirts brought from the land of the Cambebas. They sacrificed prisoners of war to wooden idols called Tururucari, smearing the idols with the blood of the victim they had eaten. This region also grew a variety of corn called milho yabotim and supplies were "infinite."

The Maguas Indians, called Cambebas by the Portuguese because of their custom of flattening their heads, lived another 18 leagues up the river. This was another world. "The best province, for provisions as well as for people." They worked hard and grew many crops. Their attire was different. Customarily, the males "dressed with trousers and shirts . . . the women with mantas e camisoens, shawls and long shirts, showing themselves more virtuous than the other Indians of this river who live naked and immoral." They were also great spinners and weavers, making their own clothing and a surplus for trade with other provinces. The burial of their dead, the absence of cannibalism, and a vegetarian diet set them apart from other Indians. They did, however, eat peixe boi and fish. "They have an affinity for slaves," but "they are not friends of idleness."

Heriarte considered them very ugly because of their flattened heads, but he had great admiration for what he considered their superiority over other Indians. They were governed by a great chief called Tururucari, "which means their God, and he holds himself to be such," claiming to have been born in Heaven. He lived among his followers assuming their form, but "whenever he wished he returned to Heaven . . . in spirit, leaving his body in the aldeia." When asked to describe Heaven, he said its characteristics had to remain a secret and that he was not to be asked about the subject any more. Heriarte reported that the Indians in this area "and the others of the Amazon, know about the universal flood and the creation of the earth." But they still lived as barbarians, "not understanding the real causes, the true God, three in one." Among the many favorable things Heriarte mentioned about these particular Indians was their use of a plant that supposedly preserved their teeth from decay, but he was not careful enough to pass the name on to us.

On the north bank of the Solimões at this point, Heriarte placed Lago Negro and described the Indians, whose characteristics, in one way or another, were like the others. He did not mention any Portuguese missions or other foreign influences.

Twelve leagues further up the Amazon, he reached the Rombos tribe, who lived eight or ten leagues back from the waterlogged river bank. He found the Indian women pretty and the people whiter than most other Indians.

Up river they found the Icaguates, called by the Portuguese the Encabelados because both men and women had hair reaching to the ground. The Franciscans of Quito came here in the company of Mestre de Campo Gordim and Captain Palácios. The Indians killed Palácios, the interpreter for the Spaniards, and the others returned to Quito without accomplishing much in the way of Christianization. "They are very filthy in their way of eating, more so than any of the others." They were also cannibals and drank the ground up bones of the dead in their "wine."

Still another hundred leagues upstream, the Quixós lived at the confluence of three rivers: the Coca, so named after the coca plant which was widely disseminated from this area, the Payamino, and the Napo, all in territory that remained Spanish in the final division. The Spaniards had made great missionary efforts here but only three settlements existed when Heriarte wrote: Avila, Archidona, and Baeca. The territory was well into the eastern Andes and was rough mountain terrain, rainy throughout the year except in September. He described the area as covering eighty leagues, all rough with many streams that the Indians crossed using swinging bridges called guanas.

15

SOUTHWARD EXPANSION, 1647–1700

Salvador Correia de Sá e Benevides, the rich and ambitious governor of Rio de Janeiro, gave some assistance to Pernambuco during the Dutch intervention, but he looked southward and harbored more self-serving objectives. In 1647 he offered to colonize at his own expense a hereditary captaincy in the south, in Santa Catarina, detached from the Bahia government and with himself as its captain. His offer received a hearing but was not approved by the king. His governorship of Rio remained legally under the governor-general of Bahia.

The proposed occupation of Santa Catarina, the territory extending beyond São Vicente to the left bank of the Paraná River, had another basis of support. The Portuguese professed to believe that the whole region was east of the Line of Demarcation and that both banks of the Rio de la Plata and Patagonia as far as the Tierra del Fuego might even be within the Portuguese sphere. The Spaniards naturally dissented. They could accept the view that the majority of the men in the bandeiras had no knowledge of longitude, but the Spaniards did not believe the governors, nor the Portuguese court itself, could have been so ignorant in the late seventeenth century, nor in the sixteenth even. True, longitude could not be measured at sea with accuracy before 1764, but it could be established approximately on land.

Thus, the invasion of Spanish territory could only be justified on the grounds of the war between Spain and Portugal from 1640 to 1668. It simply could not be justified on the pretense that the invaded territory was east of the Line of Demarcation, which at its most extreme extension was barely west of the city of São Paulo. The Portuguese court knew what it was doing, Spain believed, and in the long run, aided by geography, Portugal won most of the territory it wanted.

The hope of occupying the Plata region to obtain access to Peru's silver and gold was kept alive by numerous advocates. António Rodrigues de Figueiredo, for one, pointed out the relationship of the Plata and its precious metals to the slave trade with Angola. He cited the damage to Portugal from the Dutch occupation of Angola and recommended seizing the island of Maldonado at the mouth of the Plata estuary. Rodrigues de Figueiredo also pointed to the wisdom of importing horses from the Plata, since they were of superior quality, more numerous, and cheaper than in Brazil.

In 1648 Father António Vieira supported the proposed attack on Buenos Aires, advocating the use of the Paulistas. The territory to be added to Portuguese possessions would, he said, compensate for the loss of Northeast Brazil to the Dutch. The Marquês de Niza, a supporter of the proposal, referred to the Paulistas as "the most valiant soldiers of all Brazil and for that war the best in the world."

The Spaniards believed the Portuguese plan was feasible and represented a threat. Father António Ruiz de Montoya of Paraguay pointed out that such an invasion had been thwarted in 1641 with the defeat of the Portuguese at Mbororé by his Indian missions. In the end no action was taken because the Portuguese crown and the Overseas Council doubted the success of the proposed attack and refused approval.

Salvador Correia de Sá Benevides was forced to accept the rejection of his plan of colonization in the south, but he never forgot it. When João IV died and his widow was acting as regent, Sá renewed his request. Curiously, the person to whom he presented this petition to seize lands legally belonging to Spain was herself Spanish—that same wife of João IV who had encouraged her husband to revolt against

Spain. What Sá asked was a land grant with the island of Santa Catarina as the center of a captaincy one hundred leagues along the sea, fifty toward the south, and fifty north of Santa Catarina. The Conselho Ultramarino approved the plan in 1658, and it was later ratified by the provedor and procurador of the royal treasury. Even so, Sá was not given the captaincy. Intervening events explain why.

When Sá returned to Brazil in 1657, he bore the title governor of the southern division, as well as governor of his captaincy in Rio de Janeiro, which he normally ruled with strict and shrewd manipulation of the câmara and populace. He at once proposed taxes to meet the cost of raising the back pay of the garrison plus other expenses. The câmara had gained new status, however, after 1642, when it was granted the same privileges as the city of Oporto in Portugal, with the right to name an acting governor when the appointed governor was absent. Correia de Sá, believing he had arrived at an agreement with the câmara of Rio, went to São Paulo to promote his dream of discovering mines in the south. In São Paulo his ideas were greeted with enthusiasm.

In Rio, meantime, Jerónimo Barbalho, angered by the new taxes, led a revolt against Sá in 1660–61. Without haste, and without military escort, Sá returned to Rio de Janeiro to meet the arrival of a convoy from Portugal commanded by his friends. He arrested Jerónimo Barbalho and executed him in 1661. He sent other participants to Bahia and Lisbon, where some served long prison terms. The court was displeased by his conduct in office, however, and sent a new governor with instructions addressed to Agostinho Barbalho, a more moderate brother of the executed man, "or to the officials of the câmara."

Sá returned to Portugal and to royal favor, but he never saw Brazil again. He spent several years recovering the properties taken from him in Brazil. He continued as a member of the Conselho Ultramarino, however.

Agostinho Barbalho Bezerra received not only the grant to the lands in the south but the title of administrator of the Minas de São Paulo on February 4, 1664. He later recommended Fernão Dias Pais to the crown for an expedition in search of emeralds. Barbalho died a short time after receiving his grants, but the plan to push southward did not.

The difficulties in the sugar producing regions of Brazil during the last half of the seventeenth century suggested the need for developing other economic resources. One proposed remedy was to push southward toward the Plata. The trade that had existed before the revolt of Portugal from Spain had been very lucrative. Despite the alleged danger to Peru and the silver shipments from Portuguese penetration of the Plata region, the commerce was beneficial to local merchants. As the Spanish governor of Buenos Aires remarked in 1668, he did not consider the Portuguese his enemies "because they are the same people."

The Portuguese were numerous in the city. Indeed, there were not more than "six (commercial) firms that they did not own entirely, or at least half." The situation changed after 1641 because new competitors emerged—the Seville-Cádiz merchants, for example. As a result, many Portuguese were eventually expelled from Buenos Aires. But the mutual benefits could not be completely negated merely because of the opposition of the Spanish Crown.

The treaty of peace between Spain and Portugal in 1668 recognizing the independence of Portugal provided that normal commerce would continue between the nations, but under licenses issued by the king of Portugal. The law made an exception for ships coming from Río de la Plata with precious metals. These could enter Brazil ports, carry on commerce, pay in cash, and buy Brazil products. If the Spaniards failed to take the initiative in pursuing this trade, the Portuguese were permitted to do so.

Salvador Correia de Sá renewed his request for an extensive territory in the south, this time for the benefit of his second son João Correia de Sá and his grandson the Visconde de Asseca. He thought of dividing the region into discontinuous grants of ten to fifteen leagues each, covering the whole area west and south of Cananéia to La Plata. He emphasized the danger of allowing the Spaniards to colonize there.

The crown decided direct action was advisable if it wanted to get involved in the commerce and silver trade of La Plata. In making the grant, the crown reserved for itself all rights upstream along the north-bank of the estuary of La Plata. Salvador Correia de Sá acquiesced because the crown's fortification of the estuary promised to make his territories safer from Spanish attack.

According to the contemporary Portuguese view, and one still held by modern Portuguese and Brazilian historians, Spain recognized that this area was east of the Line of Demarcation. Sérgio Buarque de Holanda upheld this claim by citing a memorandum of the Conde de la Torre: "the long delay in deciding on this action is a matter of surprise. . . since the correctness of the claims of the Portuguese for possession of the north bank of the Rio de la Plata was recognized by everybody, including the Spanish geographers themselves."

The occupation of the Plata was never far from the thought of the government of Portugal, nor of those in Brazil who saw an opportunity to obtain large grants for themselves and to extend the territories of Portugal at the same time. In 1673 the Duke of Cadaval, a member of the kings council, advocated occupying an area near the island of São Gabriel, across the Plata from Buenos Aires. The plan was in accord with what King Pedro II had written to João da Silva e Sousa. He favored going inland so that the Portuguese could allege that their purpose was "to civilize the wild Indians" and win souls for God. The duke thought João da Silva should have the grant because he promised to assume it without expense to the crown.

In 1673 Matias de Mendonça advocated settling Maldonado Island and adjoining territories since it would be a convenient area to ex-pedite trade with Buenos Aires. Great expectations arose in 1674 when news spread of a great silver discovery near Paranaguá, in the present state of Paraná. The report proved false but it stimulated more think-ing about the south.

At this juncture, the Pope seemed to be siding with the Portuguese. In the bull "Romani Pontificis Pastoralis Solicitudo" of November 22, 1676, creating the diocese of Rio de Janeiro at royal request, the Pope defined the boundaries of the diocese as extending along the coast and islands from Espírito Santo to the Rio de la Plata. Portu-guese and Brazilians have hailed this bull as a papal endorsement of

Portuguese claims to the entire region. The boundaries of the diocese were, of course, outlined in the royal request to the Pope for permission to found a new diocese. It could be argued that a papal definition of an ecclesiastical boundary did not necessarily give political jurisdiction, but the original boundary set by the Treaty of Tordesillas was approved by the Pope and diocesan boundaries customarily fell within national lines. Thus, according to the Portuguese, the bull gave Portugal a solid basis for its claims.

Jorge Soares de Macedo received orders on October 30, 1677, to lead an expedition that was ostensibly to find the alleged mines of Paranaguá (in which by this time nobody believed) or those of the legendary Sabarabuçú. Its real purpose, however, was to prepare forces for an invasion of the Río de la Plata. Even before embarking from Lisbon, Macedo made no secret of the fact that he was busy organizing an expedition for "the founding of a settlement and fort that his Highness will order established in the Rio de la Plata."

Macedo arrived in São Paulo in November and speedily recruited his forces. In March 1679 he left Santos in seven ships with almost three hundred men, including many Indian bowmen from the aldeias of the missions. Nature spoiled his plans. A storm struck off Santa Catarina and drove him into São Francisco do Sul with the loss of ships and men.

While trying to repair the damage and regather his soldiers, a new governor, D. Manuel Lobo, arrived in Rio de Janeiro in May 1679, with updated instructions. The governor had received orders in November 1678 to establish a fort and a colony on the island of São Gabriel, located directly across the estuary from Buenos Aires and actually about five to seven hundred miles west of the original Line of Demarcation.

Macedo received instructions to remain in Santa Catarina until Lobo could join him with additional forces brought from Lisbon. The governor recruited more troops in Rio, including some freed from jail. He sailed from Santos on December 8, 1679, in five ships with three companies of infantry and one of cavalry, in all fewer than three hundred men. Among his forces were Indians and Blacks. His destination was Cabo de Santa Maria or Ilha do Lobo at the mouth of the Plata estuary.

Meanwhile, Macedo sailed from Santa Catarina for the same destination. He again suffered shipwreck in February 1680, this time at Cabo Santa Maria, losing his supplies and many men. Ashore with the survivors, he was captured by two Jesuits leading a force of 800 mission Indians. The Jesuits took Macedo and 24 men to Buenos Aires and delivered them to Spanish Governor José de Garro.

Meanwhile, Governor Manuel Lobo had arrived off São Gabriel Island and disembarked on January 20, 1680. He began construction of a fort, called Colônia do Sacramento, on the mainland rather than on São Gabriel as originally planned. Lobo sent out a search party to find Macedo, but it fell prisoner to a troop from Buenos Aires. Lobo then met with representatives of Governor José de Garro and they argued about the location of the Line of Demarcation.

Garro ordered Lobo to leave the region and surrounded him with a force of Spaniards, creoles, and Guarani Indians, who attempted to cut the Portuguese off from their supplies, mainly cattle. Lobo appealed for food for his men—even to Buenos Aires, which refused. The Spanish besiegers outnumbered the Portuguese ten to one. After the Portuguese surrendered, Indian allies of the Spaniards continued to slaughter and plunder, killing practically all the white Portuguese, both officers and soldiers. Governor Lobo was spared, however. A reinforcement of 150 men arrived only after the Spaniards, with Guarani allies, had captured Colônia on August 7, 1680.

The aid from Rio de Janeiro arrived on September 20, six weeks after the surrender. Lobo complained of bad treatment by Garro and accused the Jesuits of encouraging the Indians to kill the Portuguese. If true, this might have been a result of the long-felt hatred for Portuguese bandeirantes, who had killed and captured thousands of Indians.

The Portuguese lost from 112 to 125 dead, and the Spaniards five soldiers and 31 Indian allies. When Prince Pedro learned about the fall of Colônia, he was alarmed and angry. He protested to Madrid, threatening war. He demanded return of the prisoners, payment for

the lost supplies and munitions, and the return and retention of Colônia, even provisionally. Madrid took matters more calmly; after all,
the Spanish forces had won. Portugal believed, however, that the
government of Charles II feared war. Spain was threatened by France;
the latest of their numerous wars had just ended in 1678. In this
instance, England and the papacy intervened diplomatically to prevent
further hostilities.

The governor of Buenos Aires, José de Garro, was reprimanded
and removed from office—for the offense of defending Spanish territory against attack in time of peace between Spain and Portugal. Later
he regained royal favor and was named governor of Chile, at the
suggestion of Portugal itself according to Portuguese sources.

The Portuguese proposed a treaty that gave them every advantage.
Portugal's diplomats placed the Line of Demarcation on the east bank
of the Plata River opposite Buenos Aires. Portuguese geographers,
using only Portuguese maps and refusing all others, concluded that
the line should run either thirteen leagues west of Colônia, if São
Antão in the Cape Verdes was the starting point, or nineteen leagues
east of Colônia, if São Nicolas. Neither side was willing to compromise
sufficiently to reach a final agreement, and the Spaniards appealed
to the Pope. The Portuguese never submitted their case to the papacy.

The Portuguese sent an expedition promptly to repossess Colônia.
Governor Duarte Teixeira Chaves of Rio de Janeiro received orders
to embark for Colônia as soon as possible after his arrival in Rio. He
left with four ships in January 1683. By April 29, he had completed
negotiations with the Spaniards over local matters and reoccupied
Colônia.

The Portuguese demonstrated the famed diplomatic cleverness,
which had enabled them to win and maintain their independence, in
the negotiations over the fate of Colônia. The provisional treaty signed
on May 7, 1681, provided for the creation of a commission comprised
of equal numbers from both nations to decide who should hold Colônia. If they could not agree, Pope Innocent XI was to render a
decision within one year. Thus, in effect, the case went to the papacy.
The year passed and no decision came forth. The Pope was immersed
in other matters.

The provisional treaty of 1681 restored Colônia to the Portuguese, beginning a process of capture and recapture that continued until 1777. Keeping Colônia became a prime objective of the Portuguese and affected their European diplomacy. The Spaniards remained constantly on the alert about possible Portuguese violations of the terms of the treaty.

The main question on the minds of the Portuguese, particularly Prince Pedro, was whether sufficient commercial advantage could be wrung from Colônia to make it pay. Meanwhile, both sides looked to gain future military advantage and sought possession of the favorable location of Montevideo. Spain finally settled Montevideo in 1724–26.

Colônia was a fortification deep inside Spanish territory. Neither Spain nor Portugal had yet occupied the extensive area which presently forms most of Brazil south of São Paulo, Uruguay, and much of Argentina and Paraguay. There were no white women at first, and only a few single women of the *degradada* class were later introduced. Suggestions for female immigration were made but ignored because the area was too dangerous. Thus, Colônia was never truly a colony. Portuguese institutions and culture were not implanted, as they later were in Rio Grande de São Pedro (Rio Grande do Sul) and Santa Catarina.

Governor José de Garro pointed out the near impossibility of preventing trade with Colônia in his report to the Viceroy of Peru in 1682. He feared that Colônia was only the entering wedge of a broader plan to split off Buenos Aires, and perhaps Peru, from Spanish possession. In April 1682 Viceroy Melchoir de Navarro y Rocafull wrote to King Charles II echoing this fear.

Father Diego Altamirano stressed that Portuguese merchants could sell merchandise brought directly to Buenos Aires at half the normal Spanish prices, and still more advantageously those goods brought in via Peru. Furthermore, the Portuguese could obtain silver at eight reales in Buenos Aires that was worth sixteen in Brazil. The colonists in Rio de la Plata, Paraguay, Tucumán, Cuyo, Chile, and even Potosí and Charcas could also buy more cheaply in Colônia. In addition to the Portuguese, reported Father Altamirano, English, French, and Dutch traders were also present.

The Portuguese doubted at times the wisdom of holding Colônia. Some opponents of the policy in Lisbon advised the Conselho do Estado to abandon the site. Governor Duarte Teixeira himself questioned the value of Colônia, pointing out the great difficulty of defending it because the Spaniards were so close at hand. The king and the court saw otherwise and were adamant in their stand that Colônia must be held, irrespective of cost. Pedro II stood firm in spite of arguments about its small value to Portugal—and his successors were equally firm. At no time in these long conflicts and negotiations did Portugal or Spain advance an argument about the "natural boundaries" of their respective territories.

Modern geographers and geopoliticians see much logic in the Portuguese desire to hold everything up to the east bank of the Rio de la Plata-Paraná-Paraguay River system. Spain might with equal logic have claimed that it owned all the lands drained by the great rivers, but it did not advance such arguments. Effective occupation and the Line of Demarcation were the two chief bases for claiming the territory. Later it was seen that Portugal was in a better geographical situation to expand into Spanish territory than visa versa; but in the long run occupation, not theory, determined their respective holdings. Portuguese invasions west of the line, however, precipitated conflicts lasting more than a century and a half—until the boundaries were finally fixed in the nineteenth century.

The Spaniards held that, at its westernmost definition, the Line of Demarcation passed through the headwaters of the Jacuí River, cut through the Lagoa dos Patos, and extended into the ocean off the north coast of Rio Grande do Sul. The Portuguese claimed a line thirteen or fourteen leagues west of Colônia, which would have given them Buenos Aires, the entire mouth of the Plata Estuary and lands west of the Paraguay River. If some Portuguese advocated abandonment of Colônia, others thought of it as a jumping-off base for the conquest of Potosí and all of the Spanish Andes.

If this goal sounds a bit far-fetched to a modern reader, it sounded less so to contemporary Portuguese who lived in an era when a few people from a small nation had already accomplished the incredible.

The Spaniards saw the danger as real, and perhaps feasible. Potosí officials did not rule out the possibility of Portuguese capture, given the miserable state of Spain under the incompetent Charles II (The Bewitched) and his self-serving and venal advisers. Other nations also had ambitions; the English, French, and Dutch looked at Buenos Aires with avaricious eyes.

Portugal's insistence on keeping Colônia and as much territory as possible in the Plata was motivated in part by depressed economic conditions in Brazil during the last half of the seventeenth century. Portugal viewed Colônia as a center to tap the silver of Peru through contraband trade. It hoped to recover some of what had been lost upon its separation from Spain—for example, the tithes collected in Rio de Janeiro. After declining from a figure of 155,000 cruzados annually before 1640 to only 70,000 cruzados after 1665, they rebounded and averaged 93,500 over the three years (trienio) beginning in 1680. In 1686 tithes reached 140,000 cruzados.

The Portuguese were not sure they could retain Colônia. In 1684 Governor Duarte Teixeira, who was almost always skeptical, reported to the king that there remained great obstacles to continued possession despite the fertility of the soil. He saw no way of opening commerce with Buenos Aires from the island of São Gabriel, which, he said, was "the main purpose" of founding Colônia.

But the governor was overly pessimistic. True, by terms in Article 9 of the treaty, commerce was prohibited between Colônia and Buenos Aires, but Articles 7 and 8 gave the Portuguese all the rights previously enjoyed. They could sail their ships into São Gabriel, careen them, hunt and fish, make charcoal, have access to the herds of cattle, and live among the Spaniards in peace and friendship, thus in effect giving ample opportunity for trade. There were no effective means, in such a vast empty area without a large army and absolutely honest officials, both missing, to police the area and prevent trade.

Governor Duarte Teixeira Chaves of Colônia, who was so pessimistic about trade with Buenos Aires, nevertheless engaged in a substantial volume of commerce. He was accused of selling arms, munitions, and other materials for his personal profit and of carrying on an "exorbitant" amount of trade. Father Altamirano reported that Chaves returned to Rio de Janeiro "loaded with silver." Governor José de Herrera of Buenos Aires, who succeeded Garro, allowed trade with Colônia via Guardia de San Juan, a fort about five leagues distant.

Colônia was beneficial to the citizens of Buenos Aires. R. Lafuente Machain, the Argentine historian, wrote: "They needed to live off the products of the land, the only source of their income, and given the impossibility of trading . . . .in the channels prescribed by the king, they found themselves forced to trade with the Portuguese."

The cabildo of Buenos Aires wrote the king in 1699 explaining the situation. With its vast warehouses, there was no place closer than Colônia where the products of the countryside could be gathered and where there could be found adequate supplies of European goods and African slaves. The loss of revenue to the Spanish crown from illicit trade with Colônia provided a motive for attempting to dislodge the Portuguese. Numerous directives were sent from Spain to the governor of Buenos Aires ordering the suppression of contraband.

In 1699 officials in Buenos Aires asked the king for permission to drive the Portuguese out of San Gabriel. If it were not done, they said, it might become one of the largest colonies in America. "If not wiped out in its beginnings," this small outpost might "grow beyond the line and become the flame that burns up and devours all this kingdom of Peru."

16

SLAVERY

𝕿 he Indians became more difficult to conquer during the seventeenth century, after increases in the number of African slaves produced a large population of runaways. Gândavo had remarked in 1570 that Blacks were reluctant to flee from the coastal plantations because of their fear of the Indians. But the situation changed rapidly thereafter. The flight of slaves from their owners was always an important aspect of Brazilian slavery.

Runaways settled in quilombos or mocambos. Some were located on the fringes of towns, while others were many miles out in the sertão. As early as 1588, the Regimento given to Governor Giraldes cited quilombos already in existence. The Rezão do Estado of 1612 mentioned fugitive slaves. Other documents after this date indicate that quilombos were a major concern of the governors and senhores de engenho.

Slaves, far from being submissive workers, frequently resisted both actively and passively their general living conditions and mistreatment. In May 1597 the Provincial of the Jesuits in Brazil, Father Pedro Rodríguez, writing to the assistant general of the Order, stated that the Negroes of Guinea, living in quilombos in the mountains, were among his worst enemies in Brazil. His reference indicates that he was talking about quilombos of long standing. "The first enemies are the Negroes of Guinea, in rebellion and living in some mountains from which they issue to commit assaults and cause a lot of trouble." He added: "The time could come when they will dare to attack and destroy the fazendas, as their relatives have done on the island of São Tomé."

In 1625 Black slaves were very numerous in Rio de Janeiro, and many had fled to form mocambos and quilombos. "These fugitive Negroes became public dangers, for they committed acts of banditry, assaulting and robbing travelers on the roads, killing those who offered resistance, attacking small and isolated farms and attempting to induce other slaves to join them." The governor sent soldiers to seek out and destroy such quilombos. At some date earlier than 1627, a special professional hunter of escapees known as a capitão-do-mato (bush captain) had come into being.

The capitão-do-mato occasionly used other Black or mulatto slaves, or in some cases Indians, to help in the pursuit of runaways. Members of the Puris tribe were said to have an acute sense of smell that made them especially useful in locating Blacks. In other cases, especially trained dogs were used on the trail, as they were in the United States in the slave era and are still used for criminals today.

Frei Vicente wrote in 1627 that the Indians "helped against the Negroes of Guinea, slaves of the Portuguese who rebel regularly against them and go about assaulting (people) on the roads." He added that by order of Diogo Botelho, the governor-general, a band of Indians was sent to attack a quilombo of Blacks "who were in the Palm forests of the Itapucuru (or Itapicuru) River, four leagues from the Real River. . . . increasing greatly in number. But few returned to their owners because the savages killed many of them and Zorobabe (chief of the Indians) took some of them for himself and sold them."

By 1695, Palmares was the largest quilombo. Its origin is often incorrectly dated as 1630, but it actually existed much earlier. It came to be known as the Republic of Palmares; although its leader, Zumbi, displayed more of the characteristics of a dictator than a president. Two different sites were known as Palmares; one consisted of a few thousand people and the other had a much larger population estimated as high as 30,000. As the name indicates, they were situated in palm forests, located southwest of Recife and about sixty miles west of Porto Calvo. The smaller Palmares was twenty miles from Alagoas, surrounded by thick jungle, with three streets of residences in the midst of cultivated fields. Their religion was a mixture of various African beliefs flavored with Portuguese Catholic elements—a mixture common in Brazil to the present day.

The larger Palmares was twenty or thirty miles from the Aldeia de Santo Amaro and by the mountains known as Behu. At its height, it was constantly surrounded by 5,000 guards who lived in the local valleys. Many small villages had fifty to a hundred people. In periods of danger they took refuge in caverns in the mountains.

The two Palmares were a constant threat to slave-owning colonists. "In the dry season they detach some units of them to kidnap slaves from the Portuguese." During the governorship of Count Maurice, "the Negroes of Palmares did considerable damage especially to the country people in the surroundings of Alagoas, and a force was sent to conquer them, consisting of 300 musketeers, 100 mamelukes, and 700 brasileiro Indians." But it was unsuccessful.

The quilombos of Palmares consistently defeated the forces sent to suppress them. The Count of Óbidos, during his tenure as governor, expressed great surprise that the Blacks of Palmares had "put up a resistance greater than did the Dutch." When Governor Brito Freire of Pernambuco was preparing an expedition against them, the Count of Óbidos urged him to make very careful preparations so that the expedition would not suffer defeat like its predecessors "because of the great discredit it will bring to the armed forces" of the king. The hatred of the Blacks of Palmares by the citizens of Recife grew to such an extent that they vowed to put every last inhabitant of what they called "Black Troy" to the sword.

In São Paulo in June 1653, the ouvidor-geral of the Repartição do Sul, Dr. João Velho de Azevedo, ordered that varying rewards be given for the capture of runaway slaves caught in the vila, in the surrounding area, and in the sertão. It was common for citizens to take refugees into their service and keep them illegally. In June 1653, the ouvidor ordered "everybody who has refugee slaves in his house or estates must within fifteen days declare them before the court of be charged with theft, and must pay four vintens a day for their service."

In April 1656, Governor Jeronimo de Ataíde, Conde de Atouguia, appointed Luís de Góis de Mendonça as captain after the citizens of Cairu informed him that runaway Blacks were numerous and destroying crops. The câmara in Rio de Janerio offered prizes for whoever could catch fugitive Blacks. In the hope of claiming these prizes, many *capitães-do-mato* appeared.

Quilombos sprang up in many places. A report of 1659 reads:

The flight of African slaves from the estates was frequent. . . .these flights were numerous and assumed alarming proportions, taking on the aspect almost of a true exodus. The Negroes abandoned the farms and took refuge in the forests of the hinterland, establishing quilombos along the banks of the Paraíba River where they lived there in considerable numbers.

They committed the same acts of robbery and banditry that characterized the quilombos in other areas, attacking small interior settlements. The câmara had already offered rewards for the imprisonment of runaway slaves, assessing the owners for the costs. One of the most famous captains was Manoel Jordão da Silva, who received two-thirds of the value of each captured slave plus any children born in the quilombos.

Captured slaves stood trial for any crimes committed. As population expanded farther into the sertão, the problems of violent crimes and robberies increased the work of the courts. Blacks, mulattos, and Indians were often found in the court records. Escaped slaves, tramps, and highway robbers were a considerable part of the population. Some escaped slaves lived by assaulting people on roads, or even in towns. Violence was customary; the *poderosos do sertão* used violence to control their inferiors, destroying their enemies and helping their friends. The appointment of a *juiz ordinário* and the formation of new towns did not remedy the evils in this violent society.

The Código Filipino, following Roman Law, treated the slave as a dumb animal, prescribing to them the same laws applied to the sale of beasts. A slave could be returned if the buyer later found a defect in him—such as being a chronic drunk, a thief, or merely lazy. If the seller sold a slave recommended as skilled, but who in truth was not, then the buyer could return him.

The tomadia was the amount paid to the captain for a captured slave. The custom of tomadia was part of the law found in the Código Filipino: "If a runaway slave is recaptured, the captor should inform the owner or the judge of the district (Almoxarifado da Comarca) within a period of fifteen days . . . and not doing so, will be guilty of theft . . . ; the captor . . . will receive 3000 reis for a Black slave." The law furthermore provided that, since many slaves did not want to reveal the names of their masters, they were to be tortured and whipped—but not more than forty lashes.

Sergipe del-Rei, although one of the smaller captaincies, was the location of many quilombos. In January 1662, the governor-general of Brazil, Francisco Barreto, impatient about the existing situation, ordered an immediate attack. He authorized recruitment of people from Sergipe and Bahia to destroy some quilombos existing in the captaincy. All the captured Blacks were to be brought to Salvador, except those belonging to citizens of Sergipe. The latter "may be handed over to their masters, on payment of the usual amounts," but "reserving the children and the quintos" for the king's share.

Whether this order was carried out is not known, but his successor, the Conde de Óbidos, a year and a half later, in September 1663, appointed Francisco Rodrigues to liquidate the quilombos of Sergipe. Conde de Óbidos ordered him under pain of rigorous punishment to bring all the prisoners to Salvador. Rodrigues was not to turn them over to their owners until they had been processed through the government and the expenses of their restitution paid.

A captain had to be prepared to undergo all kinds of hardships in the hunt for fugitives who took refuge in the most distant mountains and, in some cases, in the densest forests. He had to know his territory as well or better than the fugitives. Sometimes the obligations of the office were combined with other assignments, such as carrying mail or messages, thus interfering with his primary duties. In other instances he was inclined to neglect his duties because, through bribes or other payoffs, he could gain more by allowing the slaves to remain free. In some cases he allowed the fugitives to remain free in return for sexual favors from wives and other female relatives.

Reference to slave revolts are numerous. For example, the governor-general of Brazil issued this notice on November 16, 1667: "The citizens of Hirajuia have notified me by petition that a crioulo named Manoel Maringue provoked a rebellion of 30 slaves with whom he went to form a mocambo in the sertão, from which they (citizens) would suffer a great loss if this damage could not be stopped."

Where there were no captains officially appointed, the citizens could take the initiative of attacking mocambos if they first got a license from the governor. In May 1669, Governor Alexandre de Sousa Freire sent Captain Fernão Carrilho to destroy two mocambos in Geremoabo and to kill "all who resisted." Carrilho had orders to proceed with great secrecy, putting out a story that his mission planned to travel to another area in order to deceive the spies that the Blacks had everywhere.

In 1671 Governor Fernão de Sousa Coutinho wrote about those runaways living in "the Palmares and matos." A rough area without roads, the terrain provided better natural fortifications than "men could build." The residents were increasing constantly in number and getting bolder. Because of continuous robberies and assaults, they were driving out many settlers living near their mocambos. "Their example and continued existence is an invitation to others who flee in order to free themselves from the rigorous captivity they suffer," he concluded.

Over the years there were improvements in organizing expeditions against the quilombos, but they were never successful in solving the fugitive problem.

PART II

FATHER BENCI'S SERMON ON SLAVERY

Father Jorge Benci, S.J., in his *Economia Cristã dos senhores no governo dos escravos*, written in 1700, reveals a great deal about the condition of Brazilian slaves and their treatment. After demonstrating that the "government of the slaves" was often cruel, he pleaded for humane treatment of slaves in accordance with the concepts of the era. Unless we assume that Benci was grossly exaggerating, his description of slave treatment exposes a harsh system.

Benci's book, published in the fashion of the times as a sermon, was directed toward the slaveowners of Brazil. He divided it into four parts, each outlining the obligations of the master of his slaves. The first part treats the duty to give proper sustenance, meaning clothing and housing as well as food; the second demonstrates the duty to give spiritual sustenance, that is, to teach them Christian doctrine; the third, the obligation and right to discipline the slaves, but within humane reason; and the fourth lays down the rules of labor—for the good of the slaves as well as the masters.

Father Serafim Leite in an introduction to Benci's work published in 1954, wrote: "Let it be said in any case—and now—that slavery in Brazil served a useful purpose. Because, without the Negro, Brazil as it is today would not exist. This is an opinion and, like any opinion, the opposite may be as legitimate as this one." Father Leite denied the view of Charles R. Boxer that the Jesuits in Africa could have done more, citing the case of Las Casas.

According to Leite, Boxer forgot that Las Casas did not write his account in America, but after he had traveled to Spain. "Furthermore, there were cases like Las Casas among the Jesuits in the sixteenth century, such as Father Gonçalo Leite, the first professor of philosophy in Brazil (1572), and Father Miguel Garcia, professor of theology in Bahia from 1576 to 1583." These men held the opinion that "no slave of Africa or Brazil was justly a captive, and both were forced to return to Europe." Father Leite added: "Slavery was not merely legalized tolerance, it was an institution sanctioned by jurisprudence . . . Discussion centered only on the just or unjust title in specific cases which, depending on the proof presented, was considered licit or illicit."

Father António Vieira, though accepting the enslavement of Blacks, spoke out against the cruelties of their treatment:

I well know that some of the enslavements are just—the only kind permitted by the laws . . . but what theology (Teologia) is there, or could be, that could justify the inhumanity and beastly cruelty of the excessive punishments with which the slaves are mistreated. Mistreated, I said, but this word is far short of signifying what it includes or covers. Tyrannized or martyred is what should be said. Because, for the miserable wretches to be burned with drops of hot lard, to have hot sealing wax put on them, to be cut to pieces, salted, and other greater excesses that I keep silent, but which merit more the word martyrdoms than punishments.

Unless we presume that Benci dreamed up an imaginary list of mistreatments in order to lecture Brazilian masters, we must believe he was depicting actual conditions. He stated specifically that he was only describing what he had actually seen. "In order to stop the crimes and offenses that the senhores commit against God who do not use their ownership and power over the slaves with the moderation that reason and Christian piety demand, I undertook as my subject and work to bring to light this book." Benci was disturbed because most senhores thought that, since they owned slaves, they had the right "of absolute and complete dominion over the slaves as if they were donkeys; so that just as the owner owes no obligation to the donkey, they likewise have no obligation to their slaves."

Benci first cited Aristotle to support the view that a master owed three things to his slave: "work, sustenance and punishment; and all three equally necessary in order to carry out fully and completely the obligations of the master to the slave." Benci also based his injunctions on the Bible. The first obligation of the master was to give his slave food. The master owed the slave bread so that he would not famish. And bread, Benci explained, included "everything that is needed for the preservation of human life, that is to say, sustenance, clothing, and medicines for illnesses."

Benci outlined the requirements "imposed by natural law, and authorized by man-made laws, and even more by Divine law." He added: "the cruelty of some senhores is withal such that they refuse even food . . . so abundantly given to brute animals, but denied to the captives." "If the slave dies of hunger, the senhor is guilty of murdering the slave," Benci charged.

Benci was equally concerned about the lack of proper clothing. Here too he resorted to the Bible for arguments about the duties of owners. "How is it that there are some senhores who do not dress their female slaves yet expect to see them very well dressed. And how are these to dress themselves? Asking alms? Where is the honor of the Portuguese?" Benci continued: "I really don't know what honor it can be for a senhora to have trailing her a large number of female slaves dressed in the livery of sin, as varied in the silks and colors as the various hands from whom they received them . . . And if there are some who say they do not have the means to dress them cheaply and decently, I say to them that they do not have the means to own them."

The treatment of sick slaves agitated Benci greatly. He devoted a great deal of space to discussing their poor health:

There are some senhores with feelings of such little compassion, and so very hard, who as soon as they see their slaves sick (especially if the illness requires long and expensive treatment), they desert them without protection, leaving them at the mercy of nature and . . . rigors of the sickness. That among Christians there could be tyranny and cruelty like this I would not have believed if experience had not made me see it with my own eyes.

Benci also lectured the senhores on their neglect of religious instruction. Slaves arrived from Africa "with rudimentary knowledge of the mysteries of our Faith, and so ignorant of the commandments of the law of God, that of Christians they have nothing but baptism, and even this is lacking in many of them." Parish priests received an admonition from Benci. "If you teach only the Whites and the free," he warned, in the expectation of rewards that the poor and slave could not give, "what other reward can you expect than eternal damnation?"

The excuses some senhores gave for not instructing their slaves were not convincing—"giving as their reason the crudeness of the slaves, saying that they are brutes, stupid (bocais), incapable of understanding the teachings and commandments of the Faith." But Christ commanded *docete omnes gentes*. Even if many were so backward that it was necessary to bless them a thousand times before they could learn to make the sign of the cross, Christ had commanded that all people, "however stupid and brutish," must be instructed in the mysteries of the faith. And if Christ commanded it, why should not the senhores carry out the commands.

If the senhores and priests failed to give regular instruction to the slaves, Benci warned that God would continue to punish the entire country. He listed wars, famines, and droughts. "What devastations and deaths did not the most of Brazil suffer with the deadly epidemic of the *bicha* (yellow fever)." Moreover, the effects had not yet been eradicated, and there was often a "recurrence of fevers and mortal illnesses."

The senhores were also obligated to see that slaves received the sacraments, but usually did not. "If the senhores of Brazil could understand well this truth, they certainly would not so frequently let the slaves die without confession, and many times without the last rites. Is there one senhor who does not want to die without the sacraments?"

The senhores failed to give their slaves the proper opportunity to marry and maintain households. "You will tell me that matrimony is not for these brutish people," Benci acknowledged, because both partners were likely to "indulge in greater sins after marriage" (presumably adultery). But Benci was not convinced that the free population behaved in any better manner in regard to the respect for marriage vows. When marriages were allowed, Benci pleaded that masters not prevent cohabitation. Too often a husband was sent to labor far from his wife so that they could not regularly live together. Occasionally the master actually sold a spouse to another owner in a different area. "It is amazing how some senhores so quickly and for trifling causes sell the male or female slave to some other place, or by some other means separate them from each other.''

Benci implored the senhores to set a good example for the slaves to follow. As it stood, the examples set by the masters were not commendable. It was easy to infer "the principal cause of the scandalous life commonly led by the slaves, men and women, of Brazil.'' Benci asked: "How can you expect them to live virtuous and chaste lives when they see their master keeping his concubine in his own home?'' And how could they teach slaves not to steal, when they witnessed their masters trying in every way to enrich themselves at the expense of others?

Benci found objectionable the system of labor demanded of many female slaves, which called upon them to supply the various needs of the house:

One must supply the manioc or the bread for the table, another the meat or fish, this one payment of rent, that one the oil for the lamp, and all of them required to join in whatever is demanded of them. And that this should be done among Christians! . . .Tell me senhores, or tell me senhoras (for it is to you I mainly direct myself), where do your female slaves find the wherewithal to pay these charges? . . .Where can it come from except from the sins and vile use of their bodies? And you living from the evil earnings from these sins; what is it that you are but a living and animated sin?

Benci was indignant about the sexual sins of the masters. "Is it not a scandal, the most abominable of all in the eyes of God, for the senhor to make his slave a mistress, forcing her to consent to this sin and punishing her when she refuses and wants to reject this offense to God? No Catholic can deny it. And does the senhor who does this expect salvation?'' How these practices might occur among Muslims, Benci could understand. "But that they could happen in Christendom, and among Christians as Christian as the Portuguese'' was too much for him to comprehend. Not only did the man who committed this act merit eternal damnation, but according to the laws of Portugal, he also was subject to execution if he "violently or by any other means forces and obliges any woman of any kind whatever, even those commonly called worldly, to sin."

After pages castigating the Portuguese for the ill treatment of slaves, Benci asserted nevertheless that among the master's obligations was also the punishment of slaves—for their own good, of course. They should not get into the "habit of erring, seeing their errors go unpunished." He added: "Just as the horse needs the spur and the donkey the bit, . . . the foolish and bad need the rod of punishment in order to make them well behaved." Ideally, the slaves should be governed with moderation. However, he conceded, "as they are usually willful, rebellious, and depraved, it is not easy to make them well behaved except with strict discipline and punishment."

Irrational punishment brought a strong dissent from Benci. After describing conditions he considered deplorable, Benci remarked: "From this it may be inferred how great is the cruelty of the senhores who, to prevent the slave from talking or groaning at the time of the punishment, put a stick in the mouth." Masters did not have to punish everything and should ignore small infractions, Benci instructed:

Everybody must think strange the injudicious senhores, or senhoras, who, like galley masters are constantly on their slaves with the whip in hand, not excusing any mistake however small it may be without punishment: and what is worse is to impute as mistakes what is not, nor even the shadow of a fault, as an excuse to punish them.

Punishment for the remedy of faults was one thing, but Benci advised that "in the punishment of the slaves one should not be cruel."

King Pedro II drew high praise from Benci. "Among the cares that require the attention of His Majesty, Senhor Dom Pedro (may God protect him) in such a large monarchy, he seems to have no greater preoccupation than to soften the yoke of servitude and captivity of the slaves who live in this and other dominions of Portugal."

Benci cited a carta real of the king to Governor João de Lencastre:

I am informed that in this captaincy it is the custom of senhores who have slaves to punish them with more rigor, to fix iron rings to some part of their

bodies to hold them more securely while they suffer the cruelties of punishment . . . I would like to know . . . if it is rational to burn or pinch the slaves
with wax (such an impious and cruel type of punishment), cut off their ears
or noses, brand them on the breast, or even the face, burn their lips or mouth
with a firebrand. I shall not mention other punishments still more inhumane
that the jealousy of the senhor or the senhora cause them to perpetrate on
the slaves, men and women, because they are too ignoble to put to pen, and
modesty does not allow them to be related in this place . . . Because the poor
slaves not being able to stand the cruelties of the senhor, in order to free them
selves of captivity, take death into their own hands, becoming their own
executioners, ending their lives either by wielding a knife with their own hands,
hanging them selves in a tree, drowning themselves or jumping from the
windows.

Benci believed a slave could be justifiably punished. "Principally,
if the slave does something he shouldn't, you can whip him . . . The
blows should not be, however, so hard and so many that they cut him
and wound him so that the blood flows in streams, as some senhores
barbarously do." How many blows were permissible? The Hebrews
prescribed forty lashes, but always gave fewer. Benci advised:

But as there could be crimes committed by slaves so grave and atrocious that
they deserve a greater number of lashes, I do not assume to forbid the senhores
the right . . . to give more . . . The blows are medicine for an offense; and if
the slave deserves a greater number of lashes than is ordinarily given, give
them in portions, thirty or forty today, an equal number two days later, and
still another equal number two days after, and so on, giving the blows separated, a number of lashes can be given that would if given in one day cause
fainting from loss of blood, or even death.

If the punished slave failed to mend his ways and quit his rebellion,
Benci recommended imprisonment. "With irons, putting him in
chains or with shackles . . . because no punishment serves better for
indoctrination and teaching of the slaves (even better than lashing)
than imprisonment."

Benci stated that "the fourth and ultimate obligation of the senhores
is to give work to the slaves, so that idleness does not make them
insolent." He knew of some senhores "who sin in this by giving too

little, but the majority sin by giving excessive labor." He added that since "the Blacks are incomparably more apt in all kinds of evil doings than the Whites, they graduate in less time with first-class degrees in vice idleness." To their tendency toward laziness, according to Benci, they added worse vices. "It is truly a pity to see how the fire of lasciviousness is inflaming the slaves of Brazil!"

The senhores were admonished for overworking slaves beyond the normal days. Benci tried to lay down rules that would permit slave-holders to work slaves on Sundays and holy days without excess. It was not necessarily a sin to work on Sunday; the difficulty came in defining necessity, such as burning cane fields or meeting unexpected crises. The senhores were inclined to treat many lesser crises as jus-tifications for unjust work. Owners also claimed that slaves who were excused from work to attend Church merely loafed and engaged in vices. Could not the senhores control this behavior? "Are there not punishments, are there not chains and fetters in your house?" Benci lamented:

There is not any reason whatever, as the senhores of Brazil claim, to send their slaves to work on Sundays and Holy days; and because this custom is so long established, that they are not moved by any reason at all to do anything else, the orders of the prelate to the contrary not being enough though fre-quently repeated. Not even the ecclesiastical penances imposed on them nor the daily reprimands of the preachers and confessors are enough to uproot this abuse.

The king was brought into the fight against the abuse of Sundays and Holy days. In a carta real to the governor, he wrote:

I am informed that neither the efforts of the prelates, nor the orders of the Visitas, are enough to compel some of the powerful of this captaincy to observe the Holy days, as Christians should. And that also on such days they do not give their slaves the necessary time to attend the Church and learn the Chris-tian doctrine. Though this is a matter normally the obligation of the bishop, I order you to try to help him.

The master could, nevertheless, allow his slaves to work for themselves "after going to Mass because generally speaking, such is the miserable state of the slaves of Brazil, even those best treated by their masters, that they lack many things . . . they cannot do without except with very great inconvenience." They were entitled to work on holy days for their own benefit.

In everything Benci saw a parallel with Biblical events. For example, he saw a linkage between the treatment of the slaves and the outbreak of smallpox: "If the ashes of the furnaces in which the Israelites were forced to work to excess by their masters were enough to introduce into Egypt this terrible sickness, what marvel is it that smallpox should come to Brazil?" After describing the poor conditions of the slaves, Benci addressed the racial issue: "What of the slaves of Brazil . . . who is black? All slaves just for being slaves are held in low consideration and treated with the scorn . . . ; but the treatment given to the black slaves is even more vile and abased, only because they are black."

Benci summed up the living conditions of the typical slave:

If he eats, it is always the worst and vilest food; if he dresses, the cloth is always the coarsest and the clothing the most pitiable; if he sleeps, the bed is often the cold earth and usually a hard board. The work is continuous, a struggle without rest, his resting periods restless and fearful, with little or no alleviation; when he is not careful, he is afraid; when he makes a mistake, he is apprehensive.

He despaired about the general situation in Brazil:

Oh, slaves! Oh, masters! Oh, unhappy slaves! Oh, inhuman masters! That the condition of the slaves should be such . . . and such the hearts and cruelty of the masters! What breast of steel or bronze could there be, which seeing so much misery, would not be moved to compassion and would not do all he could, to make the life of the slave tolerable and lighten the cup of bitterness for the slaves? Tell me, senhores (to whom I now speak), tell me, have you not just heard that the life of a slave is so full of punishments and torments that it is more death than life?

Benci did not preach manumission. In ancient times, he said, the first Christians had liberated their slaves when baptized. But he did not demand the same policy now:

Senhores, I do not seek to persuade you to give freedom to your slaves, though when you do it you will be doing what the true Christians did. I advocate only that you treat them as fellow men and as pitiable wretches; that you give them food for their bodies and souls; that you punish them only within reason; and that you give them only the work that they can do and not oppress them. This is all that I ask of you; this is all that I hope for; and this is all I want of you: Panis, et disciplina, et opus servo.

There is little, if any, evidence, however, that conditions improved because of Benci's published sermon.

17

DECLINE OF SUGAR AND DISCOVERY OF GOLD

ugar remained the principal export of Brazil after the Dutch left Pernambuco in 1654, but it suffered from the destruction during the long war and competition from Caribbean producers. The Dutch had long been the chief world carrier and refiner. When raw sugar could no longer be easily obtained in Brazil, Dutch traders shifted their buying to other markets. They already had footholds in Curaçao and the Guianas.

Meanwhile, the English captured Jamaica in 1655, during the Cromwellian period, and made it a major cane growing area. The Spanish islands also produced cane, and the French eventually made Haiti the chief raw sugar producer in the Caribbean during the eighteenth century. Portugal, beset with its war of independence from Spain from 1640 to 1668, was not in a good position to defend its interests. Brazil's economic growth, always closely interwoven with world markets for it products, felt the rivalry of other nations that were now building colonial empires—a status long held as almost a monopoly by Portugal and Spain.

Sugar exports from Brazil, which had grown rapidly between about 1570 and 1600, steadily from 1600 to 1630, steeply again to 1640 and to some extent up to the date when the Dutch abandoned Pernambuco, took a plunge in the 1650s and 1660s. Exports dropped as rapidly as they had risen. The decline continued to approximately 1710. Thereafter output slowly rose to 1760.

When, in 1655, Manuel Severim de Faria noted that "sugar is the most important income (rendimento) of the Portuguese Crown," he did not know that the immediate future would witness such a precipitous decline. The cries of distress from Brazil were shrill during the last half of the seventeenth century, perhaps exaggerating somewhat the real situation, but nevertheless it is clear that the decline in sugar production was real. Output hit bottom prior to the date gold was discovered in large quantities after 1693.

The decline of sugar production caused by Caribbean competition and lower prices was a blow to Brazil and Portugal. Sugar cane grown in the English islands was a substitute for Brazilian sugar imports into Britain. Those imports were estimated as high as 100,000 pounds at one time (perhaps a figure that should be taken as approximate rather than exact). But by the middle of the seventeenth century, the shipments to England had declined to around 30,000 pounds annually. Even if we take these figures as merely illustrative, they are still essentially true.

It was reported that Brazilian sugar known as mascavo and panela (the less refined) was eliminated entirely not only in England but all Europe because of the competition from the British colonies in Barbados and Jamaica. The better quality sugar known as branco (white) dropped to half its former price. By 1685 white sugar from Brazil had been eliminated from England and northern Europe.

The decline was not however precipitous. The process covered half a century. The English Navigation Acts, first passed in 1651, also must be reckoned as one of the causes of Portuguese-Brazilian difficulties. It limited imports into England to English ships or to ships of nations which had actually produced the product.

Despite the downward trend, there were a few years of substantial exports of sugar from Brazil. The fleet leaving Bahia in 1688 was the largest to date, for example. So large that when it reached Portugal, the cargoes created a "glut in the Lisbon market, and prices fell so much that in the ensuing year many *Engenhos* stopped."

The decline of the sugar industry naturally led the Portuguese to search for substitutes. Brazil already produced a great number of other items that made up the loss to some extent. Among those most actively advocating remedies was Father António Vieira. He influenced the crown in many ways. He promoted the transplanting of Eastern products to similarly tropical parts of Brazil, with the aim of cutting out Portugal's rivals because of the shorter sailing distance from Brazil to Europe than from the Pacific. Others also saw the possibility of bringing Eastern crops to Brazil. In 1675, Duarte Ribeiro de Macedo wrote *Obervações sobre a Transplantação dos Frutos da India no Brasil.*

William Dampier, an Englishman who distinguished himself as explorer, adventurer, and, according to the Portuguese and Spaniards, a pirate, stopped over in Bahia in 1699. His ship was the first English vessel to make port in Bahia in 12 years. He was received cordially and escorted to a safe anchorage by a Portuguese ship. Dampier's description gives no hint of the state of depression found in other writings about the period.

Dampier saw the merchants of Bahia as prosperous and numerous. There were some foreigners besides the Portuguese majority. He listed a Dane, a Frenchman or two, and an Englishman, who were all required to trade in Portuguese ships. He recorded the main exports of Bahia; not surprisingly, they were sugar, tobacco, hides, wood, tallow, and whale oil. He seems to contradict the view that Brazilian sugar was not known in England at this time. He spoke of Brazil's "clay'd" sugar as superior to sugar from the English Caribbean islands.

The oft-quoted statement of Father Vieira about economic conditions in the late seventeenth century is, though exaggerated, a good comparison with formerly more prosperous times:

Thus all is not merely going to ruin, but well nigh ruined; . . . In this emergency, prudent men advise us to wear cotton, eat manioc, and take to bows and arrows for lack of other arms, so that we shall shortly relapse in the savage state, and become Brazilians instead of Portuguese.

Brazil was in this condition when the mines came to the rescue.

DISCOVERY OF GOLD MINES

At the end of the seventeenth century Brazil was expanding along all its boundaries. This expansion was a continuation of the process of discovering the contents of a vast space—the Amazon, the interior of the northeast between Pernambuco and Maranhão, the southeast and southwest toward the Río de la Plata, and the regions directly westward where bandeirantes had earlier penetrated.

The most spectacular event was the discovery of gold in the last decade of the seventeenth century in Minas Gerais (General Mines). Later more gold and diamonds were found in the Serro Frio, north of the main deposits, in Goiás, Cuiabá, and Mato Grosso farther west. The gold and diamond discoveries were the only frontier movements not directly connected to the rivalry with Spain and France over the limits of territorial claims.

The discovery of gold and diamonds came after almost two centuries of hunting Indians and prospecting for minerals by bandeirantes. Although emeralds had been their principal aim, gold had always glittered in their eyes, beckoning them to perform heroic deeds and undergo unbearable hardships.

In 1674–81 the bandeira of Fernão Dias Pais in the São Francisco River valley and its tributaries did not make any specific and spectacular discoveries, but it increased knowledge of the interior. Others followed in his wake, and some had better luck. Several different gold strikes occurred shortly after 1690. Reports of these discoveries soon circulated in São Paulo. So many false hopes had been raised previously that not everyone believed the news.

Following the discovery of the gold mines, the economic outlook in Brazil suddenly changed. The shortage of labor became acute, and the price of slaves rose sharply.

Several different strikes occurred within a short period. The first man generally credited with the discovery leading to the gold rush was António Rodrigues Arzão, a bandeirante out of São Paulo. In 1693, while hunting for Indians, he saw "some creeks that looked as if they contained gold." His experience in the small gold fields already discovered in São Paulo, Curitiba, and other regions enabled him to pan three oitavas of gold—not a fortune but an augury of more. Attacked by the Indians before he could pan any more, he and his band returned to São Paulo. He commissioned his brother-in-law Bartolomeu Bueno de Siqueira to resume the search. Siqueira made a strike in Itaverava.

Other versions of the first strike also circulated. Father Diogo Soares heard another from José Rebelo Perdigão, secretary of the governor and captain general of Rio de Janeiro, during Governor Artur de Sá e Meneses's trip to São Paulo and Minas Gerais from 1697 to 1700. This version attributes the strikes to companions of Fernão Dias Pais, who was on an expedition in search of Sabarabuçú. After Pais died, his party headed back to Minas. According to this story Duarte Lopes, a *sertanista*, found large quantities of gold in the sands of a creek flowing into the Guarapiranga River. The success of Lopes inspired others who joined a bandeira in 1694, which included Manuel de Camargo, his son-in-law Bartolomeu Bueno de Siqueira, and others. They too were attacked by Indians and most were killed. Lopes's son Sebastião escaped and returned to São Paulo.

The two stories are compatible. Bartolomeu Bueno could have heard reports from both Arzão and Lopes. When Governor Sebastião de Castro Caldas assumed office in Rio de Janeiro early in 1695, Carlos Pedro da Silveira presented him with samples of the gold from Itaverava and was rewarded with the office of guarda-mor of the mines. Later he was named provedor do quinto at the foundry in Taubaté. Very soon thereafter much more gold was coming from the region known as Minas of Cataguases. On one occasion Silveira presented the governor with three arrôbas (about 96 pounds) of gold for the king.

New discoveries came quickly one after another. Manuel Ortiz de Camargo and Bartolomeu Bueno pushed beyond Itaverava but did not live to enjoy success. Miguel Garcia, son-in-law of Camargo, led a group to Gualacho do Sul, beyond Itatiaia, where gold was found in 1696. Manuel Garcia Velho found other deposits in Tripui; Belchior Barregão and Bento Leite were lucky in Itacolomi; and Salvador de

Mendonça Furtado made a strike in Ribeirão do Carmo, which was enlarged by João Lopes de Lima in 1699.

The abundant deposits found in Ouro Preto by António Dias de Oliveira in 1698 became a magnet for men from São Paulo, as well as other captaincies. The priest, Father João de Faria Fialho, discovered gold nearby in the creek later named for him. Still other discoverers were Francisco and António da Silva Bueno in the area named Ribeirão Bueno. Tomás and João Lopes de Camargo made strikes in the place that later became an *arraial* of the Paulistas. Felix de Gusmaõ Mendonça e Bueno made a discovery in Passa Dez.

Many strikes were made in the Gualacho do Norte, Brumado, Sumidouro, and Rio Pardo rivers, as well as in streams radiating from them. New discoveries were regularly reported between 1700 and 1706. João de Siqueira Afonso, already the discoverer of gold in Guarapiranga and around the Rio das Mortes, near present day São João del Rey, also found gold near Aiuruoca.

The king put his claims up for auction. The successful bidder obligated himself to work the claim or lose it if he failed to do so. If, after the first claims were granted, others were still available, the owners of slaves received preference. Owners were granted two and a half braças (15 feet) of ground for each slave.

In many cases claims failed to render a profit. Sometimes the superintendent and *escrivão* received more than the miners. Both officials received one *oitava* (2 drams) of gold as a fee for registering the claim. If the claim did not produce gold, the miner still paid the fee. When several hundred claims were filed, the officials often made more than the miners. Failure in one place was followed by renewed prospecting in another. As in all mining operations, some struck it rich while others worked sterile locations. As often happened in mining regions, some sold their claims for small sums only to see them yield many times the selling price. Mining was like a lottery.

Early mining concentrated largely on surface deposits. Miners sought alluvial gold, panning the loose flakes from the river and creeks with the *bateia*, the miner's pan. In some cases one dip might bring out a small fortune; elsewhere thousands of dips might bring up nothing. It was backbreaking work in a climate often very rainy and cool. Deep mining came later; and men with greater financial resources had the advantage.

The first governor to visit the new gold discoveries was captain-general Artur de Sá e Meneses, who governed from July 1697 to July 1702. He returned to Rio de Janeiro a rich man after remaining some-time in Minas. Later he was censured for his conduct. A road (or better, a trail) was traced from Rio de Janeiro to the mines. It ran roughly over the route of the Rio Belo Horizonte highway of modern times and supplemented others that went through Paratí (a port on the coast west of Rio de Janeiro) and Taubaté.

Soon after the big discoveries, it became evident that the Regimento of 1603, as amended in 1642, was not adequate for regulating the mines. A new Regimento of April 1702, with some amendments (as in 1703), became the basic mining code to the end of the colonial period. Its objectives were to prevent illegal and fraudulent practices, curb the powers of the richer miners vis-á-vis the less affluent, en-courage prospecting, and tighten the collection of the Fifths.

The office of provedor was abolished and in its place a Superin-tendent of Mines was substituted. He was more an enforcer of the laws than a mining expert. His duty was to maintain an orderly society, which would, in theory, produce more gold. A guarda-mor, with his own subordinates, acted as an assistant. When a new dis-covery was made, the discoverer received two claims, one was a pre-mium and the other his regular share. The guarda-mor chose one claim for the king "in the best location of the stream."

Other claims were distributed by lot and varied according to the number of slaves the claimant had available for work. A man with twelve slaves received a full claim, one as large as the discoverer, or 30 braças. Those with four slaves received only two and a half braças for each slave, equal to 5.5 meters per slave. All claims were marked off with boundary posts to avoid claim jumping and quarrels.

The crown became greatly concerned with limiting the number of Brazilians, Portuguese, and foreigners who poured into the fields. They made control of contraband very difficult. But it was impossible to stop the influx of people in certain areas. In 1703 a decree forbade prospecting near port cities on the ground that, if mines were discovered, other nations might be incited to intervene. The capitão-mor of Espírito Santo, for example, was ordered to remove miners from an area where a small deposit of gold had been found. Mining was also prohibited in Jacobina, Bahia.

The king forbade foreigners to emigrate to Brazil or live in Brazil. When informed that the foreigners were already living in the port cities and around the mines, he ordered them all expelled, with the exception of four English and four Dutch families protected by former treaties. The reasons stated for issuing the orders were that foreigners carried on commerce to the detriment of natives and that they would learn Brazil's secrets—the location of defenses, the capacity of ports, and the roads to gold fields.

The Regimento of 1702 did not always bring about the peace and order it had prescribed. The Superintendent of Mines and the guarda-mor enjoyed many arbitrary powers and were often in conflict with miners who wanted to choose their own claims.

Miners rushing to the gold fields thought the riches would last forever. In 1706 the ex-governor general of Bahia, Rodrigo da Costa (1702–1705), expressed the belief that the fields would not be exhausted "to the end of the world." The number of empty sites by the end of the century showed the error of this optimism. The governor had failed to understand that all mineral resources have a natural and finite limit.

The law foresaw the possibility of fraud and contraband involving the indispensable droves of cattle introduced into Minas along the São Franciso River. Cattle were sold for gold dust "that was certain to lose its way." The authorities were told to register all cattle coming into Minas. They levied a fine of nine times the value on owners of unregistered cattle. In addition, they imprisoned the guilty and punished them according to the laws governing fraud against the treasury. The superintendent was ordered to verify the sale prices of cattle and collect the taxes.

Slaves were admitted to Minas legally through Rio de Janeiro but not along the São Francisco River. Only cattle could be taken overland legally from Bahia to the mines. Rio was the designated port; from Rio the required route was via Taubaté or São Paulo in order to avoid loss of gold dust. The superintendent of mines or guarda-mor had orders to deport "everybody who is not necessary because they serve only to spirit away the quinto and use up the supplies and food of the people who are needed."

Such laws and regulations were stillborn. It was simple to avoid surveillance along the prescribed route. Besides the São Francisco route, there were other routes that escaped official control entirely. The shortest was established by João Gonçalves do Prado along the main ridge of the Serra do Espinhaço to the upper Rio das Contas. Along such routes, gold left Minas illegally; and just as illegally entered slaves, merchandise, farmers, and senhores de engenho.

According to the conventional interpretation, which is doubtful and subject to further verification, the gold rush emptied the northern captaincies, ruined the leading families, and drove prices to the sky. New immigrants did not remedy the coastal problems, for the newcomers also went to the fields with the glitter of gold in their eyes. A French traveler in Rio in 1703 estimated that 10,000 had left for the fields. He described the city as empty, the land fallow, and everything along the coast in a penurious condition. Manioc became very expensive in Bahia and almost non-existent in Rio (or sold at fabulous prices). Three days after landing, the French visitor saw four bushels sell at three escudos, or triple the usual price.

The king initially attempted to force men into gold production by forbidding them to engage in agriculture in the mining areas. Such efforts were futile and unwise. Men had to eat before they could dig for gold or diamonds.

Estimates of the number of people in Minas Gerais shortly after 1700 vary greatly. If we accept the estimate of the French traveler that 10,000 had left Rio de Janeiro by 1703, we could also believe that there were as many as 80,000 in Minas as some stated. Others listed 50,000 in 1705, counting only miners. Antonil, writing no later than 1710, reported 30,000. It is impossible to choose between these

different estimates, but we may doubt the higher figures. We do not
know, for example, whether the references are limited to free persons
or also include slaves.

The unprecedented richness of the new gold fields attracted an
extraordinary influx of people, particularly to Ouro Preto. They came
to prospect or hire others to prospect for them. Some went into business, buying and selling whatever was needed by the fast-growing
population in a region that produced little food and few supplies.
Estimates of the population a few years after the discoveries are about
as precise as estimates of the amount of gold; they are mere guesses.

The amount of gold produced in Brazil, as John Evelyn thought,
threatened to make Portugal independent of English support. He
wrote in his diary: "The King of Portugal has received so greate
returne of Treasure from Brazule that we feare he will either stand
neuter or joyne in the Interest of France!" Evelyn needlessly exaggerated the danger of such a defection.

The rush of thousands of people into an area almost completely
without agriculture, except perhaps some rudimentary Indian farming, produced a chaotic situation. Extreme hunger and even starvation
were evident. Corn and manioc were the two basic food crops, corn
being quicker and easier to grow. Corn matured in about four months
in fresh soil and could be eaten before its maturity. It served as food
for both humans and animals. It soon became the staple crop of Minas
and has remained so to this day.

At a much later date—in 1747—a writer listed fifteen foods made
from corn, among them popcorn, beer, and brandy. Manioc was also
produced but it required several months longer than corn to develop
and did not have as many uses. It was grown primarily in the coastal
captaincies.

Sugar was grown also, all laws to the contrary. An engenho was
built in Curralinho on the Rio das Velhas in 1706. The crown offered
a variety of reasons for prohibiting cane growing, among them the
fear that people might produce sugar rather than mine gold. This
reason was certainly a factor, but the desire to protect the coastal
engenhos was no doubt in the king's mind as well.

Economic and social conditions were strained by the wealth produced and by the great disparity between the rich and those on the lower rungs of society. A restive environment with little respect for law and order emerged. The social strain on the coast can be illustrated by citing the *"motins de Maneta"* in Bahia on October 19 and December 2, 1711. Stores were sacked as a protest against the high cost of living and the slowness of the governor in expelling the French, who had invaded Rio de Janeiro in two separate attacks in 1710 and 1711. Rio de Janeiro, which in the long run benefited more than other coastal cities from the gold riches, complained bitterly about the effect on its economy. In 1700 the câmara informed the king that slave prices had risen sharply because the Paulistas in the gold fields were buying them so heavily.

Conditions in São Paulo were worse, if our records are reliable. In the rush for the mines, cultivated land was abandoned and the captaincy remained prostrate for many years. Many other witnesses bear out the statements that the cities were empty, the lands fallow, and everything along the coast in a sad condition. In his historical writings, Boxer has cited many witnesses and official reports. Still, caution must be used in accepting such statements too literally. Witnesses who use such expressions as "all" or "everybody" cannot be considered reliable. The gold seekers needed an enormous volume of supplies that only the coastal towns could produce in the early days.

How much economic damage was suffered by the coastal areas remains unquantified and subject to further verification. On one hand, Antonil provided a graphic description of the rush to the gold fields, while on the other, he cited figures for the engenhos which do not present a picture of ruin. In 1710 he calculated 428 engenhos exporting 37,810 caixas of sugar, or 35 arrôbas per caixa. Using modern measures, this amount would come to 323,925 sacas of 60 kilograms each— an average of 610 sacas per engenho. Bahia exported about the same amount fifteen years later, and more by mid-century. Other statistics indicate that sugar went into sharp decline from 1650 to 1670, fell gradually to about 1710, and slowly increased thereafter. In 1760 another sharp drop came. If these statistics are approximately correct, the gold strike eventually helped, not hurt, sugar production.

Within a few years after discovery the first alluvial deposits were already exhausted. Further mining demanded more technical information than was generally known in Brazil. New processes arrived with the Portuguese and foreigners who flocked to Brazil. Some were sent by the government. A carta régia of January 26, 1700, refers to four experts in "the art of mining," who were sent at the request of Governor Sá e Meneses. Whether these were the same men referred to by Pedro Taques in his *Informações sobre as Minas de São Paulo* is not clear. Prices in the gold fields were astronomical, as is usual in such cases. Miners soon learned to wash down the gold-bearing banks of rivers and creeks with sluices brought from higher ground, and the method became widely used.

By the end of the first decade of the eighteenth century, three mining districts had been discovered. One was on the Rio das Mortes with São João del-Rei as its centers; another was around Ouro Preto and Mariana; and the third on the Rio das Velhas, with the two principal settlements at Sabará and Caeté. There were many smaller towns and mining camps. New mining discoveries were made later, of course.

Meanwhile, the problems in Brazil became more difficult because of Portugal's involvement in a war with Spain and France. Both the coastal captaincies and the mines needed workers, and this meant more slaves from Africa. The demand for slaves increased as more discoveries were made, and this development explains persistent complaints about the lack of slaves in Bahia during the early eighteenth century. Governor-general Rodrigo da Costa (1702–05) reported that agriculture in the northeastern coastal states suffered from a lack of labor because landowners sold their slaves for higher prices in the mining regions. In 1713 the governor-general of São Paulo e Minas de Ouro (Minas Gerais) recommended to the crown that two ships yearly be allowed to bring slaves directly to the port of Santos from Angola and Costa da Mina in Africa.

There were valid reasons for the fear of foreigners, especially the French. When Portugal switched sides at the beginning of the War of Spanish Succession, breaking with France and renewing the English alliance, the international situation was altered. At the outset Portugal was inclined to adhere to its alliance with France, but soon realized that France could do nothing to protect it from the English fleet. In order to have the protection of the English navy, Portugal signed three treaties with England in 1703, two covered military cooperation and one commercial matters. The latter, known for the English ambassador who negotiated it as the Methuen Treaty, provided that Portuguese wines could enter England duty free (giving them an advantage over French wines) and that English woolens would have preferential treatment in Portugal.

Following the reversal of its alliance, Portugal's army joined an invasion of Spain. It gave the Portuguese considerable satisfaction to recount that their armies were in Madrid temporarily; but no decisive blows knocked Philip V from the Spanish throne. One adverse effect of the European involvement was the renewal of conflict on Brazilian borders. Spanish forces from Buenos Aires attacked and captured Colônia do Sacramento in 1705. Thus on this occasion, and so many others, Brazilian boundaries were subject to alteration because of events in Europe.

The question of how much gold was extracted has fascinated all writers, but we have only guesses about its magnitude. The gold registered in the fleets did not necessarily agree with the production figures. Gold produced in one year might not be shipped until the next or even a subsequent year. An approximate calculation shows:

Average Annual Production

1700–1725	288 arrôbas
1726–1735	650 arrôbas
1736–1751	750 arrôbas
1752–1787	500 arrôbas
1789–1801	250 arrôbas

The relatively greater stability in mining areas, the chartering of new towns, and the presence of the captain-general made the collection of the king's Fifth easier—although never satisfactory from the royal viewpoint. When Governor Carvalho took office in June 1710 in São Paulo, he convoked the câmara, the procuradores, and nobility of other vilas of the captaincy to meet in July to advise him on measures for the more efficient collection of the Fifth. They agreed to adopt the system of *avenças*. The mine owners paid a tax on each mining pan, determined by counting the number of Indians or slaves employed in mining—with allowances for deaths, runaways, and rainy months when mining was impossible.

Governor Carvalho took other measures to assure the collections of the Fifths. On August 21, 1710, he ordered the justice of the peace of Guaratinguetá to exact the Fifth (quinto) on all gold that could not prove prior payment at the production site. Gold that escaped payment could be expropriated, with two-thirds going to the treasury and one-third to the informer. Another decree on September 3 required all gold going to Paratí and other towns on the old road to be registered with the Superintendent of Mines and to pay the Fifth.

Some of these acts were subsequently modified. The system of collection on the basis of the number of mining pans adopted in July was changed during a second meeting at Caeté in December. The governor thought the system too difficult to enforce and predicted a low return would result. Slave owners had customarily understated the number of their slaves and Indians, following the advice of the ecclesiastics who held that the quinto was a tribute that nobody in clear conscience should be forced to pay. Some of the clerics giving such advice were themselves miners. If such a view had prevailed, the crown revenues would have been seriously curtailed.

Revenues from the Fifth allegedly increased following the measures taken by Governor Carvalho. In 1711 the Fifth exceeded three arrôbas (43.5 kilograms), double the highest previous collection. Irregularities led to a change in the rules, however. In 1714 the system of fixed annual sums was set at 30 arrôbas (435 kilograms); this large increase was perhaps designed to recover amounts that had escaped the king in the early years. The 30 arrôbas assessment was collected until 1718, when it dropped to 25 arrôbas. The sum was raised again to 37 arrôbas in 1723 and 1724. In 1725 it was set at 18½ arrôbas.

The crown tried hard to stop tax evasion. At times mining was forbidden in certain areas where control was difficult—for example, in Serro do Frio where each pan sometimes brought up a half pound or even a pound of gold at one dip. Mining was stopped at that location in 1705, at least for a time. The tax evasion customarily practiced by merchants was harder to detect in mountainous areas than in the coastal cities. Without commerce, the gold fields could not exist, of course, and so the king could not stop tax evasion without halting the flow of supplies. The masses of people on the São Francisco River from Bahia and Pernambuco and the foreign goods freighted over the various routes provided great opportunities for contraband and fraud.

The clerics were notoriously the most flagrant smugglers, particularly the friars. The *"Informação sobre as Minas do Brasil,"* contemporary with the early years of mining, refers to "the great multitude of friars who go up to the mines and not only do not pay the Fifth of their gold but teach the secular priests and help them to do the same thing." If the king did not think he could stop the merchants from smuggling because they were indispensable, he did not think the same way about the friars. They were, after all, part of his structure of government. The remedy adopted was the total exclusion of friars from the mines.

A treatise on the geography of the mines spoke of smuggling by these "invidious contemptible Regulars." A letter of the Conde de Assumar to Pedro de Almeida contained orders from the king to "disinfest the mines of those men" who had used the sacraments only for self-enrichment. They preached from the pulpits, he complained to Bishop Francisco de São Jerónimo, that the king's subjects should refuse to pay taxes. The bishop replied that he had tried excommunication without effect. The offending friars and priests had ignored him, alleging he had no authority over them. His repeated censures and threats had availed nothing. He suggested that the government take action against the most scandalous friars as an example to others.

18

SOCIETY AND SOCIAL STRUCTURE IN 1700

round the turn of the eighteenth century, soon after the gold mines of Minas Gerais were discovered, is a good time to look at society in general, especially in Bahia and the coastal captaincies. Although the rush to the mines brought many strains on coastal society, the owners of engenhos, tobacco fields, and other land-owners survived the period and remained members of the leading economic and social class well into the eighteenth century.

Although sugar production did not increase, Bahia prospered in other respects. The growing slave trade, paid for in a large part with tobacco, brought wealth to many merchants. The market for every type of product sent from the coast to the mines promoted the pros-perity of merchants on all levels, wholesale and retail. Thus merchants and plantation owners became richer because of the gold discoveries.

Previously, studies of the Northeast, and of Brazilian society in general, tended to discuss seriously only two classes: slaves and their masters. Recent studies by Schwartz, Boxer, Russell-Wood, Flory, and other scholars writing in English, plus a considerable number of Brazilians and Frenchmen, are revealing a society of greater variety than previously acknowledged.

The discussion that follows concentrates on Bahia, but the other sugar-producing coastal captaincies were much the same. The Sal-

339

vador Câmara served to the end of the seventeenth century as the center of the administrative area around the Recôncavo, as well as wider regions when the Indians were driven back or killed off. Salvador was the seat of the high court of the Relação. The creation of new municipal councils (five) between 1698 and 1727 did not break this pattern. Citizens sat on the council, held public office, and carried on their financial affairs through Salvador. Rich rural residents built town houses (sobrados) and became members of the brotherhoods of the capital city.

The population of Salvador around 1730 was estimated at more than 30,000, and perhaps as high as 50,000. Its outlying area contained another 50,000 to 60,000 people. Urban households increased from around 3,000 in 1680 to double that number in 1725. Immigration into Brazil continued at varying rates, but increased greatly with the discovery of the mines. The social class of immigrants ranged from Portuguese nobles to merchants, farmers, and workmen of many trades. Northern Portugal and the Atlantic islands supplied the majority of voluntary immigrants.

The involuntary movement of African slaves increased greatly the total population. Bahia received up to 1,200,000 slaves according to some studies, which represented about one-eighth of the total slave trade. The percentage depends on which estimate of total slave migration we accept. About 80% of the arrivals came after 1700. At the beginning of the eighteenth century about half of the Bahia population was slave, in some districts the figure was perhaps 70%. Inasmuch as the number of women arriving was smaller than the number of men, irrespective of color, the mixtures produced an increasing proportion of mulattos. The Indian mixture was less discernible because, by the third or fourth generation, the Indian component was less visible.

Various terminologies distinguished the racial and occupational groupings: a crioulo was a Black born in Brazil; a reinol was a Portuguese; and a mazombo was a native-born person with Portuguese parents, also known as filho da terra. A person might identify himself in a way that would indicate his social position and economic status— such as "citizen and merchant" to show he had citizenship rights and made his living as a merchant; "noble and mill owner;" or "bacharel and farmer," revealing the distinction of being a university graduate as well as a farmer by profession.

Bahia had 80 sugar mills in 1629, and they had increased to 130 by 1676. The sugar produced amounted to about 15,000 chests. Prices varied from 800 reis an arrôba in 1634 to 1,660 reis in 1676, the highest price reported in the seventeenth century prior to the 1699–1700 season, when prices reached 2,200 reis—an all-time high for any period. There is no indication of the sugar producers suffering a disaster following the opening of the mines. Sugar prices were actually somewhat higher after 1700 than in the seventeenth century.

The cost of building an engenho was considerable. Leaving out the expense of slaves and land, in the period between 1684 and 1725, the cost of an engenho ranged from a low of 3,500 cruzados (cruzado = 400$000) for a very small mill to as much as 85,000 cruzados for a larger unit. The average for seventeen mills was 38,000 cruzados. Adding the costs of slaves, the average sum rose to 50,000 cruzados, or over twice the figure in the 1660s.

Increased demand from the mine areas pushed slave prices up. Slaves that had cost 40$000 to 100$000 before the gold strikes sold for 200$000 by the 1720s. Prices in general rose 100% to 200%. The average price of slaves sold in the coastal zone doubled from 62$000 to 123$000 between the 1690s and the 1710–25 period. Although the price of sugar was higher in the eighteenth century, new revenues did not compensate for the increased costs of slaves and other products.

The hazards of agriculture threatened the cane grower as well as other farmers. Among them were the uncertainties of the weather (too much or too little rain), floods, crop plagues, and epidemics that might kill slaves and other workers, or even the owner and his family. Finally, market conditions in Europe were an unpredictable factor; in some years the demand for sugar was curtailed or, at times, shut off entirely. Then, as now, some fell into the economic abyss while others held on or improved their status. Over the years some estates changed owners. Occasionally a prosperous merchant or mine owner (after 1700) married into the higher status of the senhor de engenho.

The normal course of business created an intricate system of debtor-creditor relationships. Normally, the same man was both debtor and creditor to different individuals and firms. The most important lenders were the religious institutions, who made about half the loans. The Santa Casa da Misericórdia alone made about one-fourth of the loans, with other orders also appearing as lenders occasionally. Merchants doubled as money-lenders, a dual role common in Europe for many centuries. Merchants accounted for about one-fourth of the loans, and people ranked as professionals made about one-eighth.

Mill owners appear much more frequently as borrowers than lenders. They borrowed about one-third of the funds available. Cane growers borrowed up to one-sixth of the total, and merchants accounted for about the same amount. In 1727 one half of the Santa Casa loans were made to mill owners and cane growers. These figures seem to confirm the oft-repeated statements that these groups customarily lived above their incomes. [*This is not necessarily a valid conclusion—the editor.]

We may ask how much continuity there was in the ownership class. Did the same families hold their properties for several generations? At the turn of the eighteenth century 56 of 80 owners in one sample were Brazilians. Among the native Brazilians, 34 had Brazilian fathers and 22 had immigrant fathers. The 24 immigrants were senhores de engenho. The data indicates considerable changes in ownership as newer men arrived and bought engenhos or married into wealthy families. All the owners were whites, mainly of Portuguese origin— with no foreigners and no men of color.

The majority of mill owners and cane farmers were descendants of the old families who had received land in the sixteenth and seventeenth centuries. For the immigrants and their sons, the usual progression was from merchant to landowner. Marriage within the mill-owner class was the general rule. The same rules that apply to other wealthy families the world over are also applicable here; both by propinquity and family design, wealth married wealth, with some publicized exceptions to prove the rule.

Gilberto Freyre and other authors have given their readers the impression that the widows and daughters who inherited engenhos often proved to be strong managers. Some were, no doubt, but the norm was different: "the usual role of senhoras de engenho was of a passive, interim nature."

Membership in the Salvador Câmara changed from 1680–89 to 1720–29. The percentage of landowners—either mill owners, cane growers, or merchants and professionals who owned land—dropped from almost 85% to 72%; the mill owners and large landowners who had composed more than 60% of the membership in 1700–09 were less than 40% by the 1720s. Merchant representation in the câmara, which was under 20% before 1720 jumped to over 40% in the following decade. The richer merchants often had great influence in the câmara. Merchants not listed as landowners rose from 2.7% to 17.5%. Tobacco growers and cattlemen never achieved much representation, accounting for only 4% in the first period and 5% in the latter.

Ten to fifteen families owned much of the land in the Recôncavo, measuring their holdings in some cases in hundreds of thousands of acres. Among them we recognize families whose names date back to the earliest days of colonization: Cavalcantis, Albuquerques, Adornos.

Around the turn of the eighteenth century tobacco growers emerged as a class of farmers distinct from cane growers and millers. This was made possible by the two factors: the use of tobacco to pay for slaves in Africa and the elimination of the menace of the Indians, which opened a large area of land suitable for cultivation. The initial sesmarias were quite large, but smaller holdings followed their division into farms of 600 to 100 acres, worked by perhaps a dozen slaves. These farms were usually called sitios, if small, and fazendas, if large. They grew a variety of crops and kept livestock.

Tobacco farming was much less difficult to enter than cane growing and milling. The capital required was relatively modest. People of a humbler station in life could become planters. The difference can be seen by noting that the average sugar mill was valued at 38,000 cruzados and the average tobacco-cattle sitio at 2,000 cruzados. In the second category some mulattos found a place. Thus was created a class of free agriculturists below senhores but above the common people.

A breakdown of the percentage of artisans in the principal crafts in Bahia during the 1680–1729 period reads: cobblers 21%, tailors 12%, joiners and carpenters combined 19%, and silversmiths and goldsmiths 9%. Other metal workers, including blacksmiths, swordsmiths, locksmiths, coppersmiths, and tinsmiths numbered approximately 15% of the free artisans. The free artisan class was mainly white; only 5% were considered black or mulatto. Immigrant artisans still came from Portugal, with about two-thirds from Portugal and the Atlantic islands. In general. both the native and immigrant artisans married women considered white, although some men married pardas (mixed). Most men married the daughters of other artisans or a girl of comparable social class.

Salvador contained a developing community of tradesmen and craftsmen. The upper level owned their own businesses. Among the artisans there were also Black slaves and free laborers, with the latter possibly manumitted slaves or mulattos. Some acquired property or land, but upward movement above the artisan class was not common. Since the commercial class was predominantly immigrant, the artisan had little chance of rising among them. They constituted the "immense population of free Brazilians, crowded in miserable shacks, and living on almost nothing on the outskirts of Salvador."

Bahia society was dynamic, but the strata of society did not change. The upper class of senhores de engenho, large landowners, and large merchants formed a top layer into which some ascended, and from which some descended, but the class remained. It held most of the wealth and dominated society. The less wealthy landowners expanded somewhat and changed in membership, but they remained above the artisans in most cases. The povo, the people, always remained in status quo ante.

The upper classes dominated in all the prestigious fields: income from property, proprietary public offices, officials of the militia, the senadores in the Senado da Câmara, or the equivalent councils in the newly formed towns. Many maintained a townhouse as well as a home on their estates, thereby wielding influence in town and country. The floor beneath the upper families was porous, and many climbed up to join the elect, but it must be noted that newcomers merely became new members of an elect that was always present. If new immigrants and wealthy merchants became more prominent in the affairs of the city and province, they did not destroy but rather strengthened the class into which they ascended.

Most who rose in status became members of the council, the Santa Casa, or other prestigious brotherhoods only after becoming land-owners. The activities of the rich overlapped. Owners of the great interior estates, senhores de engenhos, and the great mercantile firms sometimes were the same people, or were from the same families. If some antagonistic relations existed, the prevailing interests kept to-gether the privileged classes against the classes below them. No sepa-rate mercantile elite emerged because those who acquired wealth invariably joined the landed rich.

The artisans never achieved the stratified guild system of the Old World. The Portuguese immigrant tended to attain a superior posi-tion, and often acquired property. Rising above this class was possible and sometimes happened. One way was to place a son in a profession. Blacks and mulattos, even when free, were less likely to rise in status, but some did, especially mulattos.

Both Blacks and mulattos were almost entirely missing from the upper propertied classes. Their station in life was generally confined to earning their living as peddlers, street vendors, shopkeepers, bar keepers (cachaça), and small farmers who owned sitios producing manioc, tobacco, and cattle.

The system of arranging marriages among those of the favored. classes, as well as prejudice against people of color, limited the upward mobility of those whose tint was too dark. Some authors, however, believe that color alone was not the deciding factor in such exclusions. In this connection it should be noted that Blacks and mulattos did not enjoy the electoral rights held by the whites. They could belong only to their own brotherhoods and militia units.

Upward mobility into the highest classes was most likely for Old Christians of Portuguese descent, with occasionally other Europeans appearing. Those starting from a low social rank could ascend only within rather well-defined limits. The slave might acquire freedom, become a wage earner, or a small store owner. The tenant farmer might acquire a small sitio of his own; an employee might become a shopkeeper or bar owner. If white, or white enough, he could move up eventually to cane or tobacco grower, with the hope that through marriage he might ascend to the upper classes. The plantation economy with large to immense holdings combined with Portuguese domination of the large merchant class remained always a barrier preventing most people from climbing socially and economically. For those whites who acquired enough wealth, the upward climb was easier; enough wealth could buy land. Enough land could translate into an engenho and the top social standing. A very rich merchant could occupy the same social rung, but he was likely to acquire land to enhance his standing.

The very fact that there was constant immigration of Portuguese put limitations on the on the opportunities for the Brazilian-born non-white. This was also true of Spanish America and other colonial societies.

There was more stability to the institution of the upper class than its actual memberships. The engenho and the holding of immense lands was constant; the owners of engenhos changed as new elements arrived. The large wholesale merchant was always present. The men at the top changed through the ascension of employees who made good and because some small independent merchants prospered. The same family names were present for generations, but new names consistently appeared as well. Through work and intelligence, marriage, royal favors, or the favors of governors, new men came forward. But, it was a trickle, not a flood.

More quantitative data might make this conclusion easier to defend, but there is sufficient evidence to cast doubt on any contrary belief. Less data has been published for Pernambuco and the other captaincies, but there is no reason to believe that the social structure differed in these regions.

19

BATTLE FOR THE GOLD MINES: PAULISTAS VS. EMBOABAS

After spending their time, money, and lives in the effort to capture Indians and find mines for generations, the Paulistas became the first to make the principal gold strikes in the 1690s. Earlier they had opened up for settlement parts of the interior of Bahia and Pernambuco. Paulistas drove back, killed off, or captured the Indians who barred the routes, and even played a decisive part in destroying the largest and most dangerous of the quilombos, Palmares, in Pernambuco. They believed they owned the mines just as any other discoverer or conqueror is convinced he has established title. The Paulistas wanted to make certain that the king and all others acknowledged their prior rights.

In April 1700, the câmara of São Paulo sent the king a petition asking that mining sites be restricted to the Paulistas, because they "were the discoverers and conquerors of the said mines at the cost of their lives and their resources without any expense to the royal treasure." This natural desire to become the sole owners was one response to a development already well under way: the "invasion" of gold rushers from Rio de Janeiro, Bahia, Pernambuco, and all parts of Brazil, plus adventurers from across the Atlantic.

The king sent the petition to the governor of Rio de Janeiro, Artur de Sá e Meneses, for his recommendation. Meanwhile the governor was forbidden to grant sesmarias and he was to issue mining claims only in accordance with the existing Regimento. Alterations in the Regimento gave outsiders, especially Portuguese, some real advantages. Rich residents of Rio de Janeiro obtained large and valuable grants. Among the Paulista protesters was Garcia Rodrigues Pais, who had labored long and hard only to witness many of the rewards going to undeserving newcomers. The Paulistas wanted the king to roll back the tide of Brazilians and Europeans rushing into the mining area. The attempt would not have succeeded, even if tried, without an army far beyond the ability of the king to recruit and maintain.

A great immigration began after 1705. Within a short time, the "outsiders" were in the majority, and they were given the name Emboabas by the Paulistas. The origin of the name is unknown. It could have been taken from a bird with feathered legs, or it may have meant simply "outsiders," or even "enemy."

To the Paulistas, anyone but a Paulista was an outsider. The Bahianos were the principal rivals. They, or new immigrants into Brazil who landed in Bahia, could reach the mines via the São Francisco River as easily as the Paulistas. The cattle of the São Francisco valley furnished transport, food, and leather. The governor of Rio de Janeiro, who until 1710 was also governor of the mining areas, opposed the Bahian route because of the ease of contraband.

The cattle were legal trade, and indispensable, inasmuch as Rio de Janeiro and São Paulo could not supply them. But many cattle were smuggled in to avoid payment of the tax. Supplies for the mines were crucial. In the first rushes many, maybe hundreds or more, starved because they left the coast without adequate supplies. The interior, especially across the *caatinga* of Bahia's interior, did not have food for many people. Some Paulistas, forced to abandon their claims while they foraged for food, or sometimes even traveling to São Paulo for supplies, found those claims occupied by others upon their return. In this situation, where food was literally life or death, men did not put obedience to the law above contraband.

Slaves were an important element in the Bahia-Minas trade, though not necessarily contraband. In Bahia, where a decline in sugar production in the latter part of the seventeenth century had created a depression among the planters, a surplus of slaves now existed. The owners were glad to sell at the high prices paid by miners. This is not the usual historiographical view. Most historians have blamed the drop in sugar production after 1700, if it actually happened, on the loss of slaves to the mines.

Manuel Nunes Viana became an outstanding figure in the contraband trade from Bahia to Minas. An owner of extensive lands in the São Francisco River valley, with distinctive leadership qualities and culture above the average for his era, he became the organizer of Emboaba resistance against the Paulistas, who grew increasingly violent in their attacks on all considered outsiders.

In October 1708, Borba Gato, the chief local authority, ordered Viana to leave Minas, posting an order to this effect in the chapel of Caeté where Viana lived. Viana responded to the edital the following day. He denied particularly that he had failed to pay his taxes or had promoted riots as accused. Viana was perhaps not guilty of stirring up violence, since such activity was contrary to his interests. He could say with justice that he was known as a peacemaker in the São Francisco valley and wherever else he had lived. He claimed Borba Gato was at fault for failing to stop the violence.

Borba Gato naturally replied, and the give and take continued. On November 29, Borba Gato wrote the governor in Rio de Janeiro about the alleged contraband activities of Viana, including many armed convoys. The arms, it may be noted, were indispensable even in a legal cattle drive and were needed to repel robbers, Indians, or wild animals. They could be used as well to prevent officials from enforcing the laws.

Frei Francisco de Meneses, who had come to Sabará in 1707 and was involved in the monopoly of the slaughterhouses, became one of the chief contrabandists. He was associated with Francisco de Amaral, a man of dubious reputation who had obtained earlier the monopoly sought by the friar. He also had a monopoly in the sale of aguardente and tobacco, both brought in from Bahia. The new contract, which had aspects regarded by the people as unfavorable, caused a clamor, especially among the Paulistas.

The friar persisted, nevertheless, in partnership with Pascoal Moreira Guimarães and two other friars, Frei Firmo and Frei Conrado. Amaral, now rich and unwilling to put up a fight, retired to his estate. Frei Meneses sought the support of powerful cattlemen and merchants, among them Viana and the Bahian Sebastião Pereira de Aguilar, who were proprietors of the ranch in the Ribeirão das Abóbaras where the corral for counting and taxing incoming cattle was located.

Frei Meneses traveled to Rio de Janeiro to petition Governor Fernando Lencastre for the monopoly. The Paulistas were strongly opposed and sent agents to present their counter petition to the governor. They were prepared to go to Lisbon to appeal to the king if necessary. Governor Lencastre refused the monopoly and sent orders to Borba Gato to prevent price gouging on articles of prime necessity.

Angered by the opposition of the Paulistas, Frei Meneses vowed vengeance on them. The friar was closely associated with Viana hereafter, seeing in him a man of capacity and prestige and a useful ally as well. According to some early historians, the civil war that followed was caused by the friar. José Joaquim da Rocha, the supposed author of *Geográfia Histórica de Minas Gerais* published in 1781, accused him of abetting the conflict. Diogo Ribeiro de Vasconcellos claimed that the friar had "kindled the flame of discord."

In any case, the conflict, known as the "War of the Emboabas," was linked with speculation in goods of prime necessity carried by Bahians and Portuguese. The Taubaté author Bento Fernandes Furtado de Mendonçc, perhaps the first to describe the causes of the war, wrote:

Frei Francisco de Meneses and Frei Conrado, nursed the bitter memory of the lost tobacco monopoly in which they invested thirty arrôbas of gold, because of having met the opposition of some Paulistas. They then tried to get a monopoly of the fresh meat. . . . The result of the public-spirited opposition [to the monopolies] was the first cause of the discord that soon disturbed and divided the budding community.

The intensity of the feeling aroused by the threat to vital supplies among those people who believed they were in danger of starvation caused violent reactions. Events and crimes that normally might have passed unnoticed in the rough society of Minas, or at least would have been a local police matter, inflamed passions on both sides.

One incident, no doubt blown up with rumors, related to a Portuguese merchant on the Rio das Mortes married to a Paulista wife. He was murdered in 1706 by some Carijó Indians, if not by Paulistas, in retaliation for bad treatment at the hands of his wife. The fear caused by this event led neighbors to appeal to the governor in Rio de Janeiro for protection in June 1706. The governor named the Paulista Pedro de Morais Raposo to investigate, and he sent Francisco de Amaral Gurgel to Ouro Preto as capitão-mor.

The second event causing inflamed passions and fears has been cited by historian Sebastião de Rocha Pita. A Portuguese accused of stealing a musket was defended by Viana. The two factions squared off but no fighting took place at this time. Meanwhile, a mameluke son of a rich Paulista, José Pardo, assassinated an "outsider" and took refuge in his father's home. The Emboabas gathered a posse and demanded the surrender of the murderer, who had been aided by his father to escape. The posse in anger killed Pardo senior at the door of his own home. It was now the turn of the Paulistas. Rumors spread in November 1707 that they were planning a mass murder of the "outsiders" on January 15, 1708—a kind of Sicilian Vespers, as Rocha Pita named it, in imitation of the infamous massacres in Sicily in 1282.

Was the Paulista plot fact or fancy? The information concerning the plot comes from Rocha Pita and Father Manuel da Fonseca. Other contemporary chroniclers say nothing about it. In fact, Cláudio Manuel da Costa gives exactly the opposite view, stating that it was the Emboabas who were plotting to kill the Paulistas. None of these accounts seems believable, although the version citing a plot against the Paulistas is contained in a letter of January 1709 written by Bento do Amaral Coutinho, one of the Emboaba leaders, to the governor of Rio de Janeiro.

It is not necessary to believe there was a plot by either party. Both sides were so worked up and fearful that any rumor was accepted as fact. The conflicting evidence makes it difficult to know the truth; yet in regard to the animosity and intensity of feeling there can be no question. Governor Fernando de Lencastre decided in January 1709 to make a personal inspection in Minas. Meantime, the fighting had already started.

Governor Fernando Martins Mascarenhas e Lencastre went to the Rio das Mortes in April 1709 and was received by Emboabas and the Paulistas with great ceremonies. He drew up a peace agreement which both sides accepted. Taking matters in hand, he went on to Congonhas where he faced a force commanded by Viana. The details of what happened are not clear. The rumor had spread that the governor intended to mete out implacable justice to the rebels. If that was his plan, he did not carry it out. Instead, he retreated before Viana's forces and returned hastily to Rio de Janeiro. The failure of the governor to impose the forces of the king's law revealed the need for more decisive action.

There is no certainty about how much fighting took place before and after the meeting of Governor Lencastre with Viana. Skirmishes began in Sabará and later in Cachoeiro do Campo. No documents support Diogo de Vasconcelos, who records a fierce battle between Emboabas and Paulistas in his *História Ántiga das Minas Gerais*. Nor is there any support for his account of the inauguration of Viana as governor in a solemn mass at which Friar Francisco de Meneses officiated.

The Emboabas seem to have worsted the Paulistas in both reported fights, forcing them to retreat to the Rio das Mortes. Viana sent troops under the command of Bento do Amaral Coutinho to attack Paulista forces under Valentim de Barros and Pedro Pais de Barros. The first conflict at Ponta do Morro (later known as São José del-Rei and today as Tiradentes) favored the Paulistas. The tide of battle turned when the Emboabas under Bento de Amaral Coutinho broke the Paulistas into small retreating groups. One group was surrounded and persuaded to surrender under firm pledges of quarter. Nevertheless, the traditional version of the events say Coutinho disregarded his pledge and massacred them all as soon as they were disarmed.

The event was recorded in history as the massacre of the Capão de Traição (hill of treachery). Even the date of the battle is uncertain.

It could have taken place in February, or earlier in January, because Coutinho in his letter of January 15, 1709, to the governor speaks of the Paulistas as having already fled to the Rio das Mortes and taken refuge in the hills. The number of victims was probably highly exaggerated by Vasconcelos who claimed 300 were killed; no evidence supports such a high figure. The modern historian Afonso de Escragnolle Taunay believes 50 deaths to be a high estimate: "Those beheaded were probably the poor bastards, the Carijó and Tapanhuno Indians, slaves and wards of the commander on the hill." Taunay believes the whole reported episode could be fiction.

The Paulista defeat was soon followed by the disintegration of the Emboabas as a cohesive force. The Bahian Sebastião de Aguilar broke with Viana, whose troops suffered defeats around Mariana and Guarapiranga. The hostility of Borba Gato continued implacable.

These troubles arose because, until this date, the laws of the king had not been extended to Minas Gerais. Lawlessness was the rule. In the distribution of mining claims, the rich, who could command their own private troops, which were sometimes their armed slaves, took by force the claims of weaker prospectors. From the richest to the poorest, every man had to be his own protector, and so every man carried whatever arms he could buy—or rob from another. Robbery and murder were routine; no officials existed to punish such crimes.

King João V had received reports of the disorders and saw the need to take strong measures. Law enforcement was on its way, Antonil noted. "We now learn," he wrote, "that His Majesty is sending a governor and officials of justice, as well as raising a regiment of soldiers in the mines in order to bring about a better form of government."

The law came in the person of a new governor and captain-general, António de Albuquerque Coelho de Carvalho, who was sent with specific instructions to put down the rebellion in the mining districts. Taking office in Rio de Janeiro in June 1709, he set out at once to encounter the rebels. The mining district up to that time had no adequate structure of government, only a guarda-mor and a superintendent of mines first named in 1702.

Governor António de Albuquerque settled the immediate troubles with unexpected ease. Viana had lost prestige among his followers, who had split into factions. Governor Albuquerque and "Governor" Viana met in Caeté, which had been Viana's stronghold. Submitting to Governor Albuquerque, Viana retired to his estates in the São Francisco Valley. The new governor then made a tour of the mining districts, making administrative appointments and, in some cases, approving those appointments previously made by Viana.

The governor learned, while in Mariana, of Paulista preparations between April and August to obtain revenge for earlier defeats. Rocha Pita records the tradition that the Paulistas who had retreated from battle were subsequently coolly received by their families and friends and accused of cowardice. Taunay argues that no documentation yet discovered supports this story. But there is logic in Rocha Pita's statement. Paulista men had established a reputation as fighters that was respected throughout Brazil. A few years earlier they had conquered Palmares, invincible to other forces for more than sixty years. They were certainly smarting from their defeat and the loss of their mines.

Whether Rocha Pita's version of the events is true or not, the câmara of São Paulo gave Amador Bueno de Veiga command of a troop that left for the mines in August 1709 with 1300 men. Governor Albuquerque intercepted Amador Bueno's command in Guaratinguetá on the Paraiba do Sul River before he reached Minas. The governor failed to persuade the Paulistas to return to their homes, and he had no soldiers to enforce his orders. Returning to Rio de Janeiro the governor sent news of the Paulista advances to Minas.

An Emboaba force under Ambrósio Caldeira Brant, representing the legal side of the war, prepared to meet the Paulistas at Ponta do Morro on the Rio das Mortes. A letter sent by Brant and intercepted by the Paulistas reveals that he was present on November 13, 1709. After several days of fighting the Paulistas broke off the battle and retreated, motivated either by dissension among themselves or the news that reinforcements were on the way to Brant from Ouro Preto. In November 1709 the governor issued a general pardon that helped restore normalcy.

The Emboabas had meantime sent Friar Francisco de Meneses to see King João V to plead their case. They had not, in their eyes, gotten justice from the governor of Rio de Janeiro. The king heard Meneses and his fellow petitioners with sympathy, it is said, and decided to create a new captaincy for São Paulo and the mines, detached from Rio de Janeiro. Thus were joined into one government the two regions that had just concluded warring. Albuquerque received appointment as the first governor general and captain of the new captaincy, called São Paulo e Minas de Ouro. He assumed office in São Paulo in June 1710 and immediately set out to tour Minas Gerais.

Governor Albuquerque took various measures to bring about peace. In May 1711 the Paulistas were given back much of the property taken from them by the Emboabas. The governor also began raising the status of some mining camps, making them organized towns. The first three were Marianas, Ouro Preto, and Sabará, which were elevated to vilas (incorporated towns) in 1710. Some mining camps became permanent settlements. São Paulo itself was promoted from vila to cidade (city) in July 1711.

The return of Paulista lands and the granting of charters to new towns, enabling a certain numbers of Mineiros to receive recognition as a result of holding public office, may be considered the end of the War of the Emboabas. The hatred of the two groups for each other did not end, however. Moreover, this turbulent society remained resistant to the authority of royal officials.

The war ended none too soon. Brazil faced a new danger to which both Paulistas and Emboabas responded—the French invaded Rio de Janeiro in August 1710.

20

FOREIGN ATTACKS AND INTERNAL DISPUTES, 1710–1715

PART I

FRENCH ATTACKS ON RIO DE JANEIRO

After Portugal entered the War of Spanish Succession in 1703, its territories around the globe became subject to attack. The Portuguese expected the French to invade Brazil, and the most likely location for a French offensive was Rio de Janeiro. Rio had become the principal center for traffic to the mining regions, and hence the port most likely to possess the gold coveted by all.

Rio de Janeiro's beautiful and spacious harbor (Guanabara Bay) conducted commerce with much of the world by 1710. As a result of its favorable location vis-á-vis the gold mines, it had superseded in importance Paratí and other ports. The city had around 12,000 inhabitants, mostly housed in the area between the bay and today's Uruguayana Street. If a fleet had not recently called at the port, large amounts of gold normally awaited shipment by the government or individuals. A portion was contraband. Some went to Portugal, while other shipments headed for England, the European continent, Africa, and Asia. A variety of other wares also left Rio for the outside world. It was likewise the recipient of a large volume of imports, much of it also contraband.

Jean François Duclerc, commanding five French warships, approached Rio de Janeiro harbor in August 1710. Driven back by the cannon fire from forts guarding the entrance of the bay, he took refuge on the Ilha Grande toward the southwest. He sent forces by land on September 18 and 19 to take Rio from the rear. The Portuguese had ample time to scout his movements, but failed to do so. At first Duclerc had considerable success. His forces penetrated to the Largo do Carmo, today the Praça 15, but after heavy losses he surrendered. About 650 men, including Duclerc and his officers, many of them nobles of the rank of count or marquis, became prisoners.

The prisoners were allowed some freedom under escort, and Duclerc and his officers could be seen about the streets of Rió de Janeiro for some months. On March 18, 1711, he was assassinated by persons never identified and for reasons never discovered. It was commonly believed, however, that the dark and handsome Duclerc, who came from the Island of Guadalupe in the Caribbean, had become too popular with the ladies of Rio, some of whom were married. His body lies buried in the beautiful Candelária Church at one end of Avenida Getúlio Vargas. In 1712 the Conselho Ultramarino of Portugal expressed its disapproval of the treatment of Duclerc as "lacking the security that should be given to prisoners," but the effort to find his assassins was interrupted by the invasion of a second more successful French expedition.

Portugal had tried to strengthen it defenses against foreign attacks and commerce. In February 1711, the king sent firm orders to the viceroy and the governors of the captaincies to bar all foreign vessels, except those sailing with convoys in accordance with international treaties and those forced by storm or a shortage of water or food to seek a safe harbor. Such vessels were to be assisted and ordered to sail in the shortest time possible. Strong punishments were to be meted out to any officials who failed to enforce the orders to the letter. Any individual caught trading with the enemy would be punished. The Portuguese officials in Rio de Janeiro were thus alerted, but the fortifications were not strong enough to withstand the next French attack led by René Duguay-Trouin.

Duguay-Trouin, a commander with a distinguished career at sea, had organized an expedition in keeping with the customs of the time. It was official, in the sense that it was authorized by the king of France but privately financed by investors, who hoped for a handsome profit from the capture of ships at sea or sacking captured ports. This last aspect gave the Portuguese good reason for calling the expedition of Duclerc and Duguay-Trouin piratical. Among the "investors" was the Count of Toulouse, Admiral of France.

The expedition sailed from France on June 9, 1711, with 17 ships, 700 cannon, and 5,800 men. It had to leave hastily from Brest, where it was fitting out, to escape a British fleet sent to intercept it. Forewarned, Duguay-Trouin went first to La Rochelle, from which he set out for Brazil. A British ship sent to warn Portugal continued on to Rio de Janeiro with news of the coming attack. It reached Rio de Janeiro on August 30, 1711, well in advance of the French fleet.

Though well-fortified and alerted, the commander in Rio de Janeiro allowed himself to be surprised. The French fleet sailed into Guanabara Bay on September 12, 1711, under cover of fog. The attack cost the French 300 men, but they penetrated beyond the range of the forts at the harbor entrance and anchored in the bay before the city. Duguay-Trouin demanded surrender and threatened reprisals toward those guilty of killing French prisoners and General Duclerc the year before. The ultimatum was rejected by the Portuguese commander on the grounds that Duclerc and his men were pirates rather than prisoners of war. Duguay-Trouin bombarded the city and landed his forces. After some initial resistance, confusion spread among the Portuguese defenders, who abandoned their fixed positions and retreated from the city, leaving it to the attackers.

The Portuguese hoped for help from Minas Gerais, but the distance was long, and the events of the War of the Emboabas had left little time for attention to the affairs of the coast. Some forces were sent from Minas, but they did not arrive in time to help repel the French attack. The governor of Rio de Janeiro, Francisco de Castro Morais, retreated to Iguaçú, leaving the hungry, unsheltered and undefended people to shift for themselves. About 200 French prisoners from the Duclerc expedition were freed from prison.

The Portuguese governor, whose troops no longer obeyed him, negotiated with Duguay-Trouin for the ransom of the city. The convent of Santo António yielded some two million cruzados (800,000 milreis). The governor further agreed to pay 610,000 cruzados (244,000 milreis), a hundred caixas of sugar, and 200 head of cattle. The Casa de Moeda yielded 110,000 milreis, and the coffers of the department of fazenda (treasury) 67,000 milreis. In addition, the orphanage, the Jesuits, and many individuals were also forced to contribute. As a result, the name of Governor Francisco de Castro Morais became a curse on the lips of the people.

Meanwhile, Governor-General António de Albuquerque Coelho Carvalho arrived with poorly armed troops from Minas, where he had been busy restoring order after the War of the Emboabas. But he could do nothing against Duguay-Trouin. The people looked to him, however, rather than to Castro Morais.

The ransom paid, the French remained in the city, conducting themselves according to eye-witness accounts as "perfect cavaliers." They traded with the citizens of Rio de Janeiro, selling them, among other items, quantities of gunpowder. The longer-term aspirations of the French was signified by the arrival of several French merchants and a French consul. Duguay-Trouin sailed away a month and a half later, hoping to repeat his success in Bahia, but he was foiled by contrary winds that prevented him from landing.

Castro Morais was tried and condemned to confiscation of his property and perpetual imprisonment in India. His nephew was exiled, and the official who had surrendered Fort São João was condemned to death, but he escaped and was executed in effigy.

The two French invasions of Rio de Janeiro were a relatively brief episode in Brazilian history, but nevertheless a reminder of one of the major influences in Brazilian development, namely the vulnerability of its long coastline to foreign attacks.

The immediate French and Spanish danger did not end when Duguay-Trouin sailed away, nor even with the Treaty of Utrecht (1713–1715) which ended the War of Spanish Succession. Fortunately for Portugal during these years, the Spanish Council of the Indies was so preoccupied with the question of Colônia do Sacramento that it did not pay due attention to the Luso-Brazilian advances up the Amazon and into the missions in Paraguay, Chiquitos, and Moxas.

At the end of the war, Philip V was recognized as king of Spain in the treaties negotiated in 1713 and 1715. By the first of these treaties between Portugal and France, in April 1713, France dropped its claims to the territory between the north bank of the Amazon and the Oiapoc River, known to the Portuguese as the Costa do Cabo do Norte. (Later there was considerable quibbling about the true course of the river.) By the terms of the second treaty, in February 1715, Spain returned Colônia do Sacramento to Portugal. Portugal once again had its trade outpost across the river from Buenos Aires and a vast, hollow, beckoning hinterland between Côlonia and Brazil's southernmost settlement at Laguna Santa Catarina, founded in 1684.

Portugal had thus won more by clever negotiation than its military actions justified, which was one of the general characteristics of Portuguese and Brazilian diplomacy. Nothing in the treaties affected the western frontiers of Brazil, where bandeirantes from São Paulo and other parts of Brazil and Portugal were steadily pouring into the gold fields.

PART II

THE MASCATES: MERCHANTS VERSUS SENHORES DE ENGENHO

A serious conflict involving social class, economic interests, and political influence occurred in Pernambuco from 1710 to 1714. Pernambuco and its capital city, Olinda, the first and most conspicuous success among the original captaincies, had always manifested the vigorous and independent spirit of its founder, Duarte Coelho.

During the period of Dutch occupation from 1630 to 1654, Recife was built up as the center of government and commercial activity. In the post-Dutch era, its chief citizens, largely Portuguese merchants, engaged in an extended conflict with the chief citizens of Olinda, who represented the older landowning families, particularly the senhores de engenho. Olinda, the capital from the date of first settlement, resented the pretensions of Recife merchants, who were viewed as members of a lower social class. The friction was heightened because of the debts owed by landowners to these merchants.

After 1654 Portuguese governors favored Recife over Olinda, which had declined as a commercial center. When Governor Sebastião de Castro e Caldas arrived in June 1707, he practically ignored Olinda except for one controversy carried on with its câmara. The Olinda câmara appealed to King João V. The king subsequently ordered the governor to compose his differences with the câmara and treat it with proper respect.

The residents of Recife wanted their town raised to the status of "vila." They did not understand why, given the wealth of their town in comparison with Olinda, it should have to submit to the rule of the Olinda Câmara. They were not eligible to membership in the câmara, and they considered the situation a case of government without representation. They wanted the king to act on a petition, submitted in vain as early as 1700, to install a câmara of Recife. Governor Castro e Caldas supported their claims in 1709, and in November a royal decree authorized establishment of a city government for Recife. The boundaries were drawn and in February 1710 the governor erected a *pelourinho*, the symbol of authority. The câmara was installed soon thereafter with two Portuguese and two Recife citizens as members. The merchants had won their case, triumphing over landowners.

Olinda, defeated and incensed, considered the wisdom of contesting the royal action. The boundaries assigned to Recife were disputed by Olinda, with the ouvidor supporting Olinda and the governor Recife. Passions on both sides continued to heat up for months. During the night of October 10, 1710, an attempt was made on the life of the governor, who escaped with minor wounds. The governor arrested some conspirators and tried to arrest the ouvidor, who escaped to Paraiba with the bishop. Olinda citizens, disguised as Indians with feathers, attacked Recife, driving out the governor, who fled to Bahia on November 7 to seek help from the governor-general.

Olinda, having won, debated its future. Some favored independence and a republic. Some thought of seeking French aid. The French had already made the first of the two attacks on Rio de Janeiro, and a strong warning against foreign dangers had already gone out from Portugal to the governors. The crown called attention to the French menace and admonished the officials in Pernambuco to keep a close watch. Since the second attack on Rio by Duguay-Trouin in 1711 occurred in the midst of the Olinda-Recife conflict, the warning was not without meaning. The advocates of independence did not win in Olinda. Rather a long petition was sent to the king, outlining the demands of the rebels.

Trouble was also brewing in Bahia. Riots known as the "Motins de Maneta" protested the cost of living. Several groups, which included a few slaves advocating manumission, attacked and sacked stores on October 19 and December 2, 1711. Among the issues raised by the Bahia protesters was the failure of the governor to expel the French.

The extremists were pacified when the bishop returned from Paraiba. Upon opening the royal instructions detailing the succession of power, it was learned that the bishop was the newly designated governor. He was acceptable to both sides—for the moment. The governor-general in Bahia, Lourenço de Almada, sent him a letter of commendation on February 4, 1711. On seeing the strengthened position of Olinda, Recife gathered support from the capitão-mor of Paraiba, the terço Camarão, from Goianna, and other towns, and it revolted on June 18, 1711. The bishop was captured and imprisoned in the colégio of the Jesuits. He was forced to issue a circular supporting the "restored" government of Recife. The bishop escaped, however, and with the ouvidor, he took refuge in Olinda. He organized a small force to besiege and blockade Recife—a vain task since he had no naval force to close the port.

Several battles followed with neither side winning a decisive victory. Meanwhile, time favored Recife. The king was not likely to approve a "native"uprising in Brazil. At the time he also had to deal with the two French attacks on Rio de Janeiro in 1710 and 1711 and the War of the Emboabas was still unresolved. On October 6, 1711, a fleet from Portugal arrived in Recife with the new governor, Felix José Machado de Mendonça, who was empowered to grant a general pardon. He did not observe the terms of the pardon, however. Alleging a conspiracy against his life, and enlisting the aid of the *ouvidor* and *juiz de fora*, he persecuted the partisans of Olinda mercilessly. A modern historian says: "he arrested, exiled, punished." Olinda cried out to the king.

The king ordered the governor to cease his "investigations" in April 1714. The new viceroy, Marques de Angenja, intervened for Olinda. His pronouncements seemed to favor Olinda, but the government of the captaincy remained in Recife. The merchants had won. The friction between Pernambucans and Portuguese had not ended, and it remained a part of the history of Pernambuco to the end of the colonial period and was exacerbated at the moment of Brazilian independence.

The threat to Portuguese possession of Brazil—as exemplified by the many foreign "Emboabas" attracted to the mines, by the more direct and much greater danger from the two French invasions, and by the realization that some Pernambucans were thinking of a political connection with France—brought the government face-to-face with an unpleasant fact: the laws designed to act as a shield for Brazil operated more like a sieve with very large mesh. Thus it is not surprising that the crown remained no less preoccupied with foreign dangers than previously.

The Portuguese were greatly and constantly concerned about foreign goods sold in Brazil and about Brazilian products that needed a much larger market than Portugal alone afforded. Not only gold, but sugar, tobacco, cacao, hides, brazilwood, and many other products abundant in Brazil needed larger markets to stimulate expansion. The studies made by Simonsen show that, after 1710, Brazilian exports were increasing and local merchants were seeking more outlets.

Among the problems that the discovery of gold had aggravated, and which the end of the War of Spanish Succession had not solved, was the contraband trade and the participation of foreigners in the Brazil trade. Portugal had never, since the earliest days of discovery, been able to supply Brazil completely. During the first two centuries of its history a large number of foreign ships traveled to Brazil, either as part of the convoys or as blatant contrabandists. The richer and more sophisticated the commerce of Brazil, the greater the demand for expanded foreign markets. Meanwhile, the flow of gold had enhanced the Portuguese ability to supply Brazil.

In February 1711 the king once again issued intransigent orders to the viceroy and governors about violations by foreign ships. Stern punishment was prescribed for officials who permitted evasion of the law. Those carrying out the prohibited commerce were to be treated with equal rigor.

On October 2, 1715, Diego de Mendonça Furtado informed the Conselho Ultramarino of the will of the sovereign to stop all illegal trade. In 1718, the Duke de Cadaval complained, in vain, to the Council of the "bad enforcement of the king's orders." The Duke de Cadaval talked to the Conselho Ultramarino about the "indifference of the officials and the inefficient execution of the king's orders." Brazil would soon be lost, he said, because of clandestine foreign commerce. The Duke expressed surprise that the viceroy of Brazil had not already expelled all foreigners resident in Brazil.

The Conselho Ultramarino discussed the problem further in 1718. The Conselho had before it a report from the captain of Pernambuco, petitions from the merchants of Oporto and ship owners trading to Maranhão, plus information presented by Desembargador Cristóvão Gomes de Azevedo. All were alarmed at the growing foreign commerce. Three-fourths of all shipments to Brazil were sent by foreign merchants. In Maranhão, for example, the English were monopolizing commerce. The discovery of the mines had intensified foreign interest.

During the first twenty years of operation, the mines had produced more than a hundred million cruzados—and some said more than one hundred fifty million. Only ten million had remained in Portuguese hands, the rest going to foreigners. Brazil seemed to be working largely for the benefit of foreigners, not the mother country. The suggested remedies were dangerous. Portugal did not have the power to confront foreign nations, particularly England. Any effort to retract privileges granted to foreigners by treaty invited the use of military force against Portugal.

Another representation made to the king, undated but at about the same time, by the *"homens de negócio"* of the Brotherhood of the Holy Spirit in Lisbon, draws an excellent portrait of the situation. The foreigners, the Portuguese merchants said, bid more for contracts, including the supply of the militia, passed customs on their own signatures, and held shares of the ships used in Brazilian commerce. A number of English, French, Dutch, Flemish, and Italian merchants had established themselves in Brazil with correspondents in Lisbon and northern Europe.

The foreign merchants entered Brazil on various pretexts, discharging and selling their cargoes in exchange for gold and tobacco. Some returned to their own countries and others continued their voyages to the Orient, where they traded Brazilian products for clothing, spices, and specie. They returned to Brazil, and again "feigning similar pretexts," entered port, exchanged their oriental cargoes for tobacco and gold, and returned rich and opulent to their own countries. These accounts, said the petitioners, were not imagined fears or a mere metaphysical discourse: "These are pure truth, canonized by time and experience."

The master of one Portuguese ship, recently returned to Lisbon, reported that he had seen seven ships of foreign merchants enter Salvador, Bahia, in a period of four months. The Portuguese were placed in a position of inferiority, and their profits had evaporated. The sovereignty of Portugal was threatened because "the moradores and natives of Brazil, are of proud temperament and opulent in capital."

In 1719 about 30 alleged "pirates" were taken from Rio de Janeiro to Bahia and ordered hanged by Governor-general Conde de Vimeiro. But foreign commerce continued. When João VI subsequently legalized foreign commerce in 1808, he did no more than legalize what already existed.

One point should be reiterated and emphasized, however. This trade was Brazilian trade, whether legal or illegal. It created a market for Brazilian exports and produced economic growth. The Portuguese merchants viewed events in the light of their own self interest (narrowly conceived in our modern view), and there is little wonder that they complained about their inability to prevent the continuance of foreign competition.

21

MONSOONS TO THE INTERIOR

Preoccupations with the problems of the coast did not lessened the royal interest in the mines, nor did the Mineiros and Paulistas lose their faith in finding gold almost anywhere. The search for more gold continued, naturally, and many of those who had lost out in Minas Gerais turned their eyes to other possibilities. In 1716, or somewhat later, António Pires Campos explored a route toward Cuiabá looking for the Serra dos Martírios, where he had been in the company of his father, Manuel de Campos Bicudo, in 1675, while still a boy.

The crown looked with favor on gold prospectors, and particularly the Paulistas. They, said King João V in a letter directed to Governor Conde de Assumar in October 1718, "are the only men who are successful in discovering mines." The Paulistas were not impeded, he stated, by a rigid interpretation of the Regimento of 1702. The king was interested in a proper distribution of claims, more gold discoveries, and his *quinto* (Fifth). He knew he would get little if the men who knew how to find gold were impeded in their search. If they bent the laws, he recommended leniency—a little looking the other way. King João was not the first king to find his own laws slightly inconvenient at times. Constant new discoveries were required to keep gold sailing into Lisbon.

The miners, furthermore, did not submit willingly to unpopular

369

laws or taxes. In Pitangui, for example, the Paulistas forbade the entrance of Emboabas and prohibited the payment of the *quinto* on penalty of death. When the law came down on them, they migrated elsewhere rather than accede. To encourage them to return, the authorities tried persuasion rather than force. The Conde de Assumar issued pardons to all who fled.

In order to lessen the bitter rivalry between them, foreign miners were encouraged to become partners with the Portuguese. As mining became more difficult and expensive and the sources of water farther from the deposits of gold, operations demanded larger amounts of capital. The miners were encouraged to use hydraulic mining methods to increase production.

In July 1722, Bartolomeu Bueno da Silva, known as Anhaqueira II, left São Paulo with 152 men—including three priests, five or six Paulistas, a good number of Portuguese, one Bahiano, and 20 Indians—in search of the Serra dos Martírios, where, tradition held, nature had sculpted the crown of thorns, the lance, and the nails of the cross of Christ. After three years of searching, gold was discovered four leagues (12 miles) from the site of the city of Goiás. New mines soon opened nearby. Around the mines there quickly grew up farms, ranches, and towns to supply the miners.

Pascual Moreira Cabral Leme, following the same route taken in 1718 by Antonio Pires de Campos, discovered gold in Coxipé Mirim, Mato Grosso. This expedition opened the route known as the monções (monsoons) actually a variation of the bandeiras. The monsoons took advantage of the high water season, following the rivers to falls or cataracts, which were portaged over. In several cases they portaged from one river to another, whereas the bandeirantes had mainly followed the land routes.

The monsoons became the principal means of carrying supplies to the interior. The payloads of the boats were much greater than those of pack animals, which were difficult to use in any case, or of slaves, who were the beast of burden most commonly used by the bandeirantes. The principal river merchants came from Itú and Sorocaba. Their starting point was Araritaguaba (Porto Feliz) and thence by the Tieté, Paraná, and Paraguay rivers to Cuiabá.

The discovery produced a sensation. A mining camp was established where the chapel of São Gonçalo was later built. The monsoonists had no mining tools; they had not come in search of mines. Metal plates were used to pan the gold from the river. Gun barrels served as picks. Those who had nothing else dug with their hands. They were later joined by a bandeira led by António Antunes Maciel and Gabriel Antunes, two brothers from Sorocaba. When all their weapons, lead, and powder had been used up in mining, they were besieged by hostile Indians.

They were unexpectedly rescued by the bandeira of Fernando Dias Falcão consisting of 130 armed men, supplies, and mining tools. Falcão returned to São Paulo, perhaps accompanied by António Antunes Maciel, and raised money in 1719 for a new expedition with supplies, blacksmiths, carpenters, tailors, and everything available to supply a new mining camp. He had to mortgage everything he owned, borrowing heavily from friends to acquire the large amount of baggage. The gunpowder alone weighed about six arrôbas (approximately 90 kilos).

His gamble paid off. When Dias Falcão returned to São Paulo in 1723, he gave the crown its Fifth, amounting to 12 pounds and 84 oitavas of gold. More discoveries followed quickly, this time exactly where the modern city of Cuiabá now stands. The gold strikes had the usual fairy tale characteristics. In 1722, Miguel Sutil of Sorocaba sent two Indians to search for wild honey. They returned late at night without honey, being treated to Sutil's angry reprimands. When he had eased up, they asked if he preferred honey to gold, and thereupon they exhibited 23 nuggets of gold weighing a total of 120 oitavas. The gold they had found lay on the surface mixed with sand. In one day of work Sutil found an arrôba of gold, equal to 15 kilos; and his Portuguese companion João Francisco, who was nicknamed "0 Barbado," another 600 oitavas, or more than two kilos.

Almost all the miners at Coxipé-Mirím rushed to the "mines of Sutil." In a month of frantic digging, it is said that more than 400 arrôbas (6,000 kilos) of gold were found at depths that never exceeded half a meter. When the news reached São Paulo, Paulistas and Emboabas by the hundreds, perhaps thousands—for the numbers can never be known accurately—made the five-month, or longer, monsoon to Cuiabá.

The monsoon was useful in the commerce that developed in Brazil's far west—Goiás, Cuiabá, and Mato Grosso. The objective was not to find new territories or capture Indians but to carry merchandise from the Atlantic coast to the populations gathered around the mines. Monsoons were seasonal. They went in high water, when the flow of the river was right—hence the name monsoons, of Arabic origin, referring to the seasonal winds of the Indian Ocean that regulated the sailings of fleets. The seasonal winds and ocean currents along the coast of Brazil were also referred to as monsoons by the Portuguese and other sailors who were forced to reckon with them.

The term monsoon was not generally applied in São Paulo until about 1720. They usually started in March or April but might be delayed to May or June if the rains had not filled the rivers. The season of the monsoons was also the season of malaria with its alternating chills and fevers, often delaying voyages to later in the year. Porto Féliz had the atmosphere of a U.S. western town in the nineteenth century—Dodge City for example. Both the departing and arriving monsoonists whooped it up, sometimes at great damage to persons and property.

Generally speaking, São Paulo did not prosper from either the bandeiras or monsoons; rather it suffered. Diverted by visions of gold and riches, the people abandoned the cultivation of land and the sedentary way of life.

The monsooners soon learned the advantages of large convoys for defense against Indians, who had wiped out individuals or small groups in the earliest days of the gold rush. Large sums were invested in canoes, equipment, and cargoes. Government canoes that were well-armed and equipped for war accompanied the private parties. Measures to protect and preserve supplies, merchandise, and voyagers were vital.

The earliest voyages often lacked proper preparations and suffered either partial or total losses of canoes, supplies, and lives. One convoy that left São Paulo in 1720 lost everything, including the crew and passengers. Later voyages found wrecked canoes with spoiled supplies and corpses. Not one person made it to the mining camp of Coxipo in 1720, although numerous groups set out down the Tieté River. The next year was less disastrous, but some expeditions still lost their baggage, slaves, and crew members. Hunger was an implacable enemy. Captain José Pires de Almeida, so the story goes, traded a small mulatto boy he considered a son for a fish to assuage his hunger. He had already lost all his slaves and supplies.

The rain regulating the monsoons could also be a destructive force. Although the rain made it possible to use the swollen rivers, it also drenched supplies and produced mildew and rot. A partial solution was to erect a canopy, slightly wider than the canoe. The canopy was usually made of sailcloth, or wool or cotton flannel, stretched on a wooden frame in the center of the canoe. Between 1720 and 1725 the mosquito net was also introduced. Canoes with both canopy and mosquito nets offered much greater protection for supplies and the health of passengers during the long voyage to Cuiabá than earlier monsoons.

Cuiabá was lawless, as mining camps are in the beginning. To control the tumult, Pascual Moreira, with the title of guarda-mor, organized an ad hoc government, including a secretary and marshall with a dozen deputies. He attempted to do his duty and collect the king's Fifth by assessing the miners on the basis of pans—that is, by assessing the miners on the basis of each slave or Indian owned as done in Minas Gerais before the system of *finatas* was begun by Brás Baltasar da Silveira. The new governor of São Paulo, Rodrigo César de Meneses, approved the system as the most efficient for the royal service and the fairest for miners. The turbulence in Cuiabá did not end. Violence was the norm, regardless of the attempts at law enforcement. The miners broke into factions and became victims of *caudilhos*, like the brothers Lourenço and João Leme da Silva.

The long and dangerous expeditions could be facilitated by planting crops and raising livestock at convenient portages. This started as early as 1725 at the fazenda of Camapoã.

The hard life on the monsoon voyages is revealed in this statement of one who took the long route:

I left Sorocaba with fourteen Negroes and three of my own canoes. I lost two canoes enroute and arrived with one canoe and seven hundred oitavas of debt and expenses for supplies brought on the voyage. Of the Negroes, I sold six of mine that I had bought on credit in Sorocabá, four of eight given to me by my uncle, all of whom were sold to pay my debts. Of the four left, three died, leaving me with only one. . . . . And so, of 23 canoes with which we left Sorocaba, we arrived in Cuiabá with fourteen, nine having been lost; the same thing happened to the other voyages, as it happens every year on these voyages.

Cuiabá became a stable community from which the people migrated to settle other areas. By 1734 settlers had reached the Guaporé River, an affluent of the Madeira and hence open to the Amazon. Along the Guaporé, the Pais de Barros brothers discovered the mines of Mato Grosso. These gold discoveries, comprising at most a small part of the immense hinterlands, did not lead to sufficient migration to fill up the interior. Settlements of people were small and scattered, even into the twentieth century. Except for gold, there was not much exportable surplus to stimulate growth. The route to the interior was laid out, however, and when at a later date economic conditions became favorable, the population slowly increased. One matter was determined by the gold strikes: Portugal rather than Spain became the owners of these immense lands.

A few words must be said about the canoe. It was of Indian origin, as is well known. The norms of use followed Indian ways, the European contribution being only better tools. Very large tree trunks supplied the basic frame, which was hewed out and burned out to form the hollow. Smaller canoes were made of bark, but those were not used for long voyages. The favorite trees were the peroba and ximbauva. They were cut in the proper season, months without "r" (certainly not borrowed from the Indians) in the period of the waning moon, June and July being considered best. The walls were left with a maximum of six centimeters thickness. An additional strip nailed around the rim strengthened the canoe.

A month or more was required to cut down the tree, hewing and hollowing it out, putting on the canopy, and launching it. Size depended, of course, on the trees found. Suitable trees became scarce because thousands of the largest trees, which had been growing for centuries, were cut down within a few years. The canoe carpenters scoured the headwaters of the creeks ever farther from the main streams, sometimes living in the forests for months while searching for trees and making canoes. The area of the state of São Paulo where Piracicaba is now located was one of the principal regions devoted to canoe production.

The usual size of the canoes was twelve to thirteen meters long and one and a half meters clear width, giving a ratio of ten to one length-to-breadth. Both bow and stern were hewed down to a narrow edge. The cargo was loaded in the center under the canopy. In the open front were six rowers, the pilot, and the bowman. He steered the canoe, maneuvering it around rapids and water falls, and commanded the rowers, beating out the stroke on the bottom of the canoe with his heel. A local pilot or two might be employed in dangerous areas, if they were available. The rowers stood, according to Indian custom; the custom is followed in similar type boats everywhere, in the Venetian gondola for example. In small canoes the rowers kneeled.

The *proeiro* was the most important man of the crew. His duties went beyond steering the canoe. He also carried the keys to the stores of salt, meat, and liquids. He was a man of great prestige, exhibiting "all the swagger of a flattered and feared bully." In places, the canoes had to be unloaded and dragged around falls and rapids too dangerous to run. The total number of crew and passengers numbered from 20 to 30. In the first years as many as 150 men traveled in one canoe, but such canoes carried no supplies. The largest canoes could load up to 400 arrôbas, about 6,000 kilos of merchandise plus food for the crew and passengers. Canoes out of Porto Feliz put aboard fresh supplies in Camopoã.

The daily ration was a bit more than 100 grams of bacon or jerked meat, a liter of manioc or corn meal, and half a liter of beans. The passengers and crew all ate the same meals. From manioc mixed with water and, if available, honey, sugar, or even cachaça (rum of sugar cane), they made a drink. Fish from the rivers (not easily caught in

high water) plus palm shoots, fruit, and game, if available, enriched
the diet. A hazard always existed in attempting to living off the forests.
Some areas were dry, baked, and nearly desert, affording little of
substance.

Hundreds, perhaps thousands of men, died in locations which people far away and without first-hand experience believed to be lands
of plenty. Not only during the monsoons but throughout the tropics,
death from starvation was common. The story related earlier about
the man who traded his little slave for a single fish illustrates the
point. One of the recurring themes of the conquests by Portuguese,
Spaniards, and other Europeans was the starvation of conquerors.

The supply fleets numbered up to 400 canoes. The cargo outbound
to the mines was composed mainly of the necessities of life. But luxury
items were also in demand. Salt, indispensable for cooking, was very
expensive and sometimes limited to those who could afford the high
price. Others went without salt at the expense of their taste and health.
Silks and other fine cloths for festive or formal occasions also appealed
to the miners who struck it rich. From the mines came only one
product—gold. Hardly anything else of value was produced for transport to the coast or to Europe.

Food production soon began around the mines as well. But there
were serious obstacles to transplanting both crops and animals, the
latter especially. In the frenzy to get rich quickly, few wanted to carry
seed for planting a crop which took a number of months to develop,
or in the case of manioc a year. The food available to the first miners
was similar to what the Indians ate—fish, game, and fruits and nuts
from the forest. Sufficient food was not easy to find for a sedentary
society, where the population concentration soon exceeded anything
ever known in an Indian culture, which was constantly on the move
and did not exhaust the scant food resources.

Gold had to be mined in the rivers where it was found, however,
not where food was available close by. Agriculture and livestock for
consumption eventually emerged around the mines, but for the first
gold rushers the problem was immediate. The first corn mentioned
in early chronicles was produced in 1723. Beans, pumpkins, and man-

ioc were also planted. Sugar cane came in 1728, but secretly. Its production near the mines was prohibited by the government because, it was stated, sugar took slaves away from the mines. This may be one of the reasons, but another plausible reason was that the authorities wanted to prevent the distilling of rum.

The introduction of domestic breeding stock was more difficult than cultivating plants. Small animals were sent in before the large ones. The first recorded chickens and hogs arrived with the monsoon of 1723. Cattle and horses came later. The first cattle sent to the mines, either four or six young heifers, went with the monsoon of 1727. It does not take much imagination to understand the difficulties of transporting cattle for five months, standing in a canoe a meter and a half wide. Once they had arrived, an unforeseen difficulty arose; for lack of salt or sulfur or some other reason, they did not remain fertile. New stock, thus, had to be introduced in 1739.

22

COLÔNIA DO SACRAMENTO, 1725–1780

For various reasons the occupation of what is today Rio Grande do Sul and Uruguay was not pushed by either Spain or Portugal. The Spaniards were confident they owned the area by legal rights, but they were not strong enough to occupy it under the feeble rule of Carlos II during the last half of the seventeenth century because of numerous entanglements in international affairs.

Portugal was quite willing to push westward of the Line of Demarcation and had an interpretation of the meaning of the Treaty of Utrecht (1713–1715) that legalized its claims. The fear was that Spain might offer too much opposition. Spain could take reprisals against Colônia do Sacramento, and occasionally did. In fact, the forces of Buenos Aires customarily kept a close encirclement of Colônia to prevent Portuguese expansion too far inland.

The legal question of who owned this territory goes back to 1494. That Colônia was far beyond the line was without question. The original intent of the founders of Colônia was to go overland from São Paulo, and they appealed to the Paulistas for aid. After learning that an overland journey would require two years, they made the voyage by sea instead. Some deserters from the forces of Manuel Lobo made their way back to São Paulo by land. In 1703 a party required four months to travel from Colônia to Laguna (Santa Catrina).

Whereas the Portuguese drive to the west was principally to enslave Indians and discover gold, the southern expansion was brought about by the desire to occupy the immense territories between the far outpost of Colônia do Sacramento, settled in 1680, and the towns of Desterro on the western shore of Santa Catarina Island, settled in 1678, and Laguna, settled farther south on the coast in 1684.

No large numbers of settlers had been attracted to Laguna, however, and by the opening of the eighteenth century, the occupied area reached only a few miles inland. The settlers had done a considerable amount of inland exploration, however, and it gave them some knowledge of the geography. The settlement of Rio Grande do Sul actually began early in the eighteenth century at the time Domingos de Brito Peixoto established himself as a cattleman.

Portugal lost Colônia in 1705 during the War of Spanish Succession, but recovered title under the Treaties of Utrecht, 1713–1715. There were two conditions: Portugal would not allow Colônia to become a base for commerce with Spanish colonies either by Portuguese or foreign merchants and, second, the two nations would negotiate a satisfactory swap of Colônia for some valuable Spanish territory. The exchange that Spain proposed was refused by Portugal, however.

When the Treaty of Utrecht restored Colônia do Sacramento to Portugal in 1716, the people of Laguna had a good knowledge of the unoccupied lands south and west—unoccupied except by Indians and thousands (perhaps hundreds of thousands) of semi-wild cattle, horses, burros, and mules. The captain-general of Rio de Janeiro ordered the capitão-mor of Laguna to make a survey of a route connecting Colônia with Laguna. The câmara of Laguna urged the occupation of Rio Grande, noting its fertility, invigorating climate, the excellent port on the Lagoa dos Patos, the very real wealth of livestock, and, finally, the reports of mythical gold mines discovered by Spanish Jesuits of the Seven Missions east of the Uruguay River. Five years later, in 1720, the Portuguese Overseas Council made the same recommendation and used the same reasoning.

Viamão, a few miles east of present-day Porto Alegre, became the site, in 1719, of a settlement by colonists drawn from Laguna in Santa

Catarina, the southernmost point reached by the Paulistas to that date.

The colonization of the Capitania de São Pedro de Rio Grande, as it was first named, came after 1725. The ranches, known as *estâncias* rather than *fazendas de crear* as in the northeast, were created by taking possession of thousands of cattle already running wild on the grasslands and in the forest of southern Brazil. The process was essentially the same in all areas—the cattle and horses spread in ever wider circles from the points of first introduction from Europe and men followed in their trail to claim ownership. Rio Grande do Sul developed the largest cattle ranches in Brazil and a typical pastoral society emerged. The gaucho became as distinct a type in Brazil as the cowboy was in the western United States.

What interests us most about this period is the development of a flourishing cattle industry. Long before the end of the sixteenth century wild cattle and horses abounded. The Indians found both the cattle and horses a welcome addition to their meat supply. The horses were also a means of transportation. Having no animal like the bison that could be used for food, the Indians of South America found the cow and horse even more of a novelty than did North American Indians. The cattle and horses belonged to nobody when they were discovered by the Portuguese and Spaniards adventurers pushing out from the original centers of settlement. Initially, they were hunted like wild animals rather than tended like domestic herds.

About thirty large estancias of "mares as well as cows" were established between the Tramandaí and the Rio Grande. All were part of a plan to occupy lands not settled, as yet, by anybody but Indians. Both individual initiative and official promotion backed these settlements.

In 1725 a large number of people moved from Laguna to Rio Grande do Sul and settled in the Viamão area. In 1728, Frei António da Trinidade, Carmelite of São Paulo, who had lived in Laguna and Desterro, proposed settlements along the Uruguay, but they were not made. The governors of Minas Gerais and São Paulo both ordered studies of the possibility of founding a colony in the Lagoa dos Patos area. In 1728 the Conselho Ultramarino pointed out to the king the danger of losing not only the unoccupied lands but the mines too if a foreign power seized this territory.

Governor Caldeira Pimentel of São Paulo sent sargento-mor Francisco Sousa e Faria in 1728 to scout out a road to the south. Leaving Santos in a smack with thirty-five men, whites and Indians, he touched Paranagua, São Francisco do Sul, and Santa Catarina Island, gathering more forces as he went. From Santa Catarina he traveled overland to Laguna and reached the Ararangua River fifteen leagues away. Here in February 1728, at a place called Conventos, he began tracking the road to Campos Gerais de Curitiba. The going was difficult. He lost some men by desertions and was forced to wait at the Serra for reinforcements from São Paulo. He finally reached Curitiba on February 8, 1730.

Captain Cristóvão Pereira de Abreu set out at the same time as Sousa e Faria and met him in Laguna. He then returned to Colônia. From there he left with 800 mounts, reaching the site of the future Rio Grande in October 1731. This "presidio" was established six years later. Continuing to Santos and São Paulo, he interested Governor Caldeira Pimentel in his project to explore a new road. Supplied with more men, arms, munitions, and tools, he returned to the Ararangua and in three months found a new route to Curitiba. He stated that he could have made the trip in one month if he had not taken the time to "leave canoes along the river and build three hundred bridges." He drove about 3,000 mounts as well as 500 cows back toward the coast. He arrived in São Paulo in 1733. He claimed that the sale of the mounts had put an extra 10,000 cruzados in the royal treasury.

Thus two currents of population settled the south, one coming from the coast and the other going overland. Campos de Vacaria owed its existence to the overland route opened after 1735. Others fled Colônia do Sacramento to escape the wars between the Spaniards and Portuguese and became ranchers in Rio Grande do Sul. Both Spanish and Portuguese soldiers took up ranching.

Laguna became the center of clandestine cattle smuggling, with

Portuguese and Spaniards cooperating in driving cattle from the grasslands of the interior known as Vaqueria do Mar. A road was opened northward between 1727 and 1732 via Curitiba (settled 1668), Sorocaba, and São Paulo, facilitating the supply of cattle, horses, and mules to the mining camps of Minas Gerais. Both the Spaniards and the Portuguese were impelled to take possession of the interior since the market for cattle products, especially hides, grew steadily in the eighteenth century.

In 1730, the Italian missionary Cattaneo, who was engaged in founding one of the Jesuit missions, estimated that a cattle ranch might occupy 36 square miles and have 30,000 head of cattle. Diego de Álvoar described estancias with "twenty, thirty and forty thousand and even up to eighty and one hundred thousand, head of cows, bulls, horses, mules and sheep."

In 1735 a Spanish army from Buenos Aires again besieged Colônia. It was the result of a personal incident between the Spanish government and the Portuguese ambassador in Madrid, whose name was none other than Pedro Álvares Cabral. No full scale war arose out of this demonstration of touchy honor because the French government persuaded the Spaniards and Portuguese to sign an armistice in March 1737. This incident is only one more example of how events entirely unrelated to Brazil affected its history.

Under the terms of the agreement, Colônia remained in Portuguese control. There was, however, a decided difference between Spain and Portugal in interpreting the Treaty of Utrecht of 1715 that had handed Colônia back to Portugal. The Spanish interpretation was that only Colônia was Portuguese. The Portuguese held that they had received sovereignty in the area which is now Uruguay. By 1737 Portugal had occupied none of this land, whereas Spain had established both Montevideo and Maldonado east of Colônia (ca. 1720–1740) in an effort to counter Portuguese expansion.

The decision to occupy Rio Grande was made during the brief undeclared war between Spain and Portugal in 1736–37. In 1735, Brigadier José da Silva Pais, acting governor of Rio de Janeiro in the absence of Captain General Gomes Freire de Andrada, suggested to

Lisbon the establishment of settlements in the southern areas, but his advice was not taken. Silva Pais, before going to Rio Grande, authorized Domingo Fernandes de Oliveira, leader of a band of deserters and gaucho types from Laguna, to raid the Spanish herds back of Colônia and break the Spanish siege. Oliveira failed in the attempt and was captured by the Spaniards.

Silva Pais commanded an expedition sent to Colônia by sea to lift the Spanish siege of Colônia and capture Montevideo. He found the Spaniards too strong at Montevideo and drew up a report explaining the situation on January 15, 1737. Colônia was relieved, however, in part because of dissension within the Spanish besieging camp. Silva Pais attempted to build a new fort at Maldonado but was frustrated by contrary ocean currents and winds.

In 1736 Cristóvão Pereira was sent by the captain-general of São Paulo, Conde de Sarzedas, to relieve Colônia and to try again to lift the siege by the Spaniards. After four months of travel from São Paulo via Viamão, he reached the port of Rio Grande in October. He attacked the mission Indians who, even though living far from Colônia, were aiding the Spanish besiegers. He was present when Silva Pais arrived in Rio Grande, and they cooperated in establishing the fort.

The council received two proposals in 1736 from individuals to settle Rio Grande at their own expense in exchange for various privileges designed to help them recoup their costs. One of the two offers was accepted by José da Silva Pais, acting as governor of Rio de Janeiro, but blocked by Governor Gomes Freire de Andrada because of the possibly hostile attitude of Spain.

Pais then sailed to Rio Grande do Sul de São Pedro (as it was then called), where he disembarked and took possession on February 19, 1737. Although located west of the line set in the Elvas-Badajoz conference of 1682, Rio Grande was so close to the line that the Portuguese believed Spain would overlook this fact when confronted with an established Portuguese colony. The Spaniards did not have, in fact, forces sufficient to challenge the settlement; but they protested the actions of Silva Pais. The governor of Buenos Aires complained that the Portugese had not only settled Rio Grande, comprising the cattle-growing area of Curral Alto and Serra do São Miguel, but had gained control of livestock estimated at 180,000 cattle and up to 140,000 horses.

After peace was declared, Pais erected a pentagonal fort with 28 cannon and fortified the narrow isthmus between Lagoa Mirím and the sea in order to impede the passage of the Spaniards. He also won the friendship of the local Indians, the Minuanos. This fort served as an advance base for Portuguese penetration of the southern areas. In the long run, Portugal would lose Uruguay and hold on to Rio Grande do Sul, but not before thousands of men lost their lives in battle.

When Rio Grande was settled in 1737, some families were sent from Rio de Janeiro and adjoining towns such as São Gonçalo. Pais himself brought still others. Twenty men were sent from Laguna to work on the fortifications of the isthmus; two hundred Indian families came from São Paulo. Still other immigrants moved into the region from Laguna, Colônia, and Rio de Janeiro. Also significant was the im-migration of Azoreans.

After the Portuguese founded Rio Grande, new ranches radiated from it. Many Azoreans originally brought in as farmers shifted to ranching. Once the coastal and lake areas were occupied, the colonists pushed westward to the Taquarí and Jacuí rivers. The Portuguese revealed their seriousness about settlement by sending Azorean fami-lies to the Island of Santa Catarina and to the Rio Grande mainland. Rio Pardo was founded in 1751. Although records show Azoreans there in 1749, the peak of the immigration was 1752; around 100 families arrived in April and 75 more in August. Some of them went to Porto dos Casais, a name changed to Porto Alegre in 1773. In 1775 more families settled on the Rio Pardo and others, in 1777, on the Santo Amaro.

The population of Santa Catarina grew slowly. In 1749 it was es-timated at only 4,197. The crown began to offer inducements to set-tlers, and by 1753 approximately 4,000 couples emigrated from Portugal's Atlantic islands and foreign areas. By the 1760s there were 6,000 to 7,000 people. The principal occupations were still farm-ing, ranching, and fishing. The settlements reached only a few dozen miles inland, except for Lajes which the Paulistas reached in 1766.

The governor of Buenos Aires complained that Colônia was serving as a warehouse for other nations besides Portugal, and especially England. A steady traffic of small vessels of the *asiento* of Negroes made port even during blockades. At about the same date, naval captain Juan Antonio de Colina, who had been a prisoner of the Portuguese, stated that even though Colônia had only 400 residents, about 30 fully-loaded medium-sized Portuguese ships normally made port, and it was rare for them not to put into Montevideo on pretext of bad weather. When this trade was curtailed by war, several Portuguese merchants went bankrupt. His source of information, he said, was what he had learned while a prisoner in Rio de Janeiro.

Buenos Aires interests opposed to the trade made frequent protests, especially the Jesuits and the cattlemen. But they exerted less influence than the illegal traders. The same Spaniards who carried on the contraband trade in this region gave the impression in Spain that they were opponents of all illegal trade, but it was only to disguise their own complicity. The Portuguese were not the only contrabandists. Neither the governor of Rio de Janeiro nor the secretary of state of Portugal doubted that much of the silver shipped to Lisbon from Brazil had originated somewhere in Spanish America.

In 1747 José de Carvajal complained to the Portuguese ambassador in Madrid that five or six millions of patacas a year was drained from Spanish territory through Colônia. When asked how he could determine the amount, he replied that six millions was mined in Peru annually and, since little went out in the fleet, the conclusion was inescapable that it slipped out clandestinely through Buenos Aires. These statistics may not be accurate, but they express a condition that existed. The Spaniards were the guilty parties because they took part in, or permitted, the contraband. The evidence of this complicity was the great fortunes taken home by the governors and other officials of Buenos Aires.

Alexandre de Gusmão citing the advantages of the Treaty of Madrid in 1750, stated that the Treaty of Aix-la-Chapelle in 1748 had finally awakened the Spaniards to the great mass of silver drained off through Colônia and the futility of their efforts to stop the contraband. He claimed that the total, rather than being exaggerated, was more than generally believed.

Even after the settlement of Rio Grande do Sul, Colônia remained detached from other Portuguese colonies. Portugal was able to hold it mainly because Spain was preoccupied with other more pressing affairs at home and abroad.

THE TREATY OF 1750

By mid-century Portugal had extended its settlements and claims far beyond the Line of Demarcation—missionaries held the Amazon, gold had drawn a rush into Mato Grosso and Goiás (erected into captaincies in May 1748), and Portuguese soldiers and settlers were pushing toward the left bank of the estuary of Río de la Plata.

None of these settlements and claims was safe and undisputed. Spain still regarded the Treaty of Tordesillas as valid, although some of the wording of the Treaty of Utrecht (1713–15) had constituted, in the Portuguese view, an acknowledgment of the rights of Portugal west of the line. The disputes had been long and wearisome, however, and both Spain and Portugal were ready to arrive at a settlement and to place their claims on a firm basis.

The ascension of Ferdinand VI, married to a Portuguese princess, to the Spanish throne in 1746, brought an opportunity to settle lingering disputes in America. On the Spanish side José de Carvajal y Lancaster and on the Portuguese side Alexandre de Gusmão, who was secretary to João V and a Brazilian born in Santos, were the chief advisers to their respective kings. Secret negotiations through ambassadors began as early as 1746 on Portuguese initiative. Carvajal, on the Spanish side, was anxious to rid the Plata of the English danger, and an alliance with Portugal was viewed as beneficial. He hoped Portugal might be willing to trade Colônia for some other territory.

The Spanish position was that both banks of the Plata were Spanish territory. Carvajal pointed out the violations of the Treaty of Tordesillas. Gusmão, in turn, argued that Tordesillas was a dead letter; the uncontested advance of the Luso-Brazilians into the interior of Brazil beyond the line, he asserted, had canceled Spanish rights just as in the seventeenth century the Spanish occupation of the Moluccas had canceled Portuguese rights. Each side offered a series of proposals, the Spaniards calling attention to what they regarded as the absurd claims of Portugal. The respective boundaries in the Amazon and Orinoco River valleys also came into the conversations.

The Portuguese, who were the gainers in the vast territory west of the Line of Demarcation, insisted on their definition of boundaries. The Spaniards, who eventually received nothing in compensation east of it, resisted. In the long run the Portuguese won, as they had been doing since Portugal won its independence from Spain in the twelfth century, a point that aggravated the Spaniards then and still does today.

After almost four years of negotiations, Spain and Portugal signed a treaty in January 1750 agreeing to boundaries. With the customary phrases about permanent peace and friendship, the treaty called for the Spaniards to receive Colônia in exchange for the seven Jesuit missions east of the Uruguay River. Furthermore, the missions, the Jesuits, and the Indians were to be transferred to other territory recognized as belonging to Spain. The principle of Uti Possidetis was recognized, giving to each nation the settlements already made.

The terms of the treaty were kept rigorously secret to prevent English and French interference. The boundaries Spain granted to Portugal comprised all those areas explored by the bandeirantes of São Paulo, by the sertanistas in the north, by missionaries in the service of the state, and by many military missions sent by Portugal west of the Line of Demarcation.

The treaty described rivers, lakes, and mountains from Uruguay to Venezuela. Many on both sides rejected the terms of the treaty and denounced it as a surrender to the other. The contrabandists, Spanish and Portuguese, saw a probable curtailment of their illegal trade. Many who had fought to hold Colônia condemned the treaty. The most serious obstacle to carrying it out were the objections of the Spanish Jesuits to the removal of the missions.

Before the treaty could go into full force, the frontiers laid down on paper had to be surveyed throughout a vast area that was little known, and in great part entirely unknown. The joint boundary commissions needed constant instructions from their homelands. Neither side trusted the other, and both felt they had given up more than was necessary. The chance for conflict was ever present, and in the long run was not avoided. At the moment when the implementation of the treaty was critical, João V died. The new king, José I, named as his first minister Sebastīao José de Carvalho e Melo later known as the Marquis of Pombal. Alexandre de Gusmão, who had negotiated the treaty, lost favor; the new minister was skeptical of the treaty and of the Spaniards, and they of him.

Portugal recruited trained personnel from Germany and Italy to help in the survey. Three "partidas de límites" (Boundary Survey Parties) were named for the south and three for the Amazon basin and its confluents. Portugal named Gomes Freire de Andrada, àt the time captain-general of Rio de Janeiro, as chief of the boundary commission in the south. Spain sent the Marqués de Valdelirios. For the north, Portugal named Francisco Xavier de Mendonça Furtado, younger brother of Pombal, as captain-general of the Estado de Grão Pará e Maranhão and chief of the boundary survey. Spain chose José de Iturriaga, a naval captain.

The northern survey was never finished. Furtado made his way with a very large party to the upper Amazon, Rio Negro, and Branco in 1754 and waited for months for Iturriaga's party to show up. They were unable to meet him, because he was delayed by Indian wars in the Orinoco River valley and, it was charged, by the influence of the Jesuits opposed to the treaty.

Furtado, while waiting for the Spaniards, carried out a survey of vast regions with his cartographers, astronomers, and their soldier assistants. He was able to determine the best boundary lines for Portugal and to select sites for fortifications along the Negro and Branco rivers. He recommended the establishment of a separate captaincy, São José do Rio Negro, predecessor of the present-day state of Amazonas, with its capital city at Manaus.

By the time the Spanish commission arrived in 1759, Mendonça Furtado had returned to Portugal. His successor, Captain-General António Rolím de Moura of Mato Grosso, was unable to meet the Spanish party immediately because of other duties; so too he failed to meet the Spaniards. The Spanish party confined its activities to surveying the Orinoco and establishing new settlements.

In the south the survey was for the most part carried out. A great deal of difficulty was encountered in finding the rivers and other sites named in the treaty and shown on the official map (Mapa das Cortes). The real geography was quite different in many cases from that shown on the map.

The greatest difficulty came in the attempt to move the "Seven People" (Sete Povos) of Indians from their homes in order to place the area under Portuguese sovereignty. The result was the Guarani War (1754–1756). In open warfare against the combined Spanish-Portuguese troops, the Indians lost several battles and failed to prevent the survey. One mission, San Lourenzo, surrendered without fighting. The majority of Indians in the other missions fled to the forests and prepared for war or guerrilla activity.

The reaction of the Indians and their Jesuit missionaries should not have been unexpected in either Lisbon or Madrid. It was commonly known that the Spanish Jesuits were opposed to the transfer of the missions. The Jesuits were blamed by both the Spaniards and the Portuguese. Pombal had warned Gomes Freire de Andrada and instructed him to hold Colônia until the Indians were removed and Portuguese troops had occupied the territory. In the Amazon the Portuguese Jesuits were resisting and obstructing the work of Furtado. In the south, where the Jesuits were accused of causing the uprising, no one ever suggested that the Indians be left in their missions.

Both Spain and Portugal believed, or affected to believe, that the Jesuits meant to establish a Jesuit-controlled empire throughout South America. The nationalistic feelings displayed by the Jesuits working under Spanish sovereignty (in many cases not Spaniards) against those in Portuguese areas (also not all Portuguese) can be cited as evidence to counter such accusations. Ten years passed. The original negotiators either withdrew to other duties or died. Efforts to modify the terms of the treaty failed, and its execution was first suspended and then annulled by the Treaty of El Pardo in February 1761.

RENEWED CONFLICT 1760–1778

Neither side had anticipated that ending the Guaraní War would lead to a settlment of the boundary question. Don Pedro de V. Cevallos cautioned Madrid that the conduct of Gomes Freire de Andrada during the war suggested the existence of a deliberate Portuguese policy of endless delay aimed at retaining Colônia and extending their hold in Rio Grande do Sul. Smuggling around Colônia and its hinterlands continued, and even increased. In February 1760 Cevallos drew up a war plan for the expulsion of the Portuguese from Santa Catarina and all lands as far south as the Rio de la Plata.

By this date the defenders of the Treaty of 1750—Ferdinand VI, his queen, and their minister, Carvajal—had exited from the scene. The new king of Spain, Charles III (1759–1788), was no friend of the treaty, and Pombal had never favored it. When Spain proposed abrogation, Portugal agreed. They then signed the Treaty of Pardo in February 1761, restoring the status quo prior to 1750.

The Treaty of Pardo did not halt the rivalry over the boundaries. It merely moved the dispute into a new phase. Both sides continued the effort to improve their positions. The alliance of Spain and France in the Family Compact of 1761 during the Seven Years War (1756–1763), known in the United States as the French and Indian War, was a signal for reopening hostilities in South America. Spanish forces along the western boundaries of Brazil attacked the Portuguese. The Spaniards made no progress in Mato Grosso, nor in the Amazon Valley along the Rio Negro and Rio Branco. But the governor of Buenos Aires held Uruguay and captured a large part of Rio Grande do Sul. Both Spaniards and Portuguese made surveys, following the lines of the 1750 and 1761 treaties, that eventually led to a more accurate map of the disputed boundaries.

Meanwhile, the Portuguese colonization of Rio Grande and Mato Grosso proceeded, and most of the area eventually remained in Portuguese control. Portugal was not involved in the Family Compacts against England and was in better position than Spain to defend her interests in Brazil. The end of the Seven Years War in 1763 improved Spain's ability to contest Portuguese boundary claims, however. The two men most involved in the dispute, Pombal for Portugal and Grimaldi for Spain, were both intransigent in negotiations.

The situation was different than previously, however, because the Treaty of Pardo did not recognize Portuguese title to Santa Catarina and Rio Grande. General Cevallos complained that the Portuguese refused to evacuate some areas which they had not held prior to 1750. For the first time Spain was specifically questioning the rights of Portugal in Santa Catarina and Rio Grande. Cevallos put his war plan into operation—the same one previously proposed to Madrid and now approved. Madrid gave him full authority to expel the Portuguese from the "Debatable Lands."

In August 1762 Cevallos began a siege of Colônia. Learning two months later, in the midst of the siege, that Spain and Portugal were formerly at war again, he increased his pressure and on October 31 marched into Colônia, the third Spanish recapture since 1680. He repulsed a combined Portuguese-British effort to retake Colônia in January 1763. Marching north to Santa Teresa, São Miguel, and Rio Grande, he pursued the Portuguese along the peninsula north of Rio Grande.

News from Spain halted him. Portugal and Spain had agreed to suspend fighting. This agreement had been reached in the Treaty of Fontainbleau in November 1762 and the Treaty of Paris in February 1763, ending the Seven Years War. Certain clauses in the two treaties, which referred to the situation in the Brazil Rio de la Plata area were somewhat different, however, and kept unresolved the conflicting claims. Spain definitely believed that it had to limit Portugal to regions north of the Plata, thereby retaining both Uruguay and Rio Grande. Cevallos objected strongly to returning "Spanish" territory to the Portuguese.

A special report by the Marquis of Valdelirios pointed out the strong advantage of the Portuguese in the large business of cattle smuggling from the interior. Portuguese occupation of the interior of Rio Grande, said Valdelirios, was contrary to the treaties of 1494 and 1761. Later in 1763, Madrid learned of Cevallos's conquest of Rio Grande and the renewed siege of Colônia, and it approved. Thus did the slow exchange of information between the battlegrounds in America and the conference tables in Europe confound the commanders of troops. Pombal reacted by accusing Cevallos of acting as a tool of the Jesuits (still in Spain for a few years more, but already expelled from Portugal and Brazil). He called Grimáldi unscrupulous.

Pombal demanded the faithful execution of the Treaty of Paris, as he interpreted it, and he sent orders to Brazil to make the same demands on Cevallos. But Cevallos had enlarged his concepts, and he ordered the Portuguese to evacuate Moxos between Peru and Brazil and to return the Tape Indians still held by Portugal. Pombal asked in vain for Great Britain to intervene on Portugal's side. A period of anxious peace followed. Spain continued to hold Rio Grande and besieged, more or less, Colônia. Portugal was forced to await the next opportunity to press its claim. The Spanish hold on Rio Grande seriously hindered the emergence of a steady livestock supply for São Paulo and Minas Gerais.

For three years following the Treaty of Paris, the Spanish and Portuguese forces engaged in backbiting and scrimmaging. In May 1767 the Portuguese commander in Rio Grande do Sul, Governor Colonel José Custódia de Sá e Faria, attacked the Spaniards, but he was frustrated by bad weather and alert Spanish defenses. Officially the courts of Spain and Portugal were at peace. A common bond was temporarily created between them, when Spain expelled the Jesuits in March 1767 just as the Portuguese had done in 1759. Portugal suggested that the two nations join in pressuring the Pope to dissolve the Jesuit Order and to settle as well the boundary dispute.

Spain, in turn, sought an alliance with Portugal if France could also be brought in as an ally. Pombal made an indirect reply, stating that the first order of business was the Jesuit question. Spain renewed the offer of an alliance and suggested that, as a reward, Portugal could look to a favorable American settlement.

Spain's major aim was to gain Portuguese aid in a war of revenge on Britain. Portugal was susceptible to suggestions because Britain had not been sympathetic or helpful in the conflict with Spain. Portugal also suggested that Britain might have designs on Brazil—if not territorial, at least commercial. British resentment against Portugal had been aroused by Pombal's attempts to promote economic policies, including the monopoly companies, designed to undermine British economic dominance. Pombal also believed Britain might be conspiring with the Jesuits to invade Brazil.

Beginning in 1766 and thereafter, Pombal resolved to strengthen the defenses of Brazil. He sent two able military men, General J. H. Böhm, an Austrian who had been in British service, and Jacques Funk, a Swedish expert in fortifications. He also sent three of Portugal's best regiments to Brazil. Thus a common fear of Great Britain promoted a warm new friendship between Spain and Portugal; but it was an unnatural friendship not destined to last. Portugal, meanwhile, sent instructions to officials in Brazil to take advantage of any situation short of war to reoccupy places held by Spain, under the pretext of protecting them from British raids. Pombal renewed his protest about the tight Spanish circle around Colônia.

When, in 1768, Spain made it clear that Portuguese adherence to the Family Compact was the price of continued amiability and the modification of boundaries, the ephemeral friendship bubble burst. After much delay, Pombal replied that Portugal would not join Spain and France. Spain no longer doubted that the Portuguese reinforcements sent to Brazil were directed against them—not the British.

Portugal still held that part of the Rio Grande recovered by José Custódio and refused to give it back despite promises to Spain. Nor did it punish Custódio for unauthorized attacks after a new viceroy, Dom Luís de Almeida, Marquês do Lavradio, arrived in 1769. Lavradio received from Pombal extensive instructions about economic policies, but nothing very precise about the border situation. Colônia remained under close Spanish encirclement, and the contraband trade suffered. The Portuguese conducted raids on inland cattle and horses and established *estâncias* with guards to protect them. Spain fortified the entrance to the Lagoa dos Patos to prevent invasion of Portuguese ships. Incidents between the forces were endlessly argued.

Viceroy Lavradio sent an inspector, Francisco José da Rocha, to Rio Grande in 1771 to report on the state of the defenses. He found virtually undefended guard positions where the "termites have eaten their gun stocks." He also found the Indians under Portuguese control mistreated and despised by the whites. In an attempt to remedy this situation, he encouraged the marriage of Portuguese men with Indian girls and recommended the designation of priests to educate them. Rocha reported wholesale corruption by officials and citizens in cattle and horse roundups, depriving the king of his full revenues. He concluded that Rio Grande do Sul was "a nest of thieves."

Rocha observed that land was being distributed to the favorites of Governor António de Veiga e Andrade, rather than to the enlisted men who deserved it. He strongly recommended an investigation of the situation. The king refused Lavradio permission to go to Rio Grande do Sul and personally attempt to bring order to the military situation and end the corruption.

The Spanish governor of Buenos Aires, Juan Vértiz y Salcedo, finally obtained permission to repel the Portuguese who had penetrated an area of Rio Grande south of the Jacuí River. Many Portuguese ranches had been established there, and "Spanish" cattle were constantly rustled. Late in 1773 and early 1774, he conducted an expedition across Uruguay and into Rio Grande do Sul, reaching the Jacuí River. He turned back after the defeat of two scouting parties.

When Viceroy Lavradio heard about the Vértiz expedition in late 1773, he sent reinforcements to Rio Grande do Sul. His appeal to Portugal for more aid was couched in unusually strong language. His situation was desperate. The court received his requests—strong language and all—with sympathy, and it promised aid, including the right to choose men from two shiploads of degredados bound for the East. Pombal wrote Lavradio a warm personal letter. He appealed to Britain for aid, offering various arguments to persuade the British of their own interest in helping Portugal.

More arms went to Brazil. Pombal ordered three regiments to Rio Grande do Sul. The Portuguese army was ordered to recover only what Vértiz had taken a few years earlier, after which the troops were to assume a defensive stance in order to give Portugal a superior moral position during subsequent negotiations.

Colônia was not reinforced. Meanwhile, Lavradio replaced the commander who did not have his confidence with his confidential aid, Francisco da Rocha. A naval squadron was placed under the command of Captain Robert MacDouall. As a general policy to strengthen Lavradio's position, the new governors of several captaincies were placed directly under his authority.

In stating that Portugal lacked manpower for the effort needed, Pombal thought it reasonable to assume that the Brazilians would be willing to help in defending their own homes. This position was taken by Britain, in another content, in its struggle with the French in North America. Lavradio and many officers were promoted in rank to give them more spirit for accomplishing the job. Spain again sent reinforcements to La Plata.

General Böhm left for Rio Grande in December 1774. Lavradio learned of Spanish troops enroute to Montevideo and Colonia. Captain MacDouall sailed late in February 1775 to convoy aid to Colônia. He encountered a Spanish fleet in Montevideo but did not dare attack superior forces. General Böhm did not regard the armed forces and forts in Rio Grande do Sul as capable of offensive action, or even much defense. The Spanish fortifications seemed formidable. Captain George Hardcastle had only limited success when he attempted to run reinforcements through the entrance to the Lagoa dos Patos in April 1775. The Spaniards had better luck in running past the Portuguese forts some ten days later.

Francisco José da Rocha, recently appointed commander of Colônia in March 1775, quickly came to the conclusion reached by previous commanders, specifically that it was indefensible. He sent Viceroy Lavradio a copy of a report made by one of his predecessors, Alexandre de Gusmão, showing the weakness of the position. He called it "more of a prison" for the Portuguese than a fortress. If, he thought, the king intended to use it as a springboard to capture Montevideo and other Spanish areas, there was merit in holding it; otherwise it should be abandoned.

Whether or not Lavradio passed on Rocha's recommendation, it coincided with Pombal's line of thought. He had already decided on a plan designed to make Spain appear the aggressor. While Portuguese guerrilla forces were to continue their attack on the Spaniards, he had determined that the defense of Colonia was "chimerical and impossible."

Pombal ordered its defenders to return to Rio de Janeiro, ostensibly for recruits and training. Governor Rocha was ordered to inform the Spaniards that he was leaving Colônia because Spain and Portugal were on the verge of signing a new agreement settling their differences over boundaries. If attacked by the Spaniards before he could depart Colônia, he was to make merely a token defense and then protest that the attack broke the peace prevailing between the two countries. Pombal's intricate thinking cannot be penetrated with assurance, but it seems possible that he hoped a Spanish attack on Colônia would help bring England to his aid. With Colônia ungarrisoned, it seemed wise to send reinforcements to Santa Catarina. On October 14, 1775, the garrison left Colônia and sailed to Rio de Janeiro where they arrived, it seems, the second week in November.

Eight days later they returned to Colônia. Why? Circumstances that neither nation could foresee brought about new negotiations in 1775. Events had produced a change in Spanish policy. Spain sought to regain the prestige it had lost when defeated in the Falkland Islands dispute with Britain (1770) and in the revolt in Algiers. A quick and powerful blow in Algiers could revive respect for Spanish arms. The Spanish army was defeated, however, in early July, turning the hoped-for gain in prestige into an even more serious humiliation. Spain had learned of Portuguese reinforcements in South Brazil and wanted to settle outstanding differences. Grimaldi, the foreign minister of Spain, suggested to the Portuguese ambassador in Madrid that they make a new effort to settle disputes. Thus a new round began in the old fight.

Pombal considered the consequences of Spain's defeat in Algiers and came to the conclusion that Grimaldi was proposing peace. He thought Spain was too weak to start a new war. So, reversing his decision to abandon Colônia, he sent new aggressive instructions to Lavradio in July 1775. Meanwhile, Spain had ordered its commander to hold the line. Pombal's new instructions meant that the war in Rio Grande would be continued with added vigor and that Colônia would be "defended, secured, and maintained against any and all Castilian attacks."

Meanwhile, he delayed his response to Grimaldi. Finally on January 16, 1776, Sousa Coutinho, the Spanish ambassador in Madrid, gave Grimaldi the formal Portuguese response. It was a long memorandum divided into four parts, setting forth again the Portuguese version of the boundary dispute reaching back three centuries. The Portuguese accused Buenos Aires of aggression. Grimaldi, in return, accused the Portuguese of illegal possession of all lands held west of the Line of Demarcation of 1494. Sousa Coutinho cited the treaties of Utrecht (1715) and Paris (1763), in which Spain had made concessions west of the 1494 line.

Again we must remember that the Portuguese military preparations in the south of Brazil were concurrent with the negotiations among Spain, Portugal, France, and England to bring about a settlement without further war. The first attempt of Captain MacDouall to penetrate the Lagoa do Patos in February 1776 had been a failure, and he had returned to his station on Santa Catarina Island. He was criticized severely by Lavradio but upheld by the Portuguese court.

Important Portuguese victories were on the horizon. One victory had already encouraged the Portuguese. Major Rafael Pinto Bandeira captured San Martín (São Martinho), an important post between the old Spanish missions and their livestock estancias thirty leagues west of Rio Pardo. In March 1776 the fort of Santa Tecla surrendered to Major Bandeira, the same officer who had captured São Martinho. General Böhm won a greater battle on March 31 and April 1. Mounting a surprise attack, his forces were ferried across the entrance to Lagoa dos Patos in pre-daylight hours, where they captured the Spanish fortifications and drove them out of Lagoa for the last time. General Böhm, criticized earlier by superiors for his Fabian tactics, optimistically awaited their praises—which were not forthcoming.

Negotiations, of which the general knew nothing, were in progress, and by coincidence the orders of Pombal for the suspension of hostilities in Rio Grande do Sul had reached Rio de Janeiro the very day of Böhm's victory. Viceroy Lavradio, knowing nothing of Böhm's success, but having received news of MacDouall's failure, forwarded the orders for suspension of activity and told General Bohm to retreat slowly and remain on the alert for Spanish double-dealing.

Lavradio soon received news of the capture of Tecla. The victories were now an embarrassment. They had been achieved after the official suspension of hostilities. The Spaniards could not understand why the Portuguese in America were not up-to-date about recent developments since they had received and obeyed the orders a month earlier. Such were the consequences of slow communications when combined with ill will on both sides.

The news of the Portuguese victories arrived in Lisbon in the midst of the diplomatic effort to bring about a definite settlement in America, in which the French and British were involved. Madrid received the news late in June and Lisbon in July. Spain refused to believe that Pombal could not have sent news of the suspension of hostilities earlier, thereby preventing the Portuguese offensive in February and March 1776. Lacking any faith in Portuguese good intentions, Spain resolved to send a large expedition, large enough to assure Spanish victory. The fear of British aid in Portugal had abated.

Not entirely uninterested in a peaceable settlement, but having no trust whatever in each other, Grimaldi and Pombal prepared for war. In Spain the ministers discussed whether the simplest way to deal with Portugal, for so many centuries a thorn in the flesh of the Spaniards, might be a direct invasion to incorporate Portugal again in a united Iberian Peninsula.

Portugal's status was weakened by the American War for Independence. Britain could not in these circumstances aid Portugal against Spain. In 1776, with a clearer view ahead, Spain decided to make a major effort to force a favorable settlement of the boundary issue. Pedro de Cevallos became viceroy of the newly-created viceroyalty of La Plata with its capital in Buenos Aires, and he sailed with a fleet of 97 merchant ships, 19 men of war carrying 632 cannon, and a total contingent of 19,000 men.

Portugal's excellent spy service knew more about the Spanish plans than all but a few high Spanish officials. Spain's objective was not merely recovery of Colônia but the entire area from Santa Catarina southward. Sailing on November 13, 1776, Cevallos's fleet reached Santa Catarina Island on February 20, 1777. In possession of advanced information, Viceroy Lavradio protested the Spanish action during a period termed peaceful between the two crowns.

Cevallos occupied Santa Catarina easily, its defenders fleeing to the mainland. Their attempt to retreat to Laguna or elsewhere became a disaster; after an attempt to obtain favorable terms, they capitulated on March 5, 1777. General Cevallos agreed to permit the officers, down to the non-commissioned level, and their families to go free and make their way at their own expense to Rio de Janeiro, Buenos Aires, or Montevideo on condition that they not take up arms against Spain for the duration of the war. Most enlisted men deserted rather than surrender.

Cevallos planned to penetrate the entrance of the Lagoa dos Patos. But after his fleet left Santa Catarina, it was caught in a bad storm and forced into Montevideo. After regrouping, he besieged and captured Colônia on June 4, destroying it utterly. The garrison surrendered and was transported to Rio de Janeiro. Cevallos was preparing to march on Rio Grande when informed of the treaty of peace and orders to cease warring on the Portuguese.

The usual negotiations had been taking place in Europe while the armies fought in America. In the midst of negotiations, however, Grimaldi was forced out of office, and the Count of Floridablanca became the prime minister to King Charles III of Spain in February 1777. Note that Cevallos had landed on Santa Catarina Island the next day. José I of Portugal died February 24, leading to the fall of Pombal on March 5. New men took center stage. The way was open for peace.

Portugal and Spain signed an armistice June 5. It was an uncertain armistice, but Spain ordered its forces in America to stop offensive activity. Spain had known of the fall of Santa Catarina before signing the armistice. Considering the superiority of Spanish forces on the field, it is difficult to understand why Floridablanca so quickly consented to give up territory that Spain had always claimed as lawfully its own.

When the Treaty of San Ildefonso was signed in October 1777, both nations, at the time, and their historians ever since, have considered themselves as victims of the other's aggression. Spain once and for all time gave up claims to the extensive area west of the Line of Demarcation. Portugal bemoaned its failure to gain everything on the left bank of the Plata River. But the treaty proved impossible to carry out as written, although the war over boundaries was not reignited. The terms of the treaty were not greatly different from those in 1750. Colônia returned to Spanish sovereignty, as did the Sete Povos that had been the issue in the Guarani War. Spain did not retain all it considered legally Spanish; Portugal had not won all it claimed.

Four commissions were named to survey the boundaries. Again, as in 1750, the realities of geography as compared with the maps presented by both sides caused disputes, with each side engaging in recriminations against the other. The threat of war was constantly present. The survey parties on both sides made extensive contributions to the knowledge of geography.

After twenty years of bickering, a valuable report entitled *História de las demarcaciones de límites en la América entre los domínios de Espāna y Portugal* detailed their findings. A map, now in the Library of Congress of the United States, was the best drawn to that date. The boundaries were not well enough defined to prevent disputes in the nineteenth century, however.

23

COMMERCIAL COMPANIES, 1755–1777

ombal's solution for the economic problems of northern Brazil was the creation of monopolistic companies. They were to take over the marketing of goods overseas and encourage new production. He thought that the special problems could be solved only by an overall system of control. Furthermore, he was assuming power over the estates controlled by the missions and needed to put something in their place. He also hoped that the companies would compete on favorable terms with foreigners who, through indirect methods and contraband, were allegedly skimming the cream of Brazilian commerce. He planned to rescue Portugal from the terms of the Methuen Treaty, which he considered the source of all economic woes.

Pombal organized two companies to promote and develop the Amazon, Maranhão, and the Northeast. The first, the Companhia Geral do Grão Pará e Maranhão, was chartered in 1755. He thought this company would improve upon the performance of the missions. In his opinion, the natural, uncultivated forest products required only an organized marketing system to make them much more valuable. Given a good market, the cultivated crops would likewise prosper.

Sugar produced under the burden of taxation was forced to compete with the older sugar-producing areas of Northeastern Brazil and the

403

Caribbean colonies of foreign nations, which were closer to Europe and thus could sell at lower prices in England, Holland, and northern Europe generally. Larger populations in those countries afforded a better market than less-populated Portugal. Tobacco produced in the Amazon was a royal monopoly because it was easily taxed. The crown had previously preferred to give more attention to the mining areas since they generated large revenues. African slaves, regarded as essential to commercial farming, sold for higher prices at the mines, which prevented the farmers from easy access to a cheap supply of labor. The fleets that supposedly sailed on a regular schedule for Brazil rarely did so, often leaving Brazil without an overseas market for its products and without needed imports. Pombal blamed the organization of the economic system and thought of ways to improve it.

The Estado do Maranhão e Grão Pará produced a variety of forest products commonly called "drogas do sertão," which included spices of many kinds, cacao, cinnamon (canela), cloves, carnaúba wax, and other oils from trees. Life was hard, brutish, and usually short for the workers who went into the forests to gather these products. The Northeast with its sugar, tobacco, and cultivated cacau lived much better. In some ways it was a luxurious life for the few who owned large acreages of land or operated successfully as wholesale merchants. Those lower on the social scale, and particularly the slaves, fared much less well. Reliable and regular shipping seldom touched the northern captaincies, and buyers were lacking for their meager production. Maranhão was less favored than Pará. Money in the form of metal coins hardly existed before 1749. Other items were used as a medium of exchange: cotton seed, cacao beans, hides, cotton, and especially cloth. When Furtado assumed office in Grão Pará and Maranhão in 1750 and was charged with the "restoration" of the north, he made a series of reports, already quoted extensively, revealing economic and social conditions which truly cried out for remedies.

The residents of Maranhão had already petitioned the câmara of São Luís for permission to form a company with local capital aimed at the import of African slaves. A royal order of November 1752 acceded to the request, but specified that anybody not wanting to invest in the company could import slaves on his own. The same petition had asked for permission to establish Brazilian shipping. This too was granted and extended to Pará, specifying that each captaincy should have its own ships. The petitioners were more ambitious than conditions justified, however. Local capital was insufficient to procure the ships or invest heavily in the slave trade.

Once it became clear that local efforts were failing, Furtado proposed a plan of cooperation between Maranhão and Pará. But the combined capital proposed—300,000 cruzados—fell short of the needs. Furtado next proposed a company with participation by the merchants of Lisbon and Oporto. The result of these gestures was the Companhia Geral do Grão Pará e Maranhão formed in June 1755. Lisbon was designated as the headquarters, with branch offices in Oporto, Belém, and São Luís. The charter granted a 20–year monopoly with a capital of 1,200,000 cruzados.

The company dominated the commerce of Pará and Maranhão, leaving only a small share for individuals, particularly in the early years when the company was first organized. Opposition came quickly from those interests threatened by the privileges granted to the company. The Mesa do Comun, successor of the Junta de Comércio, protested to Pombal that the Companhia do Grão Pará e Maranhão threatened free navigation. Pombal abolished the Mesa and imprisoned the lawyer who drew up the protest. The Jesuits, accused of opposing the company, received a reprimand.

From 1758 to 1777 the company exported 75% of the products shipped from the two port cities. Individual participation in the total commerce increased from 1769 to 1774, however. Cacao became by far the most important export. Cacao exports varied from lows of 40% in 1756 and 38% in 1774 to highs of 82% in 1762, 75% in 1763, and 72% in 1773. Over the life of the company, cacao amounted to some 61% by value of its exports, or 3,309,808 milréis. Cloves during the same period came to 233,516 milreis and coffee 225,497, with neither product showing any upward tendency. Other products, including rice, cotton, and hides, added to the export total. Over the twenty year period, 138 ships entered and sailed from Belém's harbor.

From 1760 through 1778 about 180 vessels sailed from São Luís, Maranhão. Shipping activity increased in the 1770's with 103 of 180 sailings taking place in the last seven years of the firm's life. Fifty ships in all took part in the trade, some obviously making the voyage more than once. The chief exports of São Luís were cotton, rice, and tanned hides; of lesser importance were copaiba (an oleoresin used as dieuretic and stimulant), raw hides, ginger, cacao, indigo, wax, tapioca, coffee, tobacco, tallow, cloves, turtle shells, and fine woods. Rice appeared in 1767 for the first time and spurted in 1772. The company encouraged planting a new type of rice—white rice. Farmers suffered fines if they did not plant the new type, their preference being the local rice (arroz da terra).

The export of hides was greater in the first half of the company's life than the second. Cotton began a big upswing in 1766 and was about six times greater in the last five years of the period than in the first five. Neither cotton nor rice had been exported before the organization of the company.

The 1755 law emancipating the Indians and the determination of Furtado and Francisco de Melo e Póvoas, nephew of Pombal, to enforce this law and other laws to the hilt were two factors that prompted the colonists to buy African slaves. The two principal sources of slaves for Pará and Maranhão were Portuguese Guinea (Cacheu and Bissau) and Angola, with about two-thirds from the former and one third from the latter. Black slaves had existed in Pará and Maranhão before the organization of the company, but in relatively small numbers compared to the captaincies of Brazil's eastern seaboard from Rio Grande do Norte southward. The company became the first regular supplier of slaves to the north.

The first lot of slaves brought in by the company, a modest 94 in 1756 came from Cacheu, Guinea. They cost the company 6,670 milréis and sold for 7,108 milréis, rendering a profit of 438 milréis. Larger numbers and regular imports began in 1757. The total listed from 1757 to 1778 was 25,365, although there is uncertainty about the true number of people imported. The total broke down as follows: 9,229 from Bissau, 8,363 from Cacheu, and 7,774 from Angola. Total sales amounted to 1,736,208 milréis, an average of 68 milréis per slave. Maranhão paid 761,296 milréis of the total and Pará 974,912. Shipping costs amounted to 16 milréis for each slave imported.

The average sales price obviously reflected the number who arrived alive. In 1774, for example, the *São Pedro Gonçalves* shipped 221 people and only 186 arrived, with 35 lost enroute. They had cost 3,275 milréis and sold for a total 12,808 milréis, an impressive difference not consonant with the stated requirement to sell at cost on time payments. In 1759 Pombal ordered the company to lend money at 5% interest, later lowered to 3%. In the case of slaves, no interest was charged during the first year after purchase.

As a further measure to bring slaves into Brazil, Pombal had required the company to make sales, as of 1773, at their cost in Africa plus the expense of shipping. The company used sixteen ships in the slave trade. From 1770 to 1774, there were 40 shiploads comprising 5,028 slaves, which reportedly lost 50,570 milréis. The policy of the company, it was alleged, was to assume losses on slave shipments but to regain the profits from the product of their labor. On the face of the statistics, it is not possible to determine the exact situation. Much of the trade was reckoned in goods, particularly cloth; little regular money circulated, and sometimes none. Moreover, the system facilitated the manipulation of the statistics.

The problem of retaining slaves in Pará and Maranhão continued. Slaves sold for 200 milréis in Mato Grosso, or even as much as 200 oitavas of gold, which was equivalent to 300 milréis. Some cases were cited of slaves selling in other locations for two arratéis (two pounds of approximately 16 ounces each), a figure equal to 384 milréis.

One aspect of the company's activities not usually taken into account regards the fleets sent to foreign countries. Purchasing and sales departments were maintained in the Mediterranean and North Europe, and even as far as the Baltic. The company bought overseas, transshipped the goods to Pará and Maranhão, and then on to Mato Grosso. There is a great deal of additional information on this aspect of the business which is not included in this account.

The book balance of the slave trade shows that from 1756 to 1766, except in 1761, the company made profits. From 1767 to 1774 losses were the rule, except in 1768. The heaviest loss came in 1773, amounting to 120,046 milréis and more than canceling all the profits for the entire period from 1756 to 1774.

The overall profits of the company, including the losses on the slave trade, averaged 88,000 milréis from 1756 to 1774. The least profitable year was 1763 (26,906 milréis), and the most profitable was 1761 (218,660 milréis). Dividends were paid at the rate of 11.5% annually.

As a function of government, the company served national and patriotic ends—as interpreted in Lisbon. Money diverted to national defense or spent on emergencies unconnected with normal commercial activities affected the profits of the company. Fortifications were built, or rebuilt, from company funds; emergencies such as the prolonged drought in the Cape Verde Islands required the shipment of supplies costing 37,239 milréis. The company's ships numbered 13 in 1759, of which were two warships valued at 52,868 milréis. By 1774 the number had risen to 38 ships worth 130,209 milréis. Meanwhile, 13 ships, the equivalent of its original fleet, had been lost during the same period.

Because of these extraneous factors, it is impossible to judge the company on its accounting alone. The military costs illustrated above emphasize the point. Its favorable balances ranged from a low of 64,000 milréis in 1756 (15% of capital) to a high of 238,000 milréis in 1761 (50% of capital). At the time of its extinction shortly after the death of José I and the fall of Pombal in 1777, the company had stocks of goods in Pará, Maranhão, Angola, Guinea, Cabo Verde, and other places; the largest in Pará amounted to 1,262,310 milréis.

In making a final assessment, it appears that the evidence favored those who defended the company and wanted its continuance. Its extinction was a result of the political reaction against anything done by Pombal; the company's economic performance was not disputed.

Meanwhile, the residents of the Northeast submitted a petition to the king in June 1759 requesting the organization of a company for Pernambuco and Paraíba. The king approved the statutes of the Companhia Geral de Pernambuco e Paraíba in August the same year. The structure of the two companies was similar. The authorized capital was 3,400,000 cruzados (2.5 cruzados to a milréis). Some business elements strongly opposed the new organization from the outset.

The company received a monopoly over the supply of goods to the captaincies and their shipping. All free navigation was suspended between Portugal and the captaincies. The company held navigation rights and could establish feitorias in Africa to facilitate the buying of slaves. The state supplied some of the ships from its own fleet, and the company was empowered to buy others. The crews, even the chief officers, could be recruited on the same basis as those drafted for government service. Foreigners were made eligible for service.

No limit was placed on the amount of money any person could invest. Foreigners residing in Portugal were granted the same rights as citizens. The government furnished the buildings, shipyards, warehouses, and other structures in Portugal and overseas. Raw materials, wood especially, could be requisitioned at the going price. The regulations limited profits on dry goods, except flour and edible drygoods, to 40% over the Lisbon cash price, with 5% interest allowed for the extension of credit. What were known as liquid provisions—flour and other edibles measured by dry volume—were limited to 15% profit. The producers only, not middlemen, could sell to the company. The strict rules, with heavy penalties for infringement, sought to insure compliance with the law.

Large investors gained social preferment. Shareholders of ten thousand cruzados or more were entitled to homage in their houses. Those with ten shares or more enjoyed the privileges of nobles, as did higher officials. They could not be arrested except in *flagrante delito*. Employees carried arms on duty. Foreigners who were stockholders were exempt from arrest even if Portugal was at war with their country.

The Pernambuco company was accused of many shortcomings: selling its merchandise and slaves at exorbitant prices; introducing spoiled products that customers were forced to buy because they had no choice; underpricing the products of Brazil; failing to put enough coinage into circulation for local needs; defrauding the customs; and providing an insufficient market for the products of Pernambuco and Paraíba. In addition, it was blamed for causing a broad decline in the market for sugar and other products. The câmaras of Olinda, Recife, and Paraíba complained often to the king and finally petitioned for the abolition of the company. The company cited statistics to show that such accusations were false.

The senhores de engenho who attacked the company refused to admit that the ills were a result of their system of conducting business and their excessive expenditures on articles of conspicuous consumption in social competition with one another. They constantly asked and received loans from the company. Living beyond their means was the root of their economic problems.

There were 267 engenhos in the area monopolized by the company at its inception in 1759. Only 80 were in good working condition; 74 were heavily mortgaged and almost bankrupt. Ten years after the establishment of the company, there were allegedly 390 engenhos milling at full capacity. If so, the figures for production do not reflect the increase in number of engenhos. Over the prior ten years, 55,580 caixas were exported in seven fleets; from 1762 to 1771, the number rose to 72,052 caixas, a meager increase of 720 caixas a year. Between 1772 and 1775, however, annual exports rose to about 10,000 caixas, or an increase of one-third over the prior ten year period.

The tobacco business is equally difficult to assess. Tobacco was said to be decadent by 1759, which is strange because it was the main currency for buying slaves in Africa. The main producer had always been Bahia, since the region was more fertile for tobacco than Pernambuco. The company aided the planters and brought in an expert to improve production. In 1762 only 20 or 25 arrôbas were exported; by 1775 exports had risen to 68 arrôbas.

Raw hide exports increased moderately, from 366,495 units during the ten years preceding the formation of the company to 500,925 units over the following decade. Tanned hide exports averaged 43,000 units per year during the prior fifteen years and 91,000 units per year over the next decade. Indigo, cotton, and rice all increased as well.

Between 1750 and 1759, 70 ships imported 21,845 slaves, of which 13,385 went to Rio de Janeiro. From 1761 to 1770, imports from Angola alone amounted to 21,229, and from the Costa da Mina the figure was 2,920. Of the total, only 5,975 slaves were sold in Rio de Janeiro. All sales were on credit.

Results could be measured in various ways. Merchandise imports increased. From 1762 to 1771, cloth imports amounted to 4,608,584 milréis. Recife increased in population; new buildings went up, including some sumptuous structures and new churches. New towns sprang up in the interior. Paraíba enjoyed the same improvements. A historian generally unfriendly to the company wrote: "Commerce revived; the houses in the city were improved, and others were built, principally in the Varadoura. The customs house, up to that time almost always closed, began to function regularly . . . and public revenues increased. The port was frequented by a large number of ships, until then unknown."

A conclusion about the importance of the Pernambuco-Paraíba company is less easy to draw than about the Pará-Maranhão company. But the demise of the company, successful or not, came from the same source—the hatred of anything that Pombal had done.

24

CHALLENGING THE JESUITS IN THE AMAZON

I n the 1750s Francisco Xavier de Mendonça Furtado was sent to the Amazon by his brother, Sebastião José de Carvalho e Melo (Pombal), who had just become first minister of the new King José I, to find a solution for problems far more complex than settlement of the boundaries with Spanish colonies. Pombal wanted to assert the royal prerogatives of divine-right monarchy in all spheres of government, not the least being the regulation of the Jesuits, who had shown far too much independence to please the minister.

Among the first moves was the creation of the captaincy-general of Grão Pará e Maranhão with its capital in Belém. It superseded the captaincy-general of Maranhão e Grão Pará with its capital in São Luís de Maranhão. This act was more than a mere inversion of the names of the provinces. It reflected the growth of the Amazon area, and the intent of Pombal to build up the great river basin. Sending his younger brother as captain-general was an indication of his determination to do what none had done before. He decided that royal dominance could not be established as long as the Indians remained under the control of the missions, and above all the Jesuits. To accomplish his ends, Pombal counted on the help of the secular clergy.

Governor-general Mendonça Furtado had the aid of Bishop Frei

Miguel de Bulhões, who had already concluded that members of the Regular Clergy were too firmly entrenched in their positions of power to be amenable to control by a bishop or civil powers. Furtado was a stern, strict disciplinarian who reported almost daily to his brother in letters explaining the problems he met and his proposed solutions. Imbued with a deep conviction that the king's laws must be obeyed to the letter, strongly attached to his elder brother, and determined to contribute to his program of government—for both men were new in office and their futures yet to be made—Mendonça Furtado interpreted every sign of resistance to royal policy (actually Pombal's policy) as *lèse majesté*.

The royal policy, as devised by Pombal and refined in the Amazon to a large extent by Mendonça Furtado, was to take the aldeias (villages) of Indians out of the control of the Regular orders and convert them into towns and villages with Portuguese rather than Indian names, plus a saint's name, and to create civil administrations in which Indians held office. He also wanted to impose the Portuguese language in the place of the Indian languages. In 1750, at the beginning of Pombal's service as prime minister, there were 63 aldeias in the Amazon River valley—19 Jesuit, 15 Carmelite, 26 Franciscan, and 3 Mercedarians.

The emancipation of the Indians would, in Pombal's opinion, coincide with the importation of African slaves. With Africans to do the work and the illegally-held church property distributed to the *moradores*, leading citizens who were Portugese or of Portuguese descent, he intended to stimulate agriculture and manufacturing and thereby exports and imports.

Conflict with the vested interests in the Amazon and Maranhão mainly the regular clergy was expected; but the bitterness of the fight with the regulars, especially the Jesuits, was perhaps not foreseen. The continuous and acrimonious conflicts with the regulars became the hallmark of Pombal's regime and of Mendonça Furtado's governorship in the Amazon. Both men considered, or soon came to consider, the Jesuits a threat to the throne.

Mendonça Furtado's various assigned tasks required him to travel very extensively in the Amazon River over a period of eight years. He visited Macapá, where he established families of Azoreans and began building a fortress. He also visited Guamá, Marajó, the Tocantíns River, and ascended the Negro and Madeira rivers in an effort to meet the Spanish boundary commissioners, who never arrived. The captaincy of Saõ José do Rio Negro was founded in March 1755 as a result of his voyage to Rio Negro.

In the lower Amazon and on Marajó Island, where natural pastures existed and more had been created by the slash and burn clearing process, many livestock ranches had been established. The religious orders owned most of them. The new policy was to expropriate the clerical properties and distribute them to selected civilians, who became known as the "contemplados," the favored ones.

For travel along the rivers, the colonists used canoes or other boats built on the Amazon and its confluents in small shipyards that followed mainly Indian methods, improved with Portuguese knowledge and tools. By the mid-eighteenth century a shipyard of Portuguese origin operated in Belem. Over a period of fifty years it turned out three brigantines, seven frigates, one nau of 74 guns, four luggars, and twelve armed sloops, as well as a number of merchantmen, after 1755, for the Companhia Geral do Grão Pará e Maranhão.

The labor was almost entirely Indian, slave or free. They were also the hunters, fishermen, canoe rowers, gathers of the forest products, workers in the shipyards, farmers, construction workers, soliders, and household servants. From mixing with whites came the meztizos. The Black slave was generally unnecessary in the Amazon basin. Only a small number were brought in before 1755 to work on farms near Belém and on the ranches of Marajó Island. Even after that date, Black slaves never formed a large part of the population.

Total immigration into the Amazon was never large. It consisted of soldiers, exiles, some colonists and artisans from Portugal, and a few other Europeans. Azorean families settled around Macapá, Braganza, Tentugal, Ourém and Belém.

The transfer of the capital to Belém brought the center of government closer to the most vital part of the vast Amazon area. This move was a recognition of the natural division that geography made between Maranhão and the Amazon basin.

Mendonça Furtado came to the Amazon not only to establish firm royal authority over the missions and free the Indians from their control, he was to survey the boundaries stipulated in the Treaty of 1750 as well. In the course of his governorship, he also was active in establishing the company that monopolized trade and development from 1755 to 1778. He intended to make the crown as supreme in fact as it was in theory. In a letter to his brother in May 1755, Pombal referred to the "three great tasks" to be accomplished: "establishing the commercial company and introduction of Negroes into this state; fixing the amount of the salaries of the Regular Orders; and the liberation of the Indians."

Mendonça Furtado's problems were difficult from the outset. The territory he was to reorganize and govern encompassed more than half Brazil—months, even a year, might be necessary to send orders to its distant settlements; the boundaries he was to survey in cooperation with the Spaniards were unknown and months away from Belém; the missions he was ordered to convert into towns under civil rule had governed themselves for so long that they were in no mood to conform to the new civilian administration. Clergy and laymen knew there was now a new king, a new prime minister, and governor, and before bending to their combined will, these Brazilians were inclined to test the temper of their metal. The Indians to be freed were fearful of change, since they had become accustomed to obeying, however unwillingly at times, the missionaries who governed the aldeias.

Mendonça Furtado was not the type of man to rely heavily upon persuasion. He was stern, authoritarian, unbending, and prone to see offense to himself and his king even where none was intended. He had been sent by an equally stern older brother with explicit ideas about what needed to be done. An obedient younger brother, he intended to carry out the commands of "Most Illustrious and most Excellent Sir: My Dearest Brother who is Close to my Heart," as he always addressed Pombal. The Jesuits were particularly inclined to resist, and the friction with them began at once. Mendonça Furtado wrote so frequently to his brother that his letters constitute a diary regarding his tenure as governor.

Beginning in 1753 Furtado began preparation of a map and a general appraisal of the resources of the Amazon, in part to assist in drawing the boundaries with Spain and in part to promote the development of the economy. Among his assistants were Pereira Caldas and Lobo d'Almeida. The Amazon was defended by forts at São José de Macapá with 107 pieces of artillery; at Óbidos, where the river narrows; São Joaquím on the Rio Branco; São Gabriel and Morabitanas on the Rio Negro; São Francisco Xavier de Tabatinga on the Solimões; and at Príncipe da Beira in Mato Grosso.

He estimated the number of Indians working for the missions at 12,000 men, not counting members of their families and those over fifty years old. "Under the pretext of being missionaries," they carried on commerce and tried to get a "monopoly" that was "totally detrimental to the commerce and collection of forest products by individuals." He claimed that, as late as 1726, civilians dispatched 150 canoes up river to collect forest products, but in 1750 there were only three private canoes and in 1751 none—whereas the same year 28 belonged to the Jesuits, 24 to the Carmelites, and others to the Capuchins. What is more, he said, they had an 80% to 100% advantage over civilian businessmen because they did not pay most of the assessed taxes.

Moreover, they charged higher prices than justified for their products, forcing starvation on the people when there was a shortage. This happened during the great smallpox epidemic of 1749, when chickens were scarce and some missionaries charged an *oitava de ouro* for a chicken. They threatened to take the chickens to other markets if they did not get their price. This action had embittered the civilians against the regular orders. The religious orders were rich, while the civilians were poor. In their ignorance of any other means of improving their status, these civilians went up river to capture Indians and sell them. Sometimes they had the aid of missionaries who later denounced the civilians and seized the Indians for their missions.

His description of the state of the captaincy was consistently pessimistic. Citizens were so poor that the richest could not pay a debt of 30 réis; fortifications were in ruins and the soldiers ill trained and cared for; incompetent and dishonest officials abounded; and few persons were available to help him clean up the mess. The Desembargador Manuel Sarmento, the ouvidor geral of Maranhão who had come to take the residência of the departing ouvidor of Pará, informed him in a long conference, really a quarrel, that he would take no orders from the governor. Among other things, he would not even respond to the governor's request to confer with him unless he had a "secretary" to take notes. Furthermore, the ouvidor retorted, he had already deposed two governors, and "anybody who had problems with him either lived a short time or had a lot of troubles."

The Jesuits caused the most trouble, however, in matters where the issue was the degree of state control over the church. Although the Portuguese church was a branch of the state after the kings of Portugal had won special powers from the papacy, a perennial conflict between civil officials and the clergy characterized Portuguese and Brazilian history. In the Amazon the governors had always been of small importance; the real rulers were the missionaries, and the Jesuits were the most important. The arrival of a governor who meant to rule was unwelcome news. Mendonça Furtado's instructions to turn the aldeias into towns with civilian governments was destined to meet missionary opposition.

Mendonça Furtado's belief that the Jesuits were the enemies of his king was expressed over and over: "These padres do not recognize the king in any way except to extort from him everything they can, and to use all means to defraud the royal treasury and reduce his subjects to the ultimate poverty in which they now are." The governor also wrote exhaustively about his other problems, such as the state of the defences. He found the officers incompetent, the soldiers useless. "There is in this fort another man called an engineer, of 70 years of age, who has completely forgotten his profession, if he ever knew anything about it."

Governor Furtado argued strongly for the use of the Amazon-Madeira-Guaporé route to supply the mines of Mato Grosso and

Goiás. He argued that the costs would be lower. The great opponents to this plan were the merchants in Rio de Janeiro, which, it was alleged, would be ruined if the inland commerce went largely through Belém. To counter their arguments, the governor claimed that, if the rivers and the interior were not colonized, the Spaniards would seize territory that "rightfully belonged to Portugal." Meanwhile the new settlements, like the one he was making on the Javari River should, of course, be under secular, not clerical, control.

His faith in the riches of the Amazon was infinite. He compiled a list of 39 products which might be the basis of industry and merchandising. Only a few were cultivated or gathered at the time. Among the items he listed were "sugar, cotton, rice, cacau, coffee, castor bean, cinnamon (a little), leather, Couranha (a little), jarzelim, and tobacco." Of these, he thought cotton, which could be grown with little labor, the most promising, because, once planted, it did not have to be renewed for several years. The processing of cotton he especially recommended because the work could be done by "women and boys of eight years old and older." Cotton was equally suitable to the Amazon and Maranhão, which produced a better grade. His hopes for cotton were, of course, later fulfilled.

The woods of the great forest appealed to him for two reasons— the ease of transport and the use of the Tapuias Indians, who lived along the river. The Indians were available to gather the logs, which could be floated downstream for sale along the coast. "The Tapuias will be lifted out of their poverty . . . , and they will learn in this way to carry on business by cultivating cane."

He extolled the possibilities of tobacco, rice, and carauá (a fiber from which hammocks and fishing nets were made). Indigo grew in the forests and, if cultivated, would produce a larger crop. Castor beans and pine nuts required no cultivation and could be gathered by women and boys. Jarzelim required more work, but not much, and it sold for a higher price than other oils.

His instructions included seeking ways to introduce Black slaves. Upon consulting the leading citizens, he found that "not one had the wherewithal to make the payments." The introduction of Black slaves, he speculated, could result in the "total ruin" of the region. The regular clergy had Indians in their aldeias, which they had obtained at a minimum cost. The civilians, on the other hand, were able to buy only a small number of slaves since they cost ten times as much as Indians. As a result, the civilians were not able to compete in the same enterprises.

Consequently he recommended that the civilians be allowed to "descend" Indians to locations around Belém and other towns. The governor would have the authority to hire them out at the going wage. He conceived of the Indians as being "free" in these new aldeias— as opposed to the status of "slave" in the aldeias of the regular clergy. Although Indians would be required to work, they would draw wages.

Wherever Furtado turned, he found the missionaries following policies and procedures that he disapproved of. For example, one bishop sent a report, a complaint, that in the seminary the regulars did not teach the students for whom they had received tuition fees. The governor explained to his brother:

And what the Bishop . . . says takes place in the seminary . . . is true of all the others, because these Fathers accept the funds to found the seminaries, and eat up the income without teaching even one poor boy to be useful to the community.

His order that the Seminary of Cametá keep at least five boys gratis, or more if the means permitted, caused a protest.

Among the problems of Amazonian economics that Furtado hoped to solve was the cost of commodities and freight rates. The price for shipping to Portugal was not established for any products but sugar and tobacco. Other rates should be regulated too, he said, because the ship captains charged "anything they please." Ships should be compelled to allot one third of their space to sasaparilha, cloves, cotton, and hides, "which are products they do not want to ship" except at exorbitant prices.

Furtado explained to his brother the functioning of the *tropas de resgate*. The resgates were authorized by a law of April 1688 to permit the rescue of Indians held prisoners by other Indians and "tied by a cord until eaten or sold to any buyer from other tribes." To rescue such prisoners, a tropa de resgate was accompanied by a padre called a missionary, "almost always one of the Company," who had absolute power to judge which Indians could be legally taken. The soldiers on these ventures were "mean men of a licentious life," whose only motive was to catch slaves. They influenced the chiefs by giving them aguardente, trifles, and tools. Sometimes the chiefs made war on their neighbors simply to capture prisoners to be turned over to the tropas de resgate.

Many participants were vitally interested in increasing the number of persons judged as "cord" Indians and thus subject to capture. Since the missionary on the spot received a large number of captives for his order, he likewise joined in the fraud. As a result of this policy, the Indians had a great hatred for the Portuguese and sometimes sought refuge in the colonies of neighboring nations (French, Dutch, and British Guiana, plus Venezuela and Colombia). Since every Indian enslaved had to be judged, the padres signed the orders in blank to be filled in later by the tropas. "I conclude," wrote Furtado, "that these tropas de resgate . . . are one of the chief reasons for the depopulation of Your Majesty's dominions."

When Furtado tried to recruit carpenters and other workers from the aldeias to make canoes and rowers to row them, he was defied by the missionaries. They put the Indians requisitioned in stocks and whipped them to prevent them from cooperating with Furtado's agents.

While preparing for one journey upriver, he learned from the fathers that he "could not get anything whatever" from them. The Jesuits, in Furtado's opinion, would do anything possible to frustrate his work. He lost 150 Indians by desertion, among them twenty carpenters. When he called on the Jesuits to bring the Indians back, they brought him two old men, one of them lame, explaining that they had been found in the aldeias.

Padre Gabriel Malagrida, on the eve of his departure for Portugal, informed Furtado that on arrival in Lisbon he planned to petition the king to grant the Jesuits the right to settle (conquista) the Tapajós

River. They already had several aldeias on this river and had tried to prevent others from using it.

Furtado recommended as follows in February 1754:

take all the fazendas of the regulars and make them crown property, giving the priests salaries (congruas) but limiting the number of regulars. "The number of slaves is the measure of riches," and as long as the Jesuits had the aldeias and fazendas, he realized they would continue to dominate local affairs. The Jesuits told the governor to his face not to seize any of the Indians in their aldeias because these Indians had been given to them by the king and only the king could take them away.

One of the governors favorite themes was the advantages of mixing the blood of whites and Indians. He thought it was "one of the best ways to civilize these unhappy people and fill up this enormous area." He recommended that the king "declare that descendants of Indians are qualified to receive all honors, blood being no impediment, and that the Principals and their children of both sexes, and whoever marries them, are nobles as such and will enjoy all the privileges to which such ranks are entitled."

The formation of a company to take over and promote the trade of the Amazon and Maranhão was one of the prime objectives of Pombal, and naturally the Jesuits objected. Pombal gave firm instructions to his brother on this matter. If he found the Jesuits trying to stir up the people against the commercial company, he was to arrest them, just as the king had done in Portugal. Furtado was to remind the regulars that the Constituições Apostólicas forbade missionaries to engage in commerce or from holding land without specific license from the king. Furtado noted in November 1755 that he thought the commercial company would have two advantages: it would keep out foreign commerce and deprive the regulars of a monopoly over the produce of the country.

Soon after its creation, Furtado rejoiced in a letter to Pombal that the commercial company had been well received in both Pará and Maranhão. Some complained, however, that it would introduce African slaves free of tariffs. The law would be of no benefit whatever to the moradores and would serve only to enrich the merchants engaged in the slave trade, since they sold slaves at excessive prices. The result was directly contrary to the intentions of the law. The directors, he argued, should be persuaded to lower prices.

The price of salt was a similar case. A few speculators bought up the whole supply, charging four or five or even six milreis an alqueire for salt that cost them only one-sixth or less. He suggested that the commercial company keep warehouses for salt in both Maranhão and Belém. Wines, vinegars, aguardentes, port wine, and olive oil were also causes for complaint.

One of Furtado's preoccupations was how to divide the land once the missions had been dismantled. He recommended formation of a junta composed of the bishop, the governor, the ouvidor-geral, and the provedor da fazenda, plus perhaps members from among the "nobreza," to decide who would receive land grants. He did not seem to consider a system of small, family farms. All the work in this instance was to be based on some form of forced labor—whether by Indians or Blacks.

In almost the same breath, he asserted that one of the curses of the entire country was that the whites who came to Brazil despised manual labor. The king, he thought, should try to destroy this "enemy." If persuasion failed, the moradores should be coerced to cultivate, with their own hands, the lands previously given to them. To encourage this policy, the king should consider removing the civil and social disabilities that prevented manual laborers from receiving honors and holding office.

The Indians needed protection in many ways. They were easily cheated. "A single bottle of brandy is enough to buy from any Indian the product of his hard work in gathering the products of the forest."**

The Bishop of Belem wrote to Furtado about the desertions of the Indians caused by harsh treatment at the hands of the settlers. And there was the matter of Indian wives; something should be done to

---

**This author [Bailey Diffie], when a boy in eastern Oklahoma, witnessed a case in which a drunk Indian offered to "sell it—all land" to my brother for a "bottle of whiskey." Fortunately for the Indian, he had no authority to make that sale.

stop their brutal treatment. The bishop made what he and Furtado both considered a useful suggestion: draft the prostitutes to marry the soldiers, thereby removing one of the great problems with soldiers, the frequent rape of the women everywhere, and simultaneously riding the province of the prostitutes, "a pestilence in any city."

In order to reconcile the moradores to the freedom of the Indians, he pointed out continually that the Indians could still be forced to labor "for wages." To provide for the transition, a set of instructions, consisting of thirty rules, was promulgated in Bahia in 1758.

The problems Furtado faced did not lessen with time, nor were they unique. Other governors had written the same kinds of reports to the crown before his time, and others would do so in the future. The struggle with the Jesuits, and to some extent with the other orders, was a clear-cut church versus state conflict. Economic interests caused the other orders, although rivals of the Jesuits, to combine with them against the civil government.

In May 1757 the governor of Maranhão reported surprise that the regulars offered resistance to the laws regarding Indian emancipation. The head of the aldeia of Maracu held up the royal mail for nine days to enable the regulars to be forewarned and to plan their reaction in advance of official orders. Maracu was to become a vila with a civil governor. The rector of the college in Maranhão alleged exemption from the new laws because of previous bulls issued by the Pope. He refused to obey the emancipation law. This rector too was to be sent to Portugal and placed at the disposition of the king.

In a junta held in Maranhão in April 1757 all the orders except the Jesuits finally accepted Indian emancipation. The Jesuits in Maranhão tried to avoid the emancipation law by transferring the titles to the aldeias to the Pope instead of the Portuguese king, thus claiming exemption from royal law. There were clerics who openly defied the laws prohibiting establishment of convents and hospices without royal consent. Furtado referred to some of the regulars as "a band of inhuman men." He opposed letting the regulars return to the aldeias in any capacity. It would be better to curtail their numbers and pay them a salary.

For Furtado these regulars were a group of bad characters. Bishops or civil officials who tried to curb them faced rebellion. Once the governor of Mato Grosso had to take up arms to protect himself from the Jesuits. He wrote to Furtado, who forwarded his letters to Lisbon. The Jesuits countered with a memorial "which contained few less insults than paragraphs."

Furtado summed up his experience before he left Amazonas: "I cannot check the Jesuits; their astute policy is too much for all my efforts."

THE EXPULSION OF THE JESUITS AND THE NEW EDUCATION

The opposition to the Jesuits swelled like the irresistible sweep of a flooded river approaching a waterfall. The likely downfall of the Jesuits was evident by 1759. The ultimate author of the measures that carried them over the brink in Portugal was the Marquis of Pombal, but he was only one of their many enemies. Indeed, he could not have expelled the Jesuits from all the Portuguese realms without the powerful aid of allies within and outside the church.

To Pombal all opposition was "lese majesté." The king's laws, in this case Pombal's laws, were sacred orders to be obeyed to the letter. For him the issue was quite clear: the Jesuits sought to become a self-governing state within the nation state, and, beyond that, they intended to be a supra-national power above all existing states. Pombal would have agreed entirely with the following statement: "There is no such thing as a Portuguese Jesuit and a Spanish Jesuit because they are all in fact the same Jesuits who recognize no other sovereign above their General, nor any nation than their own Order; because by the oath that binds them to it, they became denationalized and separated from their parents and their kinsmen." In fact, many Jesuits in both Portuguese and Spanish America were neither Portuguese nor Spaniards, but rather Germans, Italians, English, or other nationalities who had no particular reason to feel any loyalty to either nation.

Pombal's attitude toward the Jesuits dated back at least to 1744, when he was named special envoy to Vienna in an attempt, in vain, to bring about a reconciliation between Pope Benedict XIV and the court of Vienna. He blamed the Jesuits for his failure, and it obviously nurtured his hatred until he had an opportunity for revenge. It came when he became first minister to King José I. The Pombal program met Jesuit opposition everywhere. The daily conflicts of the Jesuits with Pombal's brother, Mendonça Furtado, in the Amazon, increased the level of hostility. The question was not whether Pombal or the Jesuits had right on their side, since both were unquestionably sincere in the belief that God favored them.

The Jesuits were viewed by Pombal as the principal obstacle to his Amazon policy. Furtado had written: "I cannot keep the Jesuits down; their political cunning is more than I can match." They opposed several new policies: converting the Indian aldeias under their control (as well as those controlled by other missions) into privately owned lands; taking the schools away from the missions and creating secular schools; freeing the Indians; and establishing the Companhia Geral do Grão-Pará e Maranhão, which took away from them the exclusive privilege of marketing the products of the mission estates.

As the largest landowner and slaveholder in Brazil, they incurred the envy and hatred of many civilians. Even their moral conduct— they were the only order whose members were known never to relax their strict sexual standards—brought them a few enemies. Some critics even blamed them for the decline in gold production and for the outbreak of the Guaraní War in southern Brazil.

Pombal saw the Jesuits as his chief opponents in Portugal. The Jesuits were the royal confessors and thus wielded great influence over the king and the entire royal family. (He finally removed them as royal confessors in September 1757.)

Pombal enlisted papal help in combating the Jesuits. The Pope was not averse to listening to Pombal's attack. Pombal sent an emissary to Pope Benedict XIV with a list of complaints, asking the Pope to check Jesuit power. In a papal breve of April 1, 1758, Benedict named an Apostolic Visitor with full powers to investigate every aspect of Jesuit policy and activities. The visitor was authorized to "reform" the order. Among other ruling, he prohibited them, in May 1758, from engaging in commerce, a long-standing complaint of the other orders as well as civilians. In June the same year, the cardinal-patriarch of Lisbon forbade them to preach or hear confessions, a prohibition soon extended to all of Portugal.

Much more trouble soon faced the Jesuits. They were accused of complicity in the attempt to assassinate the king on September 3, 1758, for which the Duke of Aveiro, the Marquis and Marquise of Távora, and other high nobility were tortured and executed in January 1759. Later, some of the Jesuits accused of participation in the conspiracy were also put to death, among them Father Gabriel Malagrida, who had gone to the Amazon to establish a mission and had returned to Portugal to protest the policies of Pombal's brother. Earlier he had incurred Pombal's wrath when he published a pamphlet entitled "Juizo da verdadeira causa do Terramoto," ascribing the earthquake of 1755 to the sins of the people and to Pombal's position of power. Exiled to Setúbal south of Lisbon and later accused of witchcraft and heresy, he was condemned by the Inquisition, surrendered to the secular government, and burned in September 1761.

Early in 1759 Pombal ordered the arrest of all Jesuits throughout the Portuguese Empire and the sequestering of their property. They were expelled September 3, a year to a day after the attempt on the king's life. Those expelled from Brazil totaled more than five hundred. Some ended up in prison in Portugal but most took refuge in the Vatican. In later years Pombal justified his policy by pointing out that France, in 1764, and Spain, in 1767, had also expelled the Jesuits. Almost their only friend was Catherine the Great of Russia who admitted some refugees. Later she intervened to ask for restoration of the order after it had been abolished by the Pope in 1773.

The expulsion of the Jesuits and the condemnation of their educational methods required the development of a new educational system. The significance of the difference between the new and the old educational methods is difficult for modern readers to understand unless specifically versed in the religious and pedagogic philosophies of the eighteenth century. New teachers were found among the Franciscans, Mercedarians, and Benedictines. Secular teachers from non-ecclesiastics also entered classrooms.

What mattered to Pombal was the installation of a new philosophy

of teaching. He favorea a special version of the Enlightenment imported into Portugal from Italy and northern Errope. While serving
in the foreign service in England and Austria, he had become
acquainted with the philosophies dominant among non-scholastic
thinkers. Among them, it may be noted, were ecclesiastics of the Congregação do Oratório de São Felipe Neri.

Portugal had its own native son devoted to the new philosophy.
Luís António Verney had lived for many years in Italy and other
European countries, imbibing and embracing the new trends of
thought. Verney never returned to Portugal, but he was convinced
that a new type of learning should be introduced in his homeland. In
1746 he published, without originally revealing his authorship, *Verdadeiro Metódo de Estudar*, in Naples, Italy. When the first copies arrived
in Portugal, they were seized by the Inquisition. Denounced as a
"esquadra de demonios" (squadron of devils) and vilified, the work
immediately became in spite of this condemnation, or maybe because
of it, very popular.

Verney was not the only voice demanding change, just the most
influential. Francisco de Pina e Melo wrote in 1752: "We receive with
inexplicable pleasure the innovative fashions of France, Italy, and
England, although we do not decide to follow their style of study. We
are like a flock that does not go where it should, but where directed;
thus we enter school more in appearance than in fact."

Verney had written that his purpose was "to enlighten our nation
in every way I can." He analyzed grammar, rhetoric, philosophy,
theology, medicine, and many other aspects of knowledge. Although
attacked severely by his opponents, Verney was neither heretical nor
anti-Catholic. His approach was not so revolutionary that he espoused
the existence of a mechanistic universe; he was not a Newtonian. He
followed more Italian Illuminism than French Rationalism. He called
for a new method, not a new philosophy. He was a reformer. He
objected to the long-established Jesuit domination of university pedagogy, not to their religious thought. But he found himself in their
path, or rather, they were in his. His criticism would have meant little
in an atmosphere of free discussion, but it did not exist.

Few people had the courage to challenge any aspect of the prevailing thought. Thus, Verney's criticism, under the guise of proposing a new method to supplant the grammar taught in Jesuit schools, affronted those in power. From our viewpoint today, he sought only to abbreviate the rules of syntax, illustrating them with universal principles. The result was grammatically dramatic: the 247 rules taught in Father Manuel Sánchez's *Latin Grammar*, he reduced to 15! Furthermore, the new grammar pointed out 120 errors in Sánchez. The debate over the rules of Latin grammar and syntax challenged the Jesuit educational system.

The spirit that had prevailed in learning before Verney's *Verdadeiro Metódo de Estudar* was manifest in a notice issued by the rector of the College of Arts in Coimbra in May 1746: "In the examinations or lessons, . . . no new or little-accepted opinions shall be taught, . . . such as those of René Descartes, Gassendi, Newton and others."

In June 1759, King José I issued an alvará reforming the studies of Latin, Greek, and rhetoric. He forbade the Jesuits to direct "any of these studies whatever" and extended the prohibition to "all who. . .use the method of instruction that these same Jesuits employ." The alvará called for a general reform "to restore the ancient method. . .exactly as used by the enlightened (polidas) nations of Europe." All books used in Jesuit schools were prohibited: "Anybody who uses the grammar of Father Manuel Sánchez in his school in the future will be imprisoned to be punished in accordance with the royal will and cannot again hold classes in these kingdoms and their dominions." Many were forced to forswear the use of Sánchez's grammar and other prohibited works.

The king named Tomás de Almeida to enforce the reform. Those aspiring to teach the new system in Portugal, Brazil, and elsewhere in the empire took examinations to prove their qualifications. In Bahia, for example, 19 applicants passed the examinations in 1759. Two royal appointees were sent as professors to Pernambuco the same year; Grão Pará received one and Espírito Santo two. None is reported for Rio de Janeiro but presumably this city and others held examinations.

The expulsion of the Jesuits and the closing of their colleges produced a serious educational problem in Brazil, where there had never been an adequate school system. A new staff of teachers trained in the use of the new methods could not be created by issuing an alvará. The existing teachers reluctantly changed, an observation that can be generalized for teachers in any country at any time. The difficulty was greater in Brazil because the reform was not backed by adequate planning or government financing.

A general plan devised for Brazil authorized 17 classes of reading and writing, 15 classes in Latin grammar, and six of rhetoric. Three classes of Greek and three of philosophy were founded—one each in Rio de Janeiro, Pernambuco, and Bahia. A Real Mesa Censória was created in April 1768. This board received direction from the "studios menores," those below the higher educational level, in an alvara of June 1771.

The crown levied a new tax on wine and aguardente in Portugal and on the islands to support the educational reforms. In Brazil the levy was on every pound of beef. The new tax became known as the "literary subsidy." The alvará stated that it was assessed to enable professors to have decent housing and the freedom to leave behind other occupations. Later inspection showed the system was working in some cases; in others the tax was collected, but no classes were established.

The spirit of Pombal's reforms directed the system more toward regalism and away from church domination. The *Real Mesa Censória* gave royal censorship priority over church censorship. As emphasized before, Verney had proposed a reform of teaching methods, not a revolt against Christianity. Thus Pombal's changes did not bring Portugal and its colonies to an anti-Catholic religious position. But it did stress royal control over papal authority, which was another aspect of a long trend in European intellectual life. The Jesuits, defenders of papal power, and their own, were swept away.

The state of Portugal, endowed with patronage over church appointments for centuries past, became supreme in education also. For example, the *Compéndio Histórico do Estado da Universidade de Coimbra* criticized Aristotle severely. It advocated principles followed in the philosophies propounded by Peter Ramus, Francis Bacon, René Descartes, Pietro Gassendi, and other "moderns." Nevertheless, limitations restrained the "new thought." A work by Descartes was banned because "the Portuguese people are not yet accustomed to read in their language this kind of writing (which) advocates the spirit of doubt, of free examination, of independence, of liberty and everything else that censorship implies, and which could promote any kind of excess against the State or against religion, or at the least formulate new ideas." This censorship was fully applicable to Brazil as well.

25

LIVESTOCK, VAQUEIROS, AND GAÚCHOS

Contemporary with the fighting and negotiating over boundaries separating Spanish from Portuguese territory, economic development continued. Regardless of where the boundaries were set, the thousands of livestock that roamed the lands from São Paulo to the Paraná and Paraguay rivers constituted a valuable resource over which men did battle. For the Portuguese, the areas beyond São Paulo furnished supplies for Minas Gerais and the interior. By the end of the colonial period, the livestock products of southern Brazil sold in northern Brazil and the Caribbean.

The cattle, horses and, other farm animals of Brazil and Spanish-held territories had been transplanted from Europe at very early dates. After landing on the coast, these animals spread inland on their own feet, sometimes driven by men but more often as strays. Estimated at many millions by the eighteenth century, the real numbers cannot be known. We must temper the highest estimates with the knowledge that the total was limited by the amount of water available during any given year. Extrapolations based on the numbers seen around watering places are probably too high. The numbers of livestock depended more on the water supply than the amount of pasturage available, which did seem endless.

The settlers made limited use of the cattle and horses in the late

433

sixteenth and seventeenth centuries because the population was small. When Buenos Aires was founded for the second time in 1580, there gradually came into being a commercial center, where livestock products could be gathered for shipment abroad. Hides, tallow, and horns were the first marketable products; meat had to wait for better methods of preservation in the eighteenth century. Indians as well as Europeans and escaped Africans lived from the growing herds. These herds were wild; they belonged to nobody. Killing animals for their meat and hides became a way of life for many people—who were equally wild.

The land was originally ownerless too, populated only by nomadic Indians, whose concept of land ownership can be considered non-existent. But the concept of ownerlessness was contrary to Portuguese and Spanish legal theory. Land belonged to the state until apportioned, or until seized through squatter sovereignty with the hope of recognition by the state at some later date. Both Portuguese and Spanish colonization entailed immediate concessions of land. In the Portuguese case the sesmaria was for a privileged few. In the south, livestock normally went with the land, and the herds were granted to the newcomers.

Contraband trade already made a market for the products of the range. Açarate du Biscay reported in 1658 that he "found 22 Dutch ships, and among them two English, laden homeward with bulls-hides, plate, and Spanish wool, which they had received in exchange for their commodities."

The câmara of São Paulo sought in 1659, to put a stop to the selling of hides by the Indians. "Because they were men who owned no cattle whatever, nor any other resources; the hides could be only from stolen cattle." The Indians could sell chickens and balls of wax, nothing more—a good demonstration of how the Indians had been deprived of almost everything. What had been theirs was now given to the privileged. Only those who held licenses could legally hunt the wild livestock. Nonetheless, Indians were very active in the trade. "The Charrúas, Tapés, and Minuanos became the most expert hunters of the skittish and wild cattle in order to trade the skins for merchandise and tobacco, which they loved so much.''

In the beginning, the vaqueiros hunted for wild cattle near the towns. Cattle and horses were nearby because they had lived largely unmolested by man. In step with the increasing value of hides, the animals were hunted in greater numbers and the roundups went further afield. Although Buenos Aires was exporting a few hides soon after settlement, the big demand came only in the late seventeenth and eighteenth centuries.

The settlement of Colônia in 1680 brought the Portuguese into the hide market. After 1733 it became active in contraband and smuggling. By that date as many as thirty vessels anchored in Colônia at one time.

Early in the eighteenth century, men from Santa Fé in Argentina crossed the river to Uruguay to kill cattle for the contraband trade with the Brazilians. The earliest reported incident was 1716, but doubtless there were others. This occurred before either Spain or Portugal had effectively occupied the region. Severe laws tried to prevent hunters from killing cattle merely for one meal and abandoning the major portion of the animal to carrion. There were also legal restrictions on killing cows and heifers.

As the demand for hides increased, the killing became excessive and the herds began to thin out or disappear. Hunting further and further from population centers facilitated contraband and enhanced the value of the gaúcho. The volume of cattle and hides entering Portuguese territory from the Spanish side of the Rio de la Plata provoked a law in 1758 which prohibited the customs houses from passing any ''raw or tanned hides processed outside the kingdom.'' But the contraband persisted.

A large market for cattle, horses, and mules was found in Minas Gerais. Droves of the animals went north, on their own feet naturally, for use around the mines. Sorocaba, about fifty miles west of São Paulo, became the principal cattle market. Cattle and horses formed the main part of the herds, but burros introduced into Brazil clandestinely were also included. Horses abounded in the regions south of São Paulo but were not exported in large numbers. The mule was much sought after in mining regions as a pack animal because it required less care than the horse and was bigger than the burro.

Each animal had its own special uses. Horses were preferred for riding and drawing carriages. Mules and oxen pulled the drays and carts; oxen did the heavy work around mines and engenhos. Burros could travel the steep mountain roads, or where there were no roads, and they moved better than either horses or mules.

A large amount of capital was necessary for the livestock trade, producing a new group of cattlemen and middlemen. The drover became the successor of the bandeirantes, hunting animals rather than Indians or minerals. He was part of the development that formed the great ranches. The drover was the equivalent in many respects of U.S. cowboys who made the cattle drives from the southwest to markets along the railroad lines farther north.

The drover's hard-won wealth was quickly spent. Saddles, bridles, and trimmings were often made of silver and gold. Gambling took the earnings of some men; most, if not all, paid court to the "ladies" who awaited them like attractive spiders in the "houses" at the end of the drive. It was a style of life very distinctive from that in the older coastal settlements or the mining towns. Despite the wildness of this style of life, it was less violent than previously and led to a more stable society.

The Indians, for all the mistreatment they received, fared differently from indigenous peoples in the Unites States. They became a part of, not apart from, the society in formation. Often of mixed parentage, seldom legitimate, he often joined the vaqueiros who made the cattle industry. As long as both animals and men were wild, the vaqueiros were not only needed, but legal. When the ownership of animals and land was allocated to the privileged, many of the vaqueiros became outlaws and received a new name—gaúchos.

The earliest use of the term gaúcho is unknown. They were different from the vaqueiro who operated within the law. The gaúcho poached on others. They soon achieved a bad name that comports little with the modern romantization of the breed or the proud boast of the man from Rio Grande do Sul that he was a gaúcho. We can laugh at the Brazilian joke that a gaúcho baby was capable of seducing his nurse while still in the crib; but the man from Rio Grande do Sul still is considered the Don Juan type.

The early gaúchos were often described as "killers, kidnapers of women, *maus moçs* (bad hombres), robbers of the plains, runaways, disorderly," and many other terms of disrespect. That he served a useful purpose in spite of, or maybe because of, these characteristics is evident. His range extended from southern Brazil into Uruguay, Paraguay, and Argentina; everywhere he acquired the same bad reputation, even when the names varied. Sometimes he was called gaúcho, at other times gaudario or changador. He was described as "socially marginal," a mixture of every racial element. "Society looked down on them and feared them." Pejorative descriptions could be quoted almost without end.

All the unflattering descriptions of the runaway slaves, deserting soldiers, criminal whites, and semi-civilized Indians who made up the gaúchos (and the legal vaqueiros as well) cannot disguise an important fact: they developed the south of Brazil, and the southern Spanish colonies as well. As far as these men were concerned, the herds belonged to those with the skill to take them. Meanwhile, the buyers of the hides, tallow, and other animal products did not demand a legal bill of sale.

Hides were valuable from the beginning of settlement. Brazilian historians, followers mainly of Capistrano de Abreu, have written of the "Leather Age." In the cattle country of the south (and in Spanish America too), almost every article of clothing—hat, jacket, buttons, shoes, and trousers—was made of leather. The same was true in the dry Northeast. Some houses were made of leather, including the floors, chairs, beds, and bed covering. Grain was kept in storage bins built with leather; and leather buckets were used to carry water. Cloth was rarely worn in the cattle lands until a more comfortable style of life was affordable.

The European market for animal products grew apace in the eighteenth century. Population growth outstripped local supplies. American cows, burros, and horses supplied a tougher and thicker hide than their European cousins.

After the Treaty of San Ildefonso defined the respective boundaries in 1777, the colonists on both sides of the border founded new ranches. More than 500 existed in Rio Grande do Sul by the end of the eighteenth century. The legal size of an *estância* (ranch), three square leagues (about 27 or more square miles), was exceeded in the south as it had been in northern Brazil. Ranches often measured more than 20 square leagues (200 or so square miles). The growth in size and the legality of ranch ownership did not signify an upgrading of cattle raising methods, however, because the herds continued to be semi-wild.

The increased demand for beef in the eighteenth century brought about the production of more charqui, the process of cutting meat into strips thin enough for sun drying and salting. Preserved in this way, the meat was called *carne seca* (dried meat) by the Portuguese and *tasajo* (jerked beef) by the Spaniards.

The charqui industry led to a real revolution in beef production. The meat was now preserved and marketed rather than left to rot in the grasslands, doubling the value of the animals. José Pinto Martins, from Ceará in the north of Brazil, established the first known charqueada in 1780 on the banks of the Pelotas Arroyo. Other plants soon developed around Pelotas and on the São Gonçalo River.

A document of 1783 records the history of slaughtering and curing meat as the regular work of the gaúchos. Elaborate equipment was not required. Drying frames under the open sky cured the charqui, which was sent to Rio de Janeiro, Bahia, and other parts of Brazil. A market also developed for shipment to Havana and other Caribbean areas.

Charqui produced a culinary revolution. Cooked with beans and rice, and often other parts of hogs or cattle, a new dish developed called a feijoada in Brazil because of the black beans (feijão) which constituted its base. A rich meal in itself, providing protein and many then unnamed minerals and vitamins needed by the human body, it

became the food of the slaves. In time its excellence made feijoada
the food for everybody in any part of tropical America. It remains so
to this day. The market for the charqui of southern Brazil was greatly
increased in the 1790s, when a prolonged drought in the cattle raising
lands in the São Francisco Valley, Ceará, Piauí, and the Northeast
curtailed supplies and forced buyers to turn to the gaúcho areas.

By 1800 Rio Grande do Sul exported about 600,000 arrôbas of beef
annually; by 1814 the amount had risen to 900,000. The city of Rio
Grande was the principal port of shipment. Tallow, horns, and hair
were also exported.

26

MUSIC AND LITERATURE

notable and significant development in the field of music characterized Minas society in the eighteenth century. The extension of Portuguese music in the classical tradition to Brazil began soon after discovery and settlement, albeit weaker than in Portugal owing to the lack of facilities for full musical expression. The Portuguese kings, several of whom were composers and lovers of opera and chamber music, helped to inculcate a taste for good music in the Portuguese people. Portugal possessed perhaps the largest musical library in Europe in the eighteenth century.

The Portuguese tradition carried over to the coastal captaincies —Pernambuco, Bahia, and Rio de Janeiro—in the sixteenth century and later to Pará and Maranhão, continuing during the entire colonial period. Numerous monastic orders preserved the Gregorian Chant and the organ, but the secular clergy were reluctant to accept this musical style which predominated throughout Europe in the eighteenth century. Some critics have observed, in the façades and interiors of the churches along the coast, a reflection, or correlation, true to the music that sang the praises of God.

Until nearly the middle of the twentieth century, it was not suspected that Minas Gerais had developed a rich musical life parallel to its magnificent art. The music of Minas was traditional, but with its own characteristics, and was woven into its social fabric in a way

441

not equally reflected elsewhere. The discovery of the scores of this music in Belo Horizonte, Sabará, Ouro Preto, Cachoeira do Campo, Caeté, and other towns, principally by Francisco Curt Lange, has increased our knowledge of this music greatly. Not enough is known about music along the coast to make a critical comparison with Minas, but we can compare the quality of music with the high developments in its architecture and sculpture. The musicians of Minas deserve the honor of being called the School of Composers of the captaincy of Minas Gerais. While their technique was mainly borrowed from Europe, these musicians were a product of a mixed racial society and developed their own traditions.

The discovery of gold brought to Minas Gerais the well-known mixture of Europeans, Africans, and Indians. The numbers of mulattoes and pardos (two terms indicating only a slight variation of coloring) equaled or surpassed the whites. When Black slaves and freedmen are included in the total, the percentage of whites was small. Among the whites were some "Jews" or "New Christians," a statement based on the rather loose guesses to which we are reduced in estimating this "hidden" element in the population.

The mulatto became, in this mixed society, a "European" in language, customs, mentality, and rebellion. Though obviously part African, he was not set apart entirely from whites—as in English-speaking colonies—to pursue a separate cultural development. He was able to blend-in, to ascend the social scale in many instances and to gain positions in the clergy and among public officials quite contrary to the letter of the law. The latitudinarian character of the Brazilian people, their facile ability to skirt the literal meaning of royal decrees, and in a literal sense to see "white" or "mulatto" where the English and other Europeans saw only white and black, opened opportunities for the mixed people of part African or part Indian extraction which were not accessible to such mixtures in other European colonies. This tolerance was more usual in Minas Gerais than perhaps in any other part of Brazil.

Cultural mobility was one, if not the chief, road open. Many mixed people became distinguished among their fellowmen and were noted for their "quick intelligence, ambition, fertile imagination, and a decided inclination toward the trades and arts." Music became for them, a modern scholar remarks, "as much a consolation as a profession, and one of their fondest aspirations."

The rapid rise of a large number of sizable towns around the mines produced a demand for a variety of skilled and semi-skilled artisans. The slaves around the mines were skilled in the activities designed to meet the needs of the towns. The freemen, whether freedmen who had been slaves or freemen from birth, found their opportunities at this juncture.

The building of churches, of which there were hundreds within a few years after the opening of the mining towns, created a demand for artisans and artists. The first hastily built chapels soon gave way to the elaborate and beautiful churches we see today. Public buildings also afforded work for the skilled and unskilled. The older cities were not alone in constructing public buildings and private mansions. Churches, more than public buildings and mansions, required the talents of artists for the glorification of God and the saints. There was a proliferation of shrines devoted to saints native to Brazil. Among them were Nossa Senhora do Rosário, patroness of Blacks, slave or free, and Nossa Senhora das Mercês, protectress of mulattos and crioulos.

The multiplication of *irmandades* and *confrarias* surpassed the imagination. In a rough society where the precepts of Christian morality weighed lightly on the conscience, the fervent devotion to the Virgin and the saints was the outstanding characteristic of Christian worship. An example is the Matriz de Nossa Senhora do Pilar of Vila Rica (Ouro Prêto), where there were ten brotherhoods whose rivalry with one another stimulated construction of chapels and churches. The royal prohibition against monasteries and convents, or "unattached" friars or monks in Minas Gerais, motivated by the royal fear of the smuggling of diamonds and gold (at which the regular orders were reputed to be especially adept) was reflected directly in the need for an organization to perform the functions usually done by the religious orders.

In Minas Gerais the chapels and churches were customarily financed, constructed, and adorned in accordance with the decisions of their Mesa de Irmãos (brotherhood committee) which were democratically selected in periodical elections by members of the brotherhoods. Much of the history of such organizations can be read in their account ledgers, which record receipts and expenses as well as membership rolls. These records show the ardor of the members in improving their churches, accompanied by an intense emotional attachment to their saint and their group.

The secular clergy attended almost exclusively to their normal religious functions of celebrating mass, baptizing, registering births, performing marriages, confessing penitent sinners, administering extreme unction, and burying the dead. The people largely built and cared for the churches. The influence of churchmen was strong even if their parishioners did not live strict moral lives. The clergy were employees of the crown, which considered them a branch of government and very useful in ruling the people. Failure to support the churchmen was a failure to support the divine-right monarch. Church laws were to be obeyed just as royal laws. Attendance at mass was compulsory, even if not enforceable under existing conditions.

The brotherhood comittee governed such matters as the location for building a church, its architectural plan, the location and kind of altars, the choir, the images, the sacristy, and the purchase and upkeep of the organ. The Mesa also issued the music contracts for regular services and special occasions.

Each brotherhood in Minas evolved according to its own artistic concepts and preferences, as determined by the majority. Many brotherhoods were composed of mulattoes, and some of Blacks. The principal white brotherhoods were the Third Order of Carmelites and the Third Order of Franciscans. Racial tolerance did not necessarily mean an absence of race consciousness. The admission to a white church of a mulatto or pardo brotherhood without a building of its own, as well as the burial of people of color in churches where they were not affiliated, was as natural as the employment of painters, sculptors, bell makers, and musicians of color to build and decorate the churches.

The variety of expressions of art in Minas was not the work of

Europeans educated in Coimbra, but rather of Mineiros who had assimilated and molded European art to their own environment. "The mulatto of Minas Gerais was the real director of all the artistic activity, and almost its only interpreter."

Conditions in the mining districts intensified an appreciation of music. As one consolation for their rough life, the people found the churches and chapels and their music a source of entertainment as well as solace. [In North American mining districts and on the U.S. frontier, music also played an important role, but it produced a different style molded less along traditional religious lines.]

There are many examples of the unusual development of music in Minas beginning soon after the discovery of the mines. When, in 1717, Captain General Pedro de Portugal passed through São João del Rei, a musical director named António de Carmo was given the responsibility of providing welcoming music. Farther north in Vila Rica (Ouro Preto), the captain general's host, Capitão mor Henrique Lopes, bought three slave musicians at a cost of four thousand cruzados (a small fortune even in the rich mining district) to entertain him. The number of musicians in Minas, and the level of their learning, led to the saying, *"Mineiro sabe duas coisas bem, solfejo e Latim"* (Mineiros know two things well, singing and Latin).

Little documentation has survived, unfortunately, of this music prior to the middle of the eighteenth century—or if it survives, it has not been found. Music circulated in hand written copies, there being no printing press in Brazil, and it was soon worn and tattered. In 1734 a book published in Lisbon, entitled *Triumpho Eucharistico*, by Simão Ferreira Machado, describes vocal and instrumental groups dancing to music in religious processions, the playing of a notable German trumpeter, and a mass with two choirs. Another book, *Aureo Trono Episcopal*, published in Lisbon in 1749, treats the festivities on the arrival in Mariana of the first bishop, Frei Manuel da Cruz. After Mariana became a bishopric in 1745, it gained a reputation as a center of ecclesiastical music. In many other towns, groups of professional singers contracted their services to the brotherhoods on an annual basis.

In Vila Rica musical concerts as well as church music flourished.

The twin choirs sang "the scores of music which were of the finest composition, and sung by the outstanding singers from all Minas." One outstanding musician was Licenciado António de Sousa Lobo, a mulatto who, along with his brothers, performed for the captains general and the brotherhoods over a period of thirty years.

Vila Rica between 1750 and 1800 had many confrarias of musicians, such as the Confraria da Boa Morte, the Mercês dos Perdões, Mercês de Cima, São José, and São Francisco de Paula, who played not only in their own churches but also in churches whose confrarias were exclusively white. Such groups were usually composed of 12, 14, or 16 men and boys; some of the latter sang falsetto to replace the soprano or contralto voices. The instruments were violins, violas, and basses with three strings.

The violins retained a distinct trace of the Moorish Rebecas, as they were called in Minas. Violas were called violetas and the three-string bass was a rebecão or rebeca gorda (fat rebeca). Wind instruments included trumpets, flutes, oboes, clarinets, and others. The bassoon was the favorite family instrument, judging from the large numbers sold. Kettle drums and harps were also played.

Religious processions were notable for the bands of musicians, especially those organized by the Irmandade de Nossa Senhora do Rosário dos Pretos do Alto de Cruz of Padre Faria, which featured percussion instruments. Cravos (clavicles) were more common, but less imposing, than the organs found in churches in the coastal cities. It was difficult to bring organs over the mountains once they had been landed in Rio de Janeiro or another port city. In one known case, however, a man brought an organ from Rio de Janeiro by mule pack and sold it to the church of Carmo in Sabará. When organs were built in Minas, the woodwork was done locally while the pipes usually came from Lisbon.

The Mineiros kept their pipe organs in good condition, zealously preserving them from wear and tear and the effects of climatic conditions on wood and metal. Organs brought from Lisbon suffered from the termites common in the tropics, meaning frequent repairs were necessary. The wooden parts had to be rebuilt in Brazil with indigenous woods more resistant to insects. White wine was commonly used to clean the pipes because it allegedly preserved them longer.

Governor Gomes Freire de Andrada reported to the king in 1752 on the request of some mulattos to be allowed to carry swords for self defense and prestige: "What the petitioners state in the accompanying petition is entirely true, for there are rich men here who are mulattos, with slaves of their own, and estates, and there are master mechanics, and other officials." The importance of the mulatto in music was attested to in 1780 by Desembargador José João Teixeira Coelho, who reported to the king: "these mulattoes, in order to keep them from becoming absolute idlers, should be employed as musicians, of which there are so many in the Captaincy of Minas that their number surely exceeds that in all Portugal."

It was customary to have music at all the principal religious festivals. The various confrarias of musicians made bids annually to supply the music for such occasions in the same manner that bids were taken to repair roads, build bridges, and perform other public works. At such times a list of the musicians was given to the senado da câmara, which then either accepted or rejected the entire group or any one player or singer.

At the height of musical development the directors and composers held honored positions in society. They led prosperous lives, owning substantial homes, slaves, and otherwise displaying outward signs of affluence. The militia and other armed forces often had their own bands.

Together with the religious and ceremonial music, there existed a rich popular music, exemplified in the dramatic dances of the type described in the *Aureo Trono Episcopal* and performed by "little mulatto children imitating Carijó Indians." Orchestras played chamber music, wedding music, and funeral music, as well as non-religious music of Portuguese origin. Much has been lost, unfortunately, but fragments of the leading composers still exist. Public celebrations offered occasions for music supplied by the câmara. Concerts were given in the governor's palace and even in remote areas of the hinterland where music was the favorite form of entertainment.

As early as 1740, possibly, a small theatre existed in Ouro Preto, and sometime before 1770 an opera house was built. Governor-general Luís da Cunha Meneses (1783–88) ordered production of two dramas and three operas to celebrate the double wedding of the Portuguese and Spanish princes. The music was composed by Floréncio José Ferreira Coutinho and directed by Marcos Coelho Neto and his son of the same name. The only thing noted as remarkable was the extraordinary amount of paper needed for the music sheets.

Lange reported that he found no case of an illiterate musician. The calligraphy was good, owing to the practice of frequently copying scores. He compiled a list of 250 musicians using only the scant remaining records. José Joaquim Emerico Lobo de Mesquita, who lived in Diamantina about 1782, was one of seven directors in a period of less than thirty years. He was the greatest of the Mineiro composers.

He was a man of color, as attested by his membership in the Irmandade das Mercês dos Crioulos in 1788. In 1792 one of his slaves was also a member of the same brotherhood. He left Diamantina in 1798 for Ouro Prêto, where he was musical director of the Ordem Terceira do Carmo and also of the Santissimo Sacramento da Matriz do Pilar. He left Ouro Preto the same year and was replaced by another noted director, Francisco Gomes da Rocha. Only about forty of his works survive. These show that he was undoubtedly a great musical talent. Francisco Gomes da Rocha supposedly wrote many works but only one, "a Novena de Nossa Senhora do Pilar," has survived. Of excellent quality, it shows he was a composer of the first order.

Inácio Parreiras Neves of the Irmandade do Senhor São José was an active tenor as early as 1754 and a conductor of his own works. Only one survives however. A credo composed about 1780, its quality indicates a fine musician.

Marcos Coelho Neto, a father and son of the same name, were both composers, and it is not possible to distinguish which person wrote each of their extant pieces. Jerónimo de Sousa Lobo, who died in 1803, was an organist, violinist, and composer. A number of his compositions survive. Padre José Maurício Nunes Garcia (1767–1830),

who lived most of his life in Rio de Janeiro, wrote both sacred and
secular music and was extremely productive. His mother was a slave
in Minas Gerais. There were other musicians too numerous to mention
here, and many had names suggesting that they were mulatto descendants of Portuguese fathers.

The functional purpose of music in this society, with musicians
employed throughout the year to play on numerous religious and
public occasions, explains the large number of professionals who could
find employment. They were not part-time players working at other
jobs to make a living, but regularly employed musicians who could
devote themselves to the improvement of their art.

LITERATURE AND THE ACADEMIES

Academic and literary societies came to Brazil directly from Portugal and, more distantly, from France and Italy. The objective of
such associations was to bring together the intellectuals of a city or
a nation. As early as 1540 in Italy, Cosimo the Great, Grand Duke
of Tuscany (1519–74), organized the Academia degli Umili. Its successor was the Academia della Crusca inspired by the poet Grazzini
and hailed as a "center of good taste and fine poetry" and contributor
to the first Italian dictionary.

The first such societies adapted names that may strike us as curious:
Úmidos (the wet), Imoveis (immovable), Gelados (frozen), Surdos
(deaf), Insensatos (insensible), and Ociosos (idle). One modern critic
has written: "They held meetings with all the appearance of seriousness and wrote thick and pedantic dissertations about the most ri-
diculous themes."

The movement spread to France when the Marquise de Ram-
bouillet (1585–1655) opened her salon to people with an intellectual
bent. Noted people such as Bishop Jacques-Benigne Bossuet (1627–
1704) and Pierre Corneille (1605–84) attended, as well as many of
lesser literary talents. Cardinal Richelieu (1585–1642), prime minister
of Louis XIII, put the academy on a more serious footing. In 1635
he organized the Academie Française, which was destined to have a

profound influence on French intellectual life. Spain joined in the movement with its academies of the Nocturnos (night owls?), Desconfiados (the suspicious), and Buen Gusto (good taste). The most serious was the Real Academia begun in 1714. In Spain during the reign of Philip V (1700–46), the Academia Española de la Lengua, the Academia Real de la Historia, and Bella Artes were all functioning.

Portugal also joined the academy movement. Although criticized by Almeida Garrett as "an infinity of academies of the most extravagant and incredible names" whose members wrote "absurd things," his judgment is too harsh. The men of this era gained inspiration by holding meetings in the homes of various important figures in Portugal, among them were the noted diplomat and statesman Dom Luís da Cunha (1662–1742) and Dom Francisco Xavier de Meneses, Fourth Count of Ericeira (1673–1742).

The first academy was organized in 1649 by António Álvares da Cunha (1626–90), in the time of King João IV, with the name of Generosos (the generous, magnanimous?). It flourished to 1668 with the announced purpose: "to explain the doubtful and obscure meanings of ancient authors and at the same time establish precepts of rhetoric and poetry." Another academy, the Singulares, existed as early as 1628 perhaps, but maybe only from 1661, publishing two volumes of its papers. Its mentor was the Inquisitor General Padre Duarte Ferrão. Numerous other academies were organized; a dozen or more were important in their era.

The Academia Real da História Portuguesa, founded by King João V in December 1720, was the most important organized in Portugal to this date. With 50 members, its announced purpose was to "purify of the least shadow of falsehood the narrative of the events of either type of history, ecclesiastical or secular, and to research into those things that negligence has left hidden in the archives." It did distinguished service working toward a goal not easy to reach. To supercede the kind of history usually written was a difficult task. Ecclesiastical history meant, for example, the history of the Inquisition. Who could inquire impartially into its history with impunity? Some of the inquisitors were members of the new academy. Secular history meant the history of the king; and with King João V presiding at many of the meetings, it was risky to dig too deeply into the chronicle of the royal family. The academy was a notable success, nevertheless, flourishing for sixteen years and publishing the most significant contributions to serious Portuguese history to that date.

The Real Academia da História Portuguesa merits further examination. Consider its task: to take the writing of history out of the hands of the clerics, who had made it a genuflection to the lives of the saints and religious orders and a form of literature pandering to the royal family and the nobility. The man who best exemplifies the success of the Academia Real was José da Cunha Brochado (1651–1733). He had rendered excellent service to the king as a desembargador in Lisbon and representative of Portugal in Paris (1694–1704), London (1710–15), and Madrid (1725–27).

A century and a half before Leopold von Ranke (1795–1884) produced prodigious works following his own dictum "to write history exactly as it happened," Brochado had spelled out the same scientific goal. In 1722 he said: "the historian . . . should confine himself to writing about things the way they really happened without injecting his own opinions; let the reader use his free right of judgment . . . Little or nothing that comes from the author should be found in a history."

Brazil soon joined the academic movement. By the eighteenth century many of its sons had gone to Portugal to the University of Coimbra as well as other universities in Spain, France, and England. A few went for a time to Germany and other countries. Many Portuguese who served the home country in Brazil in one capacity or another— governors or judges, for example—had also studied outside Portugal. Although those who studied in Portugal before 1772 had perforce attended the unreformed university still under Jesuit methods, they had become aware of the newer thoughts circulating in northern European countries.

The number of academies organized in the eighteenth century demonstrate the extent to which Brazil kept abreast of developments in the home country. The literary historian Sílvio Romero thought that the academies showed "a great deal of intellectual vivacity, a great desire to learn and work." If, he said, their production was not of the highest quality, they were not far behind the home country, nor the norm in other nations, which were only beginning to escape from church and royal control.

The first of the Brazilian academies was the Academia Brazílica dos Esquecidos, founded in March 1724 by Viceroy Vasco Fernandes César de Meneses. The name, "Brazilian Academy of the Forgotten," has elicited some questions, comment, and even ridicule. Some critics have alleged that its very name indicated a shallow intellectual depth. But not necessarily so.

The name was a direct reference to the Royal Academy of History organized in 1720 in Lisbon, which no Brazilian was invited to join. Perhaps this was not an intended slight inasmuch as the academy was primarily confined to Lisbon. But some of the Bahians who had studied in, or visited, Lisbon and Coimbra took the absence of any invitations to Brazilians as a slight. If the Portuguese in Lisbon had forgotten that the Brazilians were as faithful to the crown as any native-born Portuguese and that some were originally from Portugal, so much the worse. How better to remind the homeland of their existence than to rub it in and call their academy "The Forgotten."

The academy held eighteen meetings before winding down in February 1725. In the fashion of the times, its members adopted pseudonyms such as Cloudy, Busy, Unhappy, and Vago (vagabond or restless), which was the name adopted by Sebastião de Rocha Pitta (d. 1738). Pitta's first contribution to the academy was at its second meeting, when he read a paper entitled "Who demonstrated the greater love, Clytie for the Sun or Endymion for the moon?"

Figueiredo, a desembargador of the Relação of Bahia, who adopted the name of "Cloudy," contributed a "Memorandum concerning the past history of the Luso-American Colony," which was more in keeping with the main work of Rocha Pitta entitled *História da América Portuguesa* (Lisbon, 1730). The members demonstrated a wide variety of interests in various types of history—natural, military, political, and ecclesiastical—as well as in literature, especially poetry.

Rocha Pitta was highly confident about the quality of the members, and he affords us the best evaluation of the significance of the academy: "Our Portuguese America, and principally the province of Bahia, which in the production of ingenious sons can compete with Italy or Greece, did not have the literary academies known in all well-organized societies with the objective of diverting its youth from the idleness that is contrary to all the virtues and the origin of all the vices." The purpose of the academy was "to sharpen its genius." The viceroy had encouraged the formation of the academy, and Rocha Pitta hoped he would extend his protection by "giving to the press" the "serious and wise" discourses delivered by members of the academy.

Rocha Pitta was a senhor de engenho on the Paraguaçu River, which flows into the Recôncavo. His history has been almost universally condemned as more imaginative than objective; but for the modern historian wanting to understand the spirit of the times, Rocha Pitta is profitable reading. He was also a poet, "perhaps the best of his time." Some of the work of the academy has perished with attrition and neglect. But some was published, and some is in the monastery of Alcobaça and in the Instituto Histórico Geográfico Brasileiro in Rio de Janeiro.

The second academy in Brazil was the Academia dos Felizes which sat intermittently in Rio de Janeiro from 1736 to 1740. The academy was founded in the governor's palace by Dr. Matéus Saraiva, a Portuguese medical doctor and chief surgeon of the captaincy, who had been in Brazil as *físico-mor* of the fortifications of the city since 1713. Composed of thirty members, its announced purpose was "to discuss various subjects, heroic as well as lyric." Matéus Saraiva is remembered for his medical studies, among them *"América Portuguesa mais ilustrado que outro algum Domínio deste Continente Americano,"* still available for study in the Biblioteca Nacional in Rio de Janeiro.

Near mid-century Rio de Janeiro witnessed an unusual and perhaps unique event in Brazilian colonial history, the fleeting appearance of a printing press. If there was any other press in Brazil before this date, it was possibly in Recife during the Dutch period.

António Isidoro da Fonseca, owner of a printing shop in Lisbon, moved his press to Rio de Janeiro in 1747. How he had managed this forbidden act is unknown. He printed various flyers and at least one pamphlet with the title "Relação da Entrada que fez o Excellentissimo e Reverendissimo Senhor D.F. António do Desterro Malheiro, Bispo do Rio de Janeiro. . .composta pelo Doutor Luiz António Rosado da Cunha, Juiz de Fora, e Provedor dos Defuntos, e Auzentes, Capellas, e Residuos do Rio de Janeiro." This work celebrated the arrival of the new bishop from Angola. It held all the necessary local licenses for publication and went into a second edition. One title page bears the correct date M.DCC.XLVII—and the other M.DCC.XLII. The crown was not as forbearing as the governor and the bishop. On hearing of the press, the crown acted at once. It was closed, never to open again.

The next academy, Académia dos Selectos, met only once, to honor Governor-general Freire de Andrada, who presided on January 30, 1752. The most important men of Rio de Janeiro attended to pay homage to the governor "with all the pomp and splendor compatible with the circumstances of the country." Their contributions were gathered together and printed in Lisbon in 1754.

Among those who participated was the same Dr. Mateus Saraiva and a boy of twelve, José Basílio da Gama, who later wrote the nationalistic poem "Uruguay." It told the story of the war against the Sete Povos Indians, a group that the Portuguese and Spaniards were attempting to remove in accordance with the Treaty of Madrid signed in 1750.

The single session of this group perhaps does not justify calling it an academy, but the publication of its proceedings suggests its significance and reveals the quality of the talents in this era.

The Academia Brazílica dos Renascidos was founded in Bahia in June 1759 as a revival of the Esquecidos, hence the name "The Reborn." The date chosen was the birthday of King José I. The participants wished to celebrate the king's escape from assassins in September 1758 and to express their happiness upon receiving the news of his recovery. The purpose of the academia was to write the

História Universal da América Portuguesa. It held fifteen sessions, the last in April 1760. With 40 active members and 76 supernumeraries (83 according to others), its only known work was *Relação Panegirica* published in Lisbon.

Most critics agree that the contributions of the Renascidos were not great, but worthwhile work was forthcoming from some of its members. Dr. José de Mirales wrote *História militar do Brasil, 1549 to 1762*, which remains our primary published reference. Padre António de Santa Maria Jaboatão authored *Novo orbo Serafico Brasilico*. Domingos de Loreto Couto published several worthwhile works on Brazil. José Veríssimo, in his history of Brazilian literature, expressed the harsh view that most of the works of the academy had little merit: "none . . . had literary virtues that would justify them living in the memory of man." Again we may comment that Veríssimo failed to appreciate the value of such writings as sources for modern historians, however dull or puerile.

The Academia Scientífica held its first meeting in Rio de Janeiro in February 1772 under the auspices of Viceroy Marqués do Lavradio. Its first president and founder was the viceroy's personal physician, Dr. José Henriques Ferreira. The academy's objectives were expressed in its name. Medical doctors, surgeons, and pharmacists made up a large proportion of its members; one *agricultor practico*, António José Castrioto, was also a member. In correspondence with the Royal Scientific Society of Sweden, it expressed interest in physics, chemistry, natural history, medicine, surgery, and pharmacy, as well as in agriculture and all practical means of promoting the progress of Brazil. Among its projects were the promotion of indigo (anil), cochineal, cacao, and the silk worm.

Fr. José Mariano da Conceição Veloso (1742–1811), a leading botanist in colonial times, was one of the members. Born in the city now called Tiradentes after its illustrious hero (of whom Veloso was a double first cousin), he lived in Portugal for a number of years before returning to Brazil to gather his extensive collections. He returned to Portugal again in 1790 to print his books. Various misfortunes prevented publication in full of his *Flora Fluminense*. During the French invasion of Portugal, his collection was taken to France as spoils of war. There St. Hilaire was able to study them. This academy ceased to meet in 1779, after Viceroy Marquis do Lavradio retired to Portugal.

An undoubtedly valuable contribution to our knowledge of Brazil is the work of Padre Gaspar da Madre de Déus, entitled *Memórias para a história da Capitania de São Vicente*, first published in 1797. The work by Domingos Loreto Couto, entitled *Desagravos do Brazil e Glorias de Pernambuco*, explains in the preface its purpose and the reason for that title:

I wrote this history based on verifiable information of persons 80, 90, and even 100 years old; on observations and examinations that I made when I was Visitor General of his bishopric; of the cases and events that I saw, of which there are thousands of witnesses; in some memoirs which happily came into my hands; and in notes that I extracted from the public offices and notarial archives. I used little from books that treat our Brasil, for in them there are many things that belittle, many defects, many things of fiction and more than enough calumny. These compelled me to give my book the title *Desagravos do Brasil* as well as *Glorias de Pernambuco* to honor the illustrious actions of its citizens.

27

INCONFIDÊNCIA MINEIRA, 1788–1792

The political movement considered by many historians to have had the most profound significance in colonial Brazil was the Inconfidência Mineira, 1788–1792. On its face a protest against royal taxes like its model, the earlier tax revolt in the English colonies in North America, it was basically a challenge to the entire system of Portuguese colonial government.

The occasion for the protest was the announced arrival of a new governor of Minas Gerais with orders to collect the back taxes on gold production, the Fifth. The previous governor, Luís de Cunha Meneses (1783–88), had become infamous for his erratic conduct of public affairs, producing increasing dissatisfaction among the people. They were becoming more hostile to the Portuguese, particularly toward officials.

They persistently pondered this question: why they were so poor in a land so rich? They were unwilling to admit any responsibility for their own economic condition. In some cases their attitude merely reflected the anger of a middle class that considered itself overtaxed, while unjustly barred from the privileges enjoyed by the Portuguese office holders. The situation was ripe for some precipitant, and a leader to call them to rebellion.

The cause for conflict emerged with the order for a new derrama, a special levy to be assessed to make up deficits in the collection of the Fifth. It was set at 100 arrôbas of gold a year but only 68 arrôbas a year had been collected from 1774 to 1785. The accumulated deficit of 384 arrôbas of gold the Crown now proposed to exact from the captaincy. The new governor, Luís António Furtado de Mendônça, Viscount of Barbacena, arrived in July 1788 with express orders to enact the derrama.

The alarm of the people was genuine. The sum of 384 arrôbas or more threatened to bankrupt them. They regarded the proposed collection as confiscation. The crown refused to believe gold was no longer available, accusing the people of fraudulently hiding their production—a logical accusation considering the long history of contraband, but in this case only partly true. The mines and alluvial deposits had already given up the richest of their treasure.

At the moment of Governor Barbacena's arrival in Rio de Janeiro enroute to Minas Gerais, Rio had another visitor, an unnoticed, minor officer in the regiment of dragoons, the regular salaried cavalry of Ouro Preto in Minas. He was known as Tiradentes, the toothpuller— just one of his numerous and varied skills. He was a medical man, mineralogist, prospector, engineer, and an eloquent talker and advocate of his beliefs.

He clearly was knowledgeable about hydraulics, for his mission to Rio de Janeiro was to obtain a license to convert some creeks in Catete (or Laranjeiras) and the Andaraí River into a canal system. He wanted to obtain sufficient water power to build a mill in the area of Maracanã (now site of the famous football field). His full name was Joaquim José da Silva Xavier.

His military commission was minor and his social position modest. But he had a strong drive to rise above his army rank and social level. As early as 1781, when a *mascate* (a traveling peddler), he had enlisted in the army of the captaincy of Minas Gerais to further his ambitions. But he had not risen, however. Others had passed over him in promotions, and he remained in modest rank.

The historical record has not left a reliable description of him. Some described him as "ugly," pop-eyed, looked down on by superiors, frequently the butt of humor of his colleagues, and having no "compadres" (close companions). His dreams had faded. For a time, he held a mining claim and owned four slaves, but he found little gold and wound up in debt. He manifested his discontent with his own lot and Portuguese officials during the governorship of Cunha Meneses, but disappointments had not killed his spirit. He was still determined to accomplish something in life. On furlough, he went to Rio to request the license for building the water mills; he filed a petition on June 19, 1788.

At that moment José Álvares Maciel, son of the capitão-mor of Ouro Prêto, arrived from Europe, where he had been studying philosophy and natural history in Coimbra. Previously he had spent a year in England studying chemistry. While in England he became interested in local manufacturing; England was then outpacing the world in industrial progress. Tiradentes consulted him about the proposed hydraulic mills, perhaps with the hope Maciel could help him raise capital. From Maciel, Tiradentes learned something of Europe. The question arose about why Brazil, with its riches, did not follow the example of the United States.

Tiradentes and Maciel continued at other times to talk about the chances of a revolution in Brazil. No evidence remains to show which of the two men was the main protagonist. Perhaps the knowledge young Maciel had gained in Europe combined well with the inquiring mind and restless disposition of Tiradentes. Tiradentes later assumed entire responsibility for the conspiracy—the only man among those involved who had the courage to support his ideas in the face of certain death and the only one whose name is remembered by the average Brazilian today.

From Rio, Tiradentes returned to Ouro Prêto. On his route home he began the campaign for independence, with Minas Gerais in the leadership. In Ouro Prêto and surrounding towns he continued his efforts. To the people he emphasized the contrast in the wealth of the country versus their own poverty. It was nevertheless not the abject poor but a middle group that heard and understood his message. Portugal, he said, deliberately kept Brazil poor. The Viscount of Barbacena had brought instructions to limit the wealth of individual mineiros to 10,000 cruzados—obviously not a message aimed at slaves and the poor. He did not confine his allegations to statements he could verify. He talked of foreign aid to gain independence, particularly from France.

Tiradentes talked of himself as a restorer rather than a radical revolutionary. He emphasized his intent to return the land to its rightful owners; but what he meant was not clear. He certainly did not have in mind returning the land to the Indians. He did mean, it seems, to put government into the hands of Brazilians, and thus rid it of Portuguese officials.

He knew he had to secure the aid of leading Brazilians of wealth and power in Minas Gerais. His task was all the more difficult because he had to get the attention of men of a higher social class than himself. A social leveling had taken place in Minas but it had not prevented the most successful from holding themselves above most of the people. Indeed, the defense subsequently made at his trial was based on this social class distinction. He protested that he had neither the wealth nor social standing to persuade "such great people to such an asininity."

He gained the ear of Lieutenant Colonel Francisco de Paula Freire de Andrada, who was commander of the regiment of dragoons in which Tiradentes was only an *alferes* (ensign or standard bearer). Andrada was rich and descended from one of Brazil's most illustrious families, which under normal conditions would have inclined him to look forward to promotions within the existing system. But it can be noted that revolutionaries often have come from the upper ranks of societies—the Marquis of LaFayette, for example, or George Washington.

Andrada was second to the governor in command. He not only listened to Tiradentes, he supposedly believed, when told, that Rio de Janeiro was ready for revolt and would rise against the Portuguese government and follow him. Andrada and Maciel were brothers-in-law. Through them, Tiradentes won over other influential members of the upper social and intellectual classes. It was at a moment when the threatened derrama weighed heavily on their minds.

Late in December 1788 the small group met in Andrada's home. Among those present were Tiradentes, Maciel, and Padre Carlos Correia de Toledo e Melo (vicar of São José del-Rei), a rich and influential cleric. They examined the chances of success if they rose at the announcement of the derrama. The conversations covered generalities only, and they drew up no plans of revolt.

At this meeting, or later, Inácio José de Alvarenga Peixoto came into the group. He testified at his trial that Andrada believed that, if Rio de Janeiro and São Paulo joined, they could succeed. Alvarenga Peixoto also testified that Maciel assured them of foreign aid, particularly from English-speaking nations wanting to open Brazil to trade. Other men allegedly involved were Tomás António Gonzaga, Cláudio Manuel da Costa, and Luís Vieira da Silva (canon of Mariana) because such men "had influence over the spirits of the people." At some point they decided that the derrama would be the time to start the uprising because discontent among the people would create sympathy for the anti-Portuguese propaganda.

A second meeting a short time later brought in additional recruits, especially Padre José da Silva e Oliveira Rolim of Diamantina, a wealthy man who had been accused of embezzlement and other crimes, to which no great importance was apparently attached since he had kept his prestige within the community. Alvarenga, not present at the beginning of the meeting, joined later at the request of Padre Correia. At this second meeting they resolved to act alone without waiting for the help of Rio de Janeiro and São Paulo.

They chose the United States as their model, reasoning that it had sustained a long war with fewer resources than Minas possessed. Their information about the English colonies was slight, and they overlooked the great differences between the two situations. They disregarded, for example, how the English colonies had acted together (except the Canadian provinces), whereas they were persuaded by Tiradentes and Alvarenga to go it alone.

Intendant Francisco Gregório Pires Monteiro Bandeira had been strongly reproved by the king's minister, Martinho de Mello e Castro, for failure to levy the derrama. He consulted with Tomás António Gonzaga, the ouvidor, who pointed out that the derrama was very heavy, and therefore he feared an uprising. But, he said, the law required the levy, and he thought it should be announced. He advise the junta to delay enforcement until the king could be consulted. Gonzaga had been in on conversations about the proposed uprising, and he cited his advice to the intendant as a defense against accusations of complicity. But, in vain.

The plotters were anxious for action, Tiradentes most of all. Under a flag showing an Indian or a genie breaking his chains (not a Black) and a shield with the motto taken from Virgil (at Alvarenga's suggestion) *Libertas quae sera tamen*, they planned to rise when the derrama was levied. After this meeting they dispersed to await the news. Meantime, Tiradentes, Padre Correia, and Padre Oliveira Rolim continued their propaganda, seeking out those who had complaints against the government and were delinquent in their taxes. Among those recruited for the uprising was Joaquim Silvério dos Reis, who was heavily in debt for back fifths. In the home of José Rezende Costa he was toasted by Sargento-mor Luís Vaz de Toledo, brother of the *vigário* of São José, Carlos Correia de Toledo: "Here is to the health of a man who a year from now should owe nothing to the royal treasury."

Tiradentes assigned to himself the task of announcing the uprising—with the cry "Viva La Liberdade." Lieutenant Colonel Andrada, on the pretext of putting down a mob and establishing order, was then to take charge of the situation. Tiradentes was to go straight to the residence of Governor Visconde de Barbacena and arrest him. Barbacena would not be harmed but sent to Portugal. They discussed but rejected the idea of executing him.

Each conspirator was to take responsibility for assuming power in his own district. They planned other actions. For example, Maciel was to take charge of a new powder factory and other industries.

What about Black slavery? The question had been faced in the United States and the cause of manumission lost. The Brazilian conspirators did not think about freeing the slaves as a humanitarian act. Instead, they worried lest the slaves, who were a great majority, might seize the opportunity to revolt and kill their masters. Alvarenga proposed freeing mulattos only; this idea too was rejected with little discussion.

Colonel Silvério dos Reis proved a poor recruit. He denounced the plot to Viscount de Barbacena on March 15, 1789, in the expectation that his debts would be canceled, which they were. He made his accusations more definite with a letter of April 11, 1789. Other denunciations were made by Lieutenant Colonel Basílio de Brito Malheiro de Lago on April 15; the Mestre de Campo Inácio Correia de Pamplona also denounced the conspiracy on April 20. On May 1, Joaquím Silvério arrived in Rio de Janeiro and told his story to the viceroy.

Once the conspiracy was known, others made further disclosures. The governor had meantime suspended the derrama. In Rio de Janeiro, Colonel Reis was assigned to keep an eye on Tiradentes, who had gone to Rio de Janeiro at the beginning of March before the derrama was suspended and the conspiracy denounced. The alleged purpose of his visit was to obtain an answer to his application for the hydraulic works he proposed to build—a most curious procedure for a man waiting for the signal to start a revolution. Learning that he was being watched, he attempted to escape but was arrested on May 10, 1789.

The arrest of the other conspirators soon followed. Those detained included men only incidentally involved as well as some who were aware of the plans and did not denounce the accused. The leading plotters were, of course, detained.

After the conspirators learned of the denunciations, Vigário Carlos Correia de Toledo, brother of Luís Vaz, announced that he was going to rise in revolt in any case because it was better "to die with sword in hand than like a tick in the mud." He was taken prisoner the same day. Alvarenga was arrested in São José del Rei on May 19 or 20, and Gonzaga in his home on May 22. Padre Rolim vainly tried to hide.

The plotters comprised a varied lot, from all social classes. Some had studied in European universities; some had never left Minas Gerais; some were almost illiterate. There were those who occupied the highest administrative posts, military and ecclesiastical, plus inn keepers, ensigns, sergeants, and simple parish priests.

Among the implicated, Conego Luís Viera da Silva of Mariana was known for his education. A student of the history of the English colonies, he openly expressed his approval of the North American revolt. He had heard of the planned revolt in Minas in the home of João Rodrigues de Macedo. When Luís Vieira met with Gonzaga and Alvarenga and asked them about the expected uprising, he was told by Gonzaga: "The occasion for this was lost." Gonzaga undoubtedly referred to the suspension of the derrama on March 15, which took the wind out of the sails of the rich tax delinquents since they had lost their principal grievance.

When Alvarenga went to São Luís del Rei, he reported that the atmosphere for revolt had cooled because the derrama was canceled. Padre Carlos Correia de Toledo was quoted as saying: "We waited for the derrama and as this was not made, nothing was done." Desembargador Tomás António Gonzaga, the highest judicial official in Minas, Colonel Francisco de Paula de Andrada, commander of the dragoons, Dr. Domingo Vidal Barbosa, Alvarenga Peixoto, and the clerics already mentioned—Vigário Carlos Correia de Toledo, José da Silva e Oliveira Rolim, José Lopes de Oliveira, and Manuel Rodrigues da Costa—were all arrested. Dr. Cláudio Manuel da Costa hanged himself in prison. The others were sent to Rio de Janeiro for trial. Judges were appointed on August 15, 1789.

The investigation began shortly thereafter and continued for three years. During this period, the news of the bloody revolution in France created a very hostile attitude toward conspirators who challenged a king's sacred authority. Domingos Vidal Barbosa, a graduate of Bordeaux, told the story of his fellow student José Joaquim de Maia, who had written to Thomas Jefferson and talked with him about helping to gain the independence of Brazil. Jefferson had replied that the United States was on friendly terms with Portugal and could not afford the risk of war. But if Brazil revolted, it could count on a sympathetic U.S. attitude. Later, Barbosa talked with José Resende Costa Filho who said that he had changed his mind about going to Coimbra because there were plans to establish a republic and university in Minas Gerais.

In his defense, Cônego Luís Vieira declared: "As the history of English America has been written and published, . . . I might have . . . conversed about the other America, convinced that in doing this I did not commit any crime whatever." To the trial judge, he stated "that he was glad the English Americans had given a backhand slap to England." Many others cited the American example.

The books owned by some of the conspirators indicated the possible source of their political ideas. The "laws" of the United States served as guides (we do not know just what laws they possessed), and a history of the country was a source of knowledge.

They also had copies of Abbé Guillaume Raynal's *Histoire philosophique et politique des etablissments et du commerce des Européens dans les deux Indes*, a destructive work when read in an environment where the "divine right" of the king of Portugal prevailed. Raynal was perhaps the most inspirational source of their thoughts. He had "predicted" the revolt of the English colonies. Dr. Barbosa, who had studied in Bordeaux, owned a copy, and he could quote entire passages from memory. In one of the meetings in the home of Colonel Andrada, Raynal was cited as "a writer of great vision who had predicted the revolt in North America." He argued that Brazil was too big to remain tied to Portugal and should be liberated. He further stated that the Portuguese colonial system should be revamped, the monopolies abolished, and Brazilian ports opened to the world.

In addition, they had Abbé Mably's *Observations sur le gouvernement des États Unis de l'Amérique* and other histories which expressed ideas that contrasted sharply with their own condition. In a society with no printing press and consequently no newspapers, magazines, or books of its own, a few concepts drawn from a different culture was as explosive as a torch in a powder keg. Maciel admitted he owned Robertson's *History of America* that he had bought in Birmingham, England, for two shillings.

The evidence against Conego Luís Vieira for committing the crime of reading dangerous literature was convincing. He could be considered the intellectual who laid the basis for the conspiracy. "O Cônego Luís Vieira discussed and read with others the history of the revolution in English America; and they said Cônego was the teacher of the class." He "had suggested the measures necessary for the attempt easily as much as eight years ago."

The planners believed that a revolution for independence would attract much foreign sympathy. Tiradentes testified that Maciel had said to him: "In the foreign nations where he had traveled people wondered why Brazil had not followed the example of English America." The success of the United States was ever before them. Vicente de Mota quoted Tiradentes as saying: "If Minas had another government, and if this were a republic like English America, it would be the happiest country in the world." Alvarenga Peixoto shared the view that foreign aid would be forthcoming. He thought France would offer aid, just as it done for the United States during its rebellion. Padre Toledo had asserted that at least 60 international wholesale merchants in Rio de Janeiro would support independence.

No proof of any international connection has been found, nor of any contact between José Joaquim de Maia, the young man who talked with Jefferson and Tiradentes. The influence of Free Masonry, suggested by some writers, has no documental foundation. No evidence reveals that Tiradentes contacted Masons.

Tiradentes swore on trial that he premeditated the revolt and was the one who thought up the idea without outside urging—"without inspiration from anyone." Furthermore, he said, Maciel was the first person he talked to about revolt. Gonzaga, who was exonerated by everyone except Alvarenga, said of Tiradentes: "A man like that could do a lot of harm to people with his fanaticism."

Tiradentes's uneasiness about obtaining the support of the local people was revealed in his statement about the governor. Returning from Rio after the arrival of Governor Visconde de Barbacena, he had inquired about the new governor. When he received a good report, he said: "It would be better if he were the Devil, worse than his predecessors, because then things would be more inclined to the establishment of a republic."

The conspirators were much impressed with the wealth of Minas Gerais. "A country like no other anywhere, with all the riches within themselves not needing any other country for resources," said Tiradentes. Other similar statements were attributed to Tiradentes by witnesses at his trial:

Minas Gerais is unfortunate, because so much gold and many diamonds had been taken from it, that nothing was left. Everything was shipped out and the poor sons of America left bereft, without anything of their own. The natives are so stupid that they do not think of this, or at least of what happened recently in English America.

Others shared such opinions. Francisco Xavier Machado thought that "Minas Gerais because of their riches could become independent, as English America had done." Claudio Manuel da Costa agreed:

A European prince could have nothing to do with America, which was free: the king of Portugal did not spend anything on the conquest. The natives had recovered it from the Dutch, carrying on the war at their own expense without the king contributing any money whatever to it. The French took Rio de Janeiro and the people bought it back with their own money. This land should not be subjected to Portugal because the natives wanted to establish a republic.

The blame for the economic situation, in the general opinion, rested on the colonial system. Every two or three years Portugal sent "generals and ministers along with their aids, to whom they give the best positions; and they and their aids take the produce of the mines to Portugal. If this were not so, the streets could be paved with gold." Although some governors were not greedy, "they always have a few aids who are thieves."

The concept of the new republic was not very definite, and in some ways chimerical. There were to be several parliaments (there had not been a parliament in Portugal for almost two centuries): "One in Vila Rica, another in São João del Rei, and still others." There were to be no soldiers, only a militia composed of men who would return to their homes and their regular work as soon as any emergency had passed.

Barbosa had this vision: "The vicars would collect the tithes and assume the obligation to pay teachers, maintain hospitals, and other charitable institutions." Other proposals were not so sound: "diamonds would be free" and "all the poor would wear satin."

Tiradentes's defense lawyer pleaded insanity. Since he was a man "without property, without reputation, without credibility and very loquacious, he could never start a revolution." But these claims did not comport with other statements and actions by Tiradentes. The court condemned him to death:

> The Criminal Joaquim José da Silva Xavier, nicknamed Tiradentes, alferes of the regular cavalry of the Captaincy of Minas Gerais is to be taken with hangman's rope and public proclamation through the streets to the gallows to die a natural death for ever; and after death his head is to be severed from his body and taken to Vila Rica where it will be nailed up in the most prominent place on a high pole until time rots it; and his body is to be cut into four parts and nailed along the road in Varginhas and Cebólas where the criminal did most infamous acts, and in other places of large population, where they are to remain also until they rot, demonstrating the infamy of the criminal extending to his children and grandchildren also . . . and the house in which he lived in Vila Rica will be razed to the ground and the earth salted so that never again can anything be built there. . . . And on the same spot there is to be erected a pillar by which the infamy of this abominable criminal will be remembered.

And indeed, Tiradentes is remembered; the town where he was born now bears his name.

Tiradentes had insisted on assuming the whole blame. Several others were also condemned to death, but the sentences were commuted to lesser penalties—such as exile for life. Gonzaga and Vidal de Barbosa were exiled temporarily.

The fate of the clerics involved in the conspiracy was somewhat different and was incompletely known until the publication of the papers of the Counts of Galveias in 1977. Three of the clerics had originally been condemned to death. Queen Maria I ordered, however, that they all be sent to Lisbon, and the records of their trials be given directly to her. She confided these to Martinho de Melo e Castro, Minister of Ultramar (Overseas Minister) of the family of the courts of Galveias. There the papers remained unknown until 1952. Later they were brought to Rio de Janeiro, still in the possession of the family. They have now been edited along with a new edition of *Autos da Devassa da Inconfidência Mineira* by the Câmara dos Deputados under the direction of Professor Herculano Gomes Mathias.

After their arrival in Lisbon, the clerics were sent to the Convent of São Bento, home today of the Portuguese Chamber of Deputies. The clerics were not informed about their sentences. The minister died in 1795 still in possession of the secret. Two of the condemned died in São Bento. Fathers Rolim and Costa e Toledo repeatedly petitioned for clarification of their cases. With the Inconfidência in the background, the three still in prison were released. Father Rolim returned to Brazil where he died in 1835.

Recently, influenced perhaps by modern concepts of class interpretations of history, some have suggested that Tiradentes was the only one executed because he was the humblest within this class-oriented society. A full examination of this thesis would require a great deal of time and perhaps offer more opinion than documentation, the answer depending on the orientation of the historian who undertook the task. It seems logical to believe, however, that the court accepted as truth his self-proclaimed guilt and his own assertion that he was the original organizer of the conspiracy and should bear the brunt of the blame. Few can now name his fellow conspirators, prominent though they were in their time.

But rare is the Brazilian who has not been told about the hero and patriot Tiradentes. He was hanged April 21, 1792, just one day short of the 292nd anniversary of Cabral's landing in Brazil. "Tiradentes Day" is now the principal national holiday with special ceremonies held in front of the old Chamber of Deputies in Rio de Janeiro, where his statue stands in the robe worn by persons to be executed. Cabral, cast in the long nationalistic shadow of Tiradentes, is hardly noticed.

EPILOGUE

he material on the Inconfidência Mineira was the last I was able to locate in Bailey Diffie's files. His original table of contents called for several additional chapters, carrying the narrative up to 1808. It is not clear whether these later chapters were never completed or, alternatively, were actually written and subsequently mislaid.

I was privileged to be entertained (a word carefully chosen and understood by all who ever enjoyed this man's companionship) by Bailey's stimulating conversation over lunch once or twice a week at the USC faculty club for nearly a decade, and I can recall two comments Bailey made at different times during the last year or so of his life. They perhaps shed some light on the question, although they are less definitive than we might prefer.

On one occasion, he indicated that, given his advancing age, he was considering a reduction in the length of his Brazilian manuscript. It was not a remark that any of his friends took seriously since Bailey always seemed to be in the peak of good health, and we joked that he would probably outlive us all. Indeed, he remained vigorous and active right up until a massive stroke took him away so quickly in January 1983. On another occasion Bailey told me he had finished a draft of the entire manuscript and was actively seeking a publication outlet. The two comments can be reconciled, of course, if we assume the following: Bailey meant that he had completed a slightly shortened version of the original project. I believe that is, in all likelihood, the correct assumption.

Edwin J. Perkins, editor

Appendix

THE DISCOVERY OF BRAZIL

discussion of the discovery of Brazil has been omitted from the text for two principal reasons. First, except for Cabral's landing on April 22, 1500, the first discoveries are not pertinent to the subsequent development of the country. Second, an adequate discussion of all the events surrounding the first discoveries would require a large book of its own. Many have already been published.

The reader should know, however, that there are few easily verifiable "facts" concerning discoveries. Three principal disputes have engaged the attention of historians and continue to interest them: 1) whether there was a discovery prior to Cabral; 2) whether Cabral, driven by prevailing winds and ocean currents, found Brazil accidently by wandering westward off his intended route to India; or 3) whether King Manuel I gave him "secret" instructions to make a landing in Brazil, which had already been discovered by a previous Portuguese expedition, or expeditions, in order to take formal possession.[1]

One school of writers has sought to show that the Phoenicians and other ancients were in Brazil. Among them are Cyrus H. Gordon, Walter Sullivan, and others who, in recent years, have cited an alleged message found on a stone in Paraíba, Brazil. Nicolau Duarte has proven that this entire business is a hoax in his article "Cabral e os Fenécios."

Some historians have found evidence sufficient to justify their belief that, two or more years before Cabral, the noted discoverer and comographer Duarte Pacheco Pereira sailed the Brazilian coast at the order to King Manuel. Others, among them the distinguished and careful Duarte Leite, deny that any discoveries prior to Cabral were made by anybody. Still others think that Amérigo Vespucci, Diego de Lepe, Vincente Yáñez Pinzón (or even Alonso de Ojeda) touched on the Brazilian coast to the north of Cabral's landing (from Pernambuco northward) in 1499. All, including myself, have used the same evidence, and interpreted it differently. The reader who wishes to devote a great deal of time to the conflicting documentation, as I did for years, can consult the authors cited above and many others as well.

Such a careful scholar as Captain Max Justo Guedes, Director of the Museu da Marinha in Rio de Janeiro, after comparing the early maps with those of the present day, concluded that Vespucci was not in Brazil before Cabral and that Pinzón and de Lepe touched only as far south as Mucuripe in Ceará, not in Pernambuco as some have contended. I believe, nevertheless, that Vespucci did reach Brazil in the months July-September 1499.[2]

The Argentine scholar, Roberto Levillier, concluded after extensive comparisons of early and modern maps, that Vespucci made four voyages to America, including the one to Brazil in 1499, which was described in writings ascribed to him. Alberto Magnaghi, an Italian scholar, believed that Vespucci made only two voyages (not four) but that he did touch Brazil in 1499. William B. Greenlee, in *The Voyage of Pedro Álvares Cabral*, cites in translation all the known sources of the Cabral expedition. While these are the chief references, the reader can consult for varying opinions the works by Pohl, Varnhagen, Naia, Damião Peres, T. O. Marcondes de Souza, Duarte Leite, Henry Harrissee, Henri Vanaud, Germán Arciniegas, Jaime Cortesão, Gago Coutinho, Manuel Nunes Dias, and others.[3]

My own beliefs as of this writing, and I thought otherwise in earlier years, is that neither Ojeda nor Duarte Pacheco Pereira touched Brazil and that the latter never sailed to America at all. No French explorer

landed in Brazil before 1504. Cabral touched Brazil by chance sailing
an ocean that only Vasco da Gama had sailed before him. He was
driven by natural forces—winds and ocean currents but not storms—
westward to discover Brazil between 16° and 17° south latitude. The
Portuguese had no previous knowledge of Brazil's existence, nor of
America, prior to the return of Columbus to Lisbon on March 4, 1493.

ENDNOTES FOR APPENDIX

1. Consult the works by B. W. Diffie for reasons why "secrecy"
about discoveries is not tenable. I question those who support the
secrecy theory because of the unconvincing nature of their materials
and arguments.

2. The most important single source about Cabral is Pêro Vaz
de Caminha's *Carta a El Rey D. Manuel*, edited many times. Greenlee
published this text in translation along with all other pertinent documents concerning Cabral.

3. J. H. Parry's numerous works are particularly good on the
technical aspects of navigation. Volume 267 of the RIHGB (April-
June 1970) is devoted to Cabral's voyage. Parry does not confront,
however, the many contentious doubts about details of the discoveries
which occupy so much of the time of Portuguese and Brazilian (as
well as some foreign) historians.

For the principal histories of Portuguese discoveries see the works
of Charles R. Boxer, Damião Peres, Luis de Albuquerque, Duarte
Leite, Vitorino Magalhães Godinho, Armando Cortesão, Jaime Cortesão, and Diffie and Winius, all cited in the bibliography. Also see
Pierre Chaunu, *L'expansion européenne*; Jacques Heers, *L'occident au xiv°
et xv° siecles*, pp.160–65. More detailed materials can be found in Katia
Maria Abud and others, "O descobrimento do Brasil." João Capistrano de Abreu, *O descobrimento do Brasil*, makes the essential point
that the effective discovery was made by Cabral, starting Brazil on
its path of becoming Portuguese. He accepts earlier discoveries by

Vespucci, de Lepe, and Pinzón, but rightly shows that they had no effect on Brazilian development. On early maps see Isa Adonias, "A cartografia vetustíssima até 1500." Among numerous other works that may be consulted, see António Baião, Hernani Cidade, and Manuel Múrias, eds., *História da expansão portuguêsa no mundo*; António Baião, *O manuscrito Valentim Fernandes*; Antonio Ballesteros, *Cristóbal Colón*; Joaquim Bensaúde, who wrote and reedited many works on explorations, though not precisely on Brazil; Charles Michael Boland, who believes that at least eighteen discoveries were made before Columbus; Ana Maria de A. Camargo; Viriato de Sousa Campos discusses the discovery as viewed in historiography and in the schools in Portugal. Guiseppe Caraci has an excellent discussion of Vespucci as an Italian historian sees him—his views are sharply attacked by most Portuguese scholars. A. Fontoura da Costa published in a facsimile edition, *O sete únicos documentos*—documents found in Portugal about Cabral's discoveries, of which Greenlee has translations. Carlos Coimbra credits Duarte Pacheco Pereira with a voyage in 1498, and also discusses the Portuguese objectives in the Treaty of Tordesillas which bear on knowledge of Brazil.

The most influential single historian of Portuguese expansion remains Jaime Cortesão. His theory of "secrecy" about discoveries has been widely followed, causing many to accept as fact "discoveries" for which little and sometimes no evidence exists. His "Do sigilo nacional sôbre os descobrimentos," published in 1924, was followed by many other writings holding to this position. Among them are *A expedição de Pedro Álvares Cabral* and "The Pre-Columbian Discovery of America." His works were gathered in *Descobrimentos portuguêses* in 1960. Aside from the writings ascribed to Vespucci, information attesting to his discovery of Brazil in 1499 is given in *De los Pleitos de Colón*, Seville, 1964, and later. G.R. Crone is skeptical of pre-Columbian discoveries. Manuel Nunes Dias in "Descobrimento do Brasil" accepts the thesis of intentionality, as he does in a book of the same title. (It is a good summary of what I do not believe.) Faustino da Fonseca in *A descoberta do Brasil* publishes 40 interesting illustrations. Raquel Glezer examines critically the instructions of Vasco da Gama to Cabral.

The most careful recent study of discovery and early exploration is found in Max Justo Guedes, coordinator, *Historia Naval Brasileira*. The conclusions reached by Guedes in this work are different from those in his work of 1966. Valuable contributions to the technical problems of exploration and navigation have been made by La Guarda Triás, cited in the bibliography. Alexandre Marques Lobato discovered two fragments of the instructions given to Cabral, a much needed but missing document. Useful also is his *A expansão portuguêsa de 1498 a 1530*. Myoko Makino contributes, along with others of the São Paulo school, valuable examinations of the texts of discovery documents. Captain Avelino Teixeira da Mota of the Portuguese navy has written extensively of exploration, with some of his works bearing on Brazil. José Custódio de Morais contributes worthwhile studies of wind patterns in the Atlantic and the alleged storms in the path of Cabral. Samuel Eliot Morison's many brilliant works may be read on this subject, but he is less detailed than Duarte Leite or Max Justo Guedes. Alexandre Gaspar de Naia reveals his conclusions in the titles of his articles: "Não é um mito a escola náutica criada e mantida pelo Infante D. Henrique em terra Algarvia," and "Quem foi o primeiro descobridor do Rio da Prata e da Argentina?" Rubens Viana Neiva contributed a fine study in "Ensaio de crítica náutica elisses sôbre Cabral." Charles E. Nowell in "The Discovery of Brazil——Accidental or Intentional?" leans toward "intentional." Sergio J. Pacifici published the letter King Manuel sent to Ferdinand and Isabella concerning Cabral's voyage. Damião Peres and T.O. Marcondes de Souza published sharp differences of opinion, Peres being pro-intentionality and Souza pro-chance discovery.

Duarte Pacheco Pereira's *Esmeraldo de Situ Orbis*, chapter 2, is often used to hold that he claimed to have discovered Brazil in 1498, or, as Duarte Leite asserts, Yucatan and the Caribbean. The Pereira accompanying Cabral was referred to as "O mozo," and since Duarte Pacheco Pereira was about 50 years old in 1500, he would hardly have been called "The Boy." Edgar Prestage, *The Portuguese Pioneers*, first published in 1933, is less useful today. David B. Quinn offers evidence for English discoverers in America between 1480 and 1494. J. Batalha Reis is highly critical of historians who do not accept Portuguese discovery of Brazil before 1448. Francis M. Rogers strongly upholds the Cortesão school of Portuguese priority in discoveries. Luciano Pereira da Silva, who wrote extensively on discoveries, upheld Duarte Pacheco Pereira as discoverer of Brazil in 1498. All the writings attributed to Vespucci are pertinent to the controversy regarding Brazil's discovery. Henry Vignaud's *Améric Vespuce*, is still a useful work. Louis-André Vigneras has made unique contributions to an understanding of the methods of financing exploration in Spain and the early voyages to the Brazil coast.

In many ways the most useful single work on discovery and the early period is Carlos Malheiro Dias, ed., *História da colonização porttuguesa do Brasil*, 3 vols., with valuable articles showing varied viewpoints by Jaime Cortesão, H. Lopes de Mendonça, Duarte Leite, the Vaz de Caminha letter, Luciano Pereira da Silva, and by Dias himself.

For works in English on discovery and all other aspects of Colonial Brazil the most important work—the *essential* work—is Francis A. Dutra, *A Guide to the History of Brazil, 1500—1822*. Dutra's work not only has a nearly complete listing, but also valuable and trenchant summaries of many works that are rare and seldom noted.

PORTUGUESE CURRENCY, WEIGHTS, AND MEASURES

Currency:

cruzado	=	400 réis
milréis	=	1,000 réis
oitava	=	1,600 réis

Weights and Measures:

arrôba	=	about 32 lbs.
quintal	=	4 arrôbas
vara	=	about 43 inches
braşc	=	about 6 feet

BIBLIOGRAPHY

Compiled by Mario Rodríguez, University of Southern California.

My good friend Bailey W. Diffie and I spent many hours together discussing books and historical controversies about Brazilian history during the three decades that I knew him. That experience served me well in compiling the present bibliography. He left us some materials: footnotes on the first two chapters, a highly informative appendix, and an extensive bibliography—in manuscript—which he apparently utilized in the last work he published with Professor Winius (University of Minnesota series). I also had the advantage of reading Bailey's drafts of the earlier chapters, which we discussed in great detail. The mere fact that Bailey was with me at least ten years at the University of Southern California revived my enthusiasm for a field that had been my expertise at Berkeley as a graduate student—the rivalry of Spain and Portugal in southern South America throughout the sixteenth and seventeenth centuries. I reread the present manuscript twice: the second time I jotted down all the names of chroniclers, authors, as well as noting his remarks on key documents and historiographical arguments. Bailey's close friendship with Dauril Alden, Francis A. Dutra, and Stuart Schwartz also led me to reread their major works for helpful bibliographical leads. Moreover, I recalled that my old colleague had twice borrowed my doctoral dissertation of 1952; it was useful for the earlier centuries. Knowing Bailey's high evaluation of Francis A. Dutra's work: *A Guide to the History of Brazil, 1500–1822* (Santa Barbara, 1980), I perused it to advantage. As a check on myself, I likewise examined carefully: *The Cambridge History of Latin America: Colonial Period* (2 vols., London, 1984), edited by Leslie Bethell.

From on high, let us hope that my dear colleague approves of my efforts. It has been a rewarding experience for me.

Abbeville, Claude d'. *Histoire de la mission des Pères Capucins en l'Isle de Maragnan. . .* (Paris, 1614).
Abreu, João Capistrano de. *O Descobrimento do Brasil.* (Rio de Janeiro, 1929).
———. *Caminhos antigos e povamento do Brasil.* (Rio de Janiero, 1930).
———. *Capítulos de história colonial.* 3rd ed. (Rio de Janeiro, 1934).
———. *Primeira visitação do Santo Oficio as partes do Brasil . . . 1591–92.* (Rio de Janeiro, 1935).
Acuña, Cristóbal de. *Nuevo descubrimiento del río de las Amazonas (1641).* (São Paulo, 1941).
Alden, Dauril. *Royal Government in Colonial Brazil. With Special Reference to the Administration of the Marquis of Lavradio, . . . 1769–1779.* (Berkeley, 1968).
———. "Economic Aspects of the Expulsion of the Jesuits from Brazil: A Preliminary Report," Henry H. Keith and S.F. Edwards, *Conflict and Continuity in Brazilian Society.* (University of Southern Carolina Press, 1969), pp. 25–65.
———. "Manoel Luis Vieira: An Entrepreneur in Rio de Janeiro During Brazil's Eighteenth-Century Agricultural Renaissance," *HAHR*, XXXIX, No. 4 (November, 1959), 521–537.
———. "The Population of Brazil in the late Eighteenth Century: A Preliminary Survey," *HAHR*, XLIII, May, 1963, 173–205.
———. "The Marquis of Pombal and the American Revolution," *The Americas*, XVII, April, 1961, 369–382.
———. "The Growth and Decline of Indigo Production in Colonial Brazil: A Study in Comparative Economic History," *Journal of Economic History*, XXV, March, 1965, 35–60.
——— and Warren Dean. (Eds.). *Essays concerning the socioeconomic history of Brazil and Portuguese India.* (Gainesville, 1977).
Albuquerque, Luis de. *Introdução a história dos descobrimentos.* (Coimbra, 1962).
Aldridge, A. Owen. (Ed.). *The Ibero-American Enlightenment.* (Urbana, 1971).
Alexandre de Gusmão e o Tratado de Madrid. 8 vols. (Rio de Janeiro, 1950–1959).
Almeida, Candido Mendes de. *Memórias para a história do extinto Estado do Maranhão.* 2 vols. (Rio de Janeiro, 1860–1874).
Almeida, Eduardo de Castro e. *Inventário dos documentos relativos ao Brasil exis-*

tentes no Archivo de Marinha e Ultramar de Lisboa. 8 vols. (Rio de Janeiro, 1913–1936).

Almeida, Fortunato de. *História de Portugal.* 6 vols. (Coimbra, 1922–1929).

Almeida, Luis Ferrand de. *A diplomacia portuguesa e os limites meridionais do Brasil, 1, 1493–1700.* (Coimbra, 1957).

Amaral, Luis. *História geral da agricultura brasileira.* 3 vols. (São Paulo, 1939–1940).

Amaro, José Aboal. *Amérigho Vespucci, ensayo de biografía crítica.* (Madrid, 1962).

Anchieta, Fr. José de. *Informações do Brasil e de suas Capitanias (1584).* (São Paulo, 1964).

Angelis, Pedro de. *Colección de obras y documentos relativos a la historia antigua y moderna de las provincias del Río de la Plata.* 2nd ed. 5 vols. (Buenos Aires, 1910).

Anon. Jesuit. "Sumário das armadas que se fizeram e guerras que se deram na conquista do rio Paraíba" (c. 1587) in *RIHGB,* 36/1 (1873), 13–14.

Antonil, André João. *Cultura e opuléncia do Brasil por suas drogas e minas (1711).* Andrée Mansuy, (Ed.). (Paris, 1968).

Anuário to Museu da Inconfidência. (Ouro Preto, 1953).

Arana, Henrique. *Expedición de Don Pedro de Cevallos al Río Grande y Río de la Plata.* (Río Grande, 1937).

Araujo, José de Sousa de Azevedo Pizarro e. *Memórias históricas da província do Rio de Janeiro.* 10 vols. (Rio de Janeiro, 1820–1822); 2nd ed. 9 vols. (Rio de Janeiro, 1945–1948).

Armitage, John. *History of Brazil, 1808–1831.* 2 vols. (London, 1836).

Athelstane, John Smith (Conde de Carnota). *Memoirs of the Marquis of Pombal; with Extracts from His Writings, and from Despatches in the State Paper Office.* 2 vols. (London, 1843).

Autos de devassa da inconfidência mineira. 7 vols. (Rio de Janeiro, 1936–1938).

Azarola Gil, Luis Enrique. *Contribución a la crónica de Colonia del Sacramento: La epopeya de Manuel Lobo.* (Madrid, 1931).

Azevedo, João Lúcio. (Ed.). *Cartas do Padre António Vieira.* 3 vols. (Coimbra, 1928).

———. *Épocas de Portugal Económico.* (Lisbon, 1929).

———. *História dos cristãos novos portugueses.* (Lisbon, 1921).

———. *O Marquez de Pombal e a sua época.* 2nd ed. (Lisbon, 1922).

Azevedo, Thales de. *Igreja e estado em tensão e crise.* (São Paulo, 1978).

Baião, Antonio, Hernani Cidade, and Manuel Murias. (Eds.). *Historia da expansão portuguesa no mundo.* 3 vols. (Lisbon, 1937–40).

——— and Malheiro Dias. "A expedição de Christóvam Jacques," *HCP,* III, 59–91.; also see Baião's "O Comercio do pau Brazil," *ibid.,* II, 317–347.

Balbi, Adrien, *Essai statistique sur le royaume de Portugal et d'Algarve.* . . . 2 vols. (Paris, 1822).

Barros, Henrique da Gama. *Historia da administração pública em Portugal nos séculos XII–XV.* 2nd ed. 11 vols. (Lisbon, 1945–1954).

Beaglehole, J.C. *The Exploration of the Pacific.* 3rd revised ed. (Stanford, 1966).

Beazley, Charles Raymond. *Prince Henry the Navigator.* (London, 1895).
―――. *The Dawn of Modern Geography.* 3 vols. (London and Oxford, 1897–1906).
Bermejo, Antonio de la Rica. *La Colonia del Sacramento.* (Montevideo, 1940).
Berredo, Bernardo Pereira de. *Annaes históricos do Estado do Maranhão.* (Lisbon, 1749).
Bernstein, Harry. "The Lisbon *Juiz do Povo* and the Independence of Brazil, 1750–1822: An Essay on Luso-Brazilian Populism," in Keith and Edwards, (Eds.), *Conflict and Continuity,* pp. 191–226.
Betendorf, João Felippe. *Chrónica da missão dos Padres da Companhia de Jesus no Estado do Maranhão, Revista IHGB,* vol. 119 (1909, written initially around 1700).
Bettencourt, E.A. *Descobrimentos, Guerras e conquistas dos portuguêses em Terras do ultramar nos séculos XV e XVI.* (Lisbon, 1881–1882).
Bomfim, Manoel. *O Brasil.* Nova edição. (São Paulo, 1940).
Boogaart, E. van den. (Ed.). *Johan Maurits van Nassau-Siegen, 1604–1679.* (The Hague, 1979).
Boxer, Charles R. *A Great Luso-Brazilian Figure. Padre Antônio Vieira, S.J., 1608–1697.* The Fourth Canning House Annual Lecture. (London, 1957).
―――. *Four Centuries of Portuguese Expansion, 1415–1825: A Succinct Survey.* (Johannesburg, 1961).
―――. *Portuguese Society in the Tropics. The Municipal Councils of Goa, Macao, Bahia, and Luanda, 1510–1800.* (Madison, 1965).
―――. *Race Relations in the Portuguese Colonial Empire, 1415–1825.* (Oxford, 1963).
―――. *Salvador de Sá and the Struggle for Brazil and Angola, 1602–1686.* (London, 1952).
―――. *The Golden Age of Brazil 1695–1750. Growing Pains of a Colonial Society.* (Berkeley, 1962).
―――. *The Portuguese Seaborne Empire, 1415–1825.* (New York, 1969).
―――. "Some Reflections on the Historiography of Colonial Brazil," Dauril Alden, (Ed.), *Colonial Roots of Modern Brazil.* (Berkeley, 1973), pp. 3–15.
―――. "Padre Antonio Vieira, S.J. and the Institution of the Brazil Company in 1649," *HAHR,* XXIX, No. 4 (November, 1949), 474–497.
Brandão, Ambrosio Fernandes. *Os diálogos das grandezas do Brasil (1618).* (Ed.). José Antonio Gonsalves de Mello. (Recife, 1962; 2nd ed., 1966).
Brito, Lemos. *Pontos de partida para a história econômica do Brasil.* 2nd ed. (São Paulo, 1939).
Brito, Mendes de. *O Infante D. Henrique, 1394–1460.* (Lisbon, 1942).
Brito, João Rodrigues de. *Cartas econômico-políticas sobre a agricultura e o comércio da Bahia (1807).* (Lisbon, 1821; Bahia, 1924).
Brochado, José Idalino Ferreira da Costa. *Historiógrafos dos descobrimentos.* (Lisbon, 1960).
―――. *Infante D. Henrique.* (Lisbon, 1942).
Buenos Aires. Archivo General de la Nación. *Documentos referentes a la guerra*

de la independencia . . . Campaña del Brasil. Antecedentes coloniales. Series II, 3 vols. (Buenos Aires, 1931–1941).

Burns, E. Bradford. (Ed.). *A Documentary History of Brazil.* (New York, 1966).

———. *Nationalism in Brazil: A Historical Survey.* (New York, 1968).

———. "Introduction to the Brazilian Jesuit Letters," *Mid-America,* 44:3 (July, 1962), pp. 172–186.

———. "The Enlightenment in Two Colonial Brazilian Libraries," *The Journal of the History of Ideas,* 25:3 (July-September 1964), pp. 430–438.

———. "The Role of Azeredo Coutinho in the Enlightenment of Brazil," *HAHR,* 44:2 (May, 1964), pp. 145–160.

———. "The 'Kaffirs of Europe,' the Renaissance, and the Enlightenment," in C.R. Boxer, *The Portuguese Seaborne Empire, 1415–1825.* (London, 1969), 340–366.

———. "The Intellectuals as Agents of Change and the Independence of Brazil, 1724–1822," A.J.R. Russell-Wood, (Ed.), *From Colony to Nation: Essays on the Independence of Brazil.* (Baltimore, 1975), pp. 211–246.

Butler, Ruth Lapham. "Duarte da Costa, Second Governor-General of Brazil," *Mid-America,* 25:3 (July, 1943), pp. 163–179.

———. "Mem de Sá, Third Governor-General of Brazil, 1557–1572," *ibid.,* 26:2 (April, 1944), pp. 111–137.

———. "Tomé de Sousa, First Governor-General of Brazil, 1549–1553," *ibid.,* 24:4 (October, 1942), pp. 229–251.

Cabral, Alfred do Vale. (Ed.). *Cartas Jesuíticas.* 3 vols. (Rio de Janeiro, 1931).

Caetano, Marcelo. *De Conselho Ultramarino ao Conselho do Imperio.* (Lisbon, 1943).

———. "O governo e a administração central após a restauração," *História de expansão portuguesa no mundo,* III:i (Lisbon, 1940), 189–198.

Caldas, José António. *Noticia geral de toda esta capitania da Bahia desde o seu descobrimento ate o prezente anno de 1759.* Facs. ed. (Bahia, 1949).

Calmon, Pedro. *História do Brasil.* 7 vols. (Rio de Janeiro, 1959).

———. *História da civilização brasileira.* 3rd ed. (São Paulo, 1937).

———. *História social do Brasil.* 2nd ed. 3 vols. (São Paulo, 1937–1940).

Calógeras, João Pandiá. *As minas do Brasil e sua legislação.* 3 vols. (Rio de Janeiro, 1904–1905).

———. *Formação histórica do Brasil.* 3rd ed. (São Paulo, 1938).

Calvo, Carlos. (Ed.). *Colección completa de los tratados, convenciones, capitulaciones, armisticios y otros actos diplomáticos de todos los estados de la América latina.* 11 vols. (Paris, 1862–1869).

Caminha, Pero Vaz de. *Carta a el Rey D. Manuel.* (Ed.), Leonardo Arroyo. (São Paulo, 1963).

Campos, José Moreira de. *O Infante D. Henrique e os descobrimentos dos portugueses. (Da fantasia a realidade).* (Lisbon, 1957).

Canabrava, Alice P. *O comércio português no Rio da Prata, 1580–1640.* (São Paulo, 1944).

Cardim, Fernão. *Tratados da terra e gente do Brasil.* 3rd ed. (São Paulo, 1978).

Cardozo, Manoel (da Silveira Soares). "A History of Mining in Colonial Brazil, 1500–1750," (Ph.D. Dissertation: Stanford University, 1939).

———. "Azeredo Coutinho and the Intellectual Ferment of His Times," in Keith and Edwards, (Ed.), *Conflict and Continuity*, pp. 72–103.

———. "The Last Adventure of Fernão Dias Pais (1674–1681)," *HAHR*, 26:4 (November, 1946), pp. 467–479.

———. "The Brazilian Gold Rush," *The Americas*, III, No. 2 (October, 1946), 137–160.

———. "The Collection of Fifth in Brazil, 1695–1709," *HAHR*, XX, No. 3 (August, 1940), 359–379.

———. "The Guerra dos Emboabas, Civil War in Minas Gerais, 1708–1709," *HAHR*, XXII, No. 3 (August, 1942), 470–492.

———. "Dom Rodrigo de Castel-Blanco and the Brazilian El Dorado, 1673–1682," *The Americas*, 7/2 (October, 1944), 131–59.

Carnaxide, Visconde de (Antonio de Sousa Pedroso Carnaxide). *O Brasil na administração pombalina (economia e política externa)*. (Rio de Janeiro, São Paulo, 1940).

Carneiro, Edison. *Guerras de los Palmares*. (Mexico, 1946).

Carreira, António. *As companhias pombalinas de navegação, comércio e tráfico de escravos entre a costa africana e o Nordeste brasileiro*. (Bissau, 1969).

Carvajal, Gaspar de. *Descubrimiento del río de las Amazonas (1542)*. Trans., Bertram T. Lee, as *The discovery of Amazon*, (New York, 1934).

Castro, Eugénio de. *A expedição de Martim Afonso de Sousa*. (Rio de Janeiro, 1932).

———. (Ed.). *Diario da navegação de Pero Lopes de Sousa (1530–1532)*. 2 vols. (Rio de Janeiro, 1940).

Chaunu, Pierre. *L'Expansion européenne du XIIIᵉ au XVᵉ siècle*. (Paris, 1969).

———. *Conquête et exploitation des nouveaux mondes*. (Paris, 1969).

———. "Brésil et Atlantique au xvii siècle," *Annales Economie, Sociétés Civilisations*, XVI (November-December, 1961), 1176–1207.

Chapman, Charles E. "Palmares: The Negro Numantia," *The Journal of Negro History*, 3:1 (January, 1918), pp. 29–32.

Cheke, Marcus. *Dictator of Portugal. A Life of the Marquis of Pombal, 1699–1782*. (London, 1938).

Cheyney, Edward P. *The Dawn of a New Era, 1250–1453*. (New York, 1962).

Christelow, Allan. "Great Britain and the Trades from Cádiz and Lisbon to Spanish America and Brazil, 1759–1783," *HAHR*, XXVII, 1947, 2–29.

Cidade, Hernani. *A literatura portuguesa e a expansão ultramarina: As ideias, os sentimentos, as formas de arte*. (Lisbon, 1943).

Cintra, Luis Filipe Lindley. (Ed.). *Actas. III Colóquio Internacional de Estudos Luso-Brasileiros*. 2 vols. (Lisbon, 1959–1960).

Coaracy, Vivaldo. *O Rio de Janeiro no século XVII*. 2nd ed. (Rio de Janeiro, 1965).

Coelho, P.M. Laranjo. (Ed.). *Cartas de el-rei d. João IV ao conde da Vidigueira (marqués de Niza) embaixador em Francia*. 2 vols. (Lisbon, 1940–1942).

Cohen, Martin A. (Ed.). *The Jewish Experience in Latin America. Selected Studies from the Publications of the American Jewish Historical Society.* 2 vols. (New York, 1971).

Congresso Internacional de História dos Descobrimentos. Actas, 6 vols. (Lisbon, 1960–1961).

Comissão Executiva dos Centenários. *A restauração e o império colonial português.* (Lisbon, 1940).

Condamine, Charles Marie de la. *A Succinct Abridgement of a Voyage Made within the Inland Part of South America; From the Coasts of the South-Sea, to the Coasts of Brazil and Guiana, down the River of Amazons.* (London, 1747).

Conrad, Robert. *Brazilian slavery: an annotated research bibliography.* (Boston, 1977).

Cortesão, Amando. *Cartografia e cartógrafos portuguêses dos séculos XV e XVI.* 2 vols. (Lisbon, 1935).

Cortesão, Jaime. *A Expedição de Pedro Alvares Cabral e o descobrimento do Brasil.* (Lisbon, 1922).

———. *Alexandre de Gusmão e o Tratado de Madrid.* 8 vols. (Rio de Janeiro, 1950–9).

———. *A carta de Pero Vaz de Caminha.* (Rio de Janeiro, 1943).

———. *A política de sigilo nos descobrimentos.* (Lisbon, 1960).

———. *Descobrimentos portuguéses.* 2 vols. (Lisbon, 1960–62).

———. *Do Tratado de Madrid à conquista dos Sete Povos (1750–1802).* (Rio de Janeiro, 1969).

———. *Introdução a história das bandeiras.* 2 vols. (Lisbon, 1964).

———. *Jesuítas e bandeirantes no Guaíra (1594–1640).* (Rio de Janeiro, 1951).

———. *Jesuítas e bandeirantes no Itatim (1596–1760).* (Rio de Janeiro, 1952).

———. *Rapôso Tavares e a formação territorial do Brasil.* (Rio de Janeiro, 1958).

——— and Hélio Vianna. *Manuscritos da Coleção De Angelis.* (Rio de Janeiro, 1951–1970).

Costa, Afonso. "Achegas genealógicas," *Revista de Instituto Histórico e Geográfico da Bahia,* LXI (1935), 69–460.

———. "Genealogia Baíana," *RIHGB,* CXCI (1946), 1–279.

Costa, A. Fontoura da. *A ciência náutica dos portuguêses na época dos descobrimentos.* (Lisbon, 1958).

Costa, Padre Avelino de Jesus da. (Ed.). *Colóquio Internacional de Estudos Luso-Brasileiros.* 5 vols. (Coimbra, 1965–1968).

Costa, Didio J. da. *O Brasil e o ciclo das grandes navegações.* (Rio de Janeiro, 1940).

Coutinho, José Joaquim da Cunha de Azeredo. *Ensaio econômico sobre o comércio de Portugal e suas colônias (1794)* in *Obras econômicas,* (Ed.), Sérgio Buarque de Holanda. (São Paulo, 1966).

Dampier, William. *A Voyage to New Holland, & c. In the Year 1699.* (London, 1703).

Davenport, Frances Gardiner. (Ed.). *European Treaties Bearing on the History of the United States and its Dependencies to 1648.* (Washington, D.C., 1917).

Davidson, David M. "How the Brazilian West was Won: Freelance and State on the Mato Grosso Frontier, 1737–1752," in D. Alden (Ed.), *Colonial roots of Modern Brazil*. (Berkeley and Los Angeles, 1973), 61–106.

Davidson, Theresa Sherrer. "The Brazilian Inheritance of Roman Law," in James B. Watson, *et al. Brazil: Papers Presented in the Institute for Brazilian Studies, Vanderbilt University*. (Nashville, 1953), pp. 59–90.

Degler, Carl N. *Neither Black Nor White. Slavery and Race Relations in Brazil and the United States*. (New York, 1971).

———. "Slavery in Brazil and the United States: An Essay in Comparative History," *The American Historical Review*, 75:4 (April, 1970), pp. 1004–1028.

Denevan, William M. "The aboriginal population of Amazonia," in Denevan (Ed.), *The native population of the Americas in 1492*. (Madison, 1976), 205–234.

Dias, Carlos Malheiro. (Ed.). *História da colonização portuguesa do Brasil*. 3 vols. (Oporto, 1921–1926) (Hereafter HCP). This collaborative work provides an extensive treatment of sixteenth-century Brazil and the background of its discovery. See particularly Jaime Cortesão, "A expedição de Cabral," II, 1–39; H. Lopes de Mendonça, "De Reŝtelo a Vera Cruz," II, 43–71; and Carlos Malheiro Dias, "A Semana de Vera Cruz," II, 75–169, dealing with the expedition after it reached Brazil. Also see, Duarte Leite, "A exploração do litoral do Brasil na cartografia da primeira década de século XVI," II, 393–440; C. Malheiro Dias, "Introdução," to Vol. III, pp. l–lxiii; and his "A metrópole e suas conquistas nos reinados de D. João III, D. Sebastião e Cardeal D. Henrique," III, 1–47.

Dias, Manuel Nunes. *Fomento e mercantilismo. A Companhia Geral de Comércio do Grão Pará e Maranhão (1755–1778)*. (São Paulo, 1971).

———. *O capitalismo monárquico português (1415–1549)*. 2 vols. (Coimbra, 1963).

———. *O descobrimento do Brasil*. (São Paulo, 1967).

Diffie, Bailey W. *Prelude to Empire: Portugal Overseas before Henry the Navigator*. (Lincoln, 1960).

———. "Bibliography of the Principal Published Guides to Portuguese Archives and Libraries," *Actas do I Colóquio internacional de estudos Luso-brasileiros*. (Nashville, 1953), 181–88.

———. "Foreigners in Portugal and the 'Policy of Silence,' " *Terrae Incognitae. The Annals of the Society for the History of Discoveries*. 1 (1969), pp. 23–34.

———. "The Legal 'Privileges' of the Foreigners in Portugal and Sixteenth-Century Brazil," in Keith and Edwards, (Eds.), *Conflict and Continuity*, pp. 1–19.

Documentos para a história do açúcar. 3 vols. (Rio de Janeiro, 1954–63).

"Documentos relativos a Mem de Sá, governador-geral do Brasil," *ABNRJ*, XXVII (1905), 127–280.

Documentos sobre o tratado de 1750. ABNRJ, LII and LIII (1930–1931).

Dominguez, Luis L. (Ed.). *The Conquest of the River Plate (1535–1555). I. Voyage of Ulrich Schmidt to the Rivers La Plata and Paraguai. From the Original German Edition, 1567. II. The Commentaries of Alvar Núñez Cabeza de Vaca. From the Original Spanish Edition, 1555*. (London, 1891).

Duffy, James. *Shipwreck & Empire*. (Cambridge, Massachusetts, 1955).

Dutra, Francis A. "Matias de Albuquerque: A Seventeenth-Century *Capitão-Mor* of Pernambuco and Governor General of Brazil," (Ph.D., New York University, 1968).

―――. *A Guide to the History of Brazil, 1500–1822.* (Santa Barbara and Oxford, England, 1980).

―――. "Centralization vs. Donatorial Privilege: Pernambuco, 1602–1630," Dauril Alden, (Ed.), *Colonial Roots of Modern Brazil.* (Berkeley, 1973), pp. 19–60.

―――. "A New Look into Diogo Botelho's Stay in Pernambuco, 1602–1603," *Luso-Brazilian Review*, 4:1 (Summer, 1967), pp. 27–34.

―――. "Duarte Coelho Pereira, First Lord-Proprietor of Pernambuco: The Beginning of a Dynasty," *The Americas*, 29:4 (April, 1973), pp. 415–441.

―――. *Matias de Albuquerque.* (Recife, 1976).

Eça, Raul d'. "Colonial Brazil As an Element in the Early Diplomatic Negotiations between the United States and Portugal, 1776–1808," in A. Curtis Wilgus, (Ed.), *Colonial Hispanic America.* (Washington, D.C., 1936), pp. 551–558.

Edmundson, George. (Ed.). *Journal of the Travels and Labours of Father Samuel Fritz in the River of the Amazons Between 1686 and 1723.* (London, 1922).

―――. "The Voyage of Pedro Teixeira on the Amazon from Pará to Quito and Back, 1637–39," *Transactions of the Royal Historical Society*, Fourth Series. (London, 1920), III, 52–71.

―――. "The Dutch Power in Brazil (1624–1654). Part I. The Struggle for Bahia (1624–1627)," *The English Historical Review*, 11:42 (April, 1896), pp. 231–259; Part II, "The First Conquests," *ibid.*, 14:56 (October, 1899), 676–699; cont'd, *ibid.*, 15:57 (January, 1900), pp. 38–57.

Ellis, Myriam. *O monopólio do sal no Estado do Brazil (1631–1801).* (São Paulo, 1955).

―――. *A Baleia no Brasil colonial.* (São Paulo, 1969).

Ennes, Ernesto. *As guerras nos Palmares.* (São Paulo, 1938).

―――. "The Palmares 'Republic' of Pernambuco, Its Final Destruction, 1697," *The Americas*, 5:2 (October, 1948), pp. 200–216.

Espinosa, J. Manuel. "Fernão Cardim, Jesuit Humanist of Colonial Brazil," *Mid-America*, 24:4 (October, 1942), pp. 252–271.

―――. "Gouveia: Jesuit Lawgiver in Brazil," *ibid.*, 24:1 (January, 1942), pp. 27–60.

―――. "Luis da Grã, Mission Builder and Educator of Brazil," *ibid.*, 24:3 (July, 1942), pp. 188–216.

Evreux, Yves d'. *Voyage dans le nord du Brésil (1614).* (Paris, 1864).

Ferreira, Waldemar Martins. *História do direito brasileiro.* 4 vols. (São Paulo, 1956 ff).

Figueredo, Fidelino de. "The Geographical Discoveries and Conquests of the Portuguese," *HAHR*, 6:1–3 (February-August, 1926), pp. 47–70.

Fisher, H.E.S. *The Portugal Trade. A Study of Anglo-Portuguese Commerce, 1700–1770.* (London, 1971).

Fleiuss, Max. *História administrativa do Brasil.* 2nd ed. (São Paulo, 1925).

Flory, Rae Jean Dell. "Bahian Society in the Mid-Colonial Period: The Sugar Planters, Tobacco Growers, Merchants, and Artisans of Salvador and the Reconcavo, 1680–1725," (Ph.D. Dissertation: The University of Texas at Austin, 1978).

Flory, Rae and David Grant Smith. "Bahian Merchants and Planters in the Seventeenth and Early Eighteenth Centuries," *HAHR*, 58:4 (November, 1978), pp. 571–594.

Fonseca, António José Victoriano Borges da. "Nobiliarchia pernambucana," *ABNRJ*, 47 (1925) and 48 (1926) (Rio de Janeiro, 1935), I:462.

Ford, J.D.M. and L.G. Moffatt, *Letters of John III, King of Portugal, 1521–1557.* (Cambridge, Massachusetts, 1931).

Francis, A.D. *The Methuens and Portugal, 1691–1708.* (Cambridge, 1966).

Franco, Carvalho. *Bandeiras e bandeirantes de São Paulo.* (São Paulo, 1940).

Freehafer, Virginia. "Domingos Jorge Velho. Conqueror of Brazilian Backlands," *The Americas*, 27:2 (October, 1970), pp. 161–184.

Freitas, Gustavo de. *A Companhia Geral do Comércio do Brasil.* (São Paulo, 1951).

Freitas, Jordão de. "A expedição de Martim Afonso de Souza," *HCP*, III, 97–164.

Freyre, Francisco de Brito. *História da guerra brasílica.* (Lisbon, 1675).

Freyre, Gilberto. *The Masters and the Slaves. A Study in the Development of Brazilian Civilization.* (Translated from the Portuguese of the Fourth and Definitive Edition by Samuel Putnam. New York, 1946).

―――. *Casa-Grande e Senzala.* 3rd ed. (Rio de Janeiro, 1938).

Furlong, Guillermo. *Misiones y sus pueblos de guaraníes.* (Buenos Aires, 1962).

Furtado, Celso. *The Economic Growth of Brazil. A Survey from Colonial to Modern Times.* (Trans. Ricardo W. de Aguiar and Eric Charles Drysdale. Berkeley and Los Angeles, 1963).

Furtado, Mendonça. *A Amazonia na ea pombalina: Correspondência inédita . . . , 1751–1759.* (Ed.), Marcos Carneiro de Mendonça. 3 vols. (Rio de Janeiro, 1964?).

Gaffarel, Paul. *Histoire de Brésil français au XVIe siècle.* (Paris, 1878).

Gandía, Enrique de. *Antecedentes diplomáticos de las expediciones de Juan Díaz de Solís, Sebastián Caboto, y don Pedro de Mendoza.* (Buenos Aires, 1935).

Garcia, Rodolfo. *Ensaio sobre a história política e administrativa do Brasil (1500–1810).* (Rio de Janeiro, 1956).

―――. "Os Judeus no Brasil colonial," in *Os Judeus na História do Brasil.* (Rio de Janeiro, 1936), pp. 9–46.

Godinho, Vitorino Magalhães. *A economia dos descobrimentos henriquinos.* (Lisbon, 1962).

―――. *Documentos sobre a expansão portuguesa.* 3 vols. (Lisbon, 1943–1956).

―――. *L'Economie de l'empire portuguais aux XVe et XVIe siècles.* (Paris, 1969).

Goldberg, Isaac. *Brazilian Literature.* (New York, 1922).

Gonneville, Binot Paulmier de. *Relation authentique.* (Paris, 1869).

Greenlee, William Brooks. *The Voyage of Pero Alvares Cabral to Brazil and India.* (Hakluyt Society, London, 1938, Series 2, vol. 81).

————. "The First Half Century of Brazilian History," *Mid-America*, XXV (April, 1943), 91–120.

————. "The Captaincy of the Second Portuguese Voyage to Brazil, 1501–1502," *The Americas*, 2:1 (July, 1945), pp. 3–12.

Goulart, Mauricio. *A escravidão africana no Brasil.* 3rd ed. (São Paulo, 1975).

Guedes, Max Justo. *Descobrimento do Brasil.* (Rio de Janeiro, 1966).

Hakluyt, Richard. *The Principal Navigations Voyages Traffiques & Discoveries of the English Nation Made by Sea or Over-land to the Remote and Farthest Distant Quarters of the Earth at any time within the compasse of these 1600 Yeeres.* 3 vols. (London, 1598–1600).

Handelmann, Henrique. *História do Brasil.* (Eds. and Trans.: Lucia Furquim Lahmeyer, Betholdo Klinger, and Basilio de Magalhães), *RIHGB.* (Rio de Janeiro, 1931), pp. 137–168.

Hanson, Carl A. *Dissertations on Iberian and Latin American History.* (Troy, New York, 1975).

————. *Economy and society in Baroque Portugal, 1668–1703.* (Minneapolis, 1981).

————. "Monopoly and contraband in the Portuguese tobacco trade," *Luso-Brazilian Review*, 19/2 (Winter, 1968), 149–68.

Harrisse, Henry. *The Diplomatic History of America. Its First Chapter: 1452–1493–1494.* (London, 1897).

Hemming, John. *Red Gold. The Conquest of the Brazilian Indians.* (Cambridge, 1978).

Herculano, Alexandre. *History of the Origins and Establishment of the Inquisition in Portugal.* John C. Branner, trans. (Stanford, 1926).

Hoehne, F.C. *Botânica e agricultura no Brasil no século XVI.* (São Paulo, 1937).

Holanda, Sergio Buarque de. (Ed.). *História geral da civilização brasileira, I, A época colonial.* 2 vols. (São Paulo, 1960).

————. *Monções.* (Rio de Janeiro, 1945) and *Caminhos e fronteiras.* (Rio de Janeiro, 1957).

————. "Movimentos da população em São Paulo no Século XVII," in *Revista do Instituto de Estudos Brasileiros*, 1 (1966), 51–111.

————. *Raizes do Brasil.* 5th ed. (Rio de Janeiro, 1969).

Hoornaert, E. (Ed.). *História da Igreja no Brasil.* 2nd ed. (Petropolis, 1979).

Ibarguen, Roberto. "The War of Mascate, 1710–1715: Urbanizing Catalyst in the Development of Recife, Brazil," *Latinamericanist.* Gainesville, Florida, vol. IV, No. 3, (February 15, 1969), 1–2 , a digest of a projected Ph.D. dissertation at the University of Florida.

"Informação sobre as minas do Brasil," *ABNRJ*, LVII (1935), 155–186.

Jaboatão, Frei Antonio de Santa Maria. *Chrônica dos frades menores da Província de Santo António do Brasil.* 2nd ed. 2 vols. (Rio de Janeiro, 1858–1859).

Jacobsen, Jerome V. "Jesuit Founders in Portugal and Brazil," *Mid-America*, 24:1 (January, 1942), pp. 3–26.

————. "Nóbrega of Brazil," *ibid.*, 24:3 (July, 1942), pp. 151–187.

Jayne, C.K. *Vasco da Gama and His Successors: 1460–1580.* (London, 1970).

Johnson, Allan. *Sharecroppers of the Sertão.* (Stanford, 1970).

James, Preston E. *Latin America. A Human Geography.* (New York, 1942).

Johnson, H.B. "The donatary captaincy in historical perspective: Portuguese backgrounds to the settlement of Brazil," *HAHR*, 52 (1972), 203–14.

José de Anchieta, Cartas, informações, fragmentos históricos e sermões. (Ed.), Antônio de Alcántara Machado. (Rio de Janeiro, 1933).

Julien, Charles-André. *Les Voyages de découverte et les premiers éstablissements (XV-XVI siècles).* (Paris, 1948).

Júnior, Alfredo Ellis. *A evolução da economia paulista e suas causas.* (São Paulo, 1938).

———. *Meio século de bandeirismo.* (São Paulo, 1948).

———. *O bandeirismo paulista.* 3rd ed. (São Paulo, 1938).

Júnior, Augusto de Lima. *Pequena história da inconfidência de Minas Gerais.* 3rd ed. (Belo Horizonte, 1968).

———. *História dos diamantes nas Minas Gerais.* (Lisbon and Rio de Janeiro, 1945).

Júnior, José Ribeiro. *Colonização e monopólio no Nordeste Brasileiro. A Companhia Geral de Pernambuco e Paraíba (1759–1780).* (São Paulo, 1976).

Karsten, R. *The civilization of the South American Indians, with special reference to magic and religion.* (New York, 1926).

Kayserling, M. *Biblioteca Española-Portuguesa-Judaica.* (Strasbourg, 1890).

Keith, Henry H. "New World Interlopers: The Portuguese in the Spanish West Indies, From the Discovery to 1640," *The Americas*, 25:4 (April, 1969), pp. 360–371.

——— and S.F. Edwards. (Eds.). *Conflict and Continuity in Brazilian Society.* (Columbia, South Carolina, 1969).

Kieman, Mathias. *The Indian policy of Portugal in the Amazon region, 1614–1693.* (Washington, D.C., 1954).

———. "The *Conselho Ultramarino's* First Legislative Attempts to Solve the Indian Question in America, 1643–1647," *The Americas*, 14:3 (January, 1958), pp. 259–271.

Klein, Herbert S. "The Colored Freedmen in Brazilian Slave Society," *Journal of Social History*, 3 (1969), 30–52.

Knivet, Anthony. *The Admirable Adventures and Strange Fortunes of Master Antonie Knivet . . . (1591)*, in Samuel Purchas, *Hakluytus Posthumus or Purchas his pilgrimes* (1625), pt 2, bk 6, ch. 7, (Hakluyt Society, 20 vols., Glasgow, 1906).

Koster, Henry. *Travels in Brazil.* (London, 1816); Louis-François de Tollenare, *Notas dominicais tomadas durante uma viagem em Portugal e no Brasil em 1816, 1817, e 1818.* (Bahia, 1956).

Kratz, Guillermo. *El tratado hispano-portugués de Límites de 1750 y sus consecuencias.* (Rome, 1954).

Kubler, George. *Portuguese Plain Architecture. Between Spices and Diamonds, 1521–1706.* (Middletown, Connecticut, 1972).

——— and Martin Soria. *Art and Architecture in Spain and Portugal and their American Dominions, 1500–1800.* (Baltimore, 1959).

Lafuente Machain, Ricardo de. *Los portugueses en Buenos Aires (Siglo XVII).* (Madrid, 1931).

————. *Buenos Aires en el siglo XVII*. (Buenos Aires, 1944).

Laguarda Trías, Rolando A. *La aportación científica de mallorquines y portugueses a la cartografía náutica en los siglos XIV al XVI*. (Madrid, 1963).

Lane, Frederic C. "The Mediterranean Spice Trade; Further Evidence of Its Revival in the Sixteenth Century," *American Historical Review*, 45:581–590 (1939–1940).

————. "Tonnages, Medieval and Modern," *Economic History Review*, 2nd series, 17 no. 2:214–233 (1964).

————. "Pepper Prices before Da Gama," *Journal of Economic History*, 28:590–597 (December, 1968).

Leite, Duarte. *História dos descobrimentos*. 2 vols. (Lisbon, 1958–1961).

————. *Os falsos precursores de Álvares Cabral*. 2nd ed. (Lisbon, 1950).

Leite, Serafim. (Ed.). *História da Companhia de Jesus no Brasil*. 10 vols. (Rio de Janiero, 1938–1950).

————. *Cartas do Brasil e mais escritos do Padre Manuel da Nóbrega*. (Coimbra, 1955).

Léry, Jean de. *Histoire d'un voyage fait en la terre du Brésil*. (La Rochelle, 1578).

Levillier, Roberto. *Américo Vespucio - El nuevo mundo*. (Buenos Aires, 1951).

Ley, Charles David. (Ed. and Trans.). *Portuguese Voyages, 1498–1663*. (New York, 1947).

Lima, Manoel de Oliveira. *Pernambuco e seu desenvolvimento histórico*. (Leipzig, 1895).

Lisboa, João Francisco. *Crónica do Brasil Colonial: Apontamentos para a história do Maranhão*. (Petropolis, 1976).

Livermore, H.V. *A History of Portugal*. (Cambridge, 1947).

Lobo, Eulalia Maria Lahmeyer. *Administração colonial luso-espanhola nas Américas*. (Rio de Janeiro, 1952).

————. *História do Rio de Janeiro (Do capital comercial ao capital industrial e financeiro)*. 2 vols. (Rio de Janeiro, 1978).

————. *Processo administrativo Ibero-Americano*. (Rio de Janeiro, 1962).

Luis, Washington. *Capitania de São Paulo*. (São Paulo, 1938).

Lyra, A. Tavares de. *Organisação política e administrativa do Brasil*. (São Paulo, 1941).

Machado, José Pedro and Viriato Campos. *Vasco da Gama e a sua viagem de Descobrimento*. (Lisbon, 1969).

Maclachlan, Colin M. "The Indian Labor Structure in the Portuguese Amazon, 1700–1800," Dauril Alden, (Ed.), *Colonial Roots of Modern Brazil*. (Berkeley, 1973), pp. 199–230.

Magalhães, Basilio de. *Expansão geográphica do Brasil colonial* 2nd ed. (São Paulo, 1935).

Magnusson, Magnus and Herman Palsson. *The Vinland Sagas*. (Baltimore, 1959).

Malheiro, A.M. Perdigão. *A escravidão no Brasil: ensaio histórico, jurídico e social*. 3 vols. (Rio de Janeiro, 1866/7) (new ed., 1944).

Manchester, Alan K. *British Pre-eminence in Brazil—Its Rise and Decline*. (Chapel Hill, 1933).

_____. "The Rise of the Brazilian Aristocracy," *HAHR*, XI (May, 1931), 145–168.

Marcílio, M.L. *La ville de São Paulo: peuplement et population, 1750–1850 (d'après les régistres paroissiaux et les recensements anciens)*. (Rouen, 1968).

_____. *Demografia histórica*. (São Paulo, 1977); (French ed., Paris, 1979).

_____ and L. Lisanti. "Problèmes de l'histoire quantitative du Brèsil: métrologie et démographie," in Centre National de la Recherche Scientifique, *L'histoire quantitative du Brésil de 1800 à 1930*. (Paris, 1973).

Marchant, Alexander. *From Barter to Slavery: The Economic Relations of Portuguese and Indians in the Settlement of Brazil, 1500–1580*. (Baltimore, 1942).

_____. "Aspects of the Enlightenment in Brazil," in Arthur P. Whitaker, (Ed.), *Latin America and the Enlightenment*. 2nd ed. (Ithaca, New York, 1961), pp. 95–118.

_____. "Feudal and Capitalistic Elements in the Portuguese Settlement of Brazil," *HAHR*, 22:3 (August, 1942), pp. 493–512.

_____. "Tiradentes in the Conspiracy of Minas," *HAHR*, 21:2 (May, 1941), pp. 239–257.

Markham, C.R. (Trans.). *Expeditions into the Valley of the Amazons*. (Hakluyt Society, 24; London, 1859).

Marques, António H. de Oliveira. *History of Portugal*. 2 vols. (New York and London, 1972).

_____. *Daily Life in Portugal in the Late Middle Ages*. (Trans.), L.S. Wyatt. (Madison, Milwaukee, and London, 1971).

Martins, J.P. Oliveira. *Les explorations des portugais antérieures à la découverte de L'Amerique*. (Paris, 1893).

Mattos, Anibal. *Joseph de Anchieta*. (Belo Horizonte, 1935).

Mattoso, Kátia M. Queiros. *Etre esclave au Brésil, XVIe–XIXe siècles*. (Paris, 1979).

Mauro, Frédèric. *Le Portugal et l'Atlantique au xviie siecle, 1570–1670*. (Paris, 1960).

_____. (Ed.). *Le Bresil au XVIIe siècle*. (Coimbra, 1963).

Maxwell, Kenneth R. *Conflicts and Conspiracies: Brazil and Portugal 1750–1808*. (Cambridge, 1973).

_____. "The Generation of the 1790s and the Idea of Luso-Brazilian Empire," Dauril Alden, (Ed.), *Colonial Roots of Modern Brazil*. (Berkeley, 1973), pp. 107–144.

_____. "Pombal and the Nationalization of the Luso-Brazilian Economy," *HAHR*, 48:4 (November, 1968), pp. 608–631.

Mecham, John Lloyd. *Church and State in Latin America*. (Chapel Hill, 1932).

Meireles, Mario. *História do Maranhão*. (São Paulo, 1960).

Mello, Evaldo Cabral de. *Olinda Restaurada*. (São Paulo, 1975).

Mello, José António Gonsalves de. *Tempo dos Flamengos*. 2nd ed. (Recife, 1978).

_____. *Cartas de Duarte Coelho a el Rei*. (Recife, 1967).

_____. "The Dutch Calvinists and Religious Toleration in Portuguese America," *The Americas*, 14:4 (April, 1958), pp. 485–488.

"Memórias históricas e militares relativas a guerra hollandeza, 1630–1757," *ABNRJ*, XX (1898), 119–234.

Mendonça, Henrique Lopes de. *Estudos sobre navios portugueses nos séculos XV e XVI*. (Lisbon, 1892).

Mendonça, Marcos Carneiro. (Ed.). *Amazônia na era Pombalina*. 3 vols. (São Paulo, 1963).

Meneses, Luís de (Conde de Ericeira). *História de Portugal Restaurado*. 4 vols. (Oporto, 1945–1946).

Métraux, Alfred. *La Civilisation matérielle des tribus Tupi-Guaraní*. (Paris, 1928) and *La Religion des Tupinambá et ses rapports avec celle des autres tribus Tupi-Guaraní*. (Paris, 1928).

Miranda, Agenor Augusto de. *O Rio São Francisco*. (São Paulo, 1936).

Momsen, Jr., Richard P. *Routes Over the Serra do Mar*. (Rio de Janeiro, 1964).

Monteiro, Jonatas da Costa Rego. *A Colônia do Sacramento, 1680–1777*. 2 vols. (Porto Alegre, 1937).

——. *Dominação espanhola no Rio Grande do Sul, 1763–1777*. (Rio de Janeiro, 1937).

Moraes, A.J. de Mello. *Corografia histórica . . . do Império do Brasil*. (Rio de Janeiro, 1860).

Moraes, Evaristo de. *A escravidão africana no Brasil*. (São Paulo, 1933).

Moraes, Rubens Borba de. *Bibliographia Brasiliana: A Bibliographical Essay on Rare Books about Brasil Published from 1504 to 1900 and Works of Brazilian Authors Published Abroad Before the Independence of Brazil in 1822*. 2 vols. (Rio de Janeiro and Amsterdam, 1958).

——. *Bibliografia brasileira do período colonial*. (São Paulo, 1969).

—— and William Berrien. (Eds.). *Manual bibliográfico de estudos brasileiros*. (Rio de Janeiro, 1949).

Moreno, Diogo de Campos. *Livro que dá razão do Estado do Brasil (1612)*. (Rio de Janeiro, 1968).

Morison, Samuel Eliot. *Portuguese Voyages to America in the Fifteenth Century*. (Cambridge, 1940).

——. *The European discovery of America: the southern voyages, 1492–1616*. (New York, 1974).

Mörner, Magnus. *The political and economic activities of the Jesuits in the La Plata region*. (Stockholm, 1953).

Morse, Richard M. (Ed.). *The Bandeirantes: the historical role of the Brazilian pathfinders*. (New York, 1965).

Mota, Carlos Guilherme. *Atitudes de inovação no Brasil, 1789–1801*. (Lisbon, n.d. 1970?).

Motta, Arthur. *História da literatura brasileira*. 2 vols. (São Paulo, 1930).

Nash, Roy. *The Conquest of Brazil*. (New York, 1926).

Netscher, P.N. *Les Hollandais au Brésil*. (La Haye, 1853).

Novais, Fernando A. *Portugal e Brasil na crise do antigo sistema colonial (1777–1808)*. (São Paulo, 1979).

——. *Estrutura e dinámica do sistema colonial*. (Lisbon, 1975).

Nowell, Charles E. *The Great Discoveries and the First Empires*. (Ithaca, New York, 1954).

———. *History of Portugal*. 2 vols. (New York, 1971–72).

———. "Aleixo Garcia and the White King," *HAHR*, 26:4 (November, 1946), pp. 450–466.

———. "The Discovery of Brasil—Accidental or Intentional?" *HAHR*, 16:311–38 (August, 1936).

———. "The French in Sixteenth-Century Brazil," *The Americas*, 5:4 (April, 1949), pp. 381–393.

———. "The Rejection of Columbus by John of Portugal." *University of Michigan Historical Essays*. (Ann Arbor, 1937).

———. "Reservations Regarding the Historicity of the 1494 Discovery of South America," *HAHR*, 22:205–10 (February, 1942).

———. "The Treaty of Tordesillas and the Diplomatic Background of American History," in Adele Ogden and Engel Sluiter, (Eds.), *Greater America. Essays in Honor of Herbert Eugene Bolton*. (Berkeley and Los Angeles, 1945), pp. 1–18.

Oliveira, José Manuel Cardoso de. *Actos diplomáticos do Brasil, tratados do período colonial e vários documentos desde 1493*. 2 vols. in 1. (Rio de Janeiro, 1912).

Pacifici, Sergio J. (Trans.). *Copy of a Letter of the King of Portugal Sent to the King of Castile Concerning the Voyage and Success of India*. (Minneapolis, 1955).

Padre Antonio Vieira: Obras Escolhidas. 12 vols. (Lisbon, 1951–54).

Padre Antonio Vieira: Sermões. 14 vols. (Lisbon, 1679–1710); 3 vols. (Porto, 1908).

Palmatory, H.C. *The river of the Amazonas. Its discovery and early exploration 1500–1743*. (New York, 1965).

Pastells, Pablo. *Historia de la Compañía de Jesús en la provincia del Paraguay . . .* 5 vols. (tomos VII-VIII equal vol. V). (Madrid, 1912–1949).

Payne, Stanley G. *A History of Spain and Portugal*. 2 vols. (Madison, 1973).

Pereira, Nuno Marques. *Compendio narrativo do peregrino da America*. (Lisbon, 1728).

Peres, Damião. *História dos descobrimentos Portugueses*. 2nd ed. (Coimbra, 1960).

———. (Ed.). *Historia de Portugal*. 9 vols. (Barcelos, 1928–1954).

———. *O descobrimento do Brasil por Pedro Álvares Cabral: antecedentes e intencionalidade*. (Oporto and Rio de Janeiro, 1949; 2nd ed., 1968).

Pérez Embid, Florentino. *Los descubrimientos en el Atlántico y la rivalidad castellano-portuguesa hasta el tratado de Tordesillas*. (Seville, 1948).

Pierson, Donald. "The Negro in Bahia, Brazil," *American Sociological Review*, IV (August, 1938), 524–533.

Pike, Ruth. *Enterprise and Adventure: The Genoese in Seville and the Opening of the New World*. (Ithaca, 1966).

Pitta, Sebastião da Rocha. *História da America portugueza*. (Lisbon, 1724).

Pombo, José Francisco da Rocha. *História do Brasil*. 10 vols. (Rio de Janeiro, 1905).

Poppino, Rollie. "Cattle Industry in Colonial Brazil." *Mid-America*, XXXI (October, 1949), 219–247.

Porto, Afonso Aurelio. *História das missões orientais do Uruguai.* 2nd ed. 2 vols. (Porto Alegre, 1954).

Prado, Jr., Caio. *The Colonial Background of Modern Brazil.* (Trans., Suzette Macedo) (Berkeley and Los Angeles, 1967).

Prado, J.F. de Almeida. *Primeiros povoadores do Brasil 1500–1530.* 2nd ed. (São Paulo, 1939).

————. *Pernambuco e as capitanias do norte do Brasil, 1530–1630.* 4 vols. (São Paulo, 1939–1942).

Prestage, Edgar. *The Chronicles of Fernão Lopes and Gomes Eannes de Zurara.* (Watford, 1928).

————. *The Diplomatic Relations of Portugal with France, England, and Holland from 1640 to 1668.* (Watford, England, 1925).

Purchas, Samuel. *Hakluytus Posthumus or Purchas His Pilgrimes Containing a History of the World in Sea Voyages and Lande Travells by Englishmen and Others.* 20 vols. (Glasgow, 1905–1907).

Putnam, Samuel. *Marvellous Journey. A survey of four centuries of Brazilian writing.* (New York, 1948).

Pyrard, François de Laval. *Viagem de Francisco Pyrard de Laval.* Portuguese translation. 2 vols. in 1. (Oporto, 1944).

Ramos, Arthur. *The Negro in Brazil.* (Trans. by Richard Pattee) (Washington, D.C., 1939).

Rau, Virginia. *Estudos de História.* (Lisbon, 1968).

————. *Os holandeses e a exportação do sal de Setúbal nos fins do século XVII.* (Coimbra, 1950).

————. "Feitores e feitorias—instrumentos do comércio internacional português no século XVI," *Brotéria* (Lisbon), 81:458–478 (July–December, 1965).

———— and Bailey W. Diffie. "Alleged Fifteenth-Century Portuguese Joint Stock Companies and the Articles of Dr. Fitzler," in *The Bulletin of the Institute of Historical Research,* 26:181–199 (1953).

Rego, António da Silva. *Portuguese Colonization in the Sixteenth Century: A Study of the Royal Ordinances (Regimentos).* (Johannesburg, 1959).

Reis, Artur Cezar Ferreira. *História do Amazonas.* (Manaus, 1935).

————. *A política de Portugal no valle amazónico.* (Belém, 1940).

Reis Filho, Nestor Goulart. *Evolução urbana do Brasil (1500–1720).* (São Paulo, 1968).

Reis, Francisco Sotero dos. *Curso de litteratura portugueza e brasileira.* 5 vols. (Maranhão, 1866–1873).

Ribeiro, João. *História do Brasil.* (Rio de Janeiro, 1929).

Ribeiro, Jr., José. *Colonização e monopólio no nordeste brasileiro.* (São Paulo, 1976).

Ribeiro, Orlando. *Aspectos e problemas da expansão Portuguesa.* (Lisbon, 1955).

Ricard, Robert. "Prophecy and Messianism in the Works of Antônio Vieira," *The Americas,* 17:4 (April, 1961), pp. 357–368.

Rio-Branco, Barão de. *Efemérides brasileiras.* 2nd ed. (Rio de Janeiro, 1938).

Rodrigues, José Honório. *Historiografía del Brasil. Siglo XVI.* (Mexico City, 1957).

———. *Historiografía del Brasil. Siglo XVII.* (Mexico City, 1963).

———. *Historiografía e Bibliografía do domínio holandês no Brasil.* (Rio de Janeiro, 1949).

———. *O continente do Rio Grande.* (Rio de Janeiro, 1954).

———. *Brazil and Africa.* (Trans. Richard A. Mazzara and Sam Hileman) (Berkeley and Los Angeles, 1965).

Rodrigues, Nina. *Os Africanos no Brasil.* 2nd ed. (São Paulo, 1937).

Rodríguez, Mario. "Colônia de Sacramento: Focus of Spanish-Portuguese Rivalry in the Plata, 1640–1683," (Ph.D. 1952, Berkeley).

———. "The Genesis of Economic Attitudes in the Río de la Plata," *HAHR*, XXXVI (May, 1956), 171–189.

———. "Don Pedro of Braganza and Colônia de Sacramento, 1680–1705," *HAHR*, XXXVIII (May, 1958), 179–208.

Roth, Cecil. *A History of the Marranos.* (Philadelphia, 1947).

Rubio, Julián María. *Exploración y conquista del Río de la Plata, siglos XVI y XVII.* (Buenos Aires, 1942).

Ruiz, de Montoya Antonio. *Conquista espiritual hecha por los religiosos de la Compañía de Jesús en las provincias de Paraguay, Uruguay y Tape.* (Madrid, 1639).

Russell-Wood, A.J.R. *Fidalgos and Philanthropists: The Santa Casa da Misericórdia of Bahia 1550–1755.* (Berkeley, 1968).

———. "Iberian Expansion and the Issue of Black Slavery: Changing Portuguese Attitudes, 1440–1770," *The American Historical Review*, 83:1 (February, 1978), pp. 16–42.

Ruy, Alfonso. *História política e administrativa da Cidade do Salvador.* (Salvador, 1949).

Sá, Joseph Barboza de. "Relação das povoações do Cuyabá e Mato Grosso de seos principios até os prezentes tempos," *ABNRJ*, XXIII (1901), 5–58.

Sá, Mem de. "Documentos relativos a Mem de Sá, Governador Geral do Brasil," *ANBRJ*, XXVII (1905), 127–280.

Sá, Simão Pereira de. *História topográphica e béllica da nova Colonia do Sacramento do Rio da Prata.* (Rio de Janeiro, 1900).

Salvador, Fr. Vicente do. *História do Brasil.* 4th ed. (São Paulo, 1965).

Sanceau, Elaine. *Captains of Brazil.* (Porto, 1956?).

———. *Henry the Navigator.* (New York, 1947).

Santos, Corcino Madeiros dos. *Relações comerciais do Rio de Janeiro com Lisboa (1763–1808).* (Rio de Janeiro, 1980).

Santos, Joaquim Felício dos. *Memórias do Distrito Diamantino da Comarca do Serro do Frio.* 3rd ed. (Rio de Janeiro, 1956).

Saraiva, António José. *História da Cultura em Portugal.* 2 vols. (Lisbon, 1950–1955).

———. *Inquisição e cristãos-novos.* (Oporto, 1969).

Sayers, Raymond S. *The Negro in Brazilian Literature.* (New York, 1956).

Scelle, Georges. *La traite négrière aux Indes de Castille.* 2 vols. (Paris, 1906).

Schaefer, Henrique. *História de Portugal.* 7 vols. (Lisbon: 1893–1926).

Schwartz, Stuart B. *Sovereignty and Society in Colonial Brazil. The High Court of Bahia and its judges, 1609–1751.* (Berkeley, 1973).

————. "Free Labor in a Slave Economy: The Lavradores de Cana of Colonial Brazil," Dauril Alden, (Ed.), *Colonial Roots of Modern Brazil.* (Berkeley, 1973), 147–197.

————. "The Mocambo: Slave Resistence in Colonial Bahia," *Journal of Social History,* III (Spring, 1970), 313–333.

————. "The Manumission of Slaves in Colonial Brazil: Bahia, 1684–1745," *HAHR,* 54:4 (1974), 603–35.

————. "Luso-Spanish Relations in Hapsburg Brazil, 1580–1640," *The Americas,* 25:1 (July, 1968), pp. 33–48.

————. (Ed.). *A Governor and his Image in Baroque Brazil.* (Minneapolis, 1979).

Serra Rafols, Elías. "Lançarotto malocello en Canarias," Congresso Internacional de História dos Descobrimentos. *Actas,* 3:467–478 (Lisbon, 1960).

Serrão, J. Verissimo. *História de Portugal.* 5 vols. (Lisbon, 1980).

————. *O Rio de Janeiro no século XVI.* 2 vols. (Lisbon, 1965).

————. "A conquista de Ceuta no diário veneziano de António Moroseni," Congresso Internacional de História dos Descobrimentos (Lisbon, 1960), *Actas,* 3:543–550 (1960–61).

Serrão, Joel. *Dicionário da História de Portugal.* 4 vols. (Lisbon, 1963–1971).

Shillington, V.M. and Chapman, A.B. Wallis. *The Commercial Relations of England and Portugal.* (New York, 1907).

Sideri, Sandro. *Trade and Power. Informal Colonialism in Anglo-Portuguese Relations.* (Rotterdam, 1970).

Silbert, A. *Le Portugal méditerranéen à la fin de l'Ancien Régime.* 2 vols. (Paris, 1966).

Silva, Innocencio Francisco da. *Dicionário bibliográfico português.* 22 vols. (Lisboa, 1858–1923).

Silva, João Manuel Pereira da. *História da fundação do império brasileiro.* 7 vols. (Rio de Janeiro, 1864–1868); 2nd ed. 3 vols. (Rio de Janeiro, 1877).

Silva, José Justino de Andrade e. (Ed.). *Collecção chronológica da legislação portuguesa.* 11 vols. (the last one incomplete). (Lisbon, 1854–1859).

Silva, Luciano Pereira da. *Obras completas.* 3 vols. (Lisbon, 1943–45).

Simonsen, Roberto C. *História económica do Brasil, 1500–1820.* 2 vols. (São Paulo, 1937).

Siqueira, Sónia A. *A inquisição portuguesa e sociedade colonial.* (São Paulo, 1978).

Sluiter, Engel. "Dutch Maritime Power and the Colonial Status Quo, 1585–1641," *The Pacific Historical Review,* 11:1 (March, 1942), pp. 29–41.

————. (Ed.). "Report on the State of Brazil, 1612," *HAHR,* 29:4 (November, 1949), pp. 518–562.

Soares, José Carlos de Macedo. *Fronteiras do Brasil no regime colonial.* (Rio de Janeiro, 1939).

Smith, R.C. *Arquitectura colonial bahiana.* (Bahia, 1951).

Sousa-Leão, Joaquim de. *Frans Post, 1612–1680.* (Amsterdam, 1973).

Southey, Robert. *History of Brazil*. 3 vols. (London, 1810–1819).
Souza, Bernardino José de. *O pau-brasil na história nacional*. (São Paulo, 1940).
Souza, Gabriel Soares de. *Tratado Descriptivo do Brasil em 1587*, first published in Lisbon (1825) in an incomplete version, according to Bailey Diffie. Diffie also informed that the standard edition was that edited by Francisco Adolpho de Varnhagen (Rio de Janeiro) in 1851. Diffie utilized the third edition, São Paulo, 1938. He considered Souza's work the best on agriculture in sixteenth-century Brazil. The owner of a sugar mill in Baía from 1570 to 1584, Souza wrote a work that contains a minute description of the land, plants, and people; and Diffie recommended pp. 174–360 for the discussion on agricultural matters, native and transplanted plants, and animals in Brazil.
Souza, T.O. Marcondes de. *Algumas achegas à história dos descobrimentos (criticas e controvérsias)*. (São Paulo, 1958).
———. *O descobrimento do Brasil de acôrdo com a documentação histórico-cartográfica e a náutica*. 2nd ed. (São Paulo, 1956).
———. "A expedição de 1501–02 e Amérigo Vespucci. (Réplica ao Prof. Damião Peres)," *Revista de história, São Paulo*, I, 3:391–411 (July-September, 1950).
Souza, Pero Lopes de. *Diario da Navegação . . . 1530, RIHGB*, XXIV (1861), 3–111.
Staden, Hans. *The True History of His Captivity. 1557*. (Trans. and Ed.), Malcolm Letts. (London, 1928).
Taunay, Afonso d'Escragnolle. *História seiscentista da Vila de São Paulo*. 4 vols. (São Paulo, 1926–29).
———. *História geral das bandeiras paulistas*. 11 vols. (São Paulo, 1918–1951).
Tambs, Lewis A. "Brazil's Expanding Frontiers," *The Americas*, 23:2 (October, 1966), pp. 165–179.
Taylor, E.G.R. *The Haven-Finding Art: A History of Navigation from Odysseus to Captain Cook*. (London, 1956, and New York, 1971).
Taylor, Kit Sims. *Sugar and the Underdevelopment of Northeastern Brazil, 1500–1970*. (Gainesville, 1978).
Teixeira Coelho, José João. "Instrucção para o governo da capitania de Minas Geraes (1780)," *RIHGB*, XV (1852), 257–476.
Thévet, André. *Les Singularités de la France antarctique*. (Paris, 1558).
Thomas, Georg. *Die portugiesische Indianerpolitik in Brasilien, 1500–1640*. (Berlin, 1968).
Toribio Medina, José. *The Discovery of the Amazon According to the Account of Friar Gaspar de Carvajal and Other Documents*. (Trans. Bertram E. Lee, Ed. H.C. Heaton) (New York, 1934).
Vandelli, Domingos. "Sobre as minas de ouro do Brasil," *ABNRJ*, XX (1898), 266–278; and "Sobre os diamantes do Brasil," *ibid.*, 279–282.
Varnhagen, Francisco Adolfo de (Visconde de Porto Seguro). *História geral do Brasil antes da sua separação e independência de Portugal*. 5 vols. 5th ed. (São Paulo, 1956).

Vasconcellos, Simão de. *Chronica da Companhia de Jesus do Estado do Brazil.* (Lisbon, 1663; 2nd ed., 2 vols., Lisbon, 1865). .

Velloso, Queiroz. *D. Sebastião, 1554–1578.* 3rd ed. (Lisbon, 1945) and *O reinado do Cardeal D. Henrique.* (Lisbon, 1946).

Verlinden, Charles. "Navigateurs, Marchands et colons italiens au service de la découverte et de la colonisation portugaise sous Henri Le Navigateur," *Le Moyen Âge,* 64:467–497 (1958).

———. "Lanzarotto Malocello et la decouverte portugaise des Canaries," *RBPH,* 36:1173–1209 (1958).

———. *The Beginning of Modern Colonization.* (Ithaca, New York, 1970).

Verissimo, Erico. *Brazilian Literature. An Outline.* (New York, 1945).

Vianna, Francisco José Oliveira. *Populações meridionais do Brasil.* (São Paulo, 1938).

Vianna, Urbino. *Bandeiras e sertanistas bahianas.* (São Paulo, 1937).

Vieira, Antônio. "Annua da provincia do Brasil 1624–1625," *ABNRJ,* XIX (1897), 175–217.

Vignaud, Henry. *Histoire critique de la grande entreprise de Christophe Colombus.* 2 vols. (Paris, 1911).

Vilhena, Luis dos Santos. *A Bahia no século XVIII.* 3 vols. (Bahia, 1969).

———. *Cartas de Vilhena: notícias soteropolitanas e brasílicas.* Annotated by Braz do Amaral. 3 vols. (Bahia, 1921–1922).

Wätjen, Hermann. *O domínio colonial hollandez no Brasil.* (Ed. and Trans.), Pedro Celso Uchoa Cavalcanti. (São Paulo, 1938).

Willeke, Venáncio. *Missões Franciscanas no Brasil, 1500–1975.* (Petrópolis, 1974).

Willems, Emilio. "Social Differentiation in Colonial Brasil," *Comparative Studies in Society and History,* 12 (1970), 31–49. Cf.

Witte, Charles-Mártial de. *Les Bulles pontificales et l'expansion portugaise au XVe siècle.* (Louvain, 1958).

Wiznitzer, Arnold. *Jews in Colonial Brazil.* (New York, 1960).

Wright, Antônia Fernanda Pacca de Almeida. "The Impact of the American Revolution in Two Brazilian Cities: Rio de Janeiro and São Paulo," in Joseph S. Tulchin, (Ed.), *Hemispheric Perspectives on the United States. Papers from the New World Conference.* (Westport, Connecticut, 1978).

BAILEY W. DIFFIE

Experience: *Teaching and Other Activities*
Instructor, Texas Christian University, 1926–27
Grant from Forth Worth Rotary Club for study in Spain, 1927–29
Grant from American Fund for Public Service for work on book
about Puerto Rico, 1929–30
Instructor, The City College, 1930–36
Assistant Professor, The City College, 1936–46
Rockefeller Foundation Fellow, 1940–41
Visiting Lecturer, Cornell University, Summer of 1943
Economic Analyst, Foreign Economic Administation, 1943–44
Radio Script writer, O.I.A.A., 1945
Associate Professor, The City College, 1946–51
Visiting Lecturer, Yale University, 1946–47
Professor, The City College, 1951 to 1968
Elected member of Editorial Board of *Hispanic American Historical
Review* for six-year term, 1946; second term, 1954–60
Travel Grant from Social Science Research Council, 1948
Elected member of General Committee of *Conference on Latin American
History* for two-year term in 1949
Grants from SSRC and American Philosophical Society, 1949, 1952,
1958–59, 1960, 1962, 1966; Fulbright, Brazil 1966; Portugal, 1967
Visiting Professor, New York University, 1962; Columbia, 1963–

64; Texas, summer 1965; Columbia, 1966, 1967–68 and SS 1968;
University of Washington, 1968–69; University of Texas, SS
1969; Adjunct Professor, University of Miami, Coral Gables, Fla.
1969–70
Visiting and adjunct Professor, University of Southern California,
1970–1982.

Education:
Grammar school in Detroit and Clarksville, Texas
Graduated from Hugo High School, Hugo, Oklahoma, 1919
Texas Christian University, 1919–1921
Southeastern Teachers College, Durant, Oklahoma, 1921–1923;
A.B., 1923
Texas Christian University—M.A., 1926
Doctor en Filosofiã y Letras, Madrid, Spain, 1929

Foreign Travel:
Germany and Holland, summer of 1925
Spain, 1927–29
Puerto Rico, summer of 1930
Spain and Portugal, summer of 1931
France and England, summer of 1932
Spain and Portugal, summer of 1933
Cuba and Mexico, summer of 1934
Germany, France and England, summer of 1935
France and England, summer of 1936
Brazil, Uruguay, Argentina, Chile, Bolivia, and Peru, with exten-
sive travel in Brazil, 1937–38
England and France, summer of 1938
Brazil, Columbia and Panama, 1940–41
Brazil and Portugal, 1970–76, one or both every year
Portugal, Spain, France, 1948–49
Portugal, Spain, France, England, 1952
Portugal, Spain, France, and Italy, 1958, 1960
Mexico, Central America and South America, 1962
Portugal, Spain, 1964

Brazil, Paraguay, Peru, Ecuador, Panama, Mexico, 1966
Portugal and Spain, 1967; Portugal, 1969

Foreign Languages:
    Portuguese: Speak and read with ease; write fairly well
    Spanish: Speak and read with ease; write fairly well
    French: Speak and read fairly well
    Italian: Read

Publications-Books:
  Porto Rico: A Broken Pledge, New York, 1931.
  Latin American Civilization: Colonial Period, 812 pp. plus maps and
    illustrations. Stackpole Sons, 1945. Revised, 1947 and 1967 (with
    new 76 page historiography covering 1943–1966).
  Prelude to Empire: Portugal Overseas before Henry the Navigator, Univer-
    sity of Nebraska Press 1960 and 1968.
  Foundations of the Portuguese Empire, 1415–1580 (with George Winius),
    University of Minnesota Press, 1977.

Articles:
  "Spain Under the Republic *Foreign Policy Report*, Foreign Policy
    Association, Inc., New York, N.Y., December 20, 1933, Vol. IX
    #21. Revised and published in *New Governments in Europe*, edited
    by Raymond Leslie Buell, New York, 1934.
  "A Markham Contribution to the *Leyenda Negra*," *The Hispanic
    American Historical Review*, XVI, (1936), 96–103.
  "Sir Clements R. Markham as a Translator," with Harry Bernstein,
    HAHR, (1937), 546–557.
  Estimates of Potosi Mineral Production, 1545–1555, *HAHR*, XX
    (1940), 275–282.
  "Some Foreign Influences in Contemporary Brazilian Politics,"
    HAHR, Vol. XX, (August 1940), 402–429.
  "The Ideology of Hispanidad," *HAHR*, XXIII, No. 3 (August
    1943), 457–482.
  "La ideologia de la "Hispanidad," *Ultra* #89, January 1944, La
    Habana, Cuba.

"Bibliography of the Principal Guides to Portuguese Archives and Libraries," *Proceedings of the International Colloquium on Luso-Brazilian Studies*, Washington, October 15–20, 1950, The Vanderbilt University Press, Nashville, 1953.

"Alleged Fifteenth-Century Portuguese Joint-Stock Companies and the Articles of Dr. Fitzler," with Virginia Rau, *The Bulletin of the Institute of Historical Research*, Vol. XXVI (1953)

"Portugal's Preparation for Exploration: A Functional-Cultural Interpretation," *Actas*, Vol. II, *III Coloquio Internacional de Estudos Luso-Brasileiros*, Lisboa, 1960.

Commentary on "Causes of Spanish American Wars of Independence" by Charles W. Arnade and Arthur P. Whitaker," *Journal of Inter-American Studies*, April 1960.

"Two Accurate and Two Doubtful Accounts of the Portuguese in the Mediterranean During the Twelfth Century," in *Actas do, Congresso Internacional de Historia dos Descobrimentos*, Lisbon, 1961, 123–130.

"Dois Novos Documents referents ao Comercio Luso-Veneziano no Seculo XIV," *Revista Portuguesa de Historia*, X (1962), *Faculdade de Letras da Univ. de Coimbra*.

Other Writings:

Articles in *National Encyclopedia* (Colliers, 1931); *Current History; The Nation; Schoolman's Week Proceedings; La Nueva Democracia*, New York; *Claridad, Buenos Aires; The Inter-American Quarterly*, Washington, D. C.; *Bulletin of the International Institute of Education*, New York; "Foreigners in Portugal," *Terrae Incognitae*, Vol. I: 23–34 (1969)

Personal:

Born in Detroit, Texas, June 27, 1902. Father, W. O. Diffie, born in Arkansas in 1855 of parents born in Tennessee and Alabama. Mother, Mary L. Jones, born in Arkansas in 1858 of parents born in Tennessee and Mississippi.

INDEX